The Political Economy of Climate Finance Effectiveness in Developing Countries

STUDIES IN COMPARATIVE ENERGY AND ENVIRONMENTAL POLITICS

Series editors: Todd A. Eisenstadt, American University, and Joanna I. Lewis, Georgetown University

The Political Economy of Climate Finance Effectiveness in Developing Countries

Carbon Markets, Climate Funds, and the State

MARK PURDON

OXFORD
UNIVERSITY PRESS

OXFORD
UNIVERSITY PRESS

Oxford University Press is a department of the University of Oxford. It furthers the University's objective of excellence in research, scholarship, and education by publishing worldwide. Oxford is a registered trade mark of Oxford University Press in the UK and certain other countries.

Published in the United States of America by Oxford University Press
198 Madison Avenue, New York, NY 10016, United States of America.

Library of Congress Cataloging-in-Publication Data
Names: Purdon, Mark, author.
Title: The political economy of climate finance effectiveness in developing countries : carbon markets, climate funds, and the state / by Mark Purdon.
Description: New York, NY : Oxford University Press, [2024] | Series: Studies in comparative energy and environmental politics | Includes bibliographical references and index.
Identifiers: LCCN 2024009499 (print) | LCCN 2024009500 (ebook) |
ISBN 9780197756836 (hardback) | ISBN 9780197756850 (epub)
Subjects: LCSH: Environmental policy—Economic aspects—Developing countries. |
Environmental policy—Developing countries—Finance. |
Climatic changes—Economic aspects—Developing countries. |
Carbon dioxide mitigation—Economic aspects—Developing countries.
Classification: LCC HC59.72.E5 P87 2024 (print) | LCC HC59.72.E5 (ebook) |
DDC 333.709172/4—dc23/eng/20240321
LC record available at https://lccn.loc.gov/2024009499
LC ebook record available at https://lccn.loc.gov/2024009500

DOI: 10.1093/oso/9780197756836.001.0001

Printed by Integrated Books International, United States of America

To my parents

Contents

PART III: EVALUATING CLIMATE
FINANCE EFFECTIVENESS

Acknowledgments

In a book spanning over a decade of empirical research, there are too many individuals to whom I owe a debt of gratitude, including students and colleagues at the University of Toronto (Department of Political Science), Makerere University (Faculty of Forestry and Nature Conservation), University of Dar es Salaam (Department of Economics), Moldova State University, London School of Economics (Department of International Development and Grantham Research Institute), Université de Montréal (Département de science politique) as well as the Université du Québec à Montréal, better known as UQAM (particularly the Département de stratégie, responsabilité sociale et environnementale at the École des sciences de la gestion as well as the Chair in Decarbonization). The views expressed in this book are solely mine and any errors my responsibility. Research presented in this book has been supported by the Social Sciences and Humanities Research Council (SSHRC) of Canada, including a SSHRC CGS Doctoral Fellowship and SSHRC Postdoctoral Fellowship. PhD fieldwork was additionally supported by an International Development Research Centre (IDRC) Doctoral Research Awards. More recent fieldwork was supported by UQAM (Programme d'aide financière à la recherche et à la création) as well as the UQAM Chair in Decarbonization. Research ethics approvals were obtained from universities involved in addition to research permits from the Tanzania Commission for Science and Technology and Uganda National Council for Science and Technology. Of course, I would like to also acknowledge the enduring love and support of Sabriella Jacquet. The next book is for Milan.

1

Introduction

1.1. Here Be Dragons!

There is ample evidence that engaging developing countries and emerging economies on climate change mitigation would drastically reduce the global costs of avoiding dangerous climate change (Edmonds et al., 2019; Gavard et al., 2016; Mehling et al., 2018; Paroussos et al., 2019; Stern, 2007). Each dollar spent on mitigation in the developing world can arguably reduce more greenhouse gas (GHG) emissions than it would in rich countries, where costs are higher. But emissions in the developing world are on the rise. They have more than doubled since 2010 and, while developed countries per capita emissions still far exceed those of developing countries, the gap is closing (GCB, 2022). This is a major challenge given that there is a consensus that global emissions must be reduced by more than half by 2030 and reach net zero by 2050 to avoid dangerous climate change (IPCC, 2022a; Figueres et al., 2017; Rogelj et al., 2015). Though combustion of fossil fuels remains the primary source of global emissions, there are significant opportunities in developing countries to reduce or sequester emissions in the areas of agriculture, forests, and land-use change as well as through bioenergy (Shukla et al., 2019; Tubiello et al., 2021; Tubiello et al., 2015).

Extensive debate, however, surrounds the most effective strategy for unlocking these low-cost mitigation opportunities and engaging developing countries in the transition to low-carbon development. This debate is often framed as one between carbon markets and climate funds as different sets of global climate finance instruments (Cui and Huang, 2018; Jinnah et al., 2009; Michaelowa, 2012). I define "climate finance" as transboundary flows of finance triggered by public *and* private interventions (see Michaelowa and Sacherer, 2022; Stewart et al., 2009). A number of such climate finance instruments have been developed over the years under the United Nations Framework Convention on Climate Change (UNFCCC), including the Clean Development Mechanism (CDM), Reducing Emissions from Deforestation and Forest Degradation (REDD+), and Nationally Appropriate Mitigation Actions (NAMAs). While other climate finance instruments have also emerged, such as the Green Climate Fund (GCF), these three instruments can be seen as important building blocks of Nationally Determined Contributions (NDCs): comprehensive climate change mitigation and adaptation plans that nearly all countries first submitted at the 2015 Paris

The Political Economy of Climate Finance Effectiveness in Developing Countries. Mark Purdon, Oxford University Press.
© Oxford University Press 2024. DOI: 10.1093/oso/9780197756836.003.0001

Agreement (Stewart et al., 2017). The main research question motivating this book is, under what conditions are such climate finance instruments effective in reducing emissions in developing countries?

Adopted as part of the 1997 Kyoto Protocol, the CDM is among the first international climate finance instruments for engaging developing countries. It was part of an ambitious effort to establish a global carbon market under the UNFCCC and, as initially conceived, was consonant with neoliberal ideas such as private property, free-trade, and self-regulating markets—adhering to what Bernstein (2001) has described as a global environmental norm of *liberal environmentalism*. Despite numerous challenges, the CDM still remains responsible for the vast majority of emission reductions claimed by any international or transnational climate finance instrument.[1] But, as is widely known, the Kyoto Protocol's carbon market collapsed after negotiations at the 2009 UN climate change conference in Copenhagen failed to secure a meaningful extension of the Kyoto carbon market approach, a watershed moment in climate change politics (Bodansky, 2010; Dimitrov, 2010).

At the UN level, the CDM would largely be succeeded by a set of new climate finance instruments, including REDD+ and NAMAs. What is now known as REDD+ was originally expected to be included in the CDM as "avoided deforestation," but, after acrimonious UNFCCC negotiations in late 2001, it was excluded from the Kyoto Protocol's international carbon offset system (Purdon, 2010). A major reason for its exclusion was concern that avoided deforestation projects would flood the CDM market with cheap credits (Jung, 2003). What has become REDD+ was reintroduced at the 2005 UN climate change negotiations in Montreal by two rainforest nations, Papua New Guinea and Costa Rica (2005). The concept of NAMAs, for its part, was first introduced as part of the 2007 Bali Action Plan as a way of promoting climate mitigation by 2020 (Coetzee and Winkler, 2013). While initially there was a prospect that some NAMAs would be funded through carbon markets (Okubo et al., 2011: 37), so-called crediting NAMAs were never realized. As one close observer of the process explained to me in a 2014 interview: "[Crediting NAMAs] were in there the day before the end of the [2011 UN climate change negotiations]. But when we downloaded the final text, they had disappeared because some parties didn't like the idea of carbon credits coming from NAMAs."[2]

Indeed, funding for REDD+ and NAMAs would not be associated with a global carbon market but with a raft of new climate funds. I define "climate funds" as bilateral and multilateral organizations for transboundary climate finance created, largely, by governments in developed countries for supporting climate action in developing countries. Disconnected from global carbon markets and, thus, efforts by developed countries to compensate for emissions that they either could not or would not reduce at home, REDD+ and NAMAs have been freed from concerns about the circulation of bogus carbon credits that have haunted the CDM. For example, Michael Wara, an American legal scholar, argued that a climate fund model, inspired by the Multilateral Fund of the Montreal Protocol, would have certain advantages over the CDM (Wara, 2008: 1801–1802). The Multilateral Fund is based on the principle that developed countries should pay for the incremental costs faced by developing countries for phasing out ozone-depleting substances; this was initially operationalized via an official list of technologies and strategies eligible to receive funding (Patlis, 1992). With contributions reaching approximately US$137 million per year (all dollar values in this book are reported in US$), the Multilateral Fund was able to be sourced almost entirely from official development assistance (ODA) (Biermann and Simonis, 1999: 245–246).

The model for climate funds would, however, not be the Multilateral Fund but the Global Environment Facility (GEF), established in 1991, which would become the main financial mechanism of the UNFCCC as well as most other multilateral environment agreements in the 1990s. In contrast to the Multilateral Fund, the GEF has adhered to a baseline instrument design. One reason was that the development interventions pursued by the GEF were more complex than only technology deployment. But the GEF also inherited management practices from the international development regime. This regime may be defined as the "activities of UN agencies, banks, trade institutions and the OECD in relation to promoting development" that had emerged since World War II (Gupta and Van der Grijp, 2010).

While the GEF was eclipsed by carbon markets in the mid-1990s, the climate fund model it represented would regain prominence at the 2009 UN climate change conference in Copenhagen, mentioned earlier. Here the UNFCCC committed to "scaled up, new and additional, predictable and adequate funding as well as . . . a goal of mobilizing jointly USD 100 billion a year by 2020 to address the needs of developing countries. This funding will come from a wide variety of sources, public and private, bilateral and multilateral, including alternative sources of finance" (UNFCCC, 2009: para. 8).

An important idea developed in this book is that the turn toward climate. funds at Copenhagen has been part of a broader shift within the UN climate change regime toward what I call *developmental environmentalism*. While ideas associated with developmentalism have long existed in debates about international development cooperation, they gained policy traction following the 2008 financial crisis, which undermined global confidence in neoliberal economic ideas. In addition to its reliance on public funds, developmental environmentalism contrasts with liberal environmentalism through its recognition of the state as an essential partner in climate policy implementation while softening the results-based evaluation frameworks relative to that which characterized carbon market approaches. I map out characteristics of liberal environmentalism and developmental environmentalism in Table 1.1. In light of this shift in global environmental norms, a second major research question motivating this book is, then, whether REDD+ and NAMAs, which have largely been built upon norms of developmental environmentalism, have been more effective than the CDM, which has reflected ideas of liberal environmentalism. Given the effort put into designing new climate finance instruments, it is reasonable to ask whether they and the shift to developmental environmentalism have led to more effective engagement with developing countries.

Yet, despite over a decade of experience with climate finance instruments, the debate surrounding them remains mired between opposing camps. One side sees carbon markets as highly flawed (Cullenward and Victor, 2020; Green, 2017; Paulsson, 2009)—if not constituting unequal exchange and neocolonialism (Böhm and Dhabi, 2009; Pearse and Böhm, 2014). Carbon markets and carbon pricing in general are increasingly contrasted with industrial policy (Rosenbloom et al., 2020). The other side of the debate has tended to embrace carbon markets as an opportunity to realize low-cost emission reduction opportunities around the world (Chichilnisky and Bal, 2019; Mathews, 2008; Michaelowa et al., 2019).

The polarized debate on climate finance instruments is abetted by a surprising lack of field-based, empirical research in developing countries themselves, particularly about the fundamental issue of whether climate finance instruments have been effective or not in their objective of reducing emissions. *Here be dragons!* As David Victor, one of the leading observers of climate policy, observed not too long ago: "Oddly, most studies of international coordination on global warming ignore national policy and treat governments as 'black boxes.' Few analysts of international policy peer inside the box to discover how it works"

Table 1.1 Characteristics of Liberal Environmentalism and Developmental Environmentalism

Characteristic	Global Environmental Norm	
	Liberal Environmentalism	Developmental Environmentalism
Principle source of funding	Private sector	Public sector
Role of the state	Limited role	Essential partner
Evaluation framework	Rigorous results-based approach; anticipates need for carbon market fungibility	More traditional approach to development cooperation; independent of carbon markets

(Victor, 2011: 8). It is a trend that has unfortunately continued. In a recent review of carbon pricing, Green (2021) observed *few ex-post* studies of effectiveness in reducing emissions, particularly from developing countries.

However, before going further it is important to qualify my argument about developmental environmentalism. While developmental environmentalism has gained traction within the UN climate change regime, it is not the only set of global environmental norms circulating with the broader "regime complex for climate change" since the collapse of the Kyoto Protocol (Asselt and Zelli, 2014; Keohane and Victor, 2011; Kim, 2020). In particular, developmental environmentalism contrasts with what is now commonly described as transnational climate governance—interest into which has grown considerably since Copenhagen (Bernstein et al., 2010; Bulkeley et al., 2014; Jordan et al., 2018). But for those interested in the political economy of development, transnational climate governance, with its emphasis on nonstate actors, shares unsettling similarities with neoliberalism. Notably, research into transnational climate governance has been overwhelmingly focused on potential impacts and not ex-post results (Hale et al., 2021). In the Conclusion, I reflect on transnational climate governance in light of the findings in this book.

Research Design

My contribution to the debate on climate finance instruments is to bring together theory and methods of comparative political economy of development more fully into the study of climate change politics. This book is situated in the field of comparative climate change politics (Purdon, 2015a; Sowers et al., 2023; Steinberg and VanDeveer, 2012) and is part of a broader movement toward comparative approaches in public policy and area studies (Ahram et al., 2018; Engeli and Rothmayr, 2014; Roll, 2014). While theory and methods of comparative politics are emphasized, comparative climate change politics also draws on the public policy and international relations traditions in political science.

The novelty of this approach is found, in part, in growing recognition that small-N comparative approaches can be valid methods for causal inference (Beach and Rohlfing, 2018; Mahoney, 2008). Such methods are particularly well-suited for the study of new policy initiatives, such as climate finance, where data sufficient for large-N analysis are lacking. As Steinberg (2007) has argued, "Policymakers and others working in the public interest want to learn about the art of the possible, and the risk of the unthinkable, not just the trend line of the probable" (p. 185). The result is a rare, longitudinal, and comparative study of climate finance in practice as the UN climate change regime has evolved from the Kyoto Protocol through to the Paris Agreement.

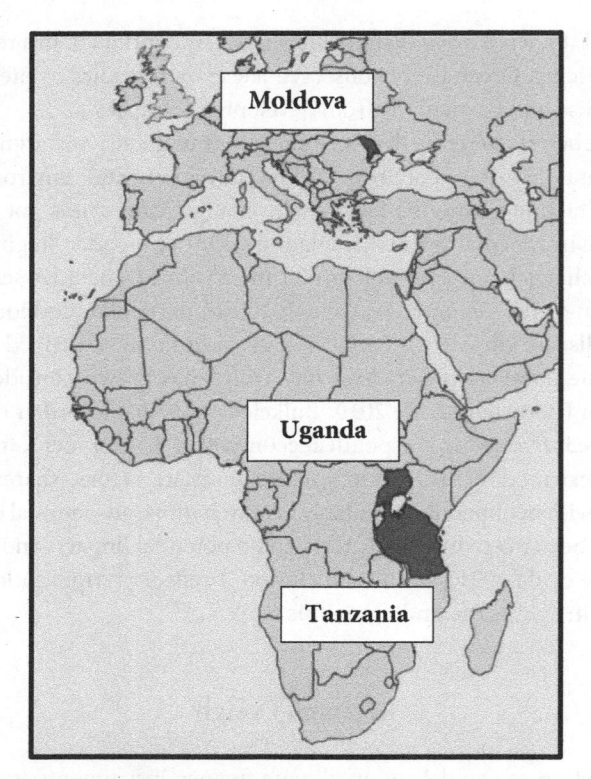

Figure 1.1 Tanzania, Uganda, and Moldova

More specifically, I draw on empirical research into the CDM, REDD+, and NAMAs over a 10-year period from 2008 through 2018 in Tanzania, Uganda, and Moldova—two countries in East Africa and one former republic of the Soviet Union (Figure 1.1). Adhering to a most-different-systems research design, my goal was not just to determine how cases differ but also to learn if, regardless of their differences, similar factors might explain outcomes across them (Anckar, 2008; Lopez, 1992: 275).

When I first initiated this research project in 2008, I designed it largely as an exploratory effort to understand the actual effectiveness of the CDM and related carbon offset projects in the forest, bioenergy, and land-use sectors (Purdon, 2015b). I cast my net widely in order to systematically evaluate climate finance instruments across countries that vary in terms of state capacity, political settlements, and development policy paradigms (Table 1.2). Each is a plausible explanatory factor in the broader literature on comparative political economy of development. Indeed, the early literature on climate and development policy suggested that state capacity would be a key explanatory factor of climate finance

Table 1.2 Key Domestic Political Economy Factors

	Tanzania	Uganda	Moldova
State organizational capacity	Low	Low	High
Political settlement	Weak dominant party	Strong dominant	Competitive clientelism
Development policy paradigm	Hybrid of classic developmentalism & neodevelopmentalism	Liberal neodevelopmentalism	Liberal neodevelopmentalism
State development interests	Limited interest in forest sector until 2016 & limited interest in renewable energy	Forest sector & limited interest in renewable energy	Forest sector & renewable energy

effectiveness. I unpack these analytical categories later in this chapter, after first describing my research design in more detail.

My initial field effort to investigate the CDM was undertaken over an eight-month period beginning in early 2009. In all three countries, I obtained a vehicle and visited almost all forest and bioenergy CDM and related carbon offset projects in operation at the time, many in remote rural locations. Drawing on contacts and documents identified in 2009, I tracked the effectiveness of my CDM projects through 2014, by which time I was able to return to all three countries for follow-up research.

For REDD+ and NAMAs, the research effort involved less project-level field-work because, given implementation challenges at both the international and domestic levels, there have been few concrete activities to investigate. It is true that there have been a number of REDD+ pilot projects in Tanzania and Uganda, often linked to voluntary carbon markets, though many collapsed after donor funding was withdrawn (Nel, 2016; Sunderlin et al., 2015). Given my focus on implementation of REDD+ and NAMAs under the UNFCCC, my field research effort into new climate finance instruments was largely comprised of interviews with key stakeholders in national capitals. This included Moldova (2013) as well as Tanzania and Uganda (2014) as implementation for REDD+ and NAMAs picked up. I carried out additional interviews during fieldwork in Tanzania and Uganda in 2018 when sufficient time had passed for evaluation of policy implementation. Interspersed between these field visits has been participation in nearly all UN climate change conferences, which has allowed me to track country efforts and maintain informal ties with various country stakeholders.

Why specifically Tanzania, Uganda, and Moldova? One reason was a pragmatic one. These three countries were all early adopters of the CDM. By October

2008, when I was selecting case-study countries for my PhD research, Tanzania and Uganda had among the highest numbers of projects under development of any country in sub-Saharan Africa (except South Africa), while CDM projects in Moldova were among the most advanced in the world (World Bank, 2012). Notably, Moldova was eligible for the CDM while, for most other transition economies in Eastern Europe and the former Soviet Union, another climate finance instrument known as "joint implementation" was intended.

State Organizational Capacity

The case-study countries were initially selected to account for differences in state capacity, or, to be more precise, state organizational capacity. Similar to the concept of administrative capacity, state organizational capacity refers to the state's ability to collect and manage information in order to design, implement, and evaluate policy (Hendrix, 2010; Savoia and Sen, 2015). But my definition extends beyond administrative tasks to also refer to operational dimensions of policy implementation, such as organizational resources like personnel, equipment, and other assets such as land. State organizational capacity contrasts with what Meckling and Nahm (2022) have described as state strategic capacity, which draws on Skocpol's (1985) definition of state capacity as a state's ability to achieve its objectives "especially over the actual or potential opposition of powerful social groups" (p. 9). For reasons explained below, I prefer the concept of political settlements to describe the relative political power of the state in developing countries.

A perceived link between state organizational capacity and effective climate policy implementation underwrites decades of capacity-building efforts on climate change. Indeed, Yohe (2001) would coin the term "mitigative capacity" (also see Winkler et al., 2007). Similarly, Victor (2011) argued that the "capabilities of governments to regulate emissions is highly correlated with interests. In general, enthusiastic countries have well-functioning systems of administrative law and regulation and control all manner of economic activities within their borders. In reluctant nations, those systems are generally much less well developed" (p. 12).

Given greater state organizational capacity in Moldova, I expected climate finance instruments would be more effectively implemented there than in East Africa. Comparing climate finance effectiveness in sub-Saharan Africa with a former republic of the Soviet Union constitutes what Eckstein (1975) described as a "crucial case-study" (also see Gerring, 2007). The failure to observe a highly likely outcome expected in light of a particular theory, like the importance accorded to state organizational capacity, is strong grounds to question it.

Before the launch in 2022 of Russia's war with its neighbor Ukraine, Moldova perhaps did not attract as much research attention as it should. But there are strong indications that it has greater state organizational capacity than the two East African countries. One pertinent indicator has been the production of technical climate policy reports, including National Communications and Biennial Update Reports. These reports are key elements of the "enhanced transparency framework" of the UN climate change regime (Gupta and Van Asselt, 2019), which I return to in Section 1.2 below. For the moment, it should be noted that Moldova submitted its First National Communication in 2000 and its fourth in 2018 (UNFCCC, 2020). Both East African countries have produced only two National Communications each since 1990 (UNFCCC, 2020a), though Uganda submitted its first Biennial Update Report in 2019 (MWE, 2019).

Another relevant indicator of state organizational capacity appropriate for this book are commitments made in climate plans submitted toward the Paris Agreement. All three countries submitted so-called Intended Nationally Determined Contributions (INDCs) ahead of Paris and, recently, updated NDCs (see Table 1.3). (Updated NDCs were adopted in 2021/2022, thus after the empirical focus period of this book, which concluded in 2018).

It should be noted that as important as NDCs are for the Paris Agreement and broader efforts to climate change cooperation, the actual NDC documents are rather short and lack detail; they are planning documents to signal to the international community how countries intend on tackling climate change mitigation and adaptation.

Different degrees and types of emission reduction commitments presented in NDCs suggest differences in state organizational capacity. Moldova would commit to a 2030 emissions reduction target below 1990 levels under the Paris Agreement, though Tanzania and Uganda would only commit to reducing theirs relative to a business-as-usual scenario. In turn, Moldova would distinguish its 2030 mitigation effort between those with and without international support. For Tanzania and Uganda, their initial Paris commitments to climate change mitigation were tied to climate finance, though in terms of its updated NDC Uganda also recognized some unconditional climate mitigation opportunities.

I also note that the CDM is referred to in all three of the updated NDCs, while those in Tanzania and Uganda also refer to REDD+ and NAMAs, despite the official intended winddown of the latter instrument by 2020. The omission of references to NAMAs in the most recent NDC of Moldova might also reflect the hope that the country will enter the EU emissions-trading system, the latter of which is conditional on it acceding to the EU itself (GoRM, 2022: 7). It should be noted that Moldova was officially granted EU candidate status in 2022.

Another indicator of state capacity, though tending toward strategic rather than organizational capacities, is the ability to extract taxes. As Skocpol has argued: "A state's means of raising and deploying financial resources tell us more than could any other single factor about its existing (and immediately potential) capacities" (Skocpol, 1985: 17). Based on the available information, I find that Tanzania and

Table 1.3 Climate Mitigation Commitments Submitted as Part of Climate Plans Submitted to the Paris Agreement

Country	INDC Commitment	Updated NDC Commitment
Tanzania*	Conditional: 10–20% reduction relative to BAU emission levels	Conditional: 30–35% reduction relative to BAU emission levels
Uganda**	Conditional: 22% reduction relative to BAU emission levels	Conditional: 18.8% reduction relative to BAU emission levels Unconditional: 5.9% reduction relative to BAU emission levels
Moldova***	Conditional: 78% reduction relative to 1990 emission levels Unconditional: 64–67% reduction relative to 1990 emission levels	Conditional: 88% reduction relative to 1990 emission levels Unconditional: 70% reduction relative to 1990 emission levels

Sources: Tanzania: INDC (United Republic of Tanzania, 2015), First NDC (United Republic of Tanzania, 2021); Uganda: INDC (MWE, 2015a), Updated NDC (MWE, 2022); Moldova: INDC (GoRM, 2015), Updated NDC (GoRM, 2022).

*Tanzania's INDC assumes a total of $60 billion for mitigation contributions and its implementation "will strongly depend on how the international community meets its commitments in terms of financial and technological support" (United Republic of Tanzania, 2015: 8); the updated NDC suggests $19 billion though does not distinguish between mitigation and adaptation (United Republic of Tanzania, 2021: 25).

**Uganda's INDC assumes that national sources cover approximately 30% of incremental costs of the activities in the next 15 years, with 70% assumed to originate from international sources (MWE, 2015a: 2); the updated NDC assumes that unconditional mitigation actions will cost 15% of total mitigation costs with the remaining 85% covered by the international community (MWE, 2022: 48).

***In both its initial and updated NDC, Moldova estimated that to reach its 2030 emission reduction target, international financial support equal to approximately $5 billion would be necessary (GoRM, 2015: 4, 2022: 9). However, in its initial NDC this was estimated at about $330 million per year though, perhaps reflecting insufficient financing accorded in the interim; the updated NDC seeks $500 million per year.

Note: BAU = Business as usual

Uganda extract much fewer taxes than Moldova. Relatedly, a functioning land cadastre exists in Moldova and is absent in Tanzania and Uganda.[3] See the Annex at the end of this chapter for additional key development indicators.

Introducing the Main Argument

The main argument I make is that despite a shift in global environmental norms from liberal environmentalism to developmental environmentalism, differences in development policy paradigms and state development interests—ideas and interests of the state—explain enduring patterns of climate finance instrument effectiveness across the three case-study countries. Over a 10-year period, I found the CDM, REDD+, and NAMAs to consistently be more effectively implemented in Uganda and Moldova than Tanzania, despite differences in state organizational capacity between East Africa and a country of the former Soviet Union. Rather, a convergence of state development policy paradigms and state development interests best explains climate finance effectiveness over the period investigated as this shapes state organizational capacity. Notwithstanding recent attention accorded to nonstate actors in the literature, my empirical findings showed them underperforming while efforts by the international development community to cater to them, to the exclusion of the state, were counterproductive.

Such findings emphasize the importance of domestic politics, particularly the state, in developing countries. By "state" I mean a set of governing institutions embedded in their respective societies that constitute a form of organized domination—sometimes legitimate, sometimes not—that provides order and public goods (Centeno et al., 2017: 2). Indeed, if there is any consensus in the literature in comparative political economy and development studies, it is the rediscovery of the state as a crucial partner in economic development (Acemoglu and Robinson, 2012b; Bates, 2008; Kohli, 2004; Stiglitz and Lin, 2013)—including in sub-Saharan Africa (Aryeetey and Moyo, 2012; Gazibo and Moumouni, 2017; Kelsall, 2013; Stiglitz et al., 2013). As Bates bluntly asserted, "No state, no development" (Bates, 2008: 709).

There are two parts to my argument about the effectiveness of climate finance instruments in developing countries. I first argue that climate finance effectiveness is related to different ideas about economic development that permeate the state apparatus—which I describe as development policy paradigms. I expand on development policy paradigms later in this chapter and defend different types of development policy paradigms in the case-study countries more fully in Chapter 7. In his classic *State-Directed Development*, Atul Kohli argued that a state's political economy orientation—that is, its guiding ideology about political economy—combined with state capacity produce what he has called "state power for development" (Kohli, 2004: 21). While not to deny the importance of environmental ideas in the developing world, ideas of modernization and industrialization continue to hold sway. For example, in climate change negotiations, leaders of developing countries have long asserted their right to economic development and the historical responsibility of rich countries for emissions (Bou-Habib, 2019; Friman and Hjerpe, 2015; Ikeme, 2003).

Policy ideas, however, are chronically understudied in developing country contexts. Rather, neopatrimonialism remains a popular concept for explaining policy failures. As defined by Clapham, neopatrimonialism is "a form of organization in which relationships of a broadly patrimonial type pervade a political and administrative system which is formally constructed on rational-legal lines. Officials hold positions in bureaucratic organizations with powers which are formally defined, but exercise those powers . . . as a form of private property" (Clapham, 1985: 48). But as Thandika Mkandawire (2015), a leading expert on African political economy, once forcefully argued, neopatrimonialism "is predisposed to downplay ideas" (p. 598). A considerable literature, much of it led by Africanists, had debunked neopatrimonialism as a valid analytical concept (Bach and Gazibo, 2013; Kelsall, 2011; Mkandawire, 2015; Pitcher et al., 2009). This is not to deny that rent-seeking behavior is not pervasive but, following Mkandawire, to ask " 'rents' for whom and with what reciprocal obligations for receivers of such rents?" (Mkandawire, 2001: 302). Looking past neopatrimonialism encourages us to seek out other reasons for policy effectiveness.

Attention to ideas about social and economic development—including the legacy of the Soviet developmental model—also discloses considerable common ground between Tanzania, Uganda, and Moldova. As observed by Robert Allen, an economic historian, the "Soviet development model" was quite attractive to leaders of newly independent developing countries after World War II: "if the USSR could transform itself from an agrarian backwater into a superpower, maybe their county could do the same" (Allen, 2003: 4).

I am able to offer evidence that development policy paradigms differ between my three case-study countries in a way that aligns with climate finance effectiveness. While Uganda and Moldova have embraced liberal neodevelopmentalism, Tanzania has aspired to a neodevelopmental paradigm that remains strongly influenced by the classic developmentalism of its first president, Julius Nyerere. Because of this ambivalence, I describe Tanzania's development policy paradigm as a hybrid of classic developmentalism and neodevelopmentalism. Despite considerable differences in state organizational capacity between Uganda and Moldova, states adhering to liberal neodevelopmentalism have treated climate finance instruments as an opportunity to engage with emerging global market opportunities in a way that more effectively harnesses existing levels of capacity, resulting in more effective implementation. In contrast, Tanzania has been more skeptical of global market opportunities offered by developed countries, which has blunted the effectiveness of implementing climate finance instruments there. Overall, the state has, in certain cases, been an effective partner in the implementation of climate finance instruments.

But an appeal to ideas alone is insufficient for explaining climate finance effectiveness. A second part of my argument is that climate finance instruments are more effectively implemented when development policy paradigms converge with state development interests. Such interests can vary significantly between different economic sectors across countries, including the forest and energy sectors I consider. In Uganda and Moldova, measures to address timber scarcity and land degradation have consistently been prioritized by central governments. In Tanzania, however, timber resources are, perhaps surprisingly, relatively abundant; rather, what has been lacking is the industrial capacity to process existing forest plantations.

Similarly, while the provision of modern energy services has been a top priority for the central governments in all three countries investigated, state development interests in decentralized renewable energy varies. As Moldova is almost entirely dependent on external sources for energy, the Moldovan central government has come to see decentralized renewable energy, particularly biomass where it has a comparative advantage, as integral to its energy security. In contrast, with considerable large-scale hydroelectric and fossil fuel resources available in East Africa, the central governments of Tanzania and Uganda have been much less interested in decentralized renewables, including modern bioenergy and improved cookstoves.

Climate finance instruments were most effective when aligned with state development interests because financial resources offered through such instruments have not yet been sufficient nor stable enough to incentivize states to fundamentally re-evaluate their pursuit of traditional carbon-intensive development pathways of modernization and industrialization. Carbon prices associated with CDM projects I investigate in this book range from $2.5 to $12.5 per tonne CO2 equivalent (tCO2e). During the period considered in this book, the World Bank Forest Carbon Partnership Facility (WB-FCPF) offered $5 per tCO2e for REDD+ (WB-FCPF, 2014: 29). Such prices are well below the social cost of carbon and prices currently observed on major carbon markets.

One reason carbon prices were so low was related to the ambition to reduce emissions in developed countries themselves, which generates a certain level of demand for CDM credits. Another has been methods that developed country experts have used for estimating what the costs of mitigation in the developing world are. For example, most studies of REDD+ potential in sub-Saharan Africa have gauged payment requirements relative to opportunity costs associated with smallholder agriculture, which tends to be quite inexpensive (Gregersen et al., 2010).

Overall, my attention to policy effectiveness and implementation on the ground allows me to offer a new perspective on the debate over climate finance instruments and to identify factors—state ideas and interests—that might be leveraged to promote more effective climate change mitigation in the developing world. Under low carbon prices observed over the period 2008–2018, climate finance instruments were most effective when used to extend the implementation of policy activities already being pursued by states for developmental purposes.

Before going further, it is important to address some terminology issues. My use of the terms "developing country" and "developing world" is clearly imperfect (see Hochstetler, 2023). However, only the two East African countries might be deemed least developing countries, while terms like the "Global South" and "Third World" overlook the former Soviet Union. I use the terms "developing country" and "developing world" in this book conscious of their limitations in order to convey broader similarities across the case-study countries. Despite differences in state organizational capacity and GDP per capita (see Annex to this chapter), Moldova remains the poorest country in Europe, and, resonating with our East African counterparts, its economy is still highly dependent on agriculture and its population largely rural. Furthermore, as Beissinger and Young (2002) have argued: "Many of the ways in which state authority has disintegrated in the countries of both [sub-Saharan Africa and the former Soviet Union] and the consequences of these cataclysms share enough similarities that meaningful insights into political processes can be generated when these situations are juxtaposed" (p. 4). The findings of this book might be expected to "resonate" (see Steinberg, 2015) with the experience of other countries still in the early process of industrialization where the economy is highly reliant on agriculture and rural peasants are still important.

1.2. Effectiveness of Climate Finance Instruments

I have organized this book to first report on the effectiveness of the CDM before moving to REDD+ and NAMAs because important lessons about policy effectiveness might first be gleaned from the CDM experience. As we shall see, only the CDM has been fully implemented among the case-studies countries, permitting evaluation of policy outcomes. For REDD+ and NAMAs, I am limited to considering how these policy instruments were implemented and programmed. I unpack policy effectiveness in this section, the dependent variable in this book, saving a more detailed presentation of political economy factors shaping the effectiveness of climate finance instruments for the next section.

Defining Policy Effectiveness

Effectiveness, though, is a difficult term in global environmental politics. As Bulkeley et al. (2014) have argued, "It is difficult, if not impossible, to tie environmental changes directly to regime activity" (p. 159). In a first generation of global environmental politics, effectiveness was generally measured as compliance with formal rules (Breitmeier et al., 2011). Many found this approach limiting. Andresen and Hey (2005) have argued that effectiveness in global environmental politics be defined as pertaining "to the ability of international regimes to solve the problems that prompted their establishment" (p. 212). But even here there are nuances. The effectiveness of an international regime might mean (1) the degree to which a global governance arrangement moves the global community toward a point where a collective-action problem is to be solved or (2) whether a governance arrangement leads to a relative improvement over what might have occurred in its absence (Wettestad, 2006: 300–301).

The approach to effectiveness taken in this book is more modest in that I consider the effectiveness of international climate finance instruments at the domestic level in a limited number of case-study countries. However, even at this level, my focus on policy effectiveness sets this book apart from much of the existing literature in global environmental politics. For example, Bernstein and Cashore (2012) argued for a shift toward understanding the "influence" of global climate governance on domestic policies and practices instead of compliance and effectiveness (p. 586). One reason is that many climate governance initiatives only produce incremental and indirect effects on emissions that are difficult to measure using traditional tools of policy analysis (Van der Ven et al., 2016). While recognizing the importance of indirect policy effects, I have striven to determine whether intended policy effects have been achieved as the result of climate finance instruments (Leroy and Crabb, 2012: 31–32). Attention to policy effectiveness over the 10-year period stretching from the Kyoto Protocol to the Paris Agreement, I submit, allows for a clearer understanding of causal processes to emerge. It is generally agreed that 10 years is sufficient for gauging policy processes and change (Jenkins et al., 2014: 192).

Drawing from Knoepfel et al. (2007), I decompose policy effectiveness into a number of stages, including policy programming/outputs, policy implementation, policy impacts, and policy outcomes (see Figure 1.2). This decomposition of policy effectiveness is not to suggest that policies always follow these stages in linear sequence. The stages are ideal types, and there can be overlap among them.

Policy programming refers to the administrative process through which a policy's constitutive elements are initially established, including a policy's objectives, evaluation framework, operational instruments, and administrative arrangements that will govern it. Ultimately, the policy program should present a reasonable solution to a public problem. Note that I include *policy outputs* as part of policy programming. Policy outputs are administrative products directly aimed at groups targeted through the policy, such as an approved project design document for a CDM project, National Program Document in the UN-REDD process, or NAMA proposals.

Policy implementation refers to the execution of a set of actions authorized in a policy program (or in specific policy outputs) that are aimed at realizing its objectives. As Grindle (1980) has observed, "a wide variety of factors . . . can and do intervene between the statement of policy goals and their actual achievement

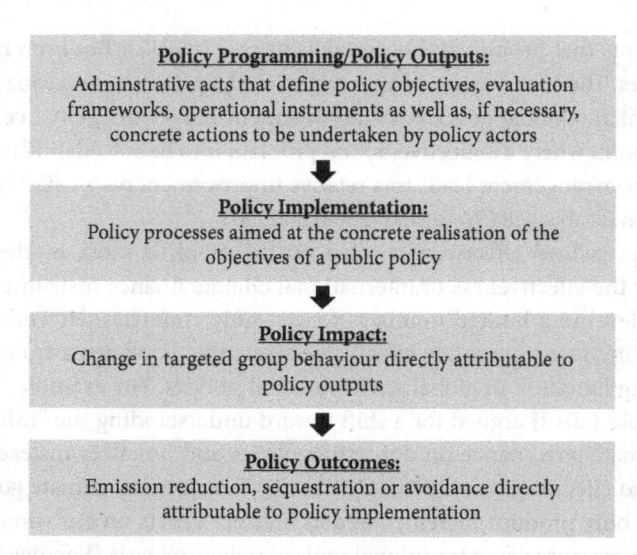

Policy Programming/Policy Outputs:
Adminstrative acts that define policy objectives, evaluation frameworks, operational instruments as well as, if necessary, concrete actions to be undertaken by policy actors

Policy Implementation:
Policy processes aimed at the concrete realisation of the objectives of a public policy

Policy Impact:
Change in targeted group behaviour directly attributable to policy outputs

Policy Outcomes:
Emission reduction, sequestration or avoidance directly attributable to policy implementation

Figure 1.2 Stages Along the Process of Policy Effectiveness

in the society" (p. 3). Furthermore, policy programming/outputs and policy implementation often occur in a series of iterative steps. For example, a national REDD+ program needs to be first articulated in broad elements, each of which needs to be implemented. Implementation of each program element might consist, however, of the development of more detailed policy outputs, each of which needs to be implemented in turn. Consequently, policy programming and policy outputs can be used interchangeably for the purposes of this book as administrative processes and products that are to be implemented.

Policy impact and policy outcomes might be considered part of the policy evaluation phase. *Policy impact* is a concept that takes into account changes in the behavior of targeted groups as a result of implementing policy; for example, a change in tree-planting rates or renewable energy production of targeted firms. Finally, *policy outcomes* refer to the results of such behavioral changes that, in context of this book, are emission reductions, avoidance, or sequestration.

Importantly, my approach to evaluating policy effectiveness varies across the three climate finance instruments, given their being found at different stages along the process of policy effectiveness (Table 1.4). For the CDM and similar carbon offset instruments, I understand effectiveness to mean the ability of carbon offset projects to lead directly to climate change mitigation by reducing, sequestering, or avoiding emissions of GHGs. That is, I focus on the

Table 1.4 Indicators of Policy Effectiveness Evaluated Across the CDM, REDD+, and NAMAs

	CDM	REDD+	NAMAs
Stage of Policy Effectiveness	Policy Outcomes	Policy Implementation	Policy Programming
Empirical Evaluation	1. Additionality 2. State coordination	1. Donor Preference 2. Level of donor support 3. Evaluation frameworks 4. State coordination	1. Number of NAMA proposals submitted 2. Sectors targeted 3. Domestic co-financing 4. Evaluation frameworks 5. State coordination

demonstration of CDM additionality—a controversial concept where emission reductions are measured against a counterfactual baseline scenario. In Chapter 8, I describe in more detail the *ex-post comparative baseline method* that I used to evaluate additionality. These results are supported by analysis of the state's coordination of the CDM in each case-study country.

For REDD+ and NAMAs, I was more limited in my evaluation of their effectiveness. By the end of the period considered (2018), neither of these climate finance instruments had been fully implemented in any of the three case-study countries. My evaluation of REDD+ focused on elements of policy implementation, including type of donor preferred and level of donor support received, the rigor of climate finance evaluation frameworks adopted, and the character of the state's coordination of the climate finance instrument. For NAMAs, my empirical investigation was even more limited given major implementation challenges the instrument has faced. Very little donor financing has been received for NAMAs among the three case-study countries. Consequently, in addition to the number of NAMA proposals submitted, I focused on programming elements discernible in NAMA proposals officially submitted to the UNFCCC. These include sectors that NAMAs target, the amount of domestic co-financing committed, and anticipated evaluation frameworks for NAMAs as well as state coordination approaches. Note that in contrast to my investigation of the CDM and REDD+, NAMAs that I considered extended beyond forest and bioenergy to include all major sectors of climate change mitigation.

My focus on climate finance effectiveness through comparative, field-based empirical research is a distinguishing feature of this book. Indeed, the vast majority of the literature on climate change politics has gauged effectiveness in terms of policy outputs (Bättig and Bernauer, 2009; Hale et al., 2021). Similarly, a close review of the published literature on the CDM reveals a dearth of field-based research on the key issue of whether the instrument has actually led to genuine emission reductions. For example, an important 2016 study commissioned by the European Commission—well known for concluding that 85% of all CDM projects were likely ineffective in reducing emissions—is essentially a desk review (Cames et al., 2016). Only a handful of studies have sought to empirically evaluate CDM projects by looking beyond information presented in CDM project documents (Calel et al., 2021; Lewis, 2010; Liu et al., 2013; Shi et al., 2021; Wara, 2008; Wara and Victor, 2008; Zhang and Wang, 2011)—none of which is comparative in perspective.

Research into new climate finance instruments has also lacked evaluation of effectiveness and whether their implementation might reasonably be expected to actually reduce emissions. With delays in their implementation, most studies of REDD+ and NAMAs have focused on institutional design and mitigation potential (Amars et al., 2017; Fridahl et al., 2015), though there have been a handful of individual case studies of NAMA potential (Boodoo and Olsen, 2018; Brandt et al., 2018; Upadhyaya, 2016). Only very recently has a comparative study of voluntary market REDD+ projects been conducted, using sophisticated synthetic control methods for causal inference, including Tanzania but not Uganda (West et al., 2023). There have also been a number of studies of REDD+ from an environmental justice and human rights perspective (Barletti and Larson, 2017; Kashwan, 2017; Myers et al., 2018; Wallbott and Recio, 2018), including Uganda (Nel et al., 2018) and Tanzania (Ece, 2021; Mukisa et al., 2020; Nantongo et al., 2019). There is not enough space in this book to address issues of environmental justice and sustainable development impacts directly, which should be taken seriously. I have discussed separately such issues with regard to a certain number of the carbon offset projects investigated here (Purdon, 2013, 2014a, 2018; Purdon and Byakagaba, 2022). I note that in a comprehensive review of human rights surrounding REDD+ projects in Tanzania, Jodoin concluded that the "overwhelming majority . . . have had some positive impacts on the rights of local communities and that very few appear to have engendered the sort of human rights violations that were feared by scholars and practitioners in the early stages of the global emergence of REDD+" (Jodoin, 2017: 171).

Climate Finance Evaluation Frameworks

When investigating the effectiveness of climate finance instruments, I also consider institutional frameworks for demonstrating the effectiveness of each. Under the UNFCCC, issues related to policy effectiveness have largely been addressed under the banner of measurement, reporting, and verification (MRV), which itself is a foundational part of the UNFCCC's broader "enhanced transparency framework" (Gupta and Van Asselt, 2019). But discussion here has been, in my view, problematic because of differences between different goals of policy effectiveness and policy transparency. Consider two different types of MRV identified by experts at the World Resources Institute: (1) MRV of GHG emissions, and (2) MRV of mitigation actions themselves (Singh et al., 2016). The first category refers to the transparent measurement of emissions as part of an emissions inventory following technical guidance developed by the Intergovernmental Panel on Climate Change (IPCC) over decades (IPCC, 2019). Only the second type of MRV entails a causal analysis endeavoring to relate policy programming/outputs to the policy outcomes of emission reductions. Given ambiguity surrounding MRV, whether it refers to policy evaluation or policy transparency, I refer to regulatory systems for measuring policy outcomes instead as "evaluation frameworks" in order to emphasize the focus on a causal relationship between policy outputs and emission reductions.

There are a number of common elements to such evaluation frameworks, which are summarized across climate finance instruments in Table 1.5. These

Table 1.5 Distinguishing Features of the CDM, REDD+, and NAMA Evaluation Frameworks

	CDM	REDD+	NAMAs
Scale	Project based (but also programmatic and sectoral approaches)	Jurisdictional (national/subnational)	National
Outcomes Sought	Emission reductions	Emission reductions	Mitigation actions
Baseline	*"A CDM project activity is additional if anthropogenic emissions of greenhouse gases by sources are reduced below those that would have occurred in the absence of the registered CDM project activity"*	*"Developing country Parties in establishing forest reference emission levels and forest reference levels should do so transparently taking into account historic data, and adjust for national circumstances"*	*Developing countries "will take nationally appropriate mitigation actions . . . aimed at achieving a deviation in emissions relative to 'business as usual' emissions in 2020"*
Source of Financing	Carbon market	Climate funds	Climate funds
Global Environmental Norm	Liberal environmentalism	Developmental environmentalism	Developmental environmentalism

include, first, the measurement of emissions associated with the implementation of a climate project, program, or policy. Second is the measurement of emissions associated with a counterfactual scenario representing conditions had the climate finance instrument not been introduced—described variably as a baseline, benchmark, reference level, or business-as-usual scenario across the three instruments considered. A third element of evaluation frameworks is attention to the cause of emissions, often referred to as "drivers." While specific factors targeted by CDM interventions are often implicitly understood to be the drivers of emissions in such projects, measurement of drivers is particularly important for REDD+ as these factors might be the target of policy interventions (Angelsen et al., 2013: 29). This is useful as it is often easier to devise policy to tackle drivers of deforestation than it is to attribute responsibility for deforestation and forest degradation to specific policy actors (as in the case of emission trading).

I distinguish evaluation frameworks from the UNFCCC's transparency framework, mentioned earlier, which has tended to focus on reporting on emissions and climate actions and not evaluation of policy effectiveness per se. Since the early stages of the UN climate change regime, all developing countries have been required to submit National Communications to the UNFCCC on a regular basis. As suggested earlier, National Communications are comprehensive documents including authoritative information on national circumstances, GHG inventories, mitigation measures, adaptation measures, and international cooperation (UNFCCC, 2003). Decisions made at the 2010 UN climate change conference required all countries to further produce Biennial Update Reports that provide more regular information on national GHG inventories and mitigation actions (UNFCCC, 2010: para. 60). In addition, the UNFCCC established the International Consultation and Analysis process to offer independent technical review of Biennial Update Reports (UNFCCC, 2010: para. 63). In addition, at the 2013 UN climate change conference, it was decided that results from REDD+ be additionally verified through a special, reinforced version of the International Consultation and Analysis process (Voigt and Ferreira, 2015: 121–122). However, Biennial Update Reports and the International Consultation and Analysis process have also blurred the lines between evaluation and transparency. For example, they both consider "mitigation actions *and their effects*" (UNFCCC, 2010: paras. 60, 63, emphasis added). Such language implies a causal analysis of policy effectiveness and did not exist in the original National Communication guidelines. This ambiguity between evaluation and transparency has permeated the implementation of REDD+ and NAMAs.

As will become clearer in later chapters, the evaluation frameworks for climate finance instruments actually share greater similarities with results-based management approaches that have been used by multilateral development agencies since the 1990s (Bester, 2012; Mayne, 2007; Vähämäki et al., 2011). As the term results-based management implies, the emphasis is on allowing implementing parties to use whatever means at their disposal to reach a policy outcome. This is often operationalized through an additionality criterion. For example, the OECD defines development additionality as the "development impacts that arise as a result of investment that otherwise would not have occurred" (Andersen et al., 2021: 18). While perhaps liberating from a managerial perspective, the main challenge is to demonstrate that a particular policy outcome is causally related to a development intervention.

Before I continue, it is important to emphasize a distinction between the climate finance instruments investigated in this book and other carbon-pricing instruments, such as emissions trading and carbon taxes. As baseline instruments, the climate finance instruments addressed in this book offer a much more eclectic array of policy interventions than those associated with carbon pricing. In contrast, carbon-pricing policies are intended to change actor behavior by requiring actors to pay for the costs of their emissions. But interventions under climate finance instruments investigated here rarely place costs on policy actors. CDM projects considered in this book, for example, include subsidies for more efficient heating systems, paying individuals or firms to plant trees, or mobilizing investments to upgrade renewable energy technology. International climate finance instruments considered here generally only focus on using financing from developed countries to pay for actions leading to emission reductions in developing countries.

1.3. Political Economy Factors of Climate Finance Effectiveness

In the preceding section, I unpacked the concept of policy effectiveness, which is the dependent variable of interest. But the book's main contribution is to identify causal political economy factors that have contributed to policy effectiveness. As already suggested, development policy paradigms and state development interests in forestry and decentralized renewable energy emerge as most important factors explaining the effectiveness of the CDM, REDD+, and NAMAs across the case-study countries. However, I also need to be able to distinguish them from other potential explanatory factors, including state organizational capacity and political settlements. Table 1.2 delineated how the three case-study countries vary in terms of these four political economy factors. While I introduced state organizational capacity earlier, this section elaborates briefly on the remaining three political economy concepts.

Development Policy Paradigms

Drawing on the work of Peter Hall (1993, 2010, 2013), I define policy paradigms as a set of economic ideas informing the *means* of achieving certain policy objectives. While such a definition might prove controversial, distinguishing between policy means and policy ends gives us considerable analytical leverage. From this point of view, development policy paradigms are a set of instrumental beliefs about how different policies—including organizational and institutional policy elements—might help achieve various economic development objectives. Development policy paradigms shape institutions and organizations responsible for policy implementation. In this way, development policy paradigms predispose developing countries to varying degrees of effectiveness in the implementation of climate finance instruments.

Since World War II development policy paradigms have followed an arc that runs from classic developmentalism, neoliberalism, neodevelopmentalism, and, most recently, what I describe as liberal neodevelopmentalism (see Ban, 2012). However, the evolution of a development policy paradigm in any one country is grounded in its historical experience. For reasons explored in Chapter 4, much of the current debate among political elites in developing countries can be found with regard to classic developmentalism, neodevelopmentalism, and liberal neodevelopmentalism. As for neoliberalism, I offer evidence demonstrating that there has been general disenchantment with this development policy paradigm since the 2008 global financial crisis.

Development policy paradigms can be thought of as differing along two dimensions (Figure 1.3). First, they differ in terms of a state's comparative advantage strategy: a *comparative advantage following* strategy or *comparative advantage defying* strategy (Lin and Chang, 2009). As I elaborate in Chapter 4, this can be observed from key economic policy strategies, including strategies regarding national asset management (nationalization/privatization), agricultural price controls, and state coordination. But second, development policy paradigms also differ in their posture relative to international trade, ranging from autarky to globalization.

Briefly, classic developmentalism, which was popular during the wave of independence during the 1960s, saw developing countries aim to defy their comparative advantage by cultivating infant industries through protectionist trade measures under a strategy known as import substitution industrialization (ISI). By the 1970s and 1980s, classic developmentalism would start to show certain strains. It would be succeeded by neoliberalism as a dominant development policy paradigm in the developing world; though, as we shall see, it is questionable to what degree it was genuinely adopted by leaders there. Neoliberalism calls for states to disassemble efforts to defy their current comparative advantage

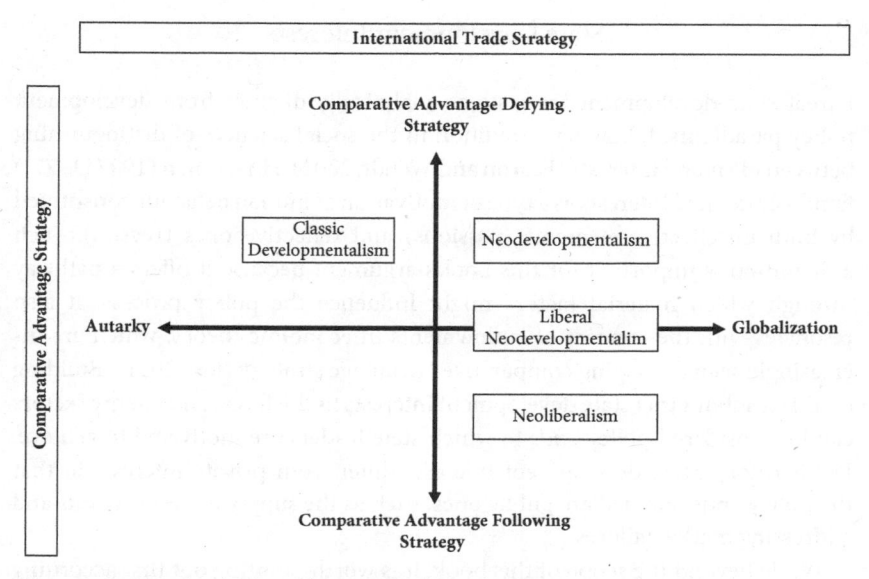

Figure 1.3 Typology of Development Policy Paradigms

and encourages developing countries to participate in the global market at their current levels. Particularly in East Asia, another development policy paradigm would emerge at this time, which I refer to as neodevelopmentalism. While sharing a *comparative advantage defying* strategy similar to classic developmentalism, it is characterized by efforts to create domestic firms capable of competing in relatively high-value segments of global and regional markets. For both classic developmentalism and neodevelopmentalism, state coordination of the economy might be more heavy-handed and top-down, given the authoritarian tendencies that such states have historically demonstrated.

Finally, states adhering to a liberal neodevelopmental paradigm share a *comparative advantage following* strategy of incrementally upgrading a country's economic capacities in order to seize existing global market opportunities. In contrast to neodevelopmentalism, such upgrading tends to be more selective and prudent; it is often based on an honest assessment of a country's competitive advantages and capacity to add value. I also submit that liberal neodevelopmentalism is characterized by a more bottom-up form of policy coordination, where the state demonstrates a certain degree of deference to existing firms already competitive in international markets. The distinction I make between neodevelopmentalism and liberal neodevelopmentalism may be controversial (see Andreoni and Chang, 2019), but I submit helps explain differences in climate finance instrument effectiveness across the case-study countries as well as between the forest and energy sectors within them.

State Development Interests

I treat state development interests as analytically distinct from development policy paradigms, following a tradition in the social sciences of distinguishing between ideas and interests (Fearon and Wendt, 2002). Hirschman (1997 [1977]) famously defined interests as a type of motivation of human behavior constituted by both unreflective elements (passions) and reflective ones (reason). Such a definition is important for this book's argument because it offers a pathway through which material factors might influence the policy process. It also resonates with the concept of endowments in economic theory, which are increasingly seen as shaping comparative advantage strategy (Lin, 2011). Building on this, I submit that state development interests in the forest and energy sectors can be considered policy *ends* to which state leaders are motivated to achieve. Furthermore, state development interests differ from private interests in that the policy ends pursued are public ones, such as the supply of public goods and addressing market failures.

While beyond the scope of this book, it is worth pointing out that according to some theorists, interests do not exist independently but are determined by individual preferences resulting from a complex cognitive process of subjective interpretation. For example, Béland and Cox (2011) argue that "interests are one form of idea" that can "change as actors alter their understanding of the changing world and recalculate their priorities" (pp. 10–11). But even leading proponents of ideational theory such as Alexander Wendt (1999) have argued that desires (a concept akin to interests) "always involve a mixture of biological drivers and beliefs, with the importance of beliefs varying along a continuum from low (a desire for water when thirsty) to high (a desire to do the right thing)" (p. 123).

There is ample evidence that material factors are politically salient in the developing world, perhaps in ways underappreciated in richer parts of the world. Most fundamentally, material scarcity constitutes a basic resource problem affecting public affairs that is often more acute than typically found in developed countries. For example, a sharp escalation in world commodity prices is widely recognized to have precipitated the global food crisis of 2007–2008, which led to violent food riots in certain—though not all—developing countries (Berazneva and Lee, 2013; Raleigh et al., 2015). Of course, environmental scarcity does not always result in conflict and is strongly mediated by institutional and ideological factors (Homer-Dixon, 1999). Furthermore, the ambition of establishing modern energy is a priority for development in all countries investigated, which cannot fully be disentangled from ideas of modernization and what it means to be "developed". But it would be an error to overlook how interests, as a distinct analytical category, help explain how material factors, like the scarcity of forest and energy resources, can independently motivate social and political behavior.

Political Settlements

Another way that material factors might affect the effectiveness of climate fi-nance instruments in developing countries is by shaping the political context in which public policy is undertaken. This insight is fundamental to the political settlements framework, which is largely associated with the work of Mushtaq Husain Khan. Khan first defined political settlements as a "combination of power and institutions that is mutually compatible and also sustainable in terms of economic and political viability" (Khan and Jomo, 1999: 4). In another useful formulation, Dye (2021) emphasized that "the political settlements approach examines the distribution of power and the alignment of different social and po-litical actors' interest with developmental outcomes" (p. 3).

Important for our purposes, political settlement provides an alternative framework for thinking about the structure of domestic politics in developing countries, particularly least developed countries. Khan (2005) pointed out that informal patron-client behavior is pervasive in the developing world; they are found in countries with vastly different historical and cultural attributes. In con-trast with neopatrimonialism and mainstream policy theory applied in devel-oped countries, the political settlements framework recognizes that political power can also be legitimately organized through such informal institutions. Rather than seeing patron-client relationships as a perversion of formal institutions, they might be better considered as coalitions with important implications for governance.

Among Khan's key innovations was to identify two pathways through which material factors might lead to the emergence of such informal, clientelistic be-havior in developing countries. First is the observation that the private sector and civil society play a smaller role in public affairs, leaving the state with dispropor-tionate weight in domestic political and economic spheres. Nonetheless, second, the state does not possess sufficient capacity—organizational nor strategic—for fundamental redistributive policies like taxing and spending. This leads to the proliferation of patron-client networks that offer elites and their clients an alter-native, albeit informal, route to the redistribution of state resources. Together, material scarcity and an underdeveloped private sector have the counterintuitive effect of concentrating political and economic power in the state while simulta-neously driving politics into informal channels where various groups compete for the state's scarce resources. The upshot is that the state plays a more central, albeit informal, role in political and economic affairs in developing countries than is the case in developed countries where dominant pluralist theories of the policy process prevail (see Smith, 1990).

However, not all political settlements are the same, which has important implications for the ability of a ruling coalition to govern. Political settlements are

Table 1.6 Typology of Political Settlements

| | | Horizontal Political Power | |
		Concentrated	Distributed
Vertical Political Power	Concentrated	Strong dominant party	Vulnerable authoritarianism
	Distributed	Weak dominant party	Competitive clientelism

Sources: Khan (2010: 64–69); Whitfield et al. (2015: 105–108).

deemed to vary along two dimensions of the distribution of political power of the ruling coalition, leading to four types of clientelist political settlements: strong dominant party, weak dominant party, vulnerable authoritarianism, and competitive clientelism (Table 1.6). Vertical power refers to the way power is distributed within the ruling coalition; for example, if the central elites have effective control over subordinates and the bureaucracy. Horizontal power refers to the political power of the ruling coalition relative to other social groups in society. The current consensus is that more transformational development policies are able to be carried out under a strong dominant party where a developmental coalition may emerge. Under these conditions, the ruling coalition exerts effective central authority and does not feel its hold on power is threatened (Khan, 2010: 66). As Hickey (2019) observes, elites tend to protect public sectors deemed integral to regime survival and legitimacy.

Overall, while there are concerns that the political settlement framework hews too close to rational choice theory (Abdulai, 2017), the framework does encourage researchers to look beyond formal institutions toward underlying political economy factors to explain policy effectiveness in developing countries.

1.4. Summary of the Main Argument

Having reviewed the independent and dependent variables around which this book is organized, in this section I summarize the main argument.

Through detailed study of the effectiveness of three different climate finance instruments in three case-study countries over a 10-year period from 2008 to 2018, this book was written to respond to questions about how to design climate finance instruments to effectively engage developing countries in reducing emissions. Under what conditions have different existing climate finance instruments been effective and have different instruments been more effective than others?

I develop my argument by first reviewing the evidence on how climate finance flows from developed to developing countries have evolved over the near decade-long transition from the liberal environmentalism of the Kyoto Protocol to the developmental environmentalism of the Paris Agreement. Here I am able to demonstrate that neither public nor private financial resources made available for climate change mitigation in developing countries have yet reached levels first promised in the 2009 Copenhagen Accord. The shift in global environmental norms has, thus far, had less material impact on global climate finance flows than anticipated. Indeed, the main policy output resulting from the 2021 UN climate change conference, the Glasgow Climate Pact, admitted "with deep regret" that rich countries had failed to live up to the $100 billion annual climate finance goal first made in Copenhagen in 2009 (Mountford et al., 2021). While in its most recent estimate, the OECD is optimistic that the $100 billion will "likely" have been met by 2022 (OECD, 2023), the war in Ukraine might affect donor financing (Strøm-Sedgwick and Tank, 2022).

One of the key arguments defended in this book is that levels of climate finance that have been on offer thus far by the international community—via climate finance instruments associated with both liberal environmentalism and developmental environmentalism—have largely been insufficient *on their own* to persuade state and nonstate actors in developing countries to abandon carbon-intensive development pathways and implement climate finance effectively. My research on the ground demonstrates that despite the institutional innovations associated with developmental environmentalism, the effectiveness of REDD+ and NAMAs across the three case-study countries is surprisingly consistent with that of the CDM.

In this context, the effectiveness of how climate finance would be implemented has depended on the interaction between the development policy paradigms and interests of the state in promoting various sectors of their economies. As for a country's political settlement, this translates into political power to push policy implementation through the state apparatus, but not the basic decision about whether to engage with climate finance instruments in the first place.

In terms of the CDM, I argue that at low carbon prices observed during the first commitment period of the Kyoto Protocol, CDM financing was insufficient to incentivize project developers to implement projects on the basis of climate finance alone. Rather, the effectiveness of the CDM and other carbon offset projects depended on the interests and capacities of project developers themselves—pockets of CDM effectiveness. Across a range of CDM project developers, I found one particular type of organization—state agencies—to possess a combination of developmental and business interests that motivated it to experiment with the carbon market as well as a latent organizational capacity that allowed climate finance to be used effectively. In effect, the state had created, albeit not purposely, organizations with capacity and interests to effectively engage with the CDM.

While I found other actors involved with the CDM, their projects were less effectively implemented. While projects by NGOs might also be effectively implemented largely on the basis of climate finance, they were precariously over-reliant on it and projects they pursued (smallholder tree planting and improved cookstoves) not well aligned with state development interests, resulting in muted government support. Private firms, however, implemented CDM projects that were only partially effective. Climate finance might have led projects to be implemented somewhat sooner than might otherwise have been the case, but it did not change the fundamentals of projects being pursued. Firms appeared to use CDM financing to implement projects already planned and, largely, financed in what appears as a bid to reduce costs and increase profits.

But state agencies associated with highly effective CDM projects were only found in Uganda and Moldova and only in the forest and not energy sectors there. State forest agencies in both countries were a product of liberal economic reforms, allowing governments to retain an interventionist foothold in their forest sectors, while these same governments fully liberalized their respective energy sectors where the state retains only a weakened regulatory role. State forest agencies were, however, absent in Tanzania at the time of my investigation of the CDM. While the Forest and Beekeeping Division (FBD) at the Ministry of Natural Resources and Tourism (MNRT) has been, until quite recently, custodian of the Tanzanian government's forest reserves and industrial forest plantations, it did not have the capacity nor interest to engage with the CDM. A state agency would subsequently be established in Tanzania, the Tanzania Forest Service (TFS), but it has also not been involved in the CDM.

I submit that the presence of state agencies is shaped by prevailing development policy paradigms and development interests of the state. That is, project-level pockets of effectiveness were contingent on state-level ideas and interests. More specifically, I attribute the retention of state organizational capacity in the forest sector in the form of state agencies—but not energy sector—of Uganda and Moldova to a development policy paradigm of liberal neodevelopmentalism. Adhering to a *comparative advantage following* strategy, the central governments in both countries had determined that they had the organizational capacity to intervene in the forest sector but not energy sector. Afforestation and renewable bioenergy were also state development priorities in Moldova, but only the CDM afforestation project in Moldova, where a state forest agency was present, proved highly effective. In contrast, a CDM bioenergy led by a government department at the Ministry of Environment simply had insufficient organizational capacity for effective implementation. State development interests were different in Uganda: while forests were a priority, decentralized renewable energy was not. Indeed, in the energy sector, the Ugandan central government has prioritized recently discovered oil deposits and large-scale hydroelectricity, albeit deferring largely to private actors for their operation. In sectors where the state does not perceive itself to have the capacity to effectively intervene, liberal neodevelopmentalism can appear like neoliberalism; it is only in comparing different economic sectors that this can be observed.

In Tanzania, the state aspires to neodevelopmentalism though prevailing economic ideas are still rooted in classic developmentalism, a situation I describe as a hybrid developmental policy paradigm of classic developmentalism and neodevelopmentalism. In this situation, while the state envisions an important role for itself in economic development, it has not sufficiently instilled organizational interest and capacity for engaging global business opportunities across the state apparatus, like those represented by the CDM. Among development practitioners, there was genuine perplexity if not frustration about the lack of constructive engagement by the Tanzanian central government with the CDM. As one in the donor explained to me in one interview in 2009: "[The Tanzanian CDM authority] is not only the bottleneck, but I mean, [the CDM authority] is the cork in the bottleneck. Seriously. And we seriously don't understand why that is. We cannot find out."[4]

Similarly, detailed investigation of REDD+ and NAMAs in the three case-study countries suggests that more effective implementation and programming, respectively, has been taking place in Uganda and Moldova than in Tanzania. In terms of REDD+, Uganda has diligently worked to implement the instrument under the more rigorous standards of the World Bank Forest Carbon Partnership Facility (WB-FCPF) that anticipates the development of carbon payments for REDD+ similar to a carbon market. REDD+ implementation would also build on Uganda's traditional strategy of more bottom-up development planning that involves a relatively broad array of policy actors. Alignment between Uganda's development policy paradigm of liberal neodevelopmental and its state development interest in the forest sector, mentioned above, has seen the Ugandan central government actively pursuing REDD+. In contrast, Tanzania became party to Norway's efforts, the world's leading financial supporter of REDD+, but prioritized the less rigorous UN-REDD framework that is unlikely to prepare the country for the demands of rigorous results-based payment system. The REDD+ file has also been centralized under the Division of Environment at the Vice-President's Office (DoE-VPO), creating tensions with arguably more appropriate organizations of the Tanzanian government. In 2016, Norway quietly admitted its REDD+ effort in Tanzania was a failure and withdrew—a major setback for what was seen as a flagship international REDD+ effort in Africa. (Note that REDD+ is not discussed with regard to Moldova, which is not engaged with the instrument given limited standing forests there and a focus instead on afforestation/reforestation.)

Finally, a similar pattern is found with regard to NAMA programming. While Uganda and Moldova have submitted numerous potential NAMAs to the UNFCCC, Tanzania has shown almost no interest in this instrument. While engagement with NAMAs is consistent with the prevalence of a liberal neodevelopmental policy paradigm in the former two countries, differences in the implementation of NAMAs between Uganda and Moldova might also be explained by state development interests. In Moldova, NAMA proposals submitted reflect urgent state development interests in the forest and energy sectors, whereas in Uganda, NAMAs have focused on decentralized renewables that tend to be at odds with a state development interest in pursuing large-scale hydroelectric and oil resources. Consequently, while both countries were engaged with the NAMA process, Moldova had committed more co-financing and invested in a more robust domestic evaluation framework.

While these results are altogether rather sobering, they also point to a better strategy for engaging with developing countries on climate change mitigation. While neither climate finance instruments derived from liberal environmentalism (CDM) nor developmental environmentalism (REDD+ and NAMAs) have proven sufficiently effective, a combination of elements of both holds promise: *liberal developmental environmentalism*. This would prioritize climate mitigation actions that states are already pursuing, like NAMAs, but also includes a more robust evaluation framework in order to attract resources from an international community that still demands results. However, carbon price floors might be introduced to ensure that climate actions supported are transformational. Furthermore, instead of privileging either state or nonstate actors, liberal developmental environmentalism would cultivate synergies between the two in the transition to low-carbon development. I discuss liberal developmental environmentalism further in the conclusion to this book.

1.5. Organization of the Book

The book is structured in three parts. In Part I, I discuss global ideas about climate and development cooperation that have circulated at the global level within the UN climate change regime. In Chapter 2, I introduce liberal environmentalism, which has underwritten the CDM as originally conceived, including review of the evaluation framework of CDM carbon offset projects—particularly in terms of CDM "additionality"—but also the relationship that architects of the CDM envisioned it would have with the state. The chapter closes with a discussion of the collapse of the CDM and Kyoto carbon market in 2012, though also noting that the CDM has continued to evolve out of the spotlight.

Chapter 3 presents developmental environmentalism, including a concise history of climate and development finance prior to it. In many ways, developmental environmentalism has represented a return to traditional development management practices that prevailed before the 1990s. But another important contribution in this chapter is to relate developmental environmentalism to the 2008 global financial crisis, which marked a critical juncture in global political economy. The global financial crisis would profoundly affect global climate politics, particularly the pivotal 2009 UN climate change conference in Copenhagen. Finally, I also demonstrate how characteristics of developmental environmentalism are reflected in new climate instruments, supporting arguments by detailed analysis of the institutional design of REDD+ and NAMAs.

In order to understand the effectiveness of climate finance instruments in developing countries I need to move beyond global environmental norms to consider the evolution of ideas about the process of development and how they have evolved in the case-study countries. This is addressed in Part II.

Beginning with Chapter 4, I unpack the concept of development policy paradigms and review major trends in their evolution since World War II. I begin by discussing the relationship between the Soviet experience of economic development, whose legacy still resonates in many developing countries; before moving to what I call classic developmentalism, which emerged post–World War II; and then to neoliberalism, which came to dominance since at least the 1980s. However, in the marketplace of ideas, neoliberalism would increasingly be challenged by the surprising success of East Asia, which shunned most neoliberal principles. I refer to this as "neodevelopmentalism." The chapter concludes with discussion of an additional development policy paradigm that falls between neoliberalism and neodevelopmentalism, which I describe as liberal neodevelopmentalism.

In Chapter 5, I begin to consider the political economy of the case-study countries of Tanzania, Uganda, and Moldova. I first discuss the political settlements of each country in greater detail. This is done to introduce the reader to the fundamental political situation in each and how they differ between one another. In Chapter 6, a similar exercise is undertaken to discuss state development interests in each country. This is based on a detailed review of the forest and energy sectors in each.

Detailed discussion of policy paradigms of the case-study countries is found in Chapter 7. While all have seen important liberal economic reforms in their recent histories, the degree to which each country has embraced neoliberalism has differed. I present initial evidence that the development policy paradigm of

Uganda and Moldova reflects many elements of liberal neodevelopmentalism while that of Tanzania demonstrates a hybrid classic developmental and neodevelopmental policy paradigm. Such differences have important implications for the effectiveness of climate finance instruments.

Part III presents empirical evaluations of climate finance effectiveness with an explanation drawing on empirical evidence of development policy paradigms and state development interests.

In Chapter 8, I present findings from the investigation of the actual effectiveness of the CDM and other types of carbon offset projects in Tanzania, Uganda, and Moldova. Key here is the identification of state agencies in the forest sectors of Uganda and Moldova as "pockets of CDM effectiveness." This chapter draws on detailed empirical evaluations of nearly all CDM and carbon offset afforestation/reforestation and bioenergy projects in operation in the three countries in the mid-to-late 2000s. I also present an argument relating project-level effectiveness of carbon offset projects to state-level variables of development policy paradigms and state development interests. Supplementary information pertinent to this chapter is found in Appendices 1 and 2.

Chapter 9 undertakes a similar analysis with regard to REDD+ implementation in Tanzania and Uganda. Given Moldova's focus on afforestation/reforestation of degraded land, as opposed to forest conservation, it has not been involved with this climate finance instrument. My results demonstrate that the implementation of REDD+ adheres to the same pattern as CDM effectiveness: it has been more effectively implemented in Uganda than Tanzania.

In Chapter 10, I consider how NAMAs have been undertaken in the three-case study countries. I find Uganda and, especially, Moldova to have sought to program NAMAs to a surprising degree in spite of almost no climate finance being offered for implementation. In contrast, Tanzania has been almost completely unengaged with the NAMA process.

In the Conclusion, presented in Chapter 11, I consider the implications of my research findings. While there are certainly limitations to their generalizability, they do demonstrate the importance of development policy paradigms and state development interests for climate policy effectiveness, which might be expected to resonate with the experience of other countries where the economy is highly reliant on agriculture and rural peasants still important. Based on my findings, I also propose a new approach to engaging developing countries on climate change mitigation that combines elements of previous global environmental norms: *liberal developmental environmentalism.*

1.6. Annex: Trends in Key Development Indicators Across Countries

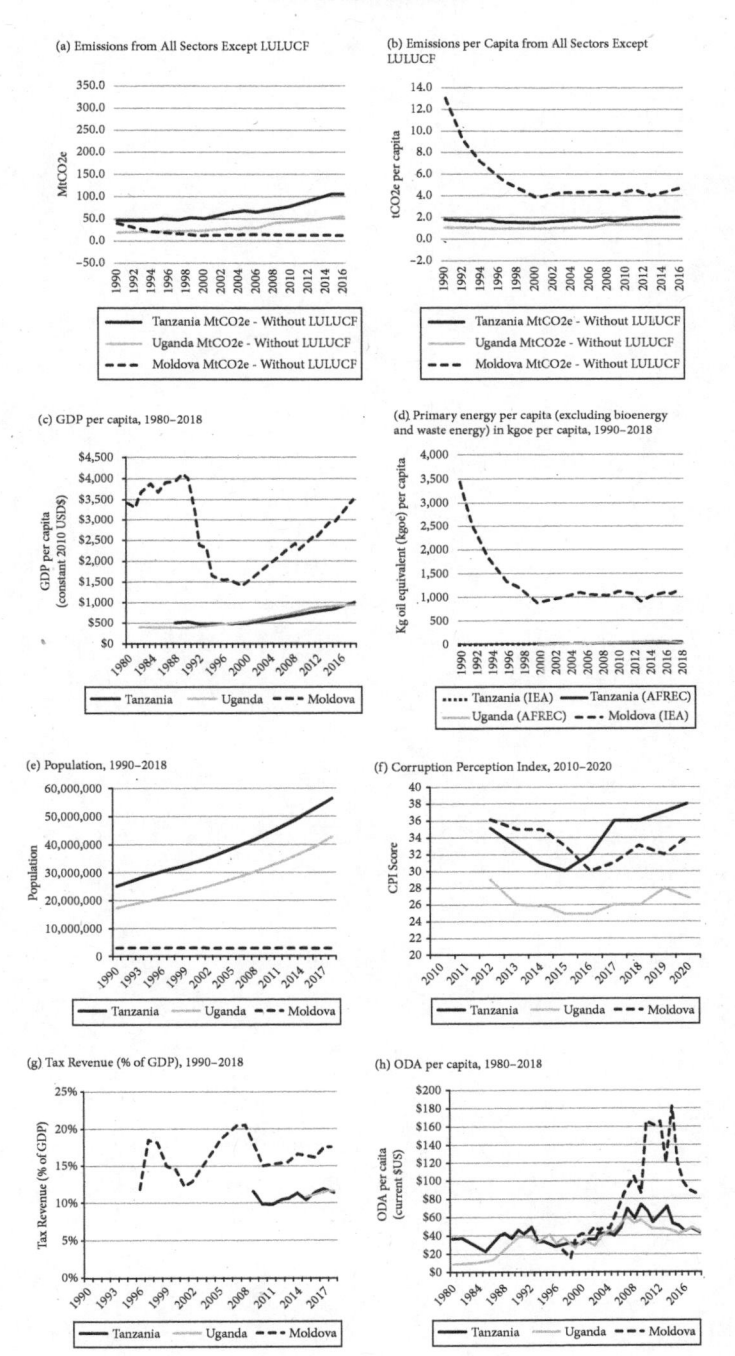

Note: LULUCF = Land Use, Land-Use Change, and Forestry

PART I

GLOBAL IDEAS ABOUT CLIMATE AND DEVELOPMENT COOPERATION

2
The CDM and Liberal Environmentalism

2.1. Introduction

In this chapter, I begin discussion of global environmental norms by reviewing the CDM as well as elements of liberal environmentalism that have underpinned it. Liberal environmentalism marked a decisive movement away from traditional practices of environmental governance toward more neoliberal market-based approaches that incorporated results-based management. As argued by Bernstein (2001), in the 1990s, liberal environmentalism prevailed over other competing ideas of sustainable development because it allowed ideas of environmental governance "to fit better" with the global neoliberal economic order and was therefore able to gain policy traction (p. 21). The carbon market in particular was consonant with neoliberal ideas such as private property, free-trade, and self-regulating markets (pp. 118–119). The CDM came to embody liberal environmentalism in terms of its reliance on the private sector, emphasis on results in the form of verifiable emission reductions, and the limited role accorded the state for implementation.

It is worth noting that, during 1997 negotiations in Kyoto, what became the CDM was originally proposed by Brazil as a clean development *fund*. In the words of Werksman (1998), the CDM was the "Kyoto surprise." Though it was not until 2001 that detailed rules were agreed upon to operationalize the CDM, the mechanism became a key instrument in a negotiated compromise between the developed and developing worlds on the costs and benefits of addressing climate change. Over 2004–2011, the value of CDM carbon credits was valued at more than $27 billion, while the instrument may have brought it $10–25 billion per year in co-financing at its peak between 2007 and 2009 (Buchner et al., 2011: 25–26; Purdon, 2014b: 318–319).

However, by 2012 the CDM carbon market would collapse, as support for a second commitment period of the Kyoto Protocol unraveled. (I discuss reasons for this in the next chapter.) Nonetheless, it is important to recognize that the CDM lives on and is widely seen now as the precursor to the Sustainable Development Mechanism (SDM), the result of negotiations on Article 6.4 of the Paris Agreement—final rules for which were only adopted in Glasgow in 2021 (Slaughter and May, 2021).

The Political Economy of Climate Finance Effectiveness in Developing Countries. Mark Purdon, Oxford University Press.

There have, of course, been many concerns with the CDM, not just about whether carbon credits generated are genuine. I briefly review these in Section 2.2 below. The rest of the chapter reviews the instrument's design characteristics including its reliance on private sector financing, limited role for the state, and a relatively rigorous results-based evaluation framework—characteristics reflecting liberal environmentalism.

2.2. Concerns with the CDM

The CDM has attracted considerable critique. A first concern has been that few CDM projects have been undertaken in least developed countries and are rather concentrated in emerging economies. The initial distribution of CDM investment flows tended to replicate traditional foreign direct investment flows with China, India, and Brazil (Cosbey et al., 2005; UNFCCC Secretariat, 2008). One reason that least developed countries have been underrepresented is the administrative burden of the CDM's initial project-based approach. All CDM projects have needed to adhere to a specific technical methodology that is subject to third-party verification. Such methodologies have been an important way for the UNFCCC to exert control over the CDM, as all have needed to be approved by the CDM Executive Board. But they are also highly technical and require considerable administrative resources to complete. In the early 2000s, the UNFCCC sought to address the administrative burden by developing "programmatic" CDM that allowed project developers to bundle together a number of projects under a common administrative umbrella (Ellis, 2006; Hinostroza et al., 2007). Programmatic CDM does appear to have alleviated some of the regional imbalances: considerably more CDM programs have been implemented in Africa than regular CDM projects (UNEP DTU, 2020: PoAanalysis).

Another reason for the skewed distribution of CDM projects has been restrictions placed on the use of land and forestry projects (Purdon, 2010). As relatively modest consumers of fossil fuels, least developed countries and low-income transition economies possess less mitigation potential in sectors such as energy and transportation relative to emerging economies. Including land-use change and forestry in the Kyoto carbon market, however, proved highly controversial (Bernoux et al., 2002). Early UNFCCC decisions put a limit on the use of afforestation and reforestation CDM credits that industrialized countries might acquire (Schlamadinger et al., 2007). Similarly, the EU never permitted the exchange of CDM credits from afforestation/reforestation projects in its emissions trading system (European Commission, 2015; Schlamadinger et al., 2005). Furthermore, as I discuss later, while what is now known as REDD+ was originally expected to be part of the CDM as "avoided deforestation," it was ultimately excluded from it at UN climate change negotiations in 2001.

As suggested in the Introduction, there is also an extensive critical literature that sees the CDM and carbon markets as forms of neocolonialism and unethical exchange (Böhm and Dhabi, 2009; Pearse and Böhm, 2014). Environmental justice and sustainable development with regard to climate finance instruments are important issues, but there is not enough room in this book to discuss them comprehensively. I have discussed separately such issues with regard to a certain number of the carbon offset projects investigated here (Purdon, 2013, 2014a, 2018; Purdon and Byakagaba, 2022).

As important as the issues of uneven project distribution and the sustainability of CDM projects and programs are, key for the CDM remains the issue of additionality and whether carbon credits issued through it are genuinely fungible with reductions of source. If not, then the entire logic of the carbon market unravels.

Here existing research has raised significant concerns. Among the first were questions about industrial gas projects. A number of early critiques of the CDM suggested that, given that reduction of one tonne of industrial gases like hydrofluorocarbons (HFCs) was equal to approximately 12,000 tonnes of CO2 (tCO2), savvy policy actors proposed to eliminate them from projects that were never really intended to be implemented in the first place (Schneider, 2011). It is worth noting that more recent research has suggested that initial concerns about HFC projects might be balanced out by conservative accounting methods (Munnings et al., 2016). But there have also been misgivings about the broader market. David Victor estimated that one-third to two-thirds of carbon credits generated through the CDM did not represent real reductions, maybe even more (Victor, 2011: 96). Perhaps the most widely cited study was commissioned by the EU, which concluded that 85% of a randomly selected sample of 90 CDM projects were unlikely to represent genuine emission reductions (Cames et al., 2016). These and other critics have suggested that CDM project developers often exaggerate baseline emissions, claiming that low-emissions projects would have been unviable without CDM financing. But most of such critique has been desk reviews based on available CDM policy documents, such as project design documents as well as validation, monitoring, and verification reports. Few have been based on empirical fieldwork to gauge the veracity of CDM policy documentation in the first placed.

2.3. Reliance on Private Sector Financing

A key distinction between liberal environmentalism and development environmentalism are different principle sources of funding. The architects of the CDM expected that the private sector would contribute the majority of funds for implementation and donors would play a very limited role. Indeed, the CDM was first designed to explicitly separate climate finance sourced through the CDM from international public financing such as official development assistance (ODA). The CDM's initial rules emphasized "that public funding for clean development mechanism projects from [developed countries] is not to result in the diversion of ODA and is to be separate from and not counted towards the financial obligations of [developed countries toward ODA]" (UNFCCC, 2001: preamble). Developing countries sought such a provision because of their concern that ODA would be diverted to the generation of carbon offsets, which were already in the interests of developed countries as means of reducing their compliance costs with the Kyoto Protocol.

In practice distinguishing between private climate finance and ODA has proven difficult. All CDM projects have required that the project developer affirm that "any public funding does not result in a diversion of ODA and is separate from and is not counted towards [ODA commitments of developed countries]" (UNFCCC, 2005a: Appendix B, para. (f)). But as close observers have pointed out, this language is unclear—particularly the purposes from which ODA is to be prevented from being diverted (Dutschke and Michaelowa, 2006).

However, there are good reasons to permit some combination of public and private climate finance. Indeed, as discussed in the next chapter, donor financing is often used as seed money to leverage co-financing from other sources—domestic and international, public and private—to create projects with larger impact. The OECD Development Assistance Committee (DAC)—a key forum where rich countries discuss and aim to coordinate their development assistance efforts—sought to legitimize such a combination. In 2004, it decided that OECD members could use donor financing for everything except the final purchase of CDM carbon credits (OECD, 2004).

Yet, as we shall also see in my investigation of CDM effectiveness in Chapter 8, the World Bank has directly purchased CDM credits through a number of affiliated entities, including the Prototype Carbon Fund, BioCarbon Fund, and Community Development Carbon Fund operating under its Carbon Finance Unit (Michaelowa and Michaelowa, 2011). Ostensibly these CDM credits might have been sold on the Kyoto or voluntary carbon markets at profit. Blurring the lines between public and private finance and organizations, the World Bank would play an outsized role in the CDM. And not without critique: as Michaelowa and Michaelowa (2011) indicate, while World Bank-supported projects were more prevalent in least developed countries, there is also evidence that it used its market power and connections in the developing world to secure contracts for the most commercially attractive projects and at CDM carbon credits prices at below market value.

2.4. Measuring CDM Emission Reductions

Another important indicator of liberal environmentalism that can be observed in the CDM's initial design was its emphasis on delivering results—carbon credits that are fully fungible with emission allowances on emissions-trading systems. In this respect, the CDM would align itself with the practice of results-based management techniques in international development cooperation that prevailed during the neoliberal period. This necessitated a complex evaluation framework, the heart of which is a counterfactual baseline against which emission reductions are measured and carbon credits claimed to be "additional." I describe technical issues involved with the CDM's evaluation framework here, which will also help the reader understand the methodology I used to evaluate CDM and related carbon offset projects in later chapters.

At its most basic level, emission reductions accredited by the CDM are to be "additional" to a counterfactual situation where the CDM did not exist, referred to as a baseline in the CDM evaluation framework. As defined by the UNFCC, a "CDM project activity is additional if anthropogenic emissions of greenhouse gases by sources are reduced below those that would have occurred in the absence of the registered CDM project activity" (UNFCCC, 2005b, para. 43). As suggested in Section 2.2 above, the concern is that if baseline emissions are overestimated or purposefully inflated, more emission reductions might be credited than justified. The emission reductions would have happened "anyway," and attributing them to the CDM is unjustified, and reason for their accreditation in the global carbon market unravels. An effective CDM project is one that reduces emissions that are additional to what would have transpired in the absence of the CDM intervention.

Until recently, CDM project developers have been largely responsible for elaborating them. Of course, detailed technical methodologies have been developed to regulate both CDM project and baseline scenarios, but information asymmetries about the development context of CDM projects has frustrated third-party verification of baselines developed by project developers. By development context, I mean the social, economic, and political conditions in which a particular CDM project is situated. For example, official documents for a CDM afforestation project that I investigated in Tanzania make little mention of large state-owned plantations directly adjacent to the project area nor the history of Tanzania's forest industry in the region. Indeed, the area is punctuated by the breathtaking Mufindi escarpment that makes the area almost ideal for plantation forestry (Figure 2.1). How could a CDM afforestation project claim there was little hope of planting trees without CDM financing if it was located adjacent to industrial, state-owned forest plantations?

(a) Tanzania government forest plantation encountered on drive to CDM afforestation project

(b) View of Mufindi escarpment from the south

Figure 2.1 Contrasting Views of Mufindi Escarpment, Tanzania

Technically, project developers have been allowed to select one of three basic approaches for developing a CDM baseline scenarios: (1) historical emissions, (2) emissions from "an economically attractive course of action" and (3) average emissions of similar project activities undertaken in the previous five years (UNFCCC, 2005a: Annex, para. 48(a-c)). Similarly, for afforestation/reforestation projects, potential baseline approaches include (1) historical trends, (2) the "most likely" land-use change expected at the time of the project's inception, and (3) expected land-use change due to economic development, taking into account barriers to investment (UNFCCC, 2005b: Annex, para. 22(a-c)). However, in practice, project developers generally "freeze" baseline conditions observed at the project's inception over a project's 7–10 year crediting period—or 20–30 years in the case of forestry projects (IEA, 2009: 69–93; Purdon, 2009a: 60–62).

This rigidity has created measurement problems. For example, the CDM Executive Board decided as early as 2005 that changes in government policy during a CDM project's crediting period would not be counted as a change in baseline conditions (CDM EB, 2005). But as some observers noted, this meant that the CDM Executive Board effectively "disabled their own additionality criteria" (WFC, 2009: 4). It has also proven technically challenging to incorporate changing baseline conditions. As Zhang and Wang (2011) have argued, many violations of CDM additionality have not been due to strategic misrepresentation of information by project developers but, rather, because of "the current CDM baseline methodology that fails to predict future emissions in a fast-changing economy" (p. 49).

It might be assumed that contextual information necessary for evaluating baselines would be provided in CDM project documents and subject to third-party review. This has not been the case, though the CDM's evaluation framework has evolved. Initially, the scope of review of third-party auditors was restricted to merely confirming if technical information submitted by project developers conformed to the requirements of a particular CDM methodology (UNFCCC, 2005b: para. 37). A number of authors argued early on that the ambit of third-party verifiers needed to be expanded (Schneider, 2007b; Wara, 2008). But it was not until 2010, as the Kyoto carbon market began to unravel, that the CDM Executive Board began to address this concern by expanding the scope of review of CDM auditors in a second version of its *CDM Validation and Verification Manual* (CDM EB, 2010: para.33(a-d)).[1] Given continuing problems with CDM additionality, subsequent rules—issued in 2014 as the *CDM Validation and Verification Standard* (CDM EB, 2014)—were even more strict about validating baselines by looking to a project's development context.

It might be gleaned from the paragraphs above that the UNFCCC sought to centralize the governance of the CDM's evaluation framework. The CDM regulatory structure as a whole is subject to the ultimate authority of the CDM Executive Board under the UNFCCC, including authorization of CDM methodologies for estimating emission reductions. This would ultimately be a target of critique as the development and authorization of CDM projects would be caught up in the notoriously slow UN administrative process, adding to concerns about administrative burdens discussed earlier. As I shall demonstrate, this contrasts with the governance of REDD+ and NAMAs. While the World Bank and UN have played a larger role in the governance of new climate finance instruments, for the CDM they were largely relegated to capacity building or, else, one of brokering and buying CDM credits. I already mentioned the blurred role of the World Bank's Carbon Finance Unit, but, to continue the example, the United Nations Development Programme (UNDP) would also establish a Millenium Development Goal Carbon Facility to broker CDM projects.

It is also interesting to note that the positive list evaluation framework of the Multilateral Fund has also been used in the CDM albeit to a limited degree. Also known as "automatic additionality," the use of positive lists was approved for certain small-scale CDM methodologies as early as 2010, as well as, subsequently, for a limited number of large-scale methodologies (Cames et al., 2016: 71–77). However, these same authors raise questions about their current use, finding that the rationale behind indicators on positive lists unclear.

It is important to realize that there have been developments with the CDM's evaluation framework since the collapse of the Kyoto carbon market, the most important of which has been the adoption of standardized baseline approaches and sectoral CDM (Hermwille, 2014; Schneider et al., 2012). Adopted in 2011, standardized baselines have only been used during the Kyoto Protocol's rather inconsequential second commitment period. I have not been able to investigate their implementation in this book. Yet these aspects of the CDM's administration saw important regulatory updates in 2014 and 2015. While initial sectoral CDM guidelines suggested a continuation of the original baseline approach (CDM EB, 2011b; Schneider et al., 2012: 5–6), key baseline parameters were subsequently required to be updated every three years (CDM EB, 2011c). Finally, CDM standardized approaches also assign a greater role to the state, which I discuss in Section 2.5 below.

Before closing this section, it is important to note the rules for the SDM agreed at the UN climate change conference in 2021 in Glasgow also maintains the additionality criterion (Slaughter and May, 2021). CDM activities are to generate "real, measurable and long-term" emission reductions as measured against a baseline scenario.

2.5. The CDM and the State

When the initial set of rules for the CDM were adopted, prevailing norms of liberal environmentalism made it difficult for the international community to conceive of a constructive role for the state in the transition to low-carbon development. Most other elements of the CDM's governance were outsourced to private agents (Doelle, 2002). As suggested above, it was private third-party auditors who were given the important task of determining whether the carbon credits claimed by individual CDM projects were genuine or not—the "additionality" criterion. States hosting CDM projects were initially allocated only limited authority over CDM projects through a domestic government body known as the Designated National Authority (DNA).

The primary function of the DNA was initially limited to the approval of individual CDM projects on the grounds of their contribution to sustainable development (see Olhoff et al., 2004). Sensing difficulty in reaching international agreement on what constitutes sustainable development, the UNFCCC decided that it would be determined by governments hosting CDM projects themselves (Curnow and Hodes, 2009: 19–38). The CDM authority in each developing country is required to produce a permit, known as a Letter of Approval, stating that the CDM project in question is assisting the country to achieve sustainable development (Lee, 2004: 40–42). However, most other matters related to the governance of emissions reductions were outsourced to other policy actors.

The DNA is also responsible for setting a definition of "forests" for CDM afforestation and reforestation projects based on minimum criteria for tree cover, land area, and tree height (Purdon, 2009b: 59). Tanzania, Uganda, and Moldova all defined "forest" under the CDM as land that has 30% tree crown cover (UNFCCC, 2014a), the upper limit permitted under this instrument. Such a definition leaves more land available for afforestation/reforestation under the CDM mechanism. However, countries might revise this definition for the purposes of REDD+ (see Sasaki and Putz, 2009). For example, Tanzania redefined "forest" for REDD+ in order to increase the amount of forestland that might qualify for it. By reducing its definition of forest to include tree crown cover to 10%, sparse forests such miombo ecosystems would qualify under REDD+ (VPO, 2013b: 20). However, Uganda's definition of "forest" for REDD+ is consistent with the definition used for the CDM (MWE, 2017c: 9).

Significant for my argument of a shift toward developmental environmentalism, the DNA has been assigned a larger role in more recently developed (and largely unimplemented) sectoral CDM using standardized baselines (Hermwille, 2014: 3–5). CDM project developers seeking to implement such projects can only propose a standardized baseline through the DNA. In turn, the DNA itself is also responsible for data quality and validity as well as keeping track of data for future revisions and updates. But given the CDM's attachment to the Kyoto Protocol and its moribund carbon market, world attention shifted to REDD+ and NAMAs that have been more open to a variety of funding sources. Indeed, the CDM carbon market has largely collapsed, though there are signs of a renewal since the UN climate change conference in 2021.

2.6. The Collapse of the CDM Carbon Market

Since hitting a high in 2008, the CDM carbon market of the Kyoto Protocol is largely now defunct. Nonetheless, trends in CDM prices tell an interesting story that will help us understand the effectiveness of CDM projects that have been implemented.

It would be noted that there is a convention of distinguishing between secondary and primary CDM markets and associated CDM credit prices. The CDM secondary market reflects prices that firms in developed countries have paid to purchase credits, which are measured in terms of tonnes CO2 equivalent (tCO2e). These prices closely tracked those on major allowance markets, particularly the European Union Emissions Trading Scheme (EU-ETS). Prices on the CDM primary market reflect prices paid to CDM project developers, which as we shall see is important for explaining CDM effectiveness on the ground. One interesting observation apparent in Figure 2.2 is that here has been more variation in secondary market prices than in the CDM primary market.

With regard to trends on the secondary CDM market, the collapse of the CDM market began with the 2008 global financial crisis, which saw CDM prices on the secondary market crash from a high of over $35 per tCO2e in mid-2008 to about $10 per tCO2e by early 2009. This was due to reduced demand in Europe and Japan for international carbon offsets as their economies slumped and emissions

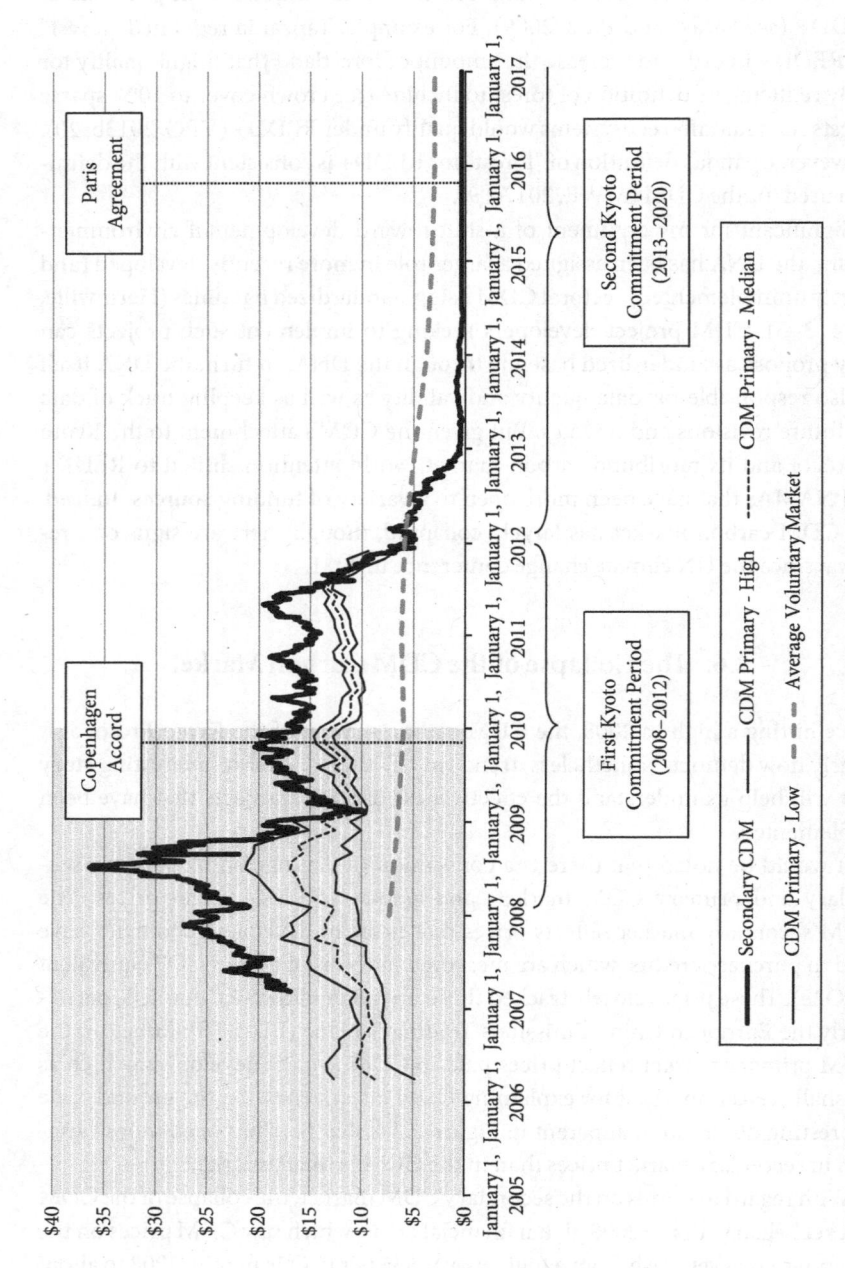

Figure 2.2 Prices for CDM Credits on Secondary and Primary Markets, 2006–2017

declined after the financial crisis (Koch et al., 2014). The important point here is to recognize that the most important drop in CDM prices occurred during 2008–2009 *before* the controversial Copenhagen UN climate conference. Indeed, after reaching a low of $10 in February 2009, CDM secondary market prices recovered to $20 by the time of the Copenhagen conference in December 2009 and hovered around $15–20 through 2011.

However, prices further collapsed in 2012 to almost zero with the World Bank reporting that CDM credits fetched between $0.15 to $0.24 per tCO2e in 2019 (World Bank, 2020a: 59). I attribute this to a lack of demand stemming from the failure of Copenhagen and subsequent UN negotiations to revive international emission reduction commitments by the close of Kyoto's first commitment period in 2012. Though a second commitment period of the Kyoto Protocol from 2013 to 2020 was salvaged in Copenhagen, the only countries who renewed emission reduction targets here were European countries and Australia—large emitters like Canada and Japan withdrew (Aakre, 2016). While the reasons for Canada's withdrawal from the Kyoto Protocol are various, it is interesting to note that the Canadian government at the time also cited concerns about additionality in its decision to not buy CDM credits (Purdon, 2014b).

Agreement on the rulebook for Article 6 of the Paris Agreement achieved in Glasgow in 2021, particularly with regard to the SDM (Article 6.4). Indeed, CDM credits issued from projects registered since 2013 are eligible for transfer into the SDM (Slaughter and May, 2021). It is unclear, however, if rich countries will allow SDM credits to be used for compliance with domestic climate policy or their Nationally Determined Contributions (NDCs).

Though secondary CDM prices are important for international climate politics, the effectiveness of CDM projects on the ground is shaped largely by prices on the primary market. As Figure 2.2 demonstrates, prices on the CDM primary market have hovered around a median of $10–15 per tCO2e for most of the mechanism's history, though also tanking in late 2011. Note that prices on the CDM primary market were obtained from a sample data set maintained by Thomson Reuters and do not represent all data at the primary market level. Indeed, price information on the primary market is difficult to obtain as prices are privately negotiated between CDM project developers and carbon brokers. Carbon prices obtained for the CDM forest and bioenergy projects investigated in this book were considerably lower than reported in Figure 2.2. During 2005–2009, prices for the CDM projects I investigated stood largely between $4–7 per tCO2e, though the World Bank appears to have paid $2.5 per tCO2e for credits from a state-agency-led afforestation project aligned with CDM efforts in Moldova while an NGO-led cookstove project brokered by the UNDP sought $12.5 per tCO2e. The latter was considered a premium price at the time.

It is useful to compare trends in CDM prices with those on other carbon markets. As can be seen in Figure 2.2, average prices of carbon credits on the voluntary carbon markets have declined since hitting a high of approximately $8 in 2008 to about $3 in late 2016. The World Bank reports prices for major voluntary schemes at between $3–$4 in 2019, though voluntary offset markets in China were transacting at $1–$2 at the same time (World Bank, 2020a: 61–64, 72–75). While initially below both CDM secondary and primary market prices, prices on the voluntary markets have been higher than the CDM since about mid-2012. Part of the reason for interest in transnational climate governance is how poorly the Kyoto carbon market has performed. Things are different on other existing emissions-trading systems. In late 2023, while completing this manuscript, prices of $35 per tCO2e were observed on the Western Climate Initiative (California-Quebec) carbon market and $90 per tCO2e on the European Union Emissions Trading System. Overall, since the Glasgow Climate Pact in late 2021, prices on most major carbon markets have seen increases (Jenkins, 2021)—though it is too soon to tell if these will be sustainable.

2.7. Conclusion

While the CDM first emerged as something of a surprise during the 1997 negotiations of the Kyoto Protocol, it came to attract significant attention given growing recognition that the developing world would need to be part of the solution to climate change. The CDM was also a product of its times, which in the 1990s and early 2000s was characterized by an abiding commitment to neoliberal economic ideas. In order to gain traction and "fit" in the global neoliberal economic order, the original CDM was designed to produce carbon credits through a market mechanism that avoided a strong role for the state in carbon offset project implementation or regulation. However, liberal environmentalism underpinning the CDM would fail to be revived at the UN climate change conference in 2009 as another set of global environmental norms, developmental environmentalism, would come to influence the design of new climate finance mechanism of REDD+ and NAMAs. This is the subject of the next chapter.

While the CDM carbon market largely collapsed after the first commitment period of the Kyoto Protocol in 2012, it is important to recognize that the CDM as an institution lives on. This is most evident with regard to the almost forgotten second commitment period of the Kyoto Protocol (2013–2020) where the UNFCCC continued to innovate with standardized baselines. Since at least 2012, the CDM has moved away from its project-based origins to embrace sectoral emission reduction efforts as well as a stronger role for the state in a manner consistent with developmental environmentalism.

Arguably, the CDM has been reborn as the SDM, rules for which were only just agreed upon at the UN climate change conference in Glasgow in late 2021. Furthermore, as we shall see in later chapters, the CDM has found a second life in NAMAs, while REDD+ still reflects many elements of its evaluation framework. Lessons learned from the CDM experience can thus contribute to our understanding of other international and transnational efforts to incite transitions to low-carbon development in the developing world.

3
The Shift to Developmental Environmentalism

3.1. Introduction

Integral to this book is the argument that since the 2008 global financial crisis, there has been a shift in global environmental norms from liberal environmentalism to developmental environmentalism within the UN climate change regime. In contrast to liberal environmentalism discussed in the previous chapter, developmental environmentalism is characterized by a greater reliance on public donor financing, the softening of evaluation frameworks, and a stronger role for the state in policy implementation.

My identification of developmental environmentalism is a novel and perhaps controversial theoretical contribution of this book, but I argue consistent with broader changes in global political economy since the financial crisis. The 2008 global financial crisis was a transformational moment in international political economy—what political scientists refer to as a "critical juncture" (Thelen, 1999). However, I do not contend that development environmentalism is the only global environmental norm permeating the climate change regime. It exists in parallel with other ideas, such as those related to transnational climate governance— issues to which I return in the Conclusion of this book.

There is also important variation in how developmental environmentalism has been implemented. Gridlock at UN climate negotiations has created a policy vacuum regarding the governance of new climate finance instruments that specialized multilateral development agencies of the UN and World Bank have sought to fill. In doing so, multilateral development agencies have been able to steer the implementation of REDD+ and NAMAs in ways consistent with their own policy preferences. This is most evident in the evaluation frameworks for new climate finance instruments that UN-REDD and the World Bank have devised, which reveal long-standing differences between UN and Bretton Woods organizations about the role of states and markets in the process of development (Kalderen, 1991; Woods, 2006). Briefly, the UN has been historically more open to alternative visions of development while the World Bank has been more favorable to market-based approaches. The upshot is that countries hosting REDD+

The Political Economy of Climate Finance Effectiveness in Developing Countries. Mark Purdon, Oxford University Press.
© Oxford University Press 2024. DOI: 10.1093/oso/9780197756836.003.0003

and NAMAs have some selectivity in how these climate finance instruments are implemented.

In the rest of this chapter, I first provide a brief history of development finance since World War II, including discussion of the evolution of development finance management practices. While climate finance is a relatively new area, development finance has figured prominently in international policy fora for decades (Gupta and Thompson, 2010; Sachs, 1992). I then discuss the impact of the global financial crisis on global environmental norms and the rise of climate funds, before reviewing the institutional design of REDD+ and NAMAs each in terms of donor support, their evaluation frameworks, and the role of the state.

3.2. Development Finance Post–World War II

International climate finance instruments build on efforts to promote international development, which took their modern form at the close of World War II with the establishment of the World Bank, the International Monetary Fund (IMF), and General Agreement on Tariffs and Trade (GATT) (Kapur et al., 2011). Originating out of a 1944 conference in New Hampshire, these institutions would be referred to collectively as the Bretton Woods institutions, given interlocking mandates for international development, finance, and trade. With financial resources that far outstrip those of UN agencies such as the United Nations Development Programme (UNDP), only established in 1966, the Bretton Woods institutions have played a decisive role in international development regime. It is important to note that the Soviet Union chose not to become member of the Bretton Woods institutions and instead sought to aid developing countries to achieve a "peaceful transition" to socialism (Guan-Fu, 1983).

Modernist development theory, popular among Western development experts after World War II, stressed the need for a "Big Push" in the form of a large expansion of economic demand for goods and services to lift developing countries out of poverty (Rosenstein-Rodan, 1943). What constitutes a Big Push is debatable, but a target for official development assistance (ODA) contributions of 0.7% gross national product (GNP) of industrialized countries was first adopted by the UN in 1970, building on discussions amongst the OECD's Development Advisory Committee (Clemens and Moss, 2007). The 0.7% GNP target has been reaffirmed on numerous occasions including in Agenda 21 of the 1992 Earth Summit, the Monterrey Consensus resulting from the 2002 International Conference on Financing for Development as well as follow-up development finance conferences (Nunnenkamp and Thiele, 2013). Notably, the target was agreed upon with the understanding that governments could not commit to, nor accurately measure, levels of private investment flowing to the developing world.

Hence the total amount of development finance is assumed to be greater than public ODA transfers. It would also be observed that Big Push policy implicitly recognized a stronger role for the state in spurring economic development. For example, Gore et al. (2018) point out that the World Bank channeled billions to central governments in the developing world for state-led power sector development (also see Vedavalli, 2007).

Also important, from at least the 1960s to the 1990s, development cooperation was based on top-down management techniques associated with financial planning and activity scheduling, such as planning, programming, and budgeting systems (Vähämäki et al., 2011). These tended to envisage a linear and hierarchical set of distinct planning phases beginning with an organization setting out its planning objectives, devising measures to achieve them, and putting measures into effect by allocating budget resources (DonVito, 1969). In practice, the focus was on managing policy inputs rather than results. Even as the World Bank would offer financing that was expected to see a policy intervention effectively implemented, and evaluation was not based on results but on implementation and operating costs (e.g., Baum, 1978).

By the 1980s, however, development finance took on a neoliberal character, accelerating into the 1990s after the end of the Cold War, in what has been commonly referred to as the "Washington Consensus" (Williamson, 2009). The World Bank and IMF are remembered at this time for "conditionality": offering development assistance to countries only in exchange for commitments to liberal economic reforms (Koeberle, 2005). Such reforms were intended to improve the business climate in developing countries, allowing for a greater influx of foreign direct investment that was expected to spur development (Morisset, 2000). It was also during this time that development cooperation began to adopt results-based management techniques (Bester, 2012; Mayne, 2007; Vähämäki et al., 2011). Important for this book's argument, the turn toward results-based management in development cooperation would be absorbed into the UN climate change regime through the CDM, discussed in the previous chapter.

In the 2000s, the Washington Consensus began to fragment, and other approaches to international development gained greater traction (Rodrik, 2006). One alternative was embodied in the Millennium Development Goals (MDGs), first adopted in 2000 (Sachs, 2012). Debate on the MDGs is mixed. On one hand, their association with Jeffrey Sachs at Colombia University suggested a return to Big Push economic ideas of the postwar period (Sachs, 2006). However, others have criticized the MDGs as advocating a major new global development initiative, albeit from within the confines of the Washington Consensus rather than fundamentally rethinking neoliberalism in the first place (Soederberg, 2005). Ultimately, it would take the 2008 global financial crisis to dislodge neoliberalism as the prevailing set of ideas about international political economy.

3.3. The 2008 Global Financial Crisis as Critical Juncture

Up to this point, I have focused on how approaches to development cooperation evolved from the Big Push approach after World War II to a more liberal,
results-based approach that was oriented toward the private sector. But there
is a growing consensus that the events of 2008 was a critical juncture in international political economy that eroded the dominance of neoliberalism (Birch
and Mykhnenko, 2010; Duménil and Lévy, 2011; Rodrik, 2011). This was largely
because of the perceived role that under-regulated financial markets played in
the global financial crisis. But it also resonated with debates in development
cooperation. As Birdsall and Fukuyama (2011) argued, "If the global financial
crisis put any development model on trial it was the free-market or neoliberal
one, which emphasized a small state, deregulation, private ownership, and low
taxes" (p. 46).

Furthermore, the response to the global financial crisis required deploying
tools that neoliberalism had long discredited. Even in the US and other Western
liberal democracies, this included unprecedented levels of government stimulus to compensate for the collapse of demand in the private sector: stimulus
funds across the OECD stood at $1.4 trillion between 2008 and 2010 (OECD,
2009a: 108, 110). Western economies also began to retreat from globalization
after the crisis. For example, global trade peaked at 51% of global GDP in 2007,
before crashing to 31% in 2008, and since then hovering around 35% of GDP
(Figure 3.1). Relatedly, economic nationalism and populism became a surprising
force in the West (Hesse, 2021). While beyond the scope of this book, there is
a compelling case to be made that the global financial crisis created conditions

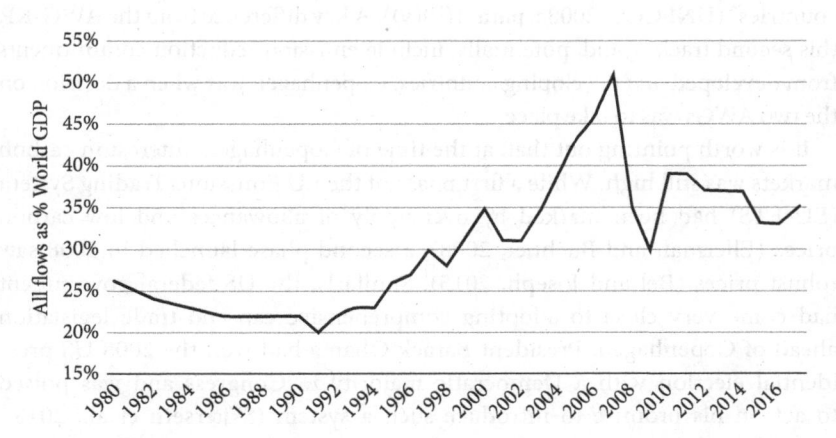

Figure 3.1 Flows of Global Goods, Services, and Finance as Percent Global GDP,
1980–2017

Source: McKinsey & Company (2018)

favouring the emergence of Brexit as well as the election of President Trump in 2016 (Cox, 2018).

Furthermore, many emerging economies that had shunned the wholesale adoption of neoliberal economic policy—particularly East Asian developmental states—appeared to emerge in a stronger position after the 2008 global financial crisis. The IMF estimated that banks in the US and EU lost at least $1 trillion in 2008 (Reuters, 2009); in contrast, China was largely perceived to have only momentarily been set back during the 2008 financial crisis before quickly returning to fast-paced growth, which pundits attributed to its lack of financial liberalization and large foreign currency reserves (Breslin, 2011). It is true that the "rise of the rest" preceded the financial crisis, but as Zakaria observes "the recession accelerated it" (Zakaria, 2011: 2).

It is helpful to reflect on the timing of the global financial crisis relative to the UN climate change negotiations. Already sensing a lack of enthusiasm for extending the Kyoto Protocol, climate negotiators had launched a two-year "dual track" approach at the 2007 UN climate change conference in Bali. One track would continue to focus on deepening emission reduction commitments of developed countries under the Kyoto Protocol, via the Ad Hoc Working Group on Further Commitments for Annex I Parties under the Kyoto Protocol (AWG-KP). This negotiating track had been officially launched in 2005 at the UN climate change conference in Montreal. But Bali negotiations also established a second, parallel track, referred to as the Ad Hoc Working Group on Long-term Co-operative Action under the Convention (AWG-LCA). The AWG-LCA was mandated to consider "various approaches, including opportunities for using markets, to enhance the cost-effectiveness of, and to promote, mitigation actions, bearing in mind different circumstances of developed and developing countries" (UNFCCC, 2008a: para. 1(b)(v)). A key difference from the AWG-KP, this second track would, potentially, include emission reduction commitments from developed *and* developing countries. Copenhagen was when a decision on the two AWGs was to take place.

It is worth pointing out that, at the time of Copenhagen, interest in carbon markets was still high. While a first phase of the EU Emissions Trading System (EU-ETS) had been marked by oversupply of allowances and low carbon prices (Ellerman and Buchner, 2008), a second phase launched in 2008 saw robust prices (Bel and Joseph, 2015). Similarly, the US federal government had come very close to adopting comprehensive cap-and-trade legislation ahead of Copenhagen. President Barack Obama had won the 2008 US presidential election with a Democratic majority in Congress and was poised to act on his promise to introduce such a system (Skjærseth et al., 2013). A number of climate change bills had been discussed in Congress in 2009, including the Waxman-Markey Bill, which contained provisions for a national emissions-trading system that was approved by the House of Representatives in July 2009.

As the impact of the financial crisis became clearer, attempts were made to combine climate efforts with those to revive national economies. For example, upon entering office in early 2009, the Obama administration sought to use economic stimulus funding to incentivize a transition to renewables and other elements of a low-carbon economy. Similarly, international agencies urged industrialized countries to use stimulus spending to promote green economies. For example, the United Nations Environment Programme (UNEP) published a *Global Green New Deal* in early 2009 (Barbier, 2010: xiii–xiv), while the OECD released a report just prior to the Copenhagen conference arguing that "the crisis is no excuse to delay tackling climate change" (OECD, 2009b: 7). Above all, this was a revolution at the level of ideas. For example, as Meckling and Allan (2020) demonstrate, while alternative ideas to liberal environmentalism, including Schumpeterian and Keynesian theories, had their audiences prior to the 2008 global financial crisis, they grew more prominent in global climate policy during and subsequent to it.

Nonetheless, the financial crisis ultimately undermined climate efforts. For example, the Waxman-Markey bill, mentioned above, never made it to the US Senate. One reason for its defeat was that public support for climate policy collapsed following the financial crisis (Scruggs and Benegal, 2012). In turn, the failure to pass major cap-and-trade legislation deprived Obama of a key bartering chip as he arrived to Copenhagen in late 2009 (Mou et al., 2010). While certainly many factors contributed to the failure in Copenhagen, "the global financial crisis sucked political attention, energy and momentum from the climate issue" (Christoff, 2010: 638).

After Copenhagen, it was apparent that a broader normative shift was taking place. For example, UNEP's 2011 *Towards a Green Economy* report broke with neoliberal tradition by urging cautious support for government interventions to stimulate a green economy. As UNEP's director wrote in the foreword to the report, "A green economy does not favor one political perspective over another. It is relevant to all economies, be they state or more market-led" (UNEP, 2011: foreward). Even the World Bank conceded in its 2010 *World Development Report* that "solving the climate change problem requires government intervention, not least because climate change is created by a large-scale negative externality. And the once in a lifetime crisis in the financial markets and the real economy calls for public spending" (World Bank, 2010b: 58).

Carbon markets were kept alive in the AWG-LCA process but lacked momentum as demand for carbon credits and allowances via the Kyoto Protocol had evaporated. Recall that a second commitment had been secured for the Kyoto Protocol in Copenhagen, though most potentially large purchasers of CDM credits, such as Canada and Japan, had exited. The 2010 UN climate change conference in Cancun also established negotiations on the New Market Mechanism (NMM) and the Framework for Various Approaches (FVA) that were eventually codified into Articles 6.2 and 6.8 of the 2015 Paris Agreement (Kulovesti, 2012). In turn, Article 6.4 established a Sustainable Development Mechanism (SDM) that many see as successor to the CDM. But it was not until the 2021 Glasgow Climate Pact that rules for operationalizing Article 6 of the Paris Agreement were finally settled (Slaughter and May, 2021). Thus from Copenhagen to Glasgow—from 2009 to 2021—carbon markets were generally characterized by chronic uncertainty and outshined by climate funds. In the rest of this chapter, I discuss the rise of climate funds, their evaluation frameworks, and the role accorded the state for their governance.

3.4. The Rise of Climate Funds

A first element of developmental environmentalism reflected in new climate finance instruments is their reliance on donor financing. This is modeled on traditional donor financing—before the results-based management revolution—which would be introduced into the UN climate change regime via the Multilateral Fund of the Montreal Protocol and, more directly, the Global Environment Facility (GEF), as suggested in the Introduction. Given that that the Multilateral Fund and GEF serve as models for climate funds, I first briefly review them before describing the broader movement toward climate funds subsequent to Copenhagen. The section concludes with a review of donor financing for REDD+ and NAMAs.

The Multilateral Fund was established in 1990, three years after the adoption of the Montreal Protocol (Patlis, 1992). With contributions reaching a total of approximately $700 million by 1996 (approximately $137 million per year), resources for the Multilateral Fund were able to be sourced almost entirely from ODA contributions of developed member countries (Biermann and Simonis, 1999: 245–246). Funds have largely been disbursed through the World Bank and the UNDP. Contributions received by the Multilateral Fund over the past 30 years have totaled over $4.4 billion (Multilateral Fund, 2022). While impressive, this amount pales in comparison to the amount of finance required to address climate change.

The GEF was established in 1991, actually prior to the establishment of the UNFCCC in 1992. Housed at the World Bank, it supports most other major international environmental conventions established in Rio, not just that for climate change. Since established, the GEF has been accorded $24.75 billion, and regular contributions have been increasing (Batra et al., 2022: 22). Interestingly,

Biermann and Simonis (1999) point out that there is little formal link between the Multilateral Fund and GEF and that, historically, developing countries had raised more concerns about the GEF because of its association with the World Bank.

The convergence of donor funding and climate change picked up speed just ahead of the UN climate change conference in Copenhagen. A set of Climate Investment Funds was first introduced at the G8 summit in June 2008 with commitments of $6 billion from OECD countries (CIF, 2018; World Bank, 2009a). The Climate Investment Funds were framed as temporary finance to complement existing bilateral and multilateral climate efforts until adoption of a climate finance framework to succeed the Kyoto Protocol (IISD, 2009). They were initially comprised of a Clean Technology Fund and Strategic Climate Fund, the latter also included a Forest Investment Program.

The shift toward climate funds was consolidated at the UN climate change conference in Copenhagen in 2009 which, as suggested earlier, was held in the shadow of the 2008 global financial crisis. Most important in the Copenhagen Accord, the UNFCCC committed to

> Scaled up, new and additional, predictable and adequate funding [and] improved access shall be provided to developing countries. . . . In the context of meaningful mitigation actions and transparency on implementation, developed countries commit to a goal of mobilizing jointly US$ 100 billion dollars a year by 2020 to address the needs of developing countries. This funding will come from a wide variety of sources, public and private, bilateral and multilateral, including alternative sources of finance. (UNFCCC, 2009: para. 8)

The emphasis on climate funds would dovetail nicely with the use of stimulus funding to restart the world economy, discussed earlier.

The move toward climate funds was reinforced in Copenhagen through agreement to establish a Green Climate Fund through which a "significant portion of [the US$100 billion a year by 2020 in] funding should flow" (UNFCCC, 2009:para 8). It is intended to "play a key role in channelling new, additional, adequate and predictable financial resources to developing countries and will catalyse climate finance, both public and private, and at the international and national levels" (UNFCCC, 2011a: annex, para. 3). With a sweeping mandate, the Green Climate Fund is coming to dominate climate funds and climate instruments including REDD+, while "NAMAs will be drawn on to provide strategic context" (GCF, 2014: 4). The Copenhagen Accord makes little reference to carbon markets except for a brief mention in paragraph 7 as one among "various approaches" to promote mitigation actions.[1]

Initial signs following the declaration of the $100 billion per year goal were promising. For example, another pledge made in Copenhagen saw rich countries commit to enhanced short-term financing: "new and additional resources, including forestry and investments through international institutions, approaching $30 billion for the period 2010 to 2012 with balanced allocation between adaptation and mitigation" (UNFCCC, 2009: para. 8; 2010: para. 95). Impressively, pledges by rich countries to such "fast start" climate finance actually surpassed the amount promised (Polycarp et al., 2012).

However, determining if the 2020 climate finance goal has been met is more difficult. First is the challenge to distinguish donor-funding pledges to climate finance from actual funding disbursements. Funding commitments made at UN climate change conferences are not always followed through. Second is the challenge of demonstrating that funds are actually "new and additional" and not the diversion of ODA from existing projects (Purdon, 2014b; Roberts et al., 2021). Compounding these problems, there are hardly any agreed tracking protocols to allow for public climate funds to be easily identified and distinguished from other forms of development assistance. These difficulties are even more prominent when seeking to measure private climate finance.

With these caveats in mind, what are the observed trends in ODA made available to developing countries to address climate change? It is important to first describe finance made available for development to gauge if climate finance is "new and additional" (Tirpak and Adams, 2008). According to OECD data, when measured in constant 2018 US dollars, there has been an overall increase in net ODA from approximately $40 billion in 1960 to nearly $175 in 2021 (OECD, 2022). However, ODA as a share of GNP of OECD member states declined during the 1990s and has hovered at about 0.3% GNP since the mid-2000s. As for climate finance itself, the OECD recently published a report estimating public climate finance rose from $38 billion in 2013 to $62 billion in 2018 (OECD, 2020: 7). In turn, the UNFCCC has gauged that public climate finance rose from $29 billion in 2011 to $41 billion in 2013 and $49 billion in 2016 (UNFCCC, 2018b: 55). However, these figures have been strongly contested by NGOs and developing countries (Roberts et al., 2021).

If public sources of climate finance are insufficient for climate change mitigation and adaptation in developing countries, might the private sector fill the gap? Climate funds were never intended to be solely reliant on donor funds; rather, they have been intended to leverage resources in the private sector. But relative to public climate finance, there are even greater concerns about the completeness of the information available on private climate finance. I produce a best estimate below.

The Climate Policy Initiative has estimated annual private flows from rich to developing countries to be between $3 to $23 billion per year over 2013–2014

(Mazza et al., 2016: 5). The broad range is indicative of the accounting difficulties involved in measuring private climate finance. The OECD recently found little change between 2013 and 2018 in the amounts of private climate finance mobilized, at an estimated $13 billion and $15 billion respectively (OECD, 2020: 7). Furthermore, information on private climate finance currently available suggests that it circulates among powerful emerging economies themselves. For example, sub-Saharan Africa and transition economies received an average of 4.1% and 3.4%, respectively, of total global foreign direct investment inflows in recent years (UNCTAD, 2017: 42).

Overall, most estimates of the total amount of climate finance that has been mobilized to support climate efforts in developing countries, including from both public and private sources, find that it has fallen short of the $100 billion per year promised in Copenhagen. For 2017 and 2018, the Climate Policy Initiative estimated a combined $72 billion reached the developing world from public and private sources in the OECD (Buchner et al., 2019: 24). The OECD has estimated comparable numbers, with total climate finance for developing countries rising from $52 billion in 2013 to $79 billion in 2018 (OECD, 2020: 7). An independent panel of experts convened by the UN estimated total climate finance rose from $53 billion in 2013 to $71 billion in 2016, concluding that the goal of mobilizing $100 billion in climate finance was unlikely to be met in 2020 (IEGCF, 2020).

On balance, the available information on climate finance indicates that while allocations to climate funds should be applauded, developed countries are yet to honor their $100 billion per year commitment. The Glasgow Climate Pact, agreed upon in late 2021, acknowledged "with deep regret" that rich countries had failed to live up to the $100 billion annual climate finance goal made in Copenhagen. The most recent estimate is that $89.6 billion was mobilized in 2021, though OECD is optimistic that the $100 billion annual will "likely" have been met by 2022 (OECD 2023). However, the onset of the war in Ukraine is likely to have diminished donor financing for international development (Strøm-Sedgwick and Tank, 2022).

Donor Financing for REDD+

The transition from carbon markets to climate funds is most evident in REDD+, where the UN and World Bank have both established multilateral REDD+ funds to channel sizeable donor contributions that have emerged. While project-based REDD+ has emerged on the so-called voluntary market, these have been limited to project-based interventions operated by transnational nonstate actors. More interest has been accorded to the development of national REDD+ policy and programs under the UNFCCC, which has taken place through more traditional state-donor channels.

I estimate that REDD+ finance pledged through various bilateral and multilateral climate funds from 2008 through 2018 stand at over \$12 billion (Table 3.1). The most important multilateral REDD+ funds include the UN-REDD program as well as the World Bank's Forest Carbon Partnership Facility (WB-FCPF)—both of which became operational in 2008—as well as, more recently, the REDD+ Results-based Payments Pilot Programme established under the Green Climate Fund. Of these three, the WB-FCPF has secured the largest budget at over \$1.1 billion, distributed between a Readiness Fund (\$0.37 billion) and Carbon Fund (\$0.74 billion). It is important to recognize that the majority of the Carbon Fund's financing comes from developed country governments and not private firms (WB-FCPF, 2023) and that emission reductions are currently unavailable for resale to third parties, including emission-trading systems. UN-REDD was established as the UN's flagship interagency effort for REDD+ implementation, galvanizing initial REDD+ capacity-building efforts, but it has attracted just under \$0.3 billion over the 10-year period considered.

Other important funding bodies include bilateral efforts, especially Norway's International Climate and Forest Initiative (NICFI). In REDD+ circles, when

Table 3.1 Distribution of Pledges to Major REDD+ Funds, 2008–2018 (M\$US)

MULTILATERAL	
GCF Pilot program for results-based payments	500
WB Forest Carbon Partnership Facility (FCPF)	1,320
Forest Investment Program (FIP)	736
UN-REDD Program	320
BILATERAL	
Norway's International Climate and Forest Initiative (NICFI)	5,500
Germany's International Climate Initiative (GICI)	1,820
SOVEREIGN MULTIDONOR	
Amazon Fund	1,748
Congo Basin Forest Fund (CBFF)	186
Total	12,130

Source: GCF (2020); Watson and Schalatek (2019).

Note: NICFI estimated at \$500 per year, GICI estimated at \$140 per year from 2008 to 2020. Some caution is necessary when interpreting these figures, as funding across funds is not necessarily independent because many bilateral funds have contributed to various multilateral and multidonor funds.

Norway talks, people listen. Through NICFI, Norway has contributed approximately $500 (NOK 3 billion) per year toward REDD+ since 2008, with funding extended through 2030 (NORAD, 2014a, 2021). Much of NICFI's resources have gone toward supporting REDD+ initiatives of multilevel development agencies rather than competing with them. For example, Norway has shouldered almost the entirety of the UN-REDD budget (87%) though only about half of WB-FCPF (CFU, 2017). It has also been the largest of provider of "results-based payments" in other key bilateral REDD+ initiatives. The most important example is the Brazilian Amazon Fund, managed by the Brazilian Development Bank (BNDES, 2021). Note that these payments are officially described as "donations" by the Brazilian Development Bank and cannot be commodified and sold to third parties.

The geographic allocation of REDD+ funding is also noteworthy as most has been concentrated in a handful of countries. Funding pledged toward REDD+ efforts in Indonesia and Brazil have each stood at over $1 billion in 2006–2014, with Peru, Guyana, and the Democratic Republic of the Congo each over $200 million (Norman and Nakhooda, 2015: 23). Indeed, the donor-driven nature of REDD+ has raised concerns about political ownership (Peskett and Brockhaus, 2009: 34).

Donor Financing for NAMAs

Compared to the billions of dollars allocated toward REDD+, NAMAs have received considerably less donor financing. I estimate that only $532 million has been made available for NAMA initiatives since 2013 (Table 3.2).

By far the most important is the NAMA Facility, which is a multilateral facility funded by European countries. It has committed nearly $460 million to NAMAs since 2013 that it has used to support 43 NAMAs (NAMA Facility, 2017b, 2021). As NAMAs were to be fully implemented by 2020, many donors of late began to present NAMAs as models for NDCs (LEDSGP, 2014; NAMA Facility, 2017a). Indeed, the NAMA Facility retained the moniker until 2022, when it was rebranded as the Mitigation Action Facility in order to focus on NDCs.

The main mechanism through which NAMAs were intended to attract donor support has been through the UNFCCC NAMA Registry. Established following a decision made at the 2010 UN climate conference, the NAMA Registry was intended "to facilitate the matching of finance, technology and capacity-building support for [NAMAs]" (UNFCCC, 2010: para. 53). Importantly it also requested that NAMA proposals include information about the "estimated costs *and emission reductions*, and the anticipated time frame for implementation" (para. 54, emphasis added).

Table 3.2 NAMA Funding Status, 2013–2018

Fund Name	Launch Year	Donor Country	Estimate Funding (M$US)
Climate-related ODA funding	2013	Germany	
International Climate Initiative (IKI)	2013	Germany	
NAMA Facility*	2013	Germany, UK, Denmark, EU	460
Global Environmental Facility (GEF)	2013	GEF	60
Latin American Investment Facility (LAIF)	2013	EU	
EU-Africa Infrastructure Trust Fund (ITF)	2013	EU and member countries	
Neighbourhood Investment Facility (NIF)	2013	EU	
Austrian NAMA Initiative	2014	Austria	3.0
Support for Activities Related to Sust. Mgmt. Forests	2014	Austria	5.8
ODA for Climate Change Measures	2014	Japan	2.9
Spanish NAMA Platform	2014	Spain	
Inter-American Development Bank	2014	Multilateral	
NEFCO Carbon Finance and Funds	2014	Finland, Norway	
FAOSTAT Emissions Database	2014	FAO	
UNDP MDG Carbon	2015	UNDP in Australia	0.3
FAOSTAT Emissions Database	2015	FAO	
Climate Technology Centre and Network (CTCN)	2015	UNFCCC	
UNDP Low Emission Capacity Building Programme	2015	EU, Germany, and Australia	
Total			**532.0**

Source: All data from UNEP DTU (2018) except (*), which is obtained from NAMA Facility (2017b, 2021).

Note: UNEP DTU only list funding contributions in terms of annual estimates. Except for the NAMA Facility, I had to estimate full funding contributions. To do so, these annual estimates were multiplied by the number of years the funds have been in operation through 2017.

What have been the fruits of the NAMA Registry? As of late 2021, 192 NAMA proposals have been submitted by developing countries where they are associated with, at least on paper, an estimated 400 megatonnes CO2 equivalent (MtCO2e) of annual emission reductions by 2030 (UNFCCC, 2021). The total estimated cost of their implementation stands at least $55 billion, with nearly three-quarters of this committed from developing countries themselves. The international community has been requested to cover the difference— approximately $14 billion. However, only eight NAMAs registered with the UNFCCC have attracted international financing—an estimated $27 million in funding 2030 (UNFCCC, 2021).

There are, however, many questions surrounding the figures listed in the NAMA Registry. Are the funds promised by developing countries being delivered? Why have donors been so hesitant to provide support? It is also not clear how many NAMAs submitted to the registry are being implemented. According to data aggregated by UNEP in late 2018, only slightly more than half are being implemented with others at more preparatory stages.[2] The upshot is that the vast majority of NAMAs submitted to the UNFCCC have not received any international financing and are ostensibly being self-funded by developing countries—if they are being implemented at all.

3.5. Softening of Evaluation Frameworks

The embrace of developmental environmentalism by the international development regime was concomitant with the softening of evaluation frameworks for climate finance, at least relative to the CDM. Constituting the second element of developmental environmentalism, the softening of evaluation frameworks is also consistent with the literature on development cooperation. It is commonly recognized that the requirements for donor financing are much less rigorous than those for trade and financial markets (Bourguignon and Sundberg, 2007; Doucouliagos and Paldam, 2009; Easterly and Pfutze, 2008). Demonstrating this softening, however, requires however a deep dive into the technical aspects of REDD+ and NAMAs as well as review of evaluation frameworks of precursors to climate funds, including the Multilateral Fund and the GEF.

In my review, I distinguish between the technical measurement of (1) baselines, (2) emissions, and (3) drivers. As has already been mentioned, the UNFCCC has been slow to provide technical guidance on these matters. With the result being that multilateral development agencies have stepped into the breach in a bid to shape the governance of these new climate finance instruments. Here divergences have emerged between the UN and World Bank with regard to the stringency of the evaluation frameworks.

Before going further, it is important to nip in the bud a common misconception that the evaluation frameworks for REDD+ and NAMAs are radically improved over the CDM. One of the early arguments in favor of a *national* evaluation framework for REDD+ was that it would reduce information asymmetries that plagued the project-based CDM (see Papua New Guinea and Costa Rica, 2005: 9). But experience to date with REDD+ suggests establishing credible baselines at the national level is also difficult. As one international expert explained:

> When you get that large-scale [jurisdictional REDD+], it's really hard to prove additionality. . . . Yet there's a knee-jerk reaction to additionality [in REDD+ policy circles, where policy actors assume that] "if we're doing large-scale [jurisdictional REDD+], then we're doing the new REDD+. Everyone had this negative reaction to project-based REDD+, so we're not going to do that. The CDM was too hard: things like additionality and leakage were too burdensome. The new large-scale REDD+ simplifies this; we don't have to worry about leakage or additionality, etc." But I think we should, otherwise it's not a good system.[3]

In addition, REDD+ and NAMAs also present regulatory challenges that contrast with cap-and-trade systems, another jurisdiction-wide climate policy instrument. The beauty of cap-and-trade is that the actual causal processes necessary to drive emission reductions at the firm level do not need to be identified by the regulator (Tietenburg, 2006). Rather, it is important that the regulator has comprehensive information on emissions in a jurisdiction and, importantly, who is emitting them—hence the importance of firm-level emissions inventories. Once emissions are measured and responsibility assigned to actors emitting them (via allocation of emission allowances), the regulator might let the market "figure out" the most cost-effective strategy of reducing emissions among actors in that jurisdiction. In the developing world, however, information and data constraints have frustrated the production of such detailed emission inventories, making cap-and-trade often impractical. However, for REDD+, it is difficult to attribute responsibility for deforestation and forest degradation to specific policy actors—like emitting firms under cap-and-trade—and assign them a REDD+ "cap" for regulatory purposes, hence the importance of identifying REDD+ drivers.

The Multilateral Fund and GEF Model

As suggested earlier, the Multilateral Fund of the Montreal Protocol and GEF have served as models for climate funds. Established prior to the UNFCCC, they embody quite different approaches to the management and evaluation of donor resources. While the Multilateral Fund would pursue a positive list approach, the GEF has designed its evaluation system around a baseline approach, albeit one that is considerably more relaxed than the results-based system of the CDM.

The Multilateral Fund is designed to fund the incremental costs of supplying and using ozone-protecting technologies in developing countries as identified in an official "Indicative List of Categories of Incremental Costs" (UNEP, 2020: 803–804). Such positive lists have certain administrative features that make them attractive for policy. While their initial development might require considerable investment, once established they facilitate evaluation frameworks considerably: if a project uses a technology identified on a positive list, the project is accepted for funding. Many observers have suggested that the CDM and other climate finance instruments adopt positive lists in addition to or instead of the current baseline approach (Erickson et al., 2014; Nguyen et al., 2010). As indicated earlier, positive lists have been used for certain small-scale CDM methodologies as early as 2010 as well as, subsequently, a limited number of large-scale methodologies (Cames et al., 2016: 71–77).

The GEF, however, has not adhered to the positive list framework of the Multilateral Fund. The exact reasons for this are unclear and beyond the scope of this book, but it would be observed that positive lists often focus on a particular set of technologies. But the GEF promotes a broad range of projects, not just technological diffusion, including "innovative business models, financial mechanisms, supportive policies regulations, strategies and institutional arrangements" (GEF, 2023). It would appear difficult to manage all this through a positive list. Rather, similar to other development agencies, the GEF measures effectiveness through three criteria.

First is the amount of co-financing that it attracts (GEF, 2018a). Average co-financing ratios have increased from approximately 2.5 in the mid-1990s to 7.5 by mid-2010s (GEF, 2018a: 2). Co-financing requirements are related to how the GEF demonstrates financial additionality. In theory, GEF funding is intended to cover the incremental costs associated with a project that promises to deliver global environmental benefits but is unable to attract local funding (Labbate, 2008). Financial additionality is thus based on a counterfactual assessment that aims to demonstrate that, in the absence of GEF financing, the project would not be implemented. However, a 2006 evaluation recommended that the counterfactual incremental cost assessment be dropped given low compliance by GEF staff in undertaking it (GEF, 2006). In justifying this recommendation, the authors of the 2006 evaluation argued that "*in practice* the additionality is achieved through co-funding" (p. 13, emphasis in the original).

Second, demonstrating that a GEF project delivers environmental benefits, what I refer to as "development additionality," is based on a more traditional baseline system. "Additionality" here is defined as "changes in the attainment of direct project outcomes at project completion that can be attributed to GEF interventions" (Batra et al., 2022: 95). For climate change mitigation, the GEF's most recent evaluation framework relies on comparing a counterfactual baseline scenario to a project scenario through recognized carbon offset methodologies or, for energy and transport projects, those developed by the GEF (GEF, 2008; 2018b; GEF STAP, 2011). However, in contrast to climate finance mechanisms such as the CDM, the GEF evaluation framework is much softer. GEF financing is accorded before project implementation and has fewer data requirements; also important, GEF funding is not revoked if emission-reduction targets for a project are not attained (GEF STAP, 2011).

Third, and most recently, the GEF has sought to develop an evaluation framework to include transformational change (Batra et al., 2022: 93–114). Transformational change is defined as those "engagements that help achieve deep, systemic and sustainable change with large-scale impact" (p. 95). To achieve transformational change, the GEF aims to support projects that are distinguished by their depth and scale of change as well as potential to catalyze market and system-level changes. Interestingly, the GEF has not jettisoned its earlier requirement to evaluate the additionality of GEF interventions in favor of transformational change. Rather, it sees the additionality of GEF interventions to be the first step in the broader demonstration of the impact of the intervention toward transformational change.

Evaluation Frameworks for REDD+

In this section I review the evaluation framework for REDD+ by first reviewing rulemaking on the issue at the UNFCCC before describing how the two leading multilateral REDD+ initiatives have sought to shape this element of the climate fund instrument.

UNFCCC Evaluation Framework for REDD+

Agreement on the technical elements of REDD+ evaluation frameworks at the UNFCCC has been convoluted as forest issues would prove to be highly politically salient. As mentioned earlier, "avoided deforestation" was excluded from the CDM at UN climate change negotiations in 2001. This also had the perverse effect of delaying improved cookstove projects under the CDM, given that reducing fuelwood would ostensibly lead to reducing deforestation (Purdon, 2010). While REDD+ as an independent climate finance instrument was introduced in 2005, it was not until the 2013 UN climate change conference that rules for operationalizing REDD+ were finalized. The Warsaw

Framework for REDD+, a set of decisions taken at the 2013 UN climate change conference in Warsaw, is largely viewed as having concluded REDD+ negotiations under the UNFCCC (Voigt and Ferreira, 2015). In the interim, from 2005 to 2013, multilateral development agencies were able to take a stronger leadership role with REDD+ implementation than was the case with the CDM.

Two observations might be made about the UNFCCC evaluation framework for REDD+. First, in contrast to the efforts to centralize technical and methodological guidance for the CDM at the UNFCCC, REDD+ has been more devolved and reliant on ad-hoc expert review. A less generous interpretation would be that UNFCCC evaluation framework for REDD+ is underspecified and insufficient for operationalization. Second, of the three elements of evaluation frameworks identified, the UNFCCC has focused on measurement of emissions using an inventory approach as well as establishing REDD+ baselines, technically referred to as "forest reference emission levels." The UNFCCC has accorded little attention to drivers of deforestation and forest degradation. I briefly discuss each of these three elements.

First, the clearest references to an inventory approach are found in the 2006 Guidelines for National Greenhouse Gas Inventories. Here emissions associated with land-use change are presented as a regular stock-taking exercise (IPCC, 2006b: 2.6–2.10). In their simplest form, the 2006 Guidelines call for the measurement of emissions as the product of human activity times an emissions factor as in the equation: Emissions = Activity Data * Emissions Factors (IPCC, 2006c: 1.6). But IPCC guidance for the production of emissions inventories alone is insufficient for baseline instruments. Indeed, IPCC Good Practice Guidance for Land Use, Land-Use Change and Forestry explicitly makes this point (see IPCC, 2003: 1.9).

Second, UNFCCC guidance on how to develop REDD+ baselines is characterized by considerable deference to expert review. At Copenhagen in 2009, the UNFCCC initially indicated that REDD+ baselines should take "into account historic data, and adjust for national circumstances" (UNFCCC, 2009: para. 7). But two years later it adopted decisions to allow countries to devise their own methodologies for establishing REDD+ baselines, which are then submitted for expert technical assessment (UNFCCC, 2011b: para. 9–13). The UNFCCC did provide brief guidelines for information that would need to be included for a REDD+ baseline (UNFCCC, 2011b: annex). Also important, the Warsaw Framework added the requirement that REDD+ emission reductions be reported through an additional technical annex to the Biennial Update Reports (Voigt and Ferreira, 2015: 121–122).

Third, however, treatment of REDD+ drivers was, strikingly, nearly absent from UNFCCC technical guidance until the Warsaw Framework. But discussion of drivers even here consists largely of a declaration of the importance of drivers and encouraging action on them, rather than technical guidance of how to address them (UNFCCC, 2013b).

Overall, while emissions from deforestation have attracted interest since at least the conception of the Kyoto Protocol, it would not be until 2013 that an evaluation framework for REDD+ would be finalized. But important gaps in technical guidelines are evident. What has emerged is a system that emphasizes emissions and, in a less standardized manner, REDD+ baselines, although REDD+ drivers are nearly absent.

UN-REDD Evaluation Framework

UN-REDD has struggled to develop a robust evaluation framework for REDD+ activities, which can be attributed to its attachment to the UNFCCC process as well as a lack of funds for actual REDD+ results-based payments.

First, UN-REDD's attachment to the UNFCCC process has limited its ability to outstanding technical gaps mentioned in the preceding section. As a UN agency, UN-REDD has had to offer technical guidance "*following guidance from the UNFCCC*" (UN-REDD, 2008: 9, emphasis added). This has proven to be a handicap. As explained by one REDD+ technical expert:

> [UNFCCC guidance on REDD+ offered through the annual Conference of Parties (COP)] is so high-level, it's so unspecific, that it puts UN-REDD in a pickle. How much guidance do they give countries? Do they go further than what the COP has said? Which might be helpful for countries because the decision texts aren't very helpful for a country to operationalize all these pieces that they're asked to put together.[4]

Most striking, UN-REDD does not require that countries identify drivers of deforestation nor develop a strategy for collecting data on them in National Program Documents—the key first step that developing countries need to go through in the UN-REDD process.

Second, UN-REDD does not have funds for results-based payments, a key difference from the WB-FCPF. As UN-REDD observed in a 2014 review: "There is currently no operational financing mechanism under the UNFCCC that provides payments for REDD+ results, although the [UNFCCC Conference of Parties] has agreed to a number of requirements that could assist in the operationalization of such a mechanism" (UN-REDD, 2014: 7). Altogether, UN-REDD has been stuck in supporting REDD+ "readiness" activities (e.g., see UN-REDD, 2014, 2015: 28). Perhaps recognizing the precariousness of this situation, UN-REDD launched the Green Gigaton Challenge in 2020 with the goal of "incentivizing corporations to purchase high-integrity carbon credits as part of their carbon offsetting portfolios"(UN-REDD, 2021). That is, UN-REDD feels compelled to tap voluntary carbon markets.

WB-FCPF Evaluation Framework

The WB-FCPF contrasts in many ways with UN-REDD above. Most importantly, it operates independently of the UNFCCC and commands far greater resources, allowing it to move from REDD+ readiness to implementation. In addition to its Readiness Fund and Carbon Fund, part of its mandate has been to pilot a performance-based payment system for REDD+ activities (WB-FCPF, 2017).

The Readiness Fund is intended to support countries in the development of an institutional framework for REDD+. Interested countries are first invited to submit a Readiness Plan Idea Note that, upon approval, is to be followed by a Readiness Preparation Proposal establishing a plan, budget, and schedule for developing elements of REDD+. The final suite of REDD+ preparations, known as the Readiness Package, is to be evaluated against a common Readiness Assessment Framework (WB-FCPF, 2013d: 8–20).

Importantly, a Readiness Package needs to include technical information pertaining to REDD+ baselines and REDD+ drivers. In terms of REDD+ baselines, the WB-FCPF adopted annual historical forest-related emissions in a REDD+ accounting area for a period of about 10 years (Van der Linden, 2014). The WB-FCPF has also emphasized drivers as integral to the construction of REDD+ baselines in the Readiness Assessment Framework: "The [REDD+ baseline] should be built around the major drivers of deforestation, forest degradation and the other REDD activities" (WB-FCPF, 2013d: 17). After evaluation, the Readiness Package also needs to be endorsed by the host country as well as the WB-FCPF before becoming eligible for the Carbon Fund (WB-FCPF, 2013d).

The Carbon Fund became operational in 2011 and has resources more than doubling those of the Readiness Fund. The Carbon Fund is designed to pilot performance-based payments for emission reductions from REDD+ programs. In an important contrast to UN-REDD, the WB-FCPF anticipated that the rules for piloting REDD+ would need to go beyond technical guidance offered by the UNFCCC:

> The Carbon Fund aims to be consistent with evolving UNFCCC decisions on REDD+. It does not intend to pre-empt international negotiations on REDD+, but seeks to provide "real life" practical insights and knowledge generated from piloting performance-based mechanisms for REDD+ and, through this, to inform ongoing negotiations. (WB-FCPF, 2013b: 6)

In order to verify the emission reductions claimed by countries for the Carbon Fund, the WB-FCPF developed its own verification system, known as the

Methodological Framework (WB-FCPF, 2013c). It contains some accounting innovations, including an uncertainty assessment procedure and buffer account. Such buffer accounts have been used as a way of managing the potential "reversibility" of forest carbon as a result of forest fires or other natural disturbances as well as a tool to manage potential changes in baseline conditions (Marland et al., 2001; VCS, 2011).

Overall, with its attention to drivers of deforestation as well as its possession of resources for results-based payments, the WB-FCPF has developed an evaluation framework that is much more robust than that offered by UN-REDD. As explained by one interviewee, the evolution of the Carbon Fund "gives some indication of the direction of travel of what the requirements might be in the future for a market because governments create [carbon] markets and those governments are the same people as those sitting at the Carbon Fund table."[5]

Evaluation Framework for NAMAs

The evaluation framework for NAMAs is considerably less rigorous than that for the CDM carbon market and even relative to REDD+. One reason is that NAMAs have been plagued by chronic uncertainty as to what they are fundamentally intended to achieve: emission reduction, mitigation actions, or both. Similar to what was developed for REDD+, a lack of technical guidance by the UNFCCC has allowed donors to play an outsized role in the development of the evaluation framework for NAMAs, which has evolved into a confounding amalgamation of approaches.

As pointed out by Coetzee and Winkler (2013), NAMAs were first proposed as part of the 2007 Bali Action Plan, and its evaluation framework was to be restricted to actions taken by developing countries and not actual emission reduction outcomes (pp. 5–7). However, uncertainty about what NAMAs were supposed to achieve set in quickly. Initial NAMAs submitted by countries in response to the 2009 Copenhagen Accord did not constitute actions but emission reduction targets (UNFCCC, 2009: para. 5; see UNFCCC, 2018a). An attempt by the UNFCCC to clarify NAMAs at the 2010 UN climate change conference only introduced more uncertainty. Here it was agreed that NAMAs were to be "aimed at achieving a deviation in emissions relative to 'business as usual' emissions in 2020" (UNFCCC, 2010: para. 48). Note that a "business as usual" scenario is comparable to baselines used in the CDM.

Adding to this complexity, decisions taken in 2010 also required all countries to produce Biennial Update Reports that provide more regular information on national greenhouse gas inventories and mitigation actions (UNFCCC, 2010: para. 60) as well as an International Consultation and Analysis process to offer independent technical review of them (UNFCCC, 2010: para. 63). Both suggest some sort of causal evaluation of NAMAs as they are required to also consider "mitigation actions *and their effects*" (UNFCCC, 2010: paras. 60,63, emphasis added). Similarly, the NAMA Registry requested developing countries to provide information about the "estimated costs *and emission reductions*, and the anticipated time frame for implementation" (UNFCCC, 2010: para. 54, emphasis added). Consequently, it was initially anticipated that least some NAMAs would be funded through carbon markets, requiring an institutional structure similar to the CDM (Okubo et al., 2011: 37).

With the objective of NAMAs in flux, multilateral development agencies would seek to fill this leadership vacuum in a manner similar to the situation with REDD+. However, in contrast to REDD+, the World Bank has been almost completely absent from the NAMA process, leaving the UNDP and the NAMA Facility as key sources of technical guidance and capacity building.

The UNDP initially recommended a two-tier approach for NAMAs that borrowed from both cap-and-trade systems and the baseline system of the CDM (Bruer et al., 2014: 5–6; LEDSGP, 2014: 6; Lütken et al., 2013: 54). The first tier focused on building an inventory of emissions and mitigation actions. This was done, ostensibly, to recognize mitigation actions that might not directly lead to emission reductions. For example, in a 2010 *How-to Guide* for NAMA implementation, the UNDP argued that "in some cases MRV is difficult, for example in the case of economic and fiscal policies and measures as they do not reduce emissions directly but induce entities or individuals to change their behaviour" (UNDP, 2010: 91–92).

A second tier of the UNDP's technical guidance focused on measuring emission reductions of individual mitigation actions, which involved establishing baselines (Bruer et al., 2014: 6). Echoing the CDM, experts emphasized that "a key issue for NAMAs will involve attributing the emissions reduction impact of the policy to the specific activity . . . MRV regulatory frameworks for NAMAs can build on existing CDM experiences with design, validation, monitoring and verification" (Bruer et al., 2014: 6–7; also see Lütken et al., 2013: 57). The UNDP initially offered a definition of NAMA baselines that was almost identical to the CDM: "The baseline scenario is that in which these parameters, including GHG emissions, continue as they would in the absence of the NAMA" (Lütken et al., 2013: 61). But in some of the same guidance documentation, the UNDP cautioned against too strong a reliance on the CDM approach, arguing that the NAMAs were national in scope and that they were disconnected from carbon markets (Lütken et al., 2013: 58, 63).

Like the UNDP, technical guidance from the NAMA Facility has combined the CDM evaluation framework with other approaches. Ironically, given critiques of project-based CDM, the NAMA Facility does not support NAMAs themselves but rather NAMA Support Projects (NSPs). These are conceived as sector-wide programs, national in scope that "contribute to the most transformational elements of the overarching NAMA in which they are embedded" (NAMA Facility, 2015: 4). As set out in the NAMA Facility's Monitoring and Evaluation Framework (NAMA Facility, 2015), NSPs are evaluated against five "mandatory core indicators," beginning with reduced GHG emissions and the number of people directly benefiting, degree to which the supported activities are likely to catalyze impacts beyond the NSPs, volume of public finance mobilized, and volume of private finance mobilized.

In terms of measuring emission reductions, the NAMA Facility promotes the measurement of emission reductions relative to baselines that "determine what would be expected to occur (the most likely scenario) in the absence of the project" (NAMA Facility, 2015: 31). Here it refers to the GHG Protocol Policy and Action Standard for baselines "although, in particular circumstances, other methodologies could be employed such as those of the Clean Development Mechanism (CDM)" (p. 31). But not all NSPs need to result in direct emission reductions: "some of the [NSPs'] activities may not result in measurable GHG reductions or may do so well after the project has been concluded" (NAMA Facility, 2015: 28).

Over time, the UNDP and NAMA Facility would both seek to promote "transformational change" through NAMAs. The UNDP has understood transformational change as being characterized by "long time lags between [a mitigation action's] implementation and the effect of emissions reduction" (Lütken et al., 2013: 66). Similarly, the NAMA Facility has defined it as a "far-reaching, structural change for delivering low-carbon sustainable development" that achieves outcomes that move the country further toward low-carbon sustainable development (NAMA Facility, 2015: 43). Key here are outcomes that the NAMA Facility associates with transformational change, which are grouped into six outcome categories (NAMA Facility, 2015: 43). Most of these outcomes are institutional: landmark decisions, creation of new financial institutions for low-carbon development, mainstreaming climate change aspects into major policies, and creating governance bodies for low-carbon development. The remaining two types of outcomes are clearly transformational: disrupting carbon-intensive path dependencies and shifting to low-carbon ones as well as scaling up low-carbon approaches or instruments.

But the devil is in the details. How do we know that an intervention is transformational? In practice, the measurement of transformational change under the NAMA Facility is based on a simple assessment by the promoter of the NSP as to whether transformational change is a likely outcome or not (NAMA Facility, 2015: 45). NSP promoters are urged to justify their assessment, but data sources suggested for measuring transformational change tend to be focused on policy outputs such as "project milestones" and the "planned course of action" (p. 45). Measurement of transformational change is surprisingly underspecified.

At the end of the day, it is hard to escape the conclusion that the evaluation framework for NAMAs is considerably softer than for the two other climate finance instruments. But as we shall see later in this book, when I investigate the actual implementation of NAMAs, policy actors have compensated for this lack of specificity by relying on CDM methodologies.

3.6. Role of the State

A final element of developmental environmentalism reflected in new climate finance instruments is the important role accorded to the state for policy implementation. Though the architects of the CDM assumed that nonstate actors would do the heavy lifting, the state has emerged as an almost natural partner for implementing REDD+ and NAMAs.

REDD+ and the State

In the initial 2005 proposal to establish what would become REDD+, a national approach was suggested on the grounds that this would resolve technical issues surrounding policy effectiveness, including additionality and leakage. For example, in their initial REDD+ proposal, Papua New Guinea and Costa Rica (2005) argued "a number of technical issues have been raised which have hampered efforts to include emissions from deforestation. Some of these issues arise out of the project-based approach to emission reductions in developing countries and national baselines would make them easier to deal with" (p. 9). Thereafter, the state increasingly came to be perceived as a natural partner for REDD+ baselines. For example, in technical guidance adopted by the UNFCCC in 2007, national-level approaches were given preeminent status; subnational approaches were recognized only insofar as they constituted "a step towards the development of national approaches, reference levels and estimates" (UNFCCC, 2008b: annex, para. 7). Even on the voluntary carbon markets, leading voluntary carbon market schemes have been pushing toward so-called jurisdictional REDD+ (VCS, 2013).

What started as a technical justification for the state in REDD+ baselines establishment soon expanded to include a broader set of functions as ideas surrounding developmental environmentalism began to crystallize after the financial crisis. An important example of this shift can be found in a book by CIFOR, the international forest policy think-tank, entitled *Realising REDD+*

(Angelsen et al., 2009). In a telling chapter, contributors write "Realising REDD+ *presupposes* a national architecture or governance structure that facilitates comprehensive actions and delivers carbon mitigation actions that are effective, efficient and equitable" (Vatn and Angelsen, 2009: 57, emphasis added). Such recognition of a large role for the state constituted a considerable departure from liberal environmentalism.

Recognition of a legitimate role for the state was formally incorporated into the 2013 Warsaw Framework for REDD+ discussed earlier. It called for the establishment of "a national entity or focal point" for REDD+ that, on first blush, is similar to the Designated National Authority of the CDM. In contrast however, the national REDD+ focal point was trusted with actually managing climate finance: it was authorized by the UNFCCC to "obtain and receive results-based payments, consistent with any specific operational modalities of the financing entities providing them with support for the full implementation of [REDD+]" (UNFCCC, 2013a, para. 1–2). The REDD+ Focal Point is also responsible for submitting Biennial Update Reports to the UNFCCC on the basis of which results-based payments are to be made (Decision 10/CP.19, para. 2; Decision 14/ CP19 para 6–14). Such a role for the state in technical and financial matters was unimaginable when the CDM was first tabled in 1997.

NAMAs and the State

NAMAs inherently require a greater role of the state to implement mitigation actions that are *nationally* appropriate. Expert advice from the UNDP and UNEP has also urged a greater level of engagement with the state than was the case for the CDM.

For example, as articulated in an early UNEP report: "The responsibility for implementation and control of NAMAs will lie with the host country. It will therefore also be the host country that defines authorizations and responsibilities to the institutions working within the NAMA" (Hinostroza et al., 2012: 19). In a later publication, UNEP went so far to describe a NAMA administrative cycle in which it ascribed a large role to the state (Sharma and Desgain, 2014). Essentially, it was anticipated that countries would undertake a national exercise to identify NAMA opportunities that would then be endorsed by central governments for submission to the NAMA Registry. This process would be administered by a so-called "NAMA Approver," an individual designated by the country's UNFCCC focal point of submitting content to the NAMA Registry. However, the term "NAMA Approver" is not to be found anywhere among official UNFCCC decisions. It only appears to have been referred to by the UNFCCC in the Manual of the NAMA Registry developed in 2014 (UNFCCC, 2014b). UNEP would concede that "there is no internationally defined or agree NAMA cycle" (Sharma and Desgain, 2014: 5).

UNDP would also promote Low-Emission Development Strategies (LEDS) as part of its Low-Emissions Capacity Building Programme, anticipating that LEDS would become a UNFCCC requirement (UNDP, 2010: 17–18). LEDS are a development planning tool that UNDP and the OECD began promoting in the wake of the Copenhagen talks (Clapp et al., 2010; UNDP, 2010, 2013). As explained by UNDP, LEDS would

> form a strategic plan to assist the country in shifting its development path to a low-carbon economy and achieve sustainable development, based on the socio-economic and development priorities of the country. . . . LEDS should contain a concrete set of measures leading to GHG emission reduction, quantification of the corresponding emission reduction for each measure and the financial requirements to implement them. For [developing countries] the set of measures can be expressed as NAMAs. Finally LEDS should outline the approach to implementation, determining concrete steps and timelines as well as provisions for monitoring, measurement, reporting and verification of results and a mechanism for further improvement on the basis of the experience in the implementation. (UNDP, 2010: 17–18)

While the Copenhagen Accord and Cancun Agreements would assert that LEDS are "indispensable to sustainable development" (UNFCCC, 2009: para. 2, 2010: Art. I.6), the UNFCC would ultimately only *encourage* and not require their development for NAMA implementation (UNFCCC, 2010: Art. III.B.64). Overall, the UNFCCC never really clarified how NAMAs were to be governed domestical; its attention wained as the instrument failed to take off. Nonetheless, recognition of the need for coordination of the NAMA process by the state is readily implied by their framing as "nationally appropriate" climate finance instrument.

3.7. Conclusion

In this chapter I first introduced a set of global environmental norms that I call developmental environmentalism, which contrasts with the liberal environmentalism upon which the CDM was first built. The key reason for this difference, I have suggested, was the impact of the global financial crisis in 2008, which resulted in the loss of neoliberalism's potency as an idea in much of the developing world. After the 2008 financial crisis, the UNFCCC was more amenable to alternatives to neoliberalism.

As evidence of the shift toward developmental environmentalism, I have demonstrated that new climate finance instruments have come to rely to a large degree on public donor financing channeled through multilateral development agencies, the softening of evaluation frameworks for showing that financing invested in REDD+ and NAMAs produces intended effects, and a stronger role for the state in policy implementation. This institutional analysis suggests that REDD+ and NAMAs have quite a different animating set of ideas behind them from what was the case with the CDM.

We have also seen that key international development agencies have been jostling for influence over REDD+ and NAMAs. These different approaches are most readily apparent for REDD+. UN-REDD technical guidance has been frustrated by almost interminable UNFCCC negotiations about what policy outcomes REDD+ is intended to achieve and how it is intended to be funded. In contrast, the World Bank has had more autonomy to pursue a more robust evaluation framework. It is particularly in terms of REDD+ drivers that the World Bank has been able to distinguish itself from UN-REDD and the UNFCCC. As for NAMAs, the World Bank has largely abandoned the implementation of this climate finance instrument to the UNDP and NAMA Facility, sensing that their evaluation framework for NAMAs would not be conducive to global carbon markets.

While this is consistent with the fragmentation of the climate change regime complex, it also appears to have accorded states in the developing world greater selectivity and, hence, agency when navigating the global climate finance landscape. Over the course of the rest of this book, I demonstrate how Tanzania, Uganda, and Moldova have been able to engage different multilateral development agencies with REDD+ and NAMAs in a way that can be best attributed to their development policy paradigms and state development interests.

PART II
COMPARATIVE POLITICAL ECONOMY OF DEVELOPMENT

4

Development Policy Paradigms in Historical Perspective

4.1. Introduction

In this chapter, I unpack the concept of development policy paradigms and review major trends in thinking about economic development that have circulated in elite political and intellectual circles in the developing world since World War II and the first major wave of independence from colonialism. In particular, there has been considerable evolution in thinking about the role of the state in the process of economic development. As discussed in the Introduction, development policy paradigms can be thought of as differing along two dimensions. First, they differ in terms of a state's comparative advantage strategy: a *comparative advantage following* strategy or *comparative advantage defying* strategy (Lin and Chang, 2009). In least developed countries, where industrialization has often been limited, this can be observed from key economic policy strategies, including national assets management (nationalization/privatization), agricultural price controls, and state strategic coordination. But second, they also differ in their posture relative to international trade, ranging from autarky to globalization. See Table 4.1.

Another objective of this chapter is to disclose the considerable common ground that has historically existed at the level of ideas between the three case-study countries, which includes two East African countries and one former republic of the Soviet Union. The economic ideas that permeated elite African circles during the initial wave of independence in the 1950s and 1960s were inspired by and shared many attributes with economic ideas associated with the industrialization of the Soviet Union. Another shared experience was the collapse of Marxism's ideological force with the dissolution of the Soviet Union and the subsequent rise of neoliberalism into the 1990s. However, especially since the 2008 financial crisis, new ideas about development associated with the exceptional success of East Asian economies have become difficult to ignore.

Before exploring the evolution of development policy paradigms since World War II, I must first defend a definition of policy paradigms as a set of ideas informing the means of achieving political objectives. I begin this chapter, then, by discussing the origins of the concept of policy paradigms as an ideational

The Political Economy of Climate Finance Effectiveness in Developing Countries. Mark Purdon, Oxford University Press.
© Oxford University Press 2024. DOI: 10.1093/oso/9780197756836.003.0004

Table 4.1 Key Economic Policy Strategies of Different Development Policy Paradigms

Development Policy Paradigm	Comparative Advantage Strategy			International Trade Strategy
	National Assets Management	Agricultural Price Controls	State Coordination	
Classic Developmentalism	Nationalization	State price controls	Top-down central planning	Import substitution industrialization
Neoliberalism	Privatization	Liberalization	Laissez-faire	Free trade
Neodevelopmentalism	Comparative advantage defying nationalization	State price controls	Top-down central planning	Export orientation
Liberal Neodevelopmentalism	Comparative advantage conforming nationalization	Strategic state price controls	Bottom-up central planning	Export orientation

factor and reviewing debates about its analytical status. The reader may observe some overlap with our discussion in this chapter and the international development régime discussed in Chapter 3. The main distinction is that development policy paradigms refer more to ideas surrounding domestic political economy than about international development cooperation.

4.2. The Concept of Development Policy Paradigms

Drawing on Peter Hall, I define "policy paradigms" as a set of ideas about the *means* of achieving state development interests. However, there is some uncertainty about the concept policy paradigms that can, in part, be attributed to Peter Hall's original definition.

Peter Hall first coined the term "policy paradigms" in an influential 1993 paper. He defined them as "a framework of ideas and standards that specifies not only the goals of policy and the kind of instruments that can be used to attain them, but also the very nature of the problems they are meant to be addressing" (Hall, 1993: 279). Note that Hall's original definition included both policy goals and the means to achieve those goals.

I submit that Hall's original interest was about connecting theories of policy change to larger debates about the role of the state and society in the policy process—in this case, the movement from Keynesian to neoliberal economic policy in the UK—in the spirit of comparative political economy. The 1993 paper where he introduced the concept of policy paradigms was published at a time when the then-dominant pluralist theory of public policy had ceded ground to critics arguing that the state could be an important and independent actor in the policy process (Evans et al., 1985). The state, critics argued, did not simply reflect the sum of society interests as pluralism suggested. But if societal pressure no longer explained state policy formation, as pluralism suggested, Hall (1993) asked, "What motivates the actions of the state[?]" (p. 275).

Hall's response to this question was policy paradigms. These were able to bridge social learning processes within the state to "much broader participation and conflict within the political system as a whole"—that is, factors that were exogenous to the policy subsystem (Hall, 1993: 276). While incremental policy change might take place through social learning within a policy subsystem, Hall sought to explain major policy change through exogenous factors—including changing material conditions, such as rates of inflation, as well as ideational structures in the "marketplace of economic ideas" (pp. 284–285, 289). It is important for the argument of this book to highlight that Hall would identify both material and ideational factors as impetus for change. While he tells us that "inflation replaced unemployment as the preeminent concern of policymakers" (p. 284), this was not simply due to policymakers preferring inflation control as a policy goal and abandoning Keynesianism. Rather the paradigm shift "initiated early in the 1970s by a series of economic developments, of which the most important was rising rates of inflation, soon to be joined by stagnating levels of growth and employment" (p. 285).

Perhaps recognizing the ambiguity in his original definition, Hall would revise policy paradigms to refer more explicitly to policy means. Hall later (2010) referred to them as "instrumental beliefs" or "means-ends schemas that describe . . . how the adoption of new institutions will affect the likelihood of achieving various types of goals, as well as the confidence with which such beliefs can be held" (p. 2018). In his most recent pronouncement on policy paradigms, Hall clearly identified them as means of policy change in contrast to exogenous political motivations and motors: "If interwar experience provided the motivation and class-based electoral competition the motor, a Keynesian paradigm provided the means for this transition" (Hall, 2013: 190).

Nonetheless, Hall's original definition of policy paradigms resonated deeply in the field of policy studies, justifying a focus on policy change within a policy subsystem to the near exclusion of exogenous political factors. Building on Lindblom's (1959) theory of incremental policy change, policy theorists found evidence of major policy change to occur within a policy subsystem in the absence of major exogenous change. For example, Cashore and Howlett (2007) argued that important reductions in timber harvesting on federal lands in the US Pacific Northwest in the early 1990s occurred in the absence of major changes in policy goals; rather it resulted from new information becoming available about the forest habitat requirements for endangered species (particularly the spotted owl).

The theoretical implications for global climate change policy are profound. Incremental policy learning that originates within the climate policy subsystem has the potential to catalyze transformational change without major paradigmatic shifts in policy goals. Climate policy can generate its own politics. The concept of policy feedbacks, first introduced by Paul Pierson (1993), has increasingly attracted attention in climate policy research.

The risk, however, is that by emphasizing endogenous sources of policy change, research into climate change politics has discounted the importance of exogenous sources of policy change—both ideational and material. This book is unique in climate change politics by drawing attention to factors exogenous to climate policy to explain policy effectiveness. In the rest of this chapter, I unpack ideal types of development policy paradigms as they have evolved since World War II.

4.3. Classic Developmentalism

Classic developmentalism is a set of economic ideas about the process of transforming rural peasant economies into industrialized ones through a comprehensive set of policies. Prior to World War II, manufacturing had been concentrated in Western Europe, North America, and Japan, with their colonies restricted to supplying primary commodities. In many ways classic developmentalism was inspired by the authoritarian and inward-looking economic policies of the Soviet Union that appeared to have allowed that former peasant economy to emerge as an industrial powerhouse. The Soviet experience offers a common point of departure linking development policy paradigms across Tanzania, Uganda, and Moldova, though other countries, now considered developed such as Germany and the United States, also pursued strategies for state-directed industrialization to catch-up with the Great Britain where the Industrial Revolution was born (Chang, 2003).

The Legacy of the Soviet Developmental Model

It is not hard to imagine the appeal of the Soviet Union after World War II, when much of the developing world found itself rapidly approaching decolonization. In addition to its long-standing critique of Western colonialism and hard-fought successes in the Great Patriotic War, the Soviet Union appeared to have succeeded in its program of economic modernization and industrialization (Allen, 2003; Jasny, 1961). The key moment had been when, in 1928, Joseph Stalin abandoned the more liberal New Economic Policy of Vladimir Lenin and turned toward centralized planning and agricultural collectivization to accelerate industrialization. Deemed by Stalin to be a "revolution from above" of equal importance to the initial Russian Revolution of 1917, Soviet industrialization in the 1930s was "a state-initiated, state-directed, and state-enforced process, which radically reconstituted the Soviet order as it had existed in the 1920s" (Tucker, 1992: xiv). By many measures of industrial output, Stalin's initial efforts toward economic modernization were a success (Allen, 2003: 89–110). While it is perhaps inappropriate to use concepts like comparative advantage in a command economy like the former Soviet Union, the effect was similar to that of defying Russia's historical comparative advantage in agriculture and achieving industrialization.

In hindsight, of course, the miracle of Soviet economic growth under Stalin was unsustainable and only achieved at a terrible human cost (Livi-Bacci, 1993; Rosefielde, 1996). While economic growth was impressive until about 1960, the system would prove unable to respond to the economic challenges of the 1970s and 1980s. Hanson (2014) argues that efforts under Stalin's successors to gradually liberalize the economy failed because of diminished administrative discipline, particularly the absence of hard budget constraints. Though the Soviet economy was able to increase its rate of economic growth, it did so largely by compelling increased production inputs, including capital and labor—what economists refer to as "extensive growth"—and lacked incentives for improving efficiency, generating innovation, and learning for productivity (Hanson, 2014; Krugman, 1995). Furthermore, the Soviet Union's modernization did not extend far beyond the military-industrial-technical sphere (Bialer, 1988). When Mikhail Gorbachev attempted to incorporate social and political modernization (*glasnost*) along with broader economic reforms (*perestroika*), the Soviet political system collapsed.

Nonetheless, the Soviet Union's economic achievements, as well as the thinking behind them, made an important impression on aspiring leaders in the developing world. After the collapse of the Soviet Union, Hughes (1992b) took stock of the appeal of Soviet Marxism for African leaders:

> The perceived remarkable achievements of the USSR in the economic sphere always held a particular fascination for African radicals faced with similar needs to transform backward colonial economies into modern industrial states. The successes of the Soviet Union were attributed to centralized planning and state ownership and direction of the means of production under the aegis of a Marxist-Leninist vanguard party. . . . Not only was the USSR's record proof of the superiority of socialist achievement but the Soviet bloc was increasingly seen as a source of practical economic assistance as well as a model for late-modernizing countries to emulate, and the means by which economic dependence on Western capitalist powers would be broken. (Hughes, 1992a: 15–16)

As Allen (2003) demonstrates, the economy of the Russian Empire that the Soviets took over in 1917 was largely a rural peasant one with social, legal, and economic institutions lagging behind those of Western Europe.

Among efforts to transform the Soviet peasant economy, four policy strategies stand out: nationalization, prices controls (particularly in the agricultural sector), central planning, and autarky. I dwell on these Soviet policy strategies as they found certain expression in the suite of policy tools adopted by leaders in sub-Saharan Africa and elsewhere in the developing world.

First, and perhaps most obvious, was the nationalization of the means of production. Under the Soviet system, the state would come to own all natural resources, almost all physical capital, and conducted virtually all industrial activity (Ericson, 1991). While nationalization was undertaken to conform with Marxist ideology, it also allowed the Soviet state to transform the fledgling industrial base the Soviets inherited. However, its options for doing so under the

Soviet system were limited to extensive growth—compelling increased inputs to increase output. Technological innovation tended to be imported from the West. This included copying and reverse-engineering US technology received during World War II, direct commercial importation, as well as what Hanson (2014) describes as "turnkey" industrial megaprojects where a Western firm assured the design, installation, training, and initial commissioning of an industrial facility. For example, "turnkey" industrial projects included a 1964 partnership with British firms to establish the Soviet petrochemical industries and 1966 Fiat-built car factory that would come to produce the iconic Lada. While learning for productivity was part of such technological upgrading, such "turnkey" projects reduced autonomous learning that might have been achieved through foreign direct investment (upon which important limits were set).

Nationalization also extended into the rural sphere through collectivization of rural peasant lands, which accelerated during 1929–1933 and allowed the Soviet state even greater control over the peasantry. Though the abolition of serfdom in 1861 increased the labor autonomy of peasants and saw the emergence of a land-owning peasantry, rural Russia remained based on a land-tenure system whereby land was not owned by individual villagers but regularly rotated among them via a village commune (Nafziger, 2016). Additional reforms were introduced to support the development of private landholdings after a 1905 revolution attempt, though to questionable effect (Pallot, 1999). Though there is scholarly debate on the matter, many of the 1905 reforms are seen to have survived under Lenin's New Economic Policy until 1928 (Davies, 1990).

In light of this, Stalin's turn toward collectivization in the early 1930s marked a radical departure. By compelling rural society into larger collective organizations—including the collectivization of land, livestock, and farm equipment—collectivization was viewed by Stalin as a means of asserting control over agricultural production while also eliminating resistance from upper class peasants. The result was initially a collapse in agricultural productivity and mass famine, particularly in the highly productive lands of Ukraine (Conquest, 1986). Nonetheless, the policy continued, and the majority of Soviet agricultural lands were collectivized by the late 1930s.

A second policy strategy adopted by the Soviets, related to collectivization efforts above though preceding them, were efforts to extract an economic surplus from the Soviet peasantry to promote industrialization. This included movement of the internal terms of trade against peasants by way of the state's monopoly of industry—the famous Soviet debate on agricultural and industrial "price scissors" in 1923 (Sah and Stiglitz, 2002). The policy obliged peasants to sell their produce to the state below market rates with the state then reselling it in urban areas and keeping the difference. Implementing the "price scissors" policy proved difficult given a national grain shortage in 1928 and refusal of peasants to relinquish their stores without compensation. But instead of changing course, Stalin embarked on a national program of collectivization mentioned above that enhanced the state's capacity to enforce the price scissors. It was only after Stalin's death that efforts were made to boost incentives for agricultural procurement, though this was limited by competing interests of the Soviet military-industrial complex who benefited from the status quo (Hanson, 2014).

A third policy strategy integral to Soviet economic development was central planning. The Soviet Union's first five-year plan was organized for 1929–1932 coinciding with the initial collectivization drive above. The State Planning Commission, known as Gosplan, would later come to play a leading role in coordinating the Soviet economy. In theory, each five-year plan was supposed to be based on robust economic data that Gosplan would use to calculate the balance of various inputs and outputs across the Soviet economy— akin to a market equilibrium. But in the absence of market forces, "the flows of intermediate material from producing firm to consuming firms must be consciously controlled by the economic planners" (Levine, 1962: 128). As is well known, because of information asymmetries, the economic planners never really had a firm understanding of the Soviet economy. Inefficiencies crept into the system with firms being asked to produce too many outputs with too few inputs or vice versa.

A fourth strategy that characterized early Soviet economic development was Stalin's policy of autarky and the shunning of international trade. While it is perhaps an exaggeration that the Soviet Union was completely autarkic, the Soviet Union initially only cultivated a system of limited international trade with a few other socialist states and maintained a strong aversion to exports (Hanson, 2014; Sanchez-Sibony, 2014). The Soviet Union also declined to participate in the Marshall Plan, through which the US assisted Europe to recover from World War II. After Stalin's death, however, Soviet foreign trade actually grew at rates comparable to other emerging economies, particularly since foreign trade was a key route for acquiring Western technology. Regardless, the prospect of spurring Western commercial ties and developing indigenously would appeal to leaders in the developing world and provide some justification for ISI.

The flip side of autarky is also important for understanding its appeal to classic developmentalists. Namely, producing goods and services for a domestic developing economy that is protected from international competition is often easier than producing for the global market. Hanson (2014) points out that Soviet managers who were required to produce for Western export markets often saw this as a punishment. To meet the rigors of the global market, considerably more effort was required.

Soviet Marxism and Classic Developmentalism in Africa

While the link between Soviet economic ideas and Moldova's experience might be evident, how were Marxist ideas associated with Soviet economic development taken up in sub-Saharan Africa? Hughes (1992a) distinguishes between two strains of African elites' affinity for Soviet Marxism. A first strain, known as African socialism, accompanied the initial wave of African independence in the 1950s and 1960s. It sought to not only adapt Marxism to the African context but also incorporate divergent philosophical positions. Though the quintessential African socialist was perhaps Ghana's first president Kwame Nkrumah (Biney, 2011), the first president of Tanzania, Julius Nyerere, has also been closely associated with African socialism through his philosophy of *ujamaa*. I unpack ujamaa in Chapter 7.

A second strain of Marxism identified by Hughes (1992a), described as "Afro-Marxism," arrived in Sub-Saharan Africa later in the 1970s. Its adherents hewed more closely to orthodox Marxist ideology and sought to respond to the perceived failures of African socialism. When he originally set out in his political career, Uganda's President Yoweri Museveni arguably fit this more orthodox Marxist mold (Melo et al., 2012; Tumusiime-Mutebile, 2009). Even a collection of Museveni's speeches from 1986 to 1991, early in his presidency, is noteworthy for themes of Afro-Marxism (Young, 2001).

Given these fertile ideational grounds, a number of the policy strategies that had been undertaken in the Soviet Union would coalesce into what I describe as classic developmentalism. For example, as I detail in Chapter 7, Nyerere's concept of *ujamaa* would be realized through nationalization of industrial assets, central planning would find expression in official five-year plans, while a policy of villagization became increasingly coercive. Classic developmentalism also aligned with the Big Push approach of the international development regime at the time, discussed in the previous chapter. While the World Bank would later become nearly synonymous with neoliberal structural adjustment policy, in years prior to this it accorded billions for state-delivered infrastructure in the developing world (Gore et al., 2018; Vedavalli, 2007).

In terms of price controls, a number of countries in sub-Saharan Africa introduced agricultural marketing boards that allowed the state to offer different prices for coffee, cocoa, and other commodities on the global market while lower ones to their producers (Bates, 2005 [1981]). This was justified as a means of generating state revenue for development purposes as well as to regulate the exposure of peasants to global commodity price fluctuations. Investments in small-scale industry and peasant agricultural productivity were viewed as offering only a "once-for-all effect" in contrast to the "continuing effect" from investments in industrialization (Dobb cited in Byres, 1979: 222).

In terms of international relations, leaders of developing countries tended to more strongly agree that it was important to pursue a more autarkic trade relationship with industrialized countries. Free trade faced considerable competition at the level of ideas after World War II, particularly from dependency theory (Cardoso and Faletto, 1979 [1969]). No country wanted to be relegated to the global periphery, producing only primary commodities. As Gordon (2006) explains, African leaders were skeptical of the Bretton Woods institutions and preferred instead to participate in the United Nations Conference on Trade and Development (UNCTAD) founded by the Argentine economist Raúl Prebisch. Prebisch's theory that declining international terms of trade kept developing countries in an inferior position in the global economy resonated strongly with African leaders. However, while the Soviet Union had turn inward to industrialize, the developing "Third World" was moving toward a set of policies that would allow developing countries to interact economically with developed countries on more favorable terms: import substitution industrialization (ISI).

Under ISI, the state would establish tariffs and other forms of trade protection so that goods produced by domestic firms would be competitive with imported ones from "core" developed countries. While Prebisch argued against protectionism and favored regional trade (Dosman, 2008), UNCTAD became a strong proponent of ISI as means of integrating developing countries on a more equal footing into the world economy (Waterbury, 1999). Significantly, the GATT originally accommodated ISI in developing countries, a feature that was reinforced during GATT negotiations as late as 1979 (Hunter, 2003).

Overall, the Soviet experience of economic development was a source of inspiration for many in the developing world, including sub-Saharan Africa. This offers a common thread linking the history of economic thinking in Tanzania, Uganda, and a former republic of the Soviet Union, Moldova. Of course, in the marketplace of ideas, classic developmentalism was challenged by an alternative set of ideas that gained greater prominence into the 1970s, to which we now turn.

4.4. The Rise of Neoliberalism

By the early 1970s, classic developmentalism started to show certain strains. The oil crisis of 1973 provoked a stagflation crisis in industrialized countries to which Keynesian economic policy, which mirrored classic developmentalism in certain ways, was unable to respond. An alternative set of economic ideas would come to dominate economic policy in developed countries, influenced by Milton Friedman whose work initially stressed monetary policy to control inflation but was soon extended to other policy areas (Shleifer, 2009). By the 1980s, with the election of Prime Minister Margaret Thatcher in the UK 1979 and President Ronald Reagan in the US in 1980, neoliberalism would become firmly incorporated into the economic policy of Western industrialized countries and international development agencies. Also important, China under Deng Xiaoping initiated preliminary liberal economic reforms in 1979.

In much of the Third World, however, neoliberal ideas were not salient until the late 1980s. Indeed, the 1973 oil crisis at first led to a surge in lending from international banks (who were reinvesting petrodollars) (Berend, 2009; Parfitt and Riley, 2010). The good times did not last long, however, and, by the 1980s, many developing countries found themselves in a debt crisis as interest rates rose. Indeed, funds borrowed during this period are now viewed as the origin of the debt crisis in many developing countries (Fole, 2003).

Particularly in least developed countries, neoliberalism first arose in discussions about rural development and urban bias theory in the 1970s. Developed by Michael Lipton (1977), urban bias theory argued that the emphasis placed on industrialization had come at the expense of rural development (also see Bradshaw, 1987). While African socialists like Nyerere also emphasized rural over urban industrial development, institutions that they espoused to protect rural peasants would be critiqued by proponents of urban bias theory—particularly agricultural marketing boards, mentioned earlier. In contrast to classic developmentalism, urban bias theorists argued for direct investments in the rural sector. Urban bias theory came to align with a broader neoliberal critique that state intervention in developing countries should be scaled back to let their comparative advantage in agriculture be realized. The World Bank's influential 1981 Berg Report—which arguably kicked-off the neoliberal period in Africa—identified one important source of underdevelopment to be "a consistent bias against agriculture in price, tax, and exchange-rate policies" (World Bank, 1981: 4).

What began as a specific reform in the agricultural sector soon grew into a broader call for rolling back the state in various parts of the economy, culminating in the Washington Consensus, introduced in Chapter 3. In addition to liberalizing price controls in key sectors such as agriculture, neoliberalism led to the reversal of other policy strategies introduced under classic developmentalism. State assets were privatized to balance budgets and improve management, often in astonishingly short periods of time. The World Bank published is "standard model" for reform of the energy sector in 1993 (World Bank, 1993). Subsequently, to receive World Bank financing for power sector development, host countries would need to introduce more transparent regulation and increase private sector involvement as well as privatization. Agricultural reform would be undertaken with a focus on individual land rights though also, given seminal contributions from Elinor Ostrom, groups rights for common property resources (Deininger and Binswanger, 1999; Dongier et al., 2003).

Central planning came into disuse, given that private economic actors were assumed to organize spontaneously in response to market forces. Nonetheless, into the 2000s, the need for development planning became evident. The World Bank would introduce a neoliberal form of development planning known as Poverty Reduction Strategy Papers (Craig and Porter, 2003). I return to these oxymoronic liberal development plans later in our discussion of liberal neodevelopmentalism.

In terms of international trade, the dissolution of the Soviet bloc and underperformance of ISI led to pressure to liberalize trade. First was the curtailment of infant industry protections via the Agreement on Agriculture negotiated under the GATT during the 1990s (Hunter, 2003). In exchange for greater access to markets in developed countries—especially for their agricultural commodities—developing countries had to agree to roll back tariffs in their industrial sectors that had originally been permitted under the GATT. Notably, the Agreement on Agriculture entered into force with the establishment of the World Trade Organization in 1995. International trade expanded considerably under the neoliberal free trade system: from 20% of global economic activity in 1980 to 37% by 2000 and peaked at 53% just before the 2008 global financial crisis (McKinsey Global Institute, 2016: 3).

Many neoliberal ideas also focused on reforming the public sector in developing countries. This was influenced by the "new public management" reforms of public administration in the developed world that had emerged during the 1980s (Hood, 1991). State agencies in particular were promoted as semi-autonomous organizations intended to adhere to more business-like, results-based management techniques (Verhoest et al., 2010). Attention to such organizations, in particular, is helpful for understanding the effectiveness of climate finance instruments.

Overall, neoliberalism marked a decisive movement away from the active promotion of industrialization by the state, including interventions in the agricultural sector that were pursued under classic developmentalism. Neoliberalism has of course been the subject of considerable critique from a variety of perspectives. Urban bias has been thoroughly contested (Byres, 1979; Jones and Corbridge, 2010), and there is a whole neo-Marxist stream of development theory that has challenged it. However, as I suggested in the previous chapter on developmental environmentalism, I think it is safe to claim that the idea of neoliberalism no longer has the same influence it once had. Indeed, even during the heyday of neoliberalism, a handful of East Asian economies would chart a different course that I call neodevelopmentalism, which differed in important ways from both neoliberalism and classic developmentalism.

4.5. Neodevelopmentalism

The success of East Asian economies, particularly since World War II, has proven difficult to explain from the vantage of either neoliberalism or classic developmentalism. In contrast to neoliberalism, it is now widely recognized that the state played a leading role in transforming the economies of Japan, Taiwan, South Korea, and most, recently, China (Amsden, 1989; Kohli, 2004). Observers originally coined the term "developmental state" to describe these characteristics in East Asia (Woo-Cummings, 1999), though for reasons, discussed below, I prefer the term neodevelopmentalism.

East Asian developmental states demonstrated similarities to two but not all the policy strategies associated with classic developmentalism. The first was the extraction of an economic surplus from the rural sector to promote industrialization. As Kay (2009) demonstrates, industrialization in South Korea was preceded by a comprehensive agricultural reform effort that allowed the state to extract an agricultural surplus to export. This was first conducted under the Japanese colonial regime though also, in a more equitable manner later, in an independent South Korea under the American security umbrella. Most East Asian developmental states would undergo land reforms that effectively removed large-scale landowners from the political landscape, allowing the state more effective control (Pempel, 1999). However, importantly, subsequent economic growth in the industrial sector allowed for the surplus to be reinvested back into the rural sector.

A second policy strategy shared with classic developmentalism was the state's use of central planning. For example, South Korea's authoritarian President Park Chung Hee argued already in 1962 that "we must take a great leap forward toward economic growth. . . . It is urgently necessary to have an economic plan or a long-range development program through which reasonable allocation of all our resources is feasible" (Park cited in Amsden, 1989: 49). Yet in contrast to Soviet planning, Park cautioned that the South Korean state "should utilize to the maximum extent the merits usually introduced by the price machinery of free competition, thus avoiding the possible damages accompanying a monopoly system" (Park cited in Amsden, 1989: 50–51). Furthermore, in contrast to the Soviet experience, the challenge of implementing complex industrial projects was welcomed by leadership because it required deep and strategic learning. Indeed, Amsden (1989) would argue that the developmental state model characterized a new mode of industrialization based on *learning* from the experiences of other countries that differed from industrialization in the UK, Germany, and America that was largely based on *innovation*.

Though sharing certain economic policy strategies of classic developmentalism, the developmental state model contrasts with it in important ways.

First, was the greater importance accorded to private property and the private sector, as suggested in the second quote from former South Korean President Park Chung Hee about the importance of "the price machinery of free competition" above. The state sought to build productive relationships with the private sector to promote the competitiveness of domestic firms so that they might upgrade their capabilities. Nonetheless, nationalization would be undertaken in certain strategic sectors, such as in the banking sector during the height of the developmental state in South Korea (Lechevalier et al., 2019). Such strategic nationalization was able to be effectively undertaken because the bureaucracy of developmental states tended to be meritocratic, highly disciplined, and retained a commitment to national developmental goals despite collaborating closely with the private sector to see these goals realized—something Evans (1995) has described as "embedded autonomy."

Another policy difference was the outward orientation of the developmental state model. As Pempel (1999) states, "Export-oriented development has become so linked in the public mind with hypergrowth of Japan, Korea and Taiwan that it has become 'a new development orthodoxy'" (p. 148). East Asian economies emblematic of the developmental state also enjoyed exceptionally close trade links to the United States, which saw the development of the region vital to its broader security interests during the Cold War. However, close observers have pointed out that export-oriented development was not an alternative to ISI; rather, the two strategies were integrated: "In East Asia, free trade, export promotion (which is, of course, not free trade), and infant industry protection were organically integrated" (Chang cited in Antonio, 2019: 276). Nonetheless, the focus was on developing a domestic market strategically in support of exportation.

While the success of East Asian development would perhaps initially be confined to comparativist academics interested in the region, there is an emerging consensus among development experts that we are witnessing the consolidation of a new development policy paradigm that more global in scope (Chang and Andreoni, 2020; Haggard, 2018; Khan and Christiansen, 2011; Schmidt, 2009; Stiglitz and Lin, 2013; Stiglitz et al., 2013; Wade, 1990, 2018). Given the association between the term "developmental state" and East Asia as well as critiques that such scholarship overlooked political settlements (see Whitfield et al., 2015: 6–14), I refer to this new development policy paradigm as "neodevelopmentalism." Similar arguments in Europe and the US have also recently been advanced in the context of climate change, often going under the label of "industrial policy" (MacNeil, 2017; Meckling, 2017). Indeed, the surprising 2022 passage of the Inflation Reduction Act—the most important piece of climate change legislation ever adopted in the US—is part of what the Biden administration describes as a "modern American industrial strategy" (Chu and Roeder, 2023).

Efforts to apply neodevelopmentalism to a broader set of countries has provoked considerable reflection. It is now recognized that neodevelopmentalism requires a set of interdependent activities requiring "strategic coordination" by the state (Andreoni and Chang, 2019: 147). Significantly, these authors distinguish between top-down and bottom-up models of coordination, though suggesting that the latter is often daunting for least developed countries that lack "diffused institutions with government organizational capabilities" (p. 147). Important for a book on global climate politics, I distinguish bottom-up state coordination from the term "orchestration." The latter has increasingly been used in the transnational climate governance literature to described a non-hierarchical governance model where states use their persuasive powers to steer climate action (e.g., Hale and Roger, 2014). Orchestration itself is drawn from what Abbott and Snidal (2009) have called "new governance" at the domestic level.

It also needs to be pointed out that despite the economic success of East Asian economies, neodevelopmentalism is not without critique. First, the association of successful developmental states with authoritarian regimes has raised questions about democratic control (Edigheji, 2010). States where neodevelopmentalism has historically been successful, South Korea after the Korean War as well as China now, have been authoritarian states capable of pushing through their agenda. Considerable attention has recently been accorded to state strategies for outmaneuvering resistance from powerful domestic actors and conflict management (Chang and Andreoni, 2020; Meckling and Nahm, 2022).

A second and related critique of neodevelopmentalism is recognition that sustained economic growth may ultimately require endogenous innovation (Evans, 2010; Mazzucato, 2011). While developed states in the past may have learned from the innovations developed in industrialized countries, continued economic growth may require *learning to innovate*. Third, the glue which makes an embedded autonomy feasible is a strong sense of national identity and purpose (Woo-Cummings, 1999). While there are signs that national identities have been increasingly supplanting ethnic ones in sub-Saharan Africa (Robinson, 2014), a weaker sense of national identity will likely continue to frustrate embedded autonomy in the region. Nonetheless, the idea of a developmental state has proven attractive in sub-Saharan Africa and the former Soviet Union, particularly since the 2008 financial crisis (Drahokoupil, 2009; ECA, 2011; Edigheji, 2010; Fritz, 2007; Stiglitz et al., 2013; Mkandawire, 2001b).

4.6. Liberal Neodevelopmentalism

As the idea of neodevelopmentalism has become more mainstream, the debate is no longer about whether the state should be involved in the economy but how. An important example of this is a debate between Justin Lin, former chief economist at the World Bank, and Ha-Joon Chang, director of the Centre of Development Studies at Cambridge University (Lin and Chang, 2009). The two debated different sides of a key question that might present itself to state leaders: Do leaders intend economic policy to defy their country's current economic endowments to build comparative advantage—a *comparative advantage defying* strategy—or should they adopt economic policy that conforms with their current comparative advantage—a *comparative advantage following* strategy? Inspired by Ban (2012), I refer to these as neodevelopmentalism and liberal neodevelopmentalism, respectively. I discussed neodevelopmentalism in the previous section, focusing on liberal neodevelopmentalism here. However, other terms have been used to describe it. Lin has since referred to liberal neodevelopmentalism as the "new structural economics" (Lin, 2011, 2021), while Andreoni and Chang (2019) describe it as the "mainstreaming of industrial policy."

The contrast between neodevelopmentalism and liberal neodevelopmentalism is a nuanced yet altogether different idea about the means of economic development. While sharing the view that the state should play an important role in economic development, states subscribing to a liberal neodevelopmental policy paradigm are more conservative about the nature of state interventions. Rather, the leadership here tends to support sectors already competitive on global markets by providing incremental regulatory, financial, and political assistance rather than pursuing risky, though potentially transformational, interventions. While a country subscribing to neodevelopmentalism might pursue growth opportunities in a new technology sector, one adhering to liberal neodevelopmentalism might rather seek to expand market share or adding value through industrialization in existing global market segments where it already has comparative advantage, such as agricultural and natural resource commodities.

I submit that there are three implications of liberal neodevelopmentalism for domestic political economy. First, liberal neodevelopmentalism implies a considerably different relationship between the state and other domestic political actors than is the case under classic developmentalism and neodevelopmentalism. While under both the latter policy paradigms, the state aims to assert its dominance over other domestic actors, a liberal neodevelopmental state might be expected to defer to them to a greater degree because of their existing economic capacities and understanding of their comparative advantage vis-à-vis global markets. Returning to the distinction between top-down and bottom-up modes of strategic coordination recognized by Andreoni and Chang (2019), the bottom-up would be expected to be more strongly associated with liberal neodevelopmentalism than neodevelopmentalism (or classic developmentalism).

A second implication of liberal neodevelopmentalism is that it suggests that the state will be more selective in the deployment of its capacities for strategic coordination of the economy than under neodevelopmentalism. Effective public policy is in part due to the ability of state leadership to understand what is politically and economically feasible given its existing capacities. This implies some sort of internal assessment by the state leadership of its comparative advantage in different economic sectors and whether it should aim to defy/follow its current comparative advantage, especially in sectors deemed within its state development interests. Such selectivity is evident in the emergence of "pockets of effectiveness" in least developed countries. Roll (2014) has defined these as "public organizations that are relatively effective in providing the public good and services the organization is officially mandated to provide, despite operating in an environment in which effective public service is not the norm" (p. 23). Such pockets of effectiveness have often been attributed to the political settlement of countries with a strong dominant party (Whitfield et al., 2015). One important contribution of this book is to offer evidence that ideational factors might also allow pockets of effectiveness to emerge: under liberal neodevelopmentalism, one might expect the state to retain pockets of effectiveness in economic sectors where it believes it has capacity to effectively intervene. I note that all the "pockets of effectiveness" identified by Roll (2014) are semi-autonomous state agencies and state-owned enterprises, which links up with the broader argument of this book.

Third, liberal neodevelopmentalism allows us to make sense of the paradoxical practice of development planning during the neoliberal period. The World Bank's Poverty Reduction Strategy Papers, mainstreamed across Bank operations in 1999, "recognize that sound growth requires investment, not least in human capital and infrastructure, as well as the right macroeconomic and structural policies, good governance, and healthy institutions" (World Bank, 2002: 2–3). Put differently, such liberal economic plans sought developmental outcomes in addition to a commitment to macroeconomic growth and stability. But this is at odds with neoliberalism. Significantly, as I discuss in Chapter 7, what I call liberal neodevelopmental economic planning was pioneered by the Ugandan government in an effort to coordinate international and domestic development interventions (Mackinnon and Reinikka, 1999; Whitworth, 2009a,b). Such development planning might also be considered more bottom-up than the more top-down processes associated with neodevelopmentalism.

While a relatively new concept in development theory, liberal neodevelopmentalism is not without critique. Andreoni and Chang (2019) point out that it is *a priori* difficult for the state to discern when and where it can credibly defy its comparative advantage; rather, "a backward economy doesn't really know what it is capable of until it tries new things" (p. 140). I readily acknowledge that liberal neodevelopmentalism appears to suffer from an omitted variable bias with regard to how the state makes strategic decisions about the comparative advantage of different firms and sectors. However, as I explain in the conclusion of this book, this is perhaps best seen as a topic for future research.

4.7. Conclusion

In this chapter, I have set the table for exploring the effectiveness of climate policy instruments in Tanzania, Uganda, and Moldova. This has included discussion of classic developmentalism, neoliberalism, but also neodevelopmentalism and liberal neodevelopmentalism. While classic developmentalism would cede ground to a neoliberal policy paradigm by the 1980s, the curious success of East Asia economies that instead embraced a more developmental role for the state in the process of economic development has proven difficult to ignore since the 2008 global financial crisis. We can now speak of a distinction between neodevelopmentalism, which sees the state as a progressive force for transforming a country's comparative advantage, and liberal neodevelopmentalism, which has similar objectives but is more cautious about state interventions and accords greater deference to other domestic policy actors. It is a distinction between development policy paradigms that emerge as a key part of the explanation for enduring trends in climate policy effectiveness across Tanzania, Uganda, and Moldova.

5

Political Settlements in Tanzania, Uganda, and Moldova

5.1. Introduction

This is the first of three chapters where I review in detail the political economy of Tanzania, Uganda, and Moldova. This chapter focuses on political settlements with the aim of introducing the reader to fundamental characteristics of the politics of the countries under study. Prevailing state ideas and interest are discussed in the subsequent two chapters.

At first glance, the domestic politics of Tanzania, Uganda, and Moldova may appear similar. Their politics have been characterized as competitive authoritarianism by Levitsky and Way (2002: 52–54). But deeper probing indicates considerable differences that might be grasped through the concept of political settlements. The reader may recall from the introduction that political settlements might be distinguished across two dimensions (horizontal and vertical political power) that gives rise to four typologies: strong and weak dominant party states, vulnerable authoritarianism, and competitive clientelism.

Uganda's political settlement might be characterized as a strong dominant party given the concentration of political power under President Yoweri Museveni. Tanzania's political settlement is best described as that of a weak dominant party. It is characterized by the dominance of the Chama Cha Mapinduzi (CCM) party, the "Revolutionary Party" that has governed Tanzania since independence—though the power of CCM has eroded considerably since the era of its first president, Julius Nyerere. Finally, I submit that Moldova's political settlement is characterized by greater competition between political parties, largely distinguishing between those favoring closer ties with Europe and those with Russia, which has led to a political settlement of competitive clientelism. In the rest of this chapter, I describe in more detail the political settlements in each country.

The Political Economy of Climate Finance Effectiveness in Developing Countries. Mark Purdon, Oxford University Press.
© Oxford University Press 2024. DOI: 10.1093/oso/9780197756836.003.0005

5.2. Tanzania's Political Settlement

I begin with Tanzania, where the current political settlement is best described as one consisting of a weak dominant party system. This finds its origins in the political settlement that first coalesced under President Nyerere after independence. In Chapter 4, I mentioned Nyerere's role as a leading proponent of African socialism or, as he would famously refer to it, *ujamaa*. Indeed, Gray (2018) speaks of a *socialist political settlement* in Tanzania that connotes an intermingling of the country's political settlement and development policy paradigm. However, as I have emphasized earlier, it is helpful to keep development policy paradigms distinct from other analytical categories.

There are different views on the political settlement in Tanzania upon independence—including Tanganyika's independence in 1961 and Zanzibar's in 1963, who united to form Tanzania in 1964. Whitfield et al. (2015) suggest that it was initially characterized by a strong dominant party system. Arguably, strong dominant party characteristics allowed the initial, post-independence Tanzania central government to muscle in certain controversial *ujamaa* policies, such as villagization. As a one-party political system, all elite factions were under the CCM tent while lower levels of the coalition were weak. Local tribal chiefs, often a vehicle for indirect colonial rule, were also abolished by Nyerere, removing a potential political rival.

Another view is that the initial political settlement established under Nyerere was weaker than often assumed, eventually undermining the CCM party's central control. First, because of a surprisingly rapid decolonization process in the 1960s, the newly independent Tanzanian leadership had little time to consolidate its authority and organizational capacity before assuming power (Gray, 2018: 84). Second, the emphasis on *African* socialism that Nyerere introduced made it difficult to create meaningful partnerships with Tanzania's business leaders, who were mostly of Asian ethnic origin at the moment of independence. Finally, Gray points out that not all elites were behind Nyerere's socialist policies, frustrating policy intervention.

Opinion is more united that, after Nyerere stepped down in 1985, characteristics of a weak dominant party political settlement would come to predominate. Under his successor, President Ali Hassan Mwinyi, the Tanzanian central government embarked on a series of democratic reforms that culminated in multiparty elections in 1992. Therkildsen and Bourgouin (2012) argue that these frustrated meaningful alliances between the state and private sector. First, competitive elections resulted in a shift towards populist policies instead of business-oriented, growth-enhancing ones. Second, competitive elections shifted power-relations within the ruling CCM party. The prospect of competitive elections instead strengthened the position of lower level party members who most directly interact with voters. Given that competition generally took place within the ruling party, it is arguably best to describe this as a weak dominant party type of political settlement.

A weak dominant party of political settlement would continue under Presidents Benjamin Mkapa (1995–2005) and Jakaya Kikwete (2005–2015). Kikwete is widely recognized as not possessing Nyerere's stature; especially in the later part of his term, clientelism appeared to increase (Babeiya, 2012: 90–91). Whitfield et al. (2015) suggest that elements of competitive clientelism are also emerging as a result of these dynamics.

President Magufuli, recently deceased after only taking office in 2015, sought to clamp down on corruption in a more authoritarian manner (Mwalupinde, 2017). Dye (2021) argues convincingly that the political settlement under Magufuli was characterized by strong elite cohesion, consistent with a strong dominant party type of political settlement (p. 3). With his untimely death in early 2021, it is unclear whether this coalition will continue or revert to weaker CCM party dominance. I submit that political settlement in Tanzania continues to be best described as weak dominant party one, though Magufuli sought to exert greater central control. Based on interviews in 2018, relations between Magufuli and the private sector appear were frayed, unsettling a key ally of any potential developmental coalition.[1]

Finally, in discussing Tanzania's political settlement, some attention to the country's remarkable history of political stability is required. Among the other recognized explanations are the adoption of its Kiswahili language policy as well as the promotion of village government institutions (Erickson, 2012; Ibhawoh and Dibua, 2003). Green (2011) also makes a convincing argument that the relative evenness of the geographic distribution of resources across Tanzania and low population density helps explain the stability the country has enjoyed.

5.3. Uganda's Political Settlement

Turning to Uganda, the current political settlement here revolves around President Museveni who came to power in 1986 after a sustained period of civil conflict.

Uganda, however, first gained independence from the British colonial regime in 1962, at which time its political settlement was characterized by competitive clientelism (Whitfield et al., 2015). Briefly, Uganda's first leader after independence in 1962, Milton Obote, held only a precarious grip on power. After increasingly turning toward authoritarian measures, he was ousted in a 1971 coup by the dictator Idi Amin who reigned until 1979. Amin's rule is largely considered disastrous. He was finally overthrown after provoking a conflict with Tanzania, which saw the Tanzanian People's Defense Force and Ugandan rebels, including Museveni, recapture Kampala. While Obote won subsequent elections held in late 1980, these were contested by the opposition led by Museveni. The dispute grew into a civil war that saw Museveni and his National Resistance Movement ultimately prevail in 1986.

The fact that Museveni acquired power through military action may explain the stronger grip that he has had on power in contrast to Tanzania and Moldova. Some have argued that Museveni's initial success with liberal economic reforms, discussed below, stemmed from his "authoritarian advantage" (Mensah, 2007: 12). From 1986 to 2000, he wielded considerable political authority, leading a number of observers to identify his regime as one with developmental potential (Hickey and Izama, 2016; Mbabazi and Taylor, 2005; Shaw, 2005). For these reasons, Museveni's initial rule is largely seen as one of a strong dominant party if not a developmental coalition.

But there are concerns that Museveni's rule is becoming increasingly authoritarian, which is a sign of his loosening grip on power. Indeed, Melo et al. (2012) speak of two Musevenis (p.23): a first Museveni who took power in 1986 and enjoyed tremendous legitimacy across the country, and a second Museveni who emerged in 2005 and who has been increasingly prone to corruption. For many, the turning point was in 2005, when Museveni changed the Ugandan Constitution to allow him to contest again for the presidency (Melo et al., 2012; Tangri and Mwenda, 2010). The issue divided the National Resistance Movement, and since then there have been indications of declining support for Museveni's rule. In order to retain his authority, Museveni has had to resort to inflationary patronage: "the need for ever-increasing amounts of money to maintain oneself in power and increasing levels of corruption to provide the required funds" (Barkan, 2011: 11). Recent elections have been criticized by international observers as flawed, while Museveni's primary opponents, Kizza Besigye and, more recently, the musician Robert Kyagulanyi Ssentamu (aka Bobi Wine), have repeatedly been harassed and imprisoned.

There is some disagreement on Uganda's current political settlement. Hickey and Izama (2016) argue that Uganda's current political settlement is characterized by a ruling coalition with transformational aspirations but which is more authoritarian and possesses less political capacity. Whitfield et al. (2015) see Museveni's authority to also be degrading such that the country's political settlement is better characterized as competitive clientelism. Since the reintroduction of multiparty elections in 2006, lower level members of the ruling coalition have grown stronger and increasingly contest Museveni's vertical power. Renewed tensions with the powerful Buganda kingdom, a traditional authority, have also made Museveni more vulnerable.

Nonetheless, my results suggest that Museveni still maintains a stronger hold on central political authority than leaders of Tanzania and Moldova. Consequently, I submit that Uganda's political settlement might still be best described as one of a strong dominant party. The prospect of recent oil discoveries coming online in the near future may also allow Museveni to continue to buy political support (Vokes, 2012).

5.4. Moldova's Political Settlement

Finally, I turn to the political settlement in Moldova, which is best characterized by competitive clientelism. Since the dissolution of the Soviet Union in 1991, Moldova has been fraught with internal divisions that have arguably hindered the consolidation of a stable political settlement.

Much of Moldova's political instability is linked to the country's geography and history. As a small country located between East and West, Moldova has for centuries been caught up in international events. Moldova was not incorporated into the Soviet Union until the end of World War II, after a complicated modern history where Moldovan territory changed hands repeatedly between Russian and Romanian powers (King, 2000). Competing ethnic, if not nationalistic, tensions have also characterized Moldova's recent history, with the central government struggling to assert a unique Moldovan national identity among competing Russian and Romanian elements.

These historical divisions manifest in the continued dispute over Transnistria, a breakaway region that retains political affinities with Russia (Crowther, 2011; Kaufman, 1996). While officially part of Moldova, Transnistria has exercised *de facto* independence since a 1992 conflict that almost transformed into civil war. Underscoring nationalist tensions, one important cause of the 1992 conflict was a call for unification with Romania by the Popular Front, an organized political movement that led Moldova through its transition to independence (Kaufman, 1996: 122–125). The issue is also complicated by the fact that Russia has maintained a sizeable number of troops in Transnistria since the Soviet era (Devyatkov, 2012; Miarka, 2020; Nygren, 2008). Since Russia's annexation of Crimea in 2014 and 2022 invasion of Ukraine, new concerns about the territorial integrity of Moldova have arisen (Vulpe et al., 2023).

Even if we set the Transnistrian issue aside, Moldova's politics since independence have been tumultuous, frustrating consolidation of vertical and horizontal dimensions of power identified in my political settlements framework. The years after independence saw a succession of changes in leadership and political institutions, including a new constitution in 1994 that introduced a form of semi-presidentialism that has proven quite unstable as the president is not elected directly but via Parliament (Crowther, 2011). Political instability was also due to a "rapacious individualism" as the government in the early years of independence pushed through rapid privatization that elites were able to turn to their advantage (Way, 2003, 2005b). During this period, Moldova found itself in an odd position of "pluralism by default" where competition among elites frustrated efforts to assert government authority despite a very weak civil society.

In contrast to the authoritarian rule of Museveni in Uganda and one-party dominance in Tanzania, political competition in Moldova has found expression in a multitude of political parties. See Figure 5.1 for a timeline of the tenure of the Moldovan presidency and Parliament from 2000 through 2020. Since independence, the country has vacillated between a Western-oriented coalition and ostensibly communist/socialist government, with the Party of Communists/ Socialist or its elements initially slowing economic reforms (Crowther, 2011; Quinlan, 2004: 499–501; Way, 2005a: 240). Having gained control of both the presidency and Parliament from 2000 to 2009, the Party of Communists might be credited with providing a certain level of political stability in a troubled nation after an initial decade of instability.

Among the most important watershed moments in recent Moldovan history, the Party of Communists surprised many by turning toward the EU in 2005 following a major disagreement with Russia over Transnistria. While Moldova is often depicted as being at the mercy of international forces, this pivot toward the EU goes far in demonstrating the agency of Moldova vis-à-vis international powers.

When first seeking office, the party's candidate for president, Vladimir Voronin, had promised to enter into direct negotiations with Moscow in order to resolve the conflict and bring Transnistria fully under control (Urse, 2009). However, the solution that Russia proposed in 2003, the "Kozak Memorandum," proved deeply unpopular in Moldova. Against the expectations of many, President Voronin broke with Russia and came to endorse EU integration by ratifying the EU-Moldova Action Plan in February 2005 (Crowther, 2007: 283– 284; Kleinschnitger and Knodt, 2018). It set out to "encourage and support Moldova's objective of further integration into European economic and social structures" and "significantly advance the approximation of Moldovan legislation, norms and standards to those of the European Union" (EU & GoM, 2005: 2). In response, Russia banned the import of agricultural products from Moldova and followed up in 2006 with a ban on Moldovan wine—both key Moldovan exports (Sanchez, 2009; Urse, 2009).

However, there has been greater competition since 2009. As Whitfield et al. (2015) explain, competitive clientelism "occurs when the ruling coalition faces strong excluded political factions, and internally, the ruling coalition is composed of strong lower-level factions and characterized by fragmentation among

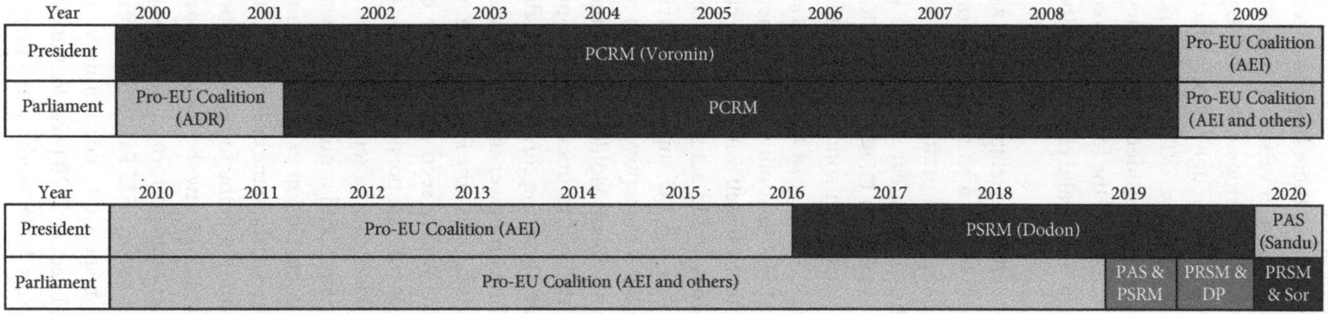

Year	2000	2001	2002	2003	2004	2005	2006	2007	2008	2009
President	PCRM (Voronin)									Pro-EU Coalition (AEI)
Parliament	Pro-EU Coalition (ADR)	PCRM								Pro-EU Coalition (AEI and others)

Year	2010	2011	2012	2013	2014	2015	2016	2017	2018	2019	2020
President	Pro-EU Coalition (AEI)						PSRM (Dodon)				PAS (Sandu)
Parliament	Pro-EU Coalition (AEI and others)									PAS & PSRM / PRSM & DP	PRSM & Sor

Figure 5.1 Moldovan Presidential and Parliamentary Authority, 2000–2020

PCRM: Party of Communists of the Republic of Moldova
AEI: Alliance for European Integration
PSRM: Party of Socialists of the Republic of Moldova
ADR: Alliance for Democracy and Reforms
PAS: Party of Action and Solidarity
DP: Democratic Party
Sor: ŞOR Party

ruling elites . . . Competitive Clientelism is typically associated with electoral democracy" (p. 106). As I detail further below, there have been regular swings in the Moldovan elections as well as outstanding levels of corruption.

From 2009 to 2012, political paralysis gripped the country again as the communist-led Parliament failed to garner enough votes to elect a president in Moldova's semi-presidential system (EurActive, 2010; New York Times, 2009). Nonetheless, Voronin ultimately ceded the presidency to the newly established Alliance for European Integration (AEI), with the leaders of three different pro-EU parties serving as "acting president" until valid election results were achieved in 2012.

The period from 2012 to 2016 saw a return to relative stability as the Moldovan presidency and Parliament were both led by a shifting coalition of parties favorable to EU integration. Unfortunately, this period also witnessed a remarkable degree of corruption (Całus, 2016). Most egregious was a $1 billion bank fraud scandal—equivalent to 12% of Moldova's GDP—in 2014 (Kottasova 2015). Corruption also tended to be associated with some of the leaders of the pro-EU coalition. For example, consider the leader of the Democratic Party (DP), Vladimir Plahotniuc. Despite aspirations for political office, he had extremely low public support and had to content himself with political control through surrogates. Support for EU integration would actually fall during this period, largely because of the perception that the EU supported corrupt albeit pro-Western politicians (Kostanyan, 2016). A perceptive analysis of Moldovan politics concludes that EU and Russian activities in Moldova at the time actually share a striking similarity: they each endeavored to uncritically support local elites, resulting in a lack of accountability and growing corruption (Nizhnikau, 2016).

While a pro-EU coalition would retain power in parliamentary elections in 2016, Igor Dodon of the Party of Socialists (not the Party of Communists) would win the presidency. His election was widely seen as evidence of popular disgust with corruption (Całus, 2018). While the president's powers are limited by Parliament, these developments also indicated a return to a more authoritarian government, efforts to centralize control, and a pivot back toward Russia. For example, just prior to the 2016 elections, Dodon explained in an interview that he aspired to become "a dictatorial leader, the same as Putin" (Nemtsova, 2016).

Though after the end of the period that is the focus of this book, it is worth noting that parliamentary elections in 2019 saw the Party of Socialists increase their seats, though not sufficiently enough to form a majority. Instead, it was forced to form a coalition with the new, pro-EU Party of Action and Solidarity (PAS) that had been established in response to corruption among other pro-EU parties. The coalition was short-lived, as 2020 presidential elections saw the leader of Party of Action and Solidarity, Maia Sandu, win a majority on an anti-corruption platform (Economist, 2020). Most recently, in June 2022, Moldova was officially granted EU candidate status, though subject to a number of economic and political conditions.

Overall, during most of the period when climate finance instruments were being implemented, Moldova's political settlement has been characterized by considerable political instability that has frustrated effective central authority. However, as we shall see, despite highly competitive clientelism, climate finance instruments have been implemented relatively effectively, which adds support to my argument about the saliency of a convergence of development policy paradigms and state development interests.

5.5. Conclusion

In this chapter I have reviewed political settlements in Tanzania, Uganda, and Moldova. Briefly, the concentration of power under President Museveni, while ebbing, contrasts with the more distributed political settlements found in Tanzania and Moldova, which are characterized by a weak dominant party and competitive clientelism political settlements respectively. As I demonstrate later in this book, such patterns in political settlements however will contrast with those for climate finance effectiveness.

6

State Development Interests in Tanzania, Uganda, and Moldova

6.1. Introduction

It might be assumed that poor countries might be eager to receive climate finance. However, my findings suggest that financial incentives offered by the international community for climate change mitigation compete with what I refer to as state development interests. Recall that I define "state development interests" as policy ends that the state leadership is motivated to attain. State development interests are shaped by history, particularly the colonial period, but also geography, such as the resource endowments.

In this chapter, I review state development interests in the forest and energy sectors of Tanzania, Uganda, and Moldova. In order to identify state development interests, I have relied on detailed analysis of forest and energy resources, national development plans, and interviews in the three case-study countries. I contend that national development plans more clearly indicate where states understand their interests lie than do official pronouncements in climate policy documents. Because interests are slow to change, I consider how state development interests in the forest and energy sectors have evolved since each country's independence. This has the virtue of demonstrating that development interests were formed prior to the advent of climate finance instruments and were surprisingly stable over the study period.

I briefly summarize my findings here before analyzing them in more detail in subsequent sections. First, state development interests in the forest sector have diverged in the three case-study countries, largely because of differences in the relative scarcity of forest resources and levels of land degradation between them. Land degradation and forest resource scarcity have made tree planting a development priority for the central governments of Uganda and Moldova. In contrast, despite the attention Tanzania's forests have received from the international community, the central government has, until relatively recently, been less interested in the forest sector.

At a certain level, the development of modern and secure energy sources is a priority for development in all countries investigated. It is difficult to fully separate this state development interests from ideas of modernization. More clarity

The Political Economy of Climate Finance Effectiveness in Developing Countries. Mark Purdon, Oxford University Press.
© Oxford University Press 2024. DOI: 10.1093/oso/9780197756836.003.0006

might be gained from considering state development interests for decentralized renewable energy, which vary considerably across countries. Almost entirely dependent on external sources for energy, the Moldovan central government has come to see renewable energy, particularly modern biomass energy, as integral to its energy security. In contrast, with considerable untapped large-scale hydroelectric and fossil fuel resources available in East Africa, the central governments of Tanzania and Uganda have been less interested in decentralized renewables.

The rest of this chapter is divided between discussion of state development interests beginning with the forest sector followed by the energy sector. Each is organized to first provide a comparative overview followed by detailed analysis of each sector in Tanzania, Uganda, and Moldova. To gauge state development interests in the forest sector, it is useful to first consider how forest cover varies across countries.

6.2. Forest Cover Across Countries

Forests cover less of Uganda and Moldova than Tanzania. However, this conclusion requires some interpretation as there are different ways of presenting information on forest cover.

First, consider the extent of forest coverage across countries as estimated through a global remote-sensing project (Hansen et al., 2013). Tanzanian's forests are significantly more extensive than in our other two case-study countries— at 329,000 km2 they are nearly 3.5 times as extensive as Uganda's forest cover (97,000 km2) and over 91 times larger than Moldova's (3,800 km2). Tanzania is just a larger country than Uganda and Moldova, which translates into greater tracts of forest. However, remote sensing also indicates that Uganda has been losing considerably more high-density forest while more than two-thirds of Tanzania's net deforestation is due to the loss of low-density miombo dryland forests. This has implications for REDD+ as miombo forest stocks have significantly less above-ground carbon than rainforests (Shirima et al., 2011).

Second, and more important for climate policy, is to consider forest cover relative to the size of a country's territory. The remote-sensing project cited above estimated that forests cover 37% of Tanzania's national territory, 48% of Uganda's, and 11.5% of Moldova's. However, estimates of forest coverage based on remote sensing are prone to fail to distinguish forests from other land uses. Measures of forest coverage based on national land-use categories are often seen as a valid alternative method (Hansen et al. 2013: supplementary material, p. 4). This appears to be particularly important in Uganda where the country's extensive wetlands are often misclassified as "forest" through remote sensing. According to land-use category data, Uganda saw its forest cover decline by an outstanding

63% from 1990 to 2015, when it was estimated to cover only 9% of the national territory compared to 48% in the remote-sensing exercise cited above (MWE, 2016: 47). A more recent estimate for Uganda's REDD+ efforts, perhaps the most precise measurement to date, found that Uganda's forest covered about 12% of the national territory (MWE, 2018: 11). Consequently, I conclude that forests cover approximately 37%, 12%, and 11.5% of the national territories of Tanzania, Uganda, and Moldova.

A third source of information on forest cover comes from technical work to establish baseline emissions from deforestation and forest degradation that Tanzania and Uganda have been submitted to the UNFCCC—what I referred to as "REDD+ baselines" in Chapter 3. These tend to align with land-use categorizations above, though direct comparisons have their limitations. With this caveat in mind, emissions from deforestation and forest degradation in Tanzania are estimated at more than seven times those of Uganda (MWE, 2018: 10, 11, and 32; United Republic of Tanzania, 2017: 6 and 31). Tanzania estimated that average annual emissions from deforestation stood at 43.7 megatonnes CO2 equivalent (MtCO2e) per year between 2002 and 2013, resulting in an estimated loss of 12% of forest cover over this time. In comparison, the Uganda government estimated that net emissions from a variety of REDD+ activities stood at 8.2 MtCO2e per year from 2000 to 2015. This amounts to a 17% forest-cover loss over 2002–2013 (the period estimated for Tanzania).

The upshot is that natural forests are scarcer in Uganda and Moldova than in Tanzania, which may reasonably be interpreted to contribute to divergent state development interests in the forest sector across the three countries.

6.3. Forest Sectors Across Countries

While forest cover is an important element of state development interests in the forest sector, governments might also be interested in forests in terms of their contribution to industrialization as well as an energy source, especially for the poor. It is from this broader vantage that I consider the forest sectors in Tanzania, Uganda, and Moldova in this section.

State Development Interests in Tanzania's Forest Sector

In addition to greater forest coverage, my investigation of Tanzania's forest sector finds that the country possesses relatively more timber plantations than the other two countries investigated and that, until quite recently, the primary state development interest has been the establishment of industrial capacity to transform standing timber into forest products. Since at least 2016, however, there has been renewed interest in plantation forestry by the central government. While this may be related to results from a national forest-monitoring exercise that highlighted that fuelwood demand highly exceeds supply, it may also be attributed to the maturation of Tanzania's timber-processing capacity.

State Interests Post-Independence

The Tanzania government inherited sizeable forest reserves and forest plantations from previous colonial regimes (Kalumanga et al., 2018; Pedersen, 2017; Sunseri, 2009). One estimate is that the British had established over 2.8 million ha of forest reserves by the time of Tanganyika's independence in 1961 (Hurst, 2003: 361; Kangalawe, 2018). German and British colonial regimes had also initiated forest plantations in the Mufindi district prior to World War II, with 6,700 ha established at the time of Tanzania's independence (Kangalawe, 2018: 108). The British anticipated growing international demand for forest products from Tanzania. It needs to be kept in mind, of course, that such forest reserves and plantations were established through unjust land expropriations. For example, Sunseri (2002) demonstrates that the establishment of forest reserves was widely resented by local populations, inciting the 1905 Maji Maji rebellion among other acts of resistance.

For reasons related to the *ujamaa* version of classic developmentalism that Nyerere espoused, discussed in the next chapter, many forest reserves established under the colonial regime were opened up for smallholder agriculture after independence. The idea that peasant agriculture should be allowed to expand into forest reserves held sway during at least the first decade of independence (1961–1971). Ultimately, forests reserves in Tanzania would be reduced to 1.25 million ha by the late 1990s—a reduction of more than half from the colonial period (GoT, 2008: 8; MNRT, 1998: 8).

As for Tanzania's forest plantations, these were nationalized following the 1967 Arusha Declaration, becoming the seed for an ambitious plan to develop the industrial forest sector, including East Africa's largest paper mill, now known as Mufindi Paper Mill (originally Southern Paper Mills). Plantations peaked in the late 1970s, with an additional 7,000 ha of plantation forest planted (Pedersen, 2017: 10). Construction of the state-owned Southern Paper Mills was officially commenced in 1977 though not finally completed until 1986, with nearly $20 million in funding from the World Bank (Christiansson and Åshuvud, 1985; Kulekana, 2008; World Bank, 2003). Annual wood consumption at the Mill would reach 300,000 m3/year once fully operational (Kulekana, 2008; World Bank, 2003: 74).

The Nyerere administration also initially demonstrated considerable interest in promoting village forestry as part of its rural development strategy. It launched a village woodlots program in 1968 (Dykstra, 1983; Skutsch, 1985) and a national tree-planting campaign in the 1980s (Ahlbäck, 1988). During the 1970s, the potential exhaustion of fuelwood also loomed as an impending crisis, further highlighting the importance of village tree-planting efforts (Dewees, 1989; Hosier et al., 1990). While the village woodlots programs led to increased village tree-planting efforts, by most estimates, their success was modest (Abdallah and Monela, 2007: 16; Ahlbäck, 1995: 306; Kulindwa and Schechambo, 1995: 115). The upshot is that, already by the 1980s, Tanzania possessed considerable state-owned timber plantations and timber-processing capacity and had taken steps to address village forest needs.

Declining Interest From the 1980s to 2000s

As the economic situation deteriorated in Tanzania into the 1980s, forestry was downgraded as a state development priority, though the central government also pursued limited economic reforms of the sector. Government support for afforestation and reforestation followed a steep downward trajectory into the 1990s (Kulindwa and Schechambo, 1995: 116). Support for village forestry also eroded because the predicted fuelwood crisis never fully realized (Johnsen, 1999). As economic conditions in Tanzania deteriorated into the 1980s, Tanzania's state-owned timber-processing capacity would also decline, particularly with the closure of the Southern Paper Mills in 1997. By 2005, processing capacity for round wood stood at half levels of 1992 (Milledge et al., 2007: 142; MNRT, 2000: 6–7).

Into the 2000s, liberal economic reforms of the forest sector incentivized a number of private firms to expand industrial plantations (Jacovelli, 2014). The contribution of the forest sector to Tanzania's GDP grew from an estimated 2–3% in 1998 to 11% by 2006 (GoT, 2008: 9; MNRT, 1998: 9). By 2010, established plantations were estimated at slightly more than 147,000 ha, (TFS, 2015b: 53). Liberal economic reforms also attracted investment into timber-processing capacity, with Southern Paper Mills being bought by private investors and reopened as Mufindi Paper Mill in 2005. Overall, by the early 2000s, private sector-led expansion of forest plantations and timber-processing capacity appeared to have sated the central government's development interest in the forest sector. As I discuss in the next chapter, the relative success of these liberal economic reforms seems due moreso to donor interests rather than those of the Tanzanian central government.

This is reflected in Tanzania's two Poverty Reduction Strategy Papers (PRSPs) submitted to the World Bank accorded modest attention to the forest sector relative to other industrial sectors such as agriculture, mining, and natural gas exploitation. The forest sector is mentioned in 2005's MKUKUTA 1, but it was not one of the "lead" sectors identified for public investment under the goal of ensuring sound economic management (GoT, 2005: annex 1, 3). In MKUKUTA 2, released in 2010, the forest sector receives little attention except for a call for greater value addition from forest concessions and licenses (MFEA, 2010: 118). The marginalization of Tanzania's forest sector continued in the central government's First Five-Year Development Plan (First FYDP), unveiled in 2011. No new forest initiatives were planned, and the government anticipated spending only a total of 72 billion Tanzanian shilling (Tsh) on forestry, which pales in comparison with other sectors such as agriculture (2,631 billion Tsh) and mining (1,383 billion Tsh) (POPC, 2011: 106–123).

The 2010s Through the Magufuli Period

The forest sector would see renewed government attention in the Second Five-Year Development Plan (Second FYDP), released in 2016 under the Magufuli regime. Released after the CDM market had collapsed and with REDD+ still embryonic, the plan would reveal a striking new interest in industrial plantation development. This included commitment to a "national tree planting and management strategy" that would see 185,000 ha of trees planted each year and a commitment to expand timber plantations to 1.85 million ha by 2025 (MPF, 2016: 59). The most recent government figures estimate industrial plantations at about 160,000 ha of which nearly two-thirds are government owned (FBD, 2021: 7). Interestingly this same report includes about 422,000 ha of individual woodlots in its tally of Tanzania's forest plantations, which would bring total forest plantations to nearly 583,000 ha.

Important for our discussion of REDD+, the area of natural forest cover was also expected to decline under the Second FYDP (MPF, 2016: 59). This suggests that industrial forestry and not forest conservation was the priority of the Magufuli regime in the forest sector. Nonetheless, while spending for environmental and natural resources would increase to 134 billion Tsh, this still pales in comparison to a 9,100 billion Tsh slated for the agricultural sector (MPF, 2016: 252, 254).

To promote the objectives of the Second FYDP, the Ministry of Natural Resources and Tourism (MNRT) drafted the National Forest Policy (MNRT, 2018a) and the National Forest Policy Implementation Strategy, 2018–2028 (MNRT, 2018b). Here MNRT committed to increasing industrial forest plantations by 200,000 ha, fuelwood plantations by nearly 30,000 ha, while also increasing natural forest reserves by 1.4 million ha (MNRT, 2018b: 20–23). The largest funding allocations anticipated in the National Forest Policy Implementation Strategy are for financing forest industries (10.0 trillion Tsh), increasing forest area under plantations and woodlots (6.4 trillion Tsh), as well as increasing protection of miombo woodland and naturally regenerating forests (2.5 trillion Tsh) (MNRT, 2018b: 27–35). To the best of my knowledge, however, the National Forest Policy remains in draft form and has not yet been formally adopted by the central government (FAO, 2021).

The renewed interest in the forest sector described above, particularly commercial plantations, is a striking recent development in Tanzania. The timing of this shift in government priorities is difficult to explain, though two possibilities present themselves. First, has been potential greater awareness by the state leadership of the scarcity of forest resources, which can be attributed to the publication in 2015 of results from the National Forest Resources Monitoring and Assessment (NAFORMA) of mainland Tanzania (TFS, 2015b). NAFORMA demonstrated that wood supply was scarcer than previously known: Tanzania was able to sustain 42.8 million m3 of wood on an annual basis but consumed 62.3 million m3, resulting in an annual wood deficit of 19.5 million m3 (TFS, 2015b: 45–46). But the cause of this imbalance is largely attributed (nearly 70%) to household fuelwood consumption of natural forests and woodlands. However, fuelwood is only partially addressed in the draft National Forest Policy Implementation Strategy, where, as indicated above, the central government focused on commercial plantations and offered only modest support for the development of fuelwood plantations. This suggests that the revival of Tanzania timber-processing capacity, particularly the Mufindi Paper Mill in 2005—though due to private investment and donors in the context of liberal economic reforms—may have piqued government interest in industrial forestry.

Overall, forests have generally not been a high priority among state development interests in Tanzania. Recently however, with renewed timber-processing capacity, as well as increased attention to forest scarcity, the state's interest in the sector appears to be growing. Nonetheless, as I demonstrate in later chapters, the Tanzanian central government has not proactively engaged forest opportunities under the CDM nor REDD+.

State Development Interests in Uganda's Industrial Forest Sector

Because of the poor state of Uganda's forest resources, they have consistently been accorded significant attention by the Museveni regime—a state development interest that transcends the period including the CDM and REDD+.

Origins of Uganda's Timber Shortage
Decades of conflict have made industrial timber resources and processing capacity highly scarce in Uganda. As explained by Webster et al. (2003: 167–168), independent Uganda inherited a functional forest department and system of forest reserves from the colonial regime. As in Tanzania, such forest reserves had largely been established by colonial authorities through unjust land

expropriations, which would invite problems with encroachment that continue to the present day. Nonetheless, forest sector institutions were generally retained by the incoming Obote regime after independence in 1962. However, when Amin took power in 1972, Uganda's industrial forestry resources saw a sharp decline. First, Amin opened up forest reserves for agriculture in a populist bid to gain political support. Second, his expulsion of Uganda's Asian population culled most of the managerial capacity for sawmilling. During the second Obote regime and subsequent civil conflict, forest reserve management was largely suspended.

As a result, Museveni would face acute timber scarcity upon coming to power. Uganda's timber demand in the 2000s was still being met by plantations established prior to Uganda's descent into civil conflict in the 1960s (Jacovelli, 2014; SPGS, 2007: 11; Webster et al., 2003: 167). One estimate has been that at least 120,000 ha of plantation forest would be needed by 2020 to meet internal demand, though this might rise to 160,000 ha if, as is more likely to be the case, less efficient saw-milling is used (SPGS, 2011: 4). At most 35,000 ha of industrial timber plantations existed in 2005, increasing to approximately 101,000 ha by 2015 as forestry came to be treated as state development interest (MWE, 2016: 47; NFA, 2005b: 10).

Forestry as a National Development Priority

Since Museveni came to power in 1986, the Ugandan central government has demonstrated considerable interest in the forest sector. As early as 1987, Museveni's regime sought, unsuccessfully, to devolve natural resource management to the districts (Turyahabwe and Banana, 2008). Museveni also took an early interest in taking stock of Uganda's forest reserves. In contrast to Tanzania, where NAFORMA was only completed by 2015, Uganda undertook its first National Biomass Study in 1990 (MWE, 2017c: 16). Perhaps on this basis, as early as 2001, in the Uganda Forest Policy, the Ministry of Water, Lands & Environment (MWLE) would acknowledge

> there is increasing concern about the deteriorating state of forestry in the country. Natural forest cover is receding; ecological services are declining; there is increasing pressure on forest land and increasing demand on forest products; management capacity is limited and institutional weaknesses constrain development. (MWLE, 2001: 1)

Such an assessment was not restricted to the MWLE. The forest sector would soon find its place in national development plans, first led by the powerful Ministry of Finance, Planning and Economic Development (MFPED) and later the semi-autonomous National Planning Authority (NPA). Uganda's 2005 Poverty Eradication Action Plan (PEAP) committed to increasing forest cover, including via linkages with carbon markets (MFPED, 2005: 77–78). Adding greater specificity, the 2010 National Development Plan committed Uganda to restoring national forest cover to 1990 levels by 2015: approximately 5 million ha, or 24%, of the national land base (NPA, 2010: 95–96). Despite increased plantation efforts, forest cover in Uganda in 2015 was well shy of this target (MWE, 2016: 47). Consequently, the 2015 National Development Plan pushed back the 24% objective to 2040 and only committed to increase forest cover to 18% of the Uganda's national land base by 2020 (NPA, 2015: 102).

Uganda also continues to lack large-scale timber-processing capacity. Instead, small-scale mobile sawmills remain the dominant method for processing timber (Turinawe, 2013). In 2009, only one major plywood manufacturer was operational in the country (Kambugu et al., 2010: 196), though two transnational private firms (GRL and the New Forests Company) launched pole-processing plants in 2010 (GRAS, 2011: 5; NFC, 2017). In 2015, GRL launched a small sawmill at its operations near Jinja (BFC, 2018). The pulp and paper industry is also underdeveloped. In the mid-2000s, the Uganda Investment Agency reported that most of the paper products in Uganda were imported (UIA, 2011a: 7). To the best of the author's knowledge, as of 2018 there were only two companies producing paper packaging in Uganda (Crane Paper Bags, 2018; Kasozi, 2007)— and even here the feedstock appears to be derived from waste paper residues and not timber.

To summarize, forest resources have been quite scarce in Uganda, and the central government has treated the sector as a priority for development. As I later demonstrate, this would converge with a development policy paradigm of liberal neodevelopmentalism in a way that would see the Ugandan central government treat climate finance instruments in the forest sector as a development opportunity.

State Development Interests in Moldova's Forest Sector

Similar to the situation in Uganda, forestry has continuously been prioritized in Moldova's national development planning. But this is not because of the government's interest in cultivating a forest industry but, rather, to address another pressing development issue that has wide-ranging implications for its agricultural-based economy: land degradation.

In Moldova, three-quarters of the land area is considered suitable for agriculture, and more than half is comprised of highly productive "black earth" soils (Potopová et al., 2016: 2080). Despite this rich natural endowment, the country has among the highest levels of land degradation of any country of the former Soviet Union (Krupenikov, 2008; Van Lynden, 2000: figure 2c). Currently, almost 40% of Moldova agricultural land is considered degraded, resulting in declining agricultural yields (Wiesmeier et al., 2015: 609). Land degradation in Moldova is largely attributed to the Soviet era practice of intensive tilling—fields were tilled as many as four to five times during a single season—as well as tilling on sloping terrain (Karbozova-Saljnikov et al., 2004; Summer and Diernhofer, 2003). Degradation was masked by the Soviet practice of intensive application of fertilizers and pesticides (Boincean, 2009). Land degradation was also exacerbated by rapid land reforms in the late 1990s that fragmented the rural land base in a way that frustrated soil conservation practices (Summer and Diernhofer, 2003). Finally, rising energy prices, particularly natural gas, have also exacerbated the exploitation of local forests and woodlots. It is estimated that 1 million m3 of fuelwood is harvested per year, almost two-thirds of it illegally and often unsustainably (World Bank, 2014: 14, 16). Figure 6.1 shows a degraded hillside in Moldova that was deforested in the 1990s during a period of fuel scarcity yet was still being used for pasture when I visited in 2009.

It is worth noting that in commercial terms, the contribution of the forest industry to the Moldovan economy is modest. While the agricultural sector has been responsible for 10–20% of GDP over the 2000s, forestry contributes less than 0.5% GDP (World Bank, 2014). Notably, Moldsilva, the state forest agency, possesses excess timber-processing capacity (World Bank, 2014: 13–14). Such excess capacity can be explained by the fact that during the Soviet era, Moldova's timber mills received raw logs from Ukraine for processing. The concerted effort to afforest degraded land has therefore been maintained despite the negligible role of Moldova's forest industry.

Figure 6.1 Degraded Hillside in Rural Moldova

Despite Moldova's fraught domestic political situation, there has been a surprising political consensus on the need to restore degraded lands through afforestation. Tree planting has long been identified as an efficient way of addressing land degradation in the former Soviet Union (Khamzina et al., 2006; Zdruli et al., 1997). In Moldova, afforestation was first promoted in what might be referred to as the 2001 Economic Revival Program of the Party of Communists, which called for halting land degradation and increasing forest area (GoRM, 2001: 13). Relatedly, the government's 2001 Strategy for the Sustainable Development of the Forestry Sector (2003–2020) set a goal of expanding forest cover to 15% of the national territory by 2020—or to afforest 130,000 ha (Gulca, 2006: 126, 2010a: 87; ICAS, 2007). I return to this 2020 forest cover target in Chapter 8 when discussing the CDM afforestation project in Moldova. Furthermore, the National Development Strategy 2008–2011 set a midterm forest cover target of 13.2% of the national territory by 2015 (GoRM, 2007: 35, 95).

The interest in addressing land degradation through afforestation remained under a pro-EU coalition government. While the National Development Strategy did not initially include a section on land degradation nor afforestation, a National Agricultural and Rural Development Strategy 2014–2020 was officially incorporated subsequently (Expert-Grup, 2017: 10). It continued to highlight the link between insufficient forest cover and soil degradation, though a forest cover goal has not been explicitly rearticulated (GoRM, 2014c: 72).

The Moldovan central government does appear to be making progress in its efforts to tackle land degradation through afforestation. National forest cover in 2016 stood at 12.6% of the national territory (FAOSTAT, 2018). This amounts to an increase of nearly 900 km2 of forest cover since 2000, of which over 40% is due to carbon offset projects that I discuss in Chapter 8. But the country is still nearly 800 km2 below the 2020 forest cover target of 15% of the national territory.

Overall, the Moldovan central government has consistently recognized tree planting and afforestation as a key strategy for restoring degraded lands, a clear national development priority. Like Uganda, such state development interests have converged with its development policy paradigm in what I find has resulted in relatively effective engagement with the CDM and NAMAs in the forest sector.

6.4. Recent Trends in Energy Supply Across Countries

To understand state development interests in renewable energy across the three case-study countries we need to first consider broad patterns in energy supply among them. This is more challenging than it first appears as primary energy needs in sub-Saharan Africa are still predominantly met through the informal use of biomass, typically fuelwood in rural areas and charcoal in urban settings.

Estimates from Tanzania and Uganda indicate that fuelwood and charcoal contributes over 90% of total energy consumption (GoT, 2017: 77; MEMD, 2002: 19; Mwandosya and Luhanga, 1993: 448). But painting a more exact comparative picture of total primary energy supply across countries is challenging as data on energy from biomass and waste, including fuelwood, is not reported consistently by Uganda.[1] The below represents a best effort.

In Tanzania, the role of fossil fuels increased from 6% to 16% of total primary energy supply between 2000 and 2018 (IEA, 2020). At nearly 200 KTOE in 2018, hydroelectricity accounted for only approximately 1% of total primary energy supply (IEA, 2020). While in Uganda it is difficult to measure the relative importance of different fuels for reasons provided above, a larger role for hydroelectricity is expected in Uganda, where it supplied nearly 300 KTOE in 2018 (AFREC, 2019). Both East African countries also have significant fossil fuel deposits that their governments are striving to exploit. In contrast, natural gas is the largest source of energy in Moldova, most of which is still sourced from Russia. Interesting for our argument about Moldova's state development interests, energy derived from biomass and waste has risen significantly in Moldova—from approximately 2% of the country's primary energy supply in 2009 to 20% by 2018 (IEA, 2020).

It is worth mentioning that natural gas and hydroelectricity in Tanzania and Uganda have been associated with outstanding recent improvements in electricity access (this is nearly universal in Moldova). In 2009, during my first round of fieldwork, Uganda had some of the lowest measures of electricity access, which reached just 10% of the population; Tanzania faired only slightly better at 11% (World Bank, 2020b). Yet by 2016, Tanzania and Uganda would post electricity access rates of 33% and 27%, respectively. Similarly, in terms of *rural* access to electricity, I observe an increase from 2% and 3% in 2009, in Tanzania and Uganda respectively, to 17% and 18% by 2016. Increased electrification rates are, of course, not only due to greater generation capacity (Cuesta Fernández, 2018; Dye, 2021). Nonetheless, rising access to electricity, much of it realized just since 2015, is an outstanding development achievement.

Tanzanian State Development Interests in the Energy Sector

The Tanzania central government has prioritized the provision of modern energy services through the development of large-scale hydroelectric power projects and, more recently, domestic natural gas and coal resources in what many observers have described as "resource nationalism" (Pedersen et al., 2020). Despite their promotion by the international community, decentralized renewable energy technologies have failed to attract significant state attention. This helps explain, in part, the lack of interest of the Tanzanian central government in pursuing climate finance initiatives in the energy sector, many of which have focused on such renewables.

A bit of history helps us understand the interests of the Tanzanian state in the energy sector. The first large power station was built under the British colonial regime at Pangani Falls in 1959 though limited to a mere 18 MW, considerably less than initial efforts in Uganda (TANESCO, No Date). Two years later, the same year that Tanganyika gained independence, another 21 MW dam was commissioned. The next major power project was only developed much later: the first phase of the Great Ruaha Hydroelectric Project, a 200 MW hydroelectric dam supported by the World Bank, was completed in 1975 and the second in 1981. However, little other generating capacity was built during the 1980s as Tanzania entered a period of economic crisis.

Into the 1990s, a preference for large-scale hydro and fossil fuel power generation would consistently be expressed in Tanzania's energy policies and national development plans. Although the 1992 National Energy Policy set a goal of arresting "woodfuel depletion by involving more appropriate land management practices and more efficient woodfuel technologies" (GoT, 1992: 5), the government's focus was on expanding hydroelectricity and fossil fuels. Together these sectors absorbed 95% of expenditures for the implementation of the policy (Mwandosya and Luhanga, 1993: 450). Arguably, little changed by the time of the 2003 National Energy Policy (GoT, 2003). It focused on institutional reform to make the energy sector more attractive to international investors with little attention to woodfuel (Lymio, 2007: 10). Rather, a key goal of the energy policy effort over the 1990s was increasing thermal power generation to compensate for depressed hydroelectric capacity due to a prolonged regional drought (Gratwick et al., 2006). Under neoliberal reforms, discussed in the next chapter, two private thermal power generation projects were initiated; one running on heavy fuel oil and the other on natural gas. The natural gas plant was notable as the first attempt to exploit Tanzania's offshore natural gas for domestic power generation—including construction of a 200 km pipeline that began delivering gas to Dar es Salaam in 2004 (TPDC, No Date). However, both were plagued with controversy and delayed significantly, only coming online in 2002 and 2004, respectively.

Indeed, natural gas has transformed Tanzania's energy landscape: estimates of Tanzania's proven natural gas reserves range from 18 to 50 trillion cubic feet—among the top-25 largest national reserves in the world (Ledesma, 2013: 13). Tanzania and neighboring Mozambique first identified promising natural gas reserves in the 1990s, though commercial exploitation did not really takeoff until the early 2000s when the costs of deep offshore drilling came down (Ledesma, 2013: 7, 12). It is also worth pointing out that Tanzania also has 304 million tonnes of proven coal reserves (Mwasumbi and Tzoneva, 2007: 4), which also follows the "resource nationalism" narrative (Jacob, 2017).

Initial development plans for the energy sector during the neoliberal period were tepid. The first version of Tanzania's PRSP, MKUKUTA 1, produced in 2005, did not offer many specific targets for the energy sector (VPO, 2005: annex, p. 13). MKUKUTA 2, released in 2010, would seek to increase electricity generation to 1700 MW by 2015, which would include natural gas development; rural electrification projects; and "harnessing wind, solar, small hydro, biogas, with emphasis on renewable sources" (MFEA, 2010: 123). However, as I discuss in the next chapter, the second PRSP would be the last of Tanzania's neoliberal planning efforts as it would subsequently return to more centralized planning.

Between MKUKUTA 1 and MKUKUTA 2, President Kikwete, a former energy minister, came to see Tanzania's natural gas and coal resources as an opportunity to build a state-led power sector. This would be foreshadowed in the 2009 Power System Master Plan. It evaluated nearly 8000 MW of new power generation potential, half of which consisted of large hydropower stations, while more than 27% derived from gas and another 20% from coal (Dye, 2021: 6). Kikwete's administration eventually succeeded in raising power capacity from 833 MW in 2005 to 1616 MW in 2015, largely from gas. The First Five-Year Development Plan (FYDP1) of 2010, which signaled a more ambitious approach to development that I discuss in the next chapter, called for an increase in power generation from 900 MW to 2780 MW between 2010 and 2015, considerably more than that considered under MKUKUTA 2, which was released nearly at the same time (POPC, 2011: 142). In the Second FYDP, President Magufuli committed to increasing power generation to 4915 MW by 2020 as well as raising urban and rural electricity access rates to 75% (MPF, 2016: 81, 138).

Indeed, President Magufuli had been bullish on harnessing Tanzania's hydro and fossil fuel resources. Upon coming to power in 2015, President Magufuli focused his energies on the controversial the 2100 MW Stiegler's Gorge Dam—renamed the Julius Nyerere Hydropower Station under his tenure—as Tanzania's "flagship electricity project" with an expected completion date of 2024. Notably it is being built by a consortium led by Egyptian firms with key support from Chinese manufacturers (Egypt Today, 2021). Finally, Tanzania's coal deposits are expected to fuel at least three new power plants slated for development (Dye, 2021; Kihwele et al., 2012: 3915).

The Tanzania central government has consistently demonstrated limited interest in decentralized renewables such as solar and wind. For example, in the 2009 Power System Master Plan, wind power is the only decentralized renewable mentioned—and here at only 2% of planned new generating capacity (Dye, 2021: 6). While, also in 2009, the central government would introduce the Small Power Producer program for renewable energy and cogeneration, its results have been modest thus far. As of 2016, 40 MW were being generated from 10 approved projects with another 32 in the pipeline (Moner-Girona et al., 2016: 309). A 2013 study of the solar sector in Tanzania observed that "the government does not seem to intend to go much beyond existing policies" given its focus on fossil fuels and large-scale hydro (MFPED, 2005: 66; Ondraczek, 2013: 412). The contribution of wind, geothermal, and biofuels—while mentioned—is left unspecified in the First FYDP (POPC, 2011: 141, 145). The Second FYDP only anticipates one 50 MW wind energy installation and a 200 MW geothermal plant (MPF, 2016: 207–209). Elite interviews reported by Dye (2021) indicate that decentralized renewables are perceived by the state as untested and expensive while also risking dependency on international actors.

While there has been a modicum of state development interest in wind and solar in Tanzania, there has been a near complete withdrawal of the central government from fuelwood and improved cookstove programmes. While village woodlot programs were pursued by the Nyerere regime after independence, improved cookstoves programs and other efforts to curb fuelwood demand were only initiated in the mid-1980s (O'Keefe et al., 1990; Otiti, 1992; Sawe, 2009). The effort was modest next to the vast scale of the problem. For example, the improved cookstove component of a major forest program disseminated only 10,500 stoves (World Bank, 1999: ii). Government interest in improved cookstoves lapsed into the 1990s. Indeed, Tanzania's planning documents have consistently suggested substituting fuelwood with coal (MPF, 2016: 152; VPO, 2005: annex, p. 17). More interest appears to be being accorded to modern biomass technologies. A domestic biogas program aims to establish 20,000 biogas plants by 2017, while two biomass cogeneration plants have been established, which supply 4.5 MW (IRENA, 2017: 22).

Much of the support for decentralized renewable energy has come from international donors. Solar and wind have been supported by the $14 million Scaling Up Renewable Energy Programme, an initiative of the Climate Investment Funds, and the more recent Sustainable Energy for All program since 2012 (Sawe, 2015). While beyond the scope of this book, it would quite interesting to see how effective these donor-financed climate finance projects are in light of the general low interest in renewables on the part of the Tanzania central government. Similarly, much of the recent support for improved cookstoves has come from international donors, development agencies, and NGOs. Indeed, one prominent donor-supported cookstove project justified its involvement in the sector by reference to the Tanzanian government's focus on rural electrification (ProBEC, 2010). However, many questions have been raised about the precarious nature of international support for cookstoves. A 2012 study would conclude that "funding [for improved cookstoves] is short-lived, sector activities are uncoordinated and there is a lack of focus on commercialization" (Clough, 2012: 29).

A more recent study referred to Tanzania's improved cookstove initiatives as "scattered" (IRENA, 2017: 21).

To summarize, the Tanzanian central government has largely been interested in augmenting modern energy supplies through the development of large-scale hydro and, increasingly, natural gas and coal. While such resource nationalism cannot easily be separated from ideas of modernization, Tanzania's focus on large-scale hydro and fossil fuels reflects the country's resource endowments that demonstrate how material factors contribute to the formation of state development interests. Such state development interests have frustrated state engagement with renewable energy opportunities made available through climate finance instruments.

Ugandan State Development Interests in the Energy Sector

With some of sub-Saharan Africa's largest hydroelectric potential, successive political regimes in Uganda have prioritized large-scale hydroelectric power generation projects. Indeed, Winston Churchill, who visited Uganda in 1907, envisioned the Nile gorge would "one day be crowded with factories and industries" (Churchill cited in MacLean et al., 2016: 113). Recent oil deposits have also attracted the growing interest of the central government, not only in terms of its export potential but also as a domestic source of energy. Decentralized renewables, though heavily supported by the international community, have struggled to attract the interests of state elites, though Uganda has shown more interest than neighboring Tanzania.

The British colonial regime began construction of the 150 MW Nalubaale dam, formerly known as the Owen Falls dam, in 1948 near the point where Lake Victoria spills into the White Nile. After independence, Obote tried unsuccessfully to develop at least two new large hydroelectric dams—what would realized only much later under Museveni as the Bujagali and Karuma dams. However, efforts to develop the power sector fell into disarray as Uganda descended into civil conflict. By the time the civil conflict was over in 1986, no new power capacity had been built since the original Nalubaale dam, which was by then operating at under half its initial capacity (Kapika and Eberhard, 2012: 90).

Upon coming to power in 1986, President Museveni would, like Obote, also come to focus on large-scale hydropower. Museveni's first major power generation project was initiated in 1991: the 200 MW extension to the Nalubaale dam, known as the Kiira Power Station (Gore, 2017: Loc 2831). Its construction under the Uganda Energy Board proved problematic, with its first turbines only becoming operational by 2000. As I discuss in the next chapter, as the Museveni regime embraced liberal economic reforms in the energy sector, attention would eventually turn to the 250 MW Bujagali dam, construction for which began in 2007. But Bujagali faced considerable delays and would come fully online only in 2012. Nonetheless, interest in large-scale hydro has persevered. Construction for the 600 MW Karuma dam began in 2013, and it is expected to be commissioned by 2022; the 180 MW Isimba dam was built over 2015–2019; while plans for the 840 MW Ayago hydropower project were formalized in 2020 (Businge, 2020; Monitor, 2019; Independent, 2020; UEGCL, 2018). Most recently, Uganda has explored the possibility of building a 360 MW dam at Uhuru Falls (Mwesigye and Redd, 2021).

The priority status accorded to large-scale hydroelectric projects has been clearly indicated in successive Ugandan national development plans. The 2005 PEAP clearly states: "The major expenditures in this sub sector are rural elec-trification and large power projects" (MFPED, 2005: 95). The 2010 National Development Plan called for an additional 3500 MW in power generation ca-pacity, with almost 66% from new large-scale hydroelectric stations—though a remaining 16% from renewables (NPA, 2010: 49). It also identified the estab-lishment of the Karuma, Isimba, and Ayago dams as "National Core Projects" that were to "take the first call of budget resources"; through this designation, the central government committed to establish public-private partnerships with it shouldering 70% of funding (NPA, 2010: 53–54). The 2015 National Development Plan continues to prioritize large-scale hydroelectricity, though it also mentions nuclear power in addition to a minor role for other renewables (NPA, 2015: 123, 137).

Oil production and refining has also received growing attention in Uganda. While oil was first discovered in 1938, it was not until 2006 that the govern-ment would confirm the discovery of large-scale deposits of 6.5 billion barrels (Hickey and Izama, 2016). It is anticipated that once operational, the Uganda central government will be capable of generating $2 billion in annual revenue (Khan, 2015). While much of the oil is destined for the export market, the 2010 National Development Plan highlighted a 700 MW thermal power plant as one of its primary development objectives in order to generate 20% of the targeted 3500 MW in power generation capacity (NPA, 2010: 49, 153). The use of oil for power generation is also mentioned in the 2015 National Development Plan (NPA, 2015: 57, 123).

In contrast to the Uganda central government's interest in large-scale hydroe-lectricity and developing its oil sector, renewables have consistently received less attention in national development plans, though interest appears to slowly be growing. Interviews undertaken by Gore (2017) in 2002 reflect the general dis-interest in renewables by the central government. An exasperated leader of an environmental NGO exclaimed in 2002 that "politicians didn't see the role of bio-mass . . . it just wasn't a priority!" (Gore, 2017: loc. 2539). Similarly, a government official explained, "It is still an uphill battle to get government to focus on [bi-omass] . . . there is a lot of bias into hydro" (Gore, 2017: loc. 2567). However, solar, small-scale hydro, and improved cookstoves are mentioned briefly as part of Uganda's efforts to promote rural electrification in the 2005 PEAP (MFPED, 2005: 66, 95–96).

Nonetheless, in 2007, the Ministry of Energy and Mineral Development published its Renewable Energy Policy (MEMD, 2007). Its vision is to make modern renewable energy a substantial part of the national energy consumption and specifically set a goal for increasing the share of renewables, including large hydropower, to 61% of national energy consumption by 2017, a target of ap-proximately of 1420 MW. The Renewable Energy Policy was also noteworthy for having introduced the first of a series of renewable feed-in tariffs by the Uganda central government. However, most accounts of these renewable feed-in tariffs (REFITs) have found that tariffs have not been sufficiently high to incentivize new or existing firms to increase renewable energy production (Meyer et al., 2018; Probst et al., 2021). To address this challenge, in 2013, a donor-backed REFIT was promoted under the Global Energy Transfer Feed-in Tariff (GET FiT) program, which I return to below.

The 2010 National Development Plan also called for the construction of 200 MW of solar, 100 MW of geothermal, and 150 MW of biomass cogeneration (NPA, 2010: 152). It also identified improved cookstoves as a strategy for re-ducing pressure on forests, but only after efforts to speed up rural electrification and increase subsidies for fossil fuels (NPA, 2010: 97). Indeed, it suggested that a reliance on fuelwood was linked to a lack of access to grid-connected electricity. A similar emphasis on large-scale hydroelectricity over decentralized renewables is also found in the 2015 National Development Plan (NPA, 2015: 182–183).

As in Tanzania, support for renewables has largely been promoted by donors. Most notable has been GET FiT Uganda mentioned above. Introduced in 2013, it is a $130 million donor-backed REFIT program to attract renewable energy (GET FiT Uganda, 2014: 3, 32–33). Relative to Uganda's previous REFIT efforts, the GET FiT tariffs have been more effective. As of 2018, it incentived 15 in-dependent power producers with capacity for producing 50 MW of renewable power (Meyer et al., 2018: 79). However, the incentives for renewable energy need to be considered compared to the government's pursuit of large-scale hy-droelectric power and oil sector projects. For example, the GET FiT program has been estimated to have leveraged $400 million in private sector financing, while the total Bujagali dam alone cost $900 million (Gore, 2017: loc. 3282, 3451). As in Tanzania, it would be insightful to investigate the effectiveness of the GET Fit program, through this is beyond the scope of the current book.

Finally, I would note the emphasis on improved cookstoves in Uganda's Green Growth Development Strategy (2017/18–2030/31), which was produced with support from the UNDP's Low Emissions Capacity Building Programme (NPA, 2017: 20–23). Like the 2015 National Development Plan, it was also produced by the NPA. This perhaps signals a turn toward greater acceptance of cookstove technology, though it appears to be the first time it has been accorded such priority status. It remains to be seen whether cookstoves will be integrated into the next National Development Plan or if, instead, other modern and renewable energies for cooking are identified.

Overall, Uganda has largely prioritized the development of its large hydroelectric capacity and more recently oil reserves. While the Uganda central government has been more open to decentralized renewables than Tanzania, including perhaps recent openness to improved cookstoves, it has not independently been willing to finance them to be effective and has largely depended on the international community to do so.

Moldovan State Development Interests in the Energy Sector

State development interests in Uganda and Tanzania, with their gravitation toward exploiting domestic energy resources, contrasts with the situation in Moldova where successive central governments—including governments formed by the Party of Communists and various pro-EU coalitions—have been seeking to reduce the country's dependency on external sources of energy, particularly from Russia. This includes reducing dependency not only on Russian natural gas but also on the energy assets in Transnistria, the semi-autonomous region of the country where Russia maintains considerable influence. Incentives to reduce dependency on Russia have surely increased since the 2022 invasion of Ukraine.

Two strategies have been developed by successive Moldovan governments to address the country's dependency on external energy resources: diversify by increasing natural gas supplies and the deployment of renewable energy, particularly biomass energy where Moldova has a comparative advantage. Importantly, such interests preceded EU integration. While there has been a surge in donor finance from the EU since 2010, EU support for renewables has been pushing on an open door as the Moldova central government has consistently demonstrated an interest in them.

Since I first visited Moldova in 2009, natural gas imported from Russia via Ukraine has dominated Moldova's energy supply, constituting 97% of its energy supply at the time (Government of Moldova, 2007: 8). Furthermore, Russia's Gazprom has been a majority shareholder of Moldovagaz, the only distributor of natural gas in the country (Woehrel, 2009). Moldova has also relied on a massive 2520 MW natural gas–powered power plant in Transnistria, which amounted to 50–70% of the country's total power generation in the mid-2000s (enerCEE, 2011; Government of Moldova, 2007: 11). Also significant, a Russian firm gained ownership of the natural gas power plant in Transnistria in 2004 (Jirušek and Kuchyňková, 2018; Popovici, 2007).

Moldova's dependency on Gazprom has given Russia considerable political leverage. A first strategy deployed by Russia was to subsidize natural gas to Moldova to stifle competition (Nuțu and Cenușă, 2016). For example, in late 2005, prices paid for natural gas in many former Soviet Republics stood at $50–80 per thousand of cubic meters (MCM), considerably below prices in the EU (Stern, 2006). But since the Moldovan Party of Communists turned away from Russia in early 2005, Russia insisted that all former Soviet republics should pay EU prices—nearly triple the previous rate at about $160–230 mcm (Jirušek and Kuchyňková, 2018: 829). This led to a situation in January 2006 where Gazprom briefly cut off natural gas supply to Ukraine and Moldova (Stern, 2006).

In 2011, the long-term gas supply contract with Gazprom expired, which Russia has since been refusing to sign (Całus et al., 2018: 22). Though a number of short-term natural gas agreements have kept natural gas flowing, Russia has conditioned renewal of a long-term contract on Moldova's suspension of energy sector reforms required for EU integration. In particular, Russia objects to competitiveness provisions that would require Moldovagaz be split into two companies and the establishment of an independent gas transmission operator. I discuss these reforms in more detail in the next chapter.

Natural gas supply in Moldova is further complicated by the fact that the main Russian pipeline passes through Transnistria. Altogether, Moldova consumes about 3.5 billion cubic meters of gas per year, but only around one-third is used in the Chisinau-controlled portion of the country (Jirušek and Kuchyňková, 2018). The bulk of Moldovan natural gas is consumed by the power plant in Transnistria. Furthermore, due to a contractual agreement preceding the 1992 Transnistria conflict, Gazprom recognizes Moldovagaz as the client for natural gas consumed in Transnistria and not the Transnistrian government. The debt to Gazprom for consumption in Transnistria is estimated at $6 billion (Całus et al., 2018: 22).

A first strategy to address reliance on Russian natural gas has been to diversify natural gas supply. Even the 2001 Economic Revival Program, published by the Party of Communists before their break with Russia, prioritized the "consistent implementation of measures to secure the country with energy" (GoRM, 2001: 11–12). The National Development Strategy for 2008–2011 announced that "the diversification of gas and electric energy suppliers as a measure of ensuring energy security" was a major task of the nominally communist government (GoRM, 2007: 65). With the election of a pro-EU government in 2009, opportunities for diversifying supply have increased. Examples include the construction of an interconnector gas pipeline in 2014 to tap recent Romanian natural gas discoveries (Mihalache, 2014; Nuțu and Cenușă, 2016) and an effort to connect with a major pipeline transporting natural gas from Azerbaijan (Molnar, 2012; Urse, 2009). Overall, there have been a number of efforts to import natural gas from other partners to reduce reliance on Russia.

A second strategy to address Moldova's dependency on external energy resources has been increasing the deployment of renewable energy, particularly bioenergy resources. In 2005, renewable energy represented just 0.8 MTOE or 3.6% of Moldova's primary energy supply (Government of Moldova, 2007: 15). However, already at this time, it was estimated that there was potential to generate 2.7 MTOE in modern renewable energy (Government of Moldova, 2007: 15). Interestingly, of the different types of renewables, solar was identified in this 2007 report as having the most potential with wind and biomass energy next. However, among the various renewables, Moldova has seen significant increases in biomass energy production since 2009, which has reached approximately 20% by 2010 and 25% by 2016 of total energy supply (Tirsu and Uzun, 2018: 28).

Successive central governments in Moldova have supported greater use of renewable energy as part of an interest in energy security over the past 20 years. This is important for our argument because it demonstrates that the state's interest in renewables existed prior to the EU's accelerated support since the 2009 elections. While there was no mention of biomass or alternative forms of energy in the 2001 Economic Revival Program produced by the Party of Communists, it encouraged "the introduction of resources, energy-saving technologies, and the use of advanced materials" (GoRM, 2001: 11–12). The 2004 Economic Growth and Poverty Reduction Strategy Paper was the first national development plan to make official mention of the role that "non-traditional sources of energy (such as solar, wind, biogas)" might play in this transition (GoRM, 2004: 78, 161). Interest in renewable energy would continue to grow under the Party of Communists. This is reflected in a new development plan, Energy Strategy and Law on Renewables, being announced in 2007. For example, the Energy Strategy would commit Moldova to drawing 6% of its energy from renewable sources by 2010 and 20% by 2020 (: 43). The subsequent Law on Renewable Energy sought to create an appropriate legal framework to incentivize rural energy.

State interest in renewable energy continued under the pro-EU governing coalition that came into power in 2009. The 2012 National Development Plan committed the country to deriving 20% of its final energy consumption from renewable energy and 10% biofuel utilization (GoRM, 2012: 45). That same year, the Moldovan central government established the National Renewable Energy Action Plan 2013–2020 as well as National Energy Efficiency Program 2011–2020 (NEEP 2011–2020). The objectives of the latter have been to reduce primary energy consumption by 20%, increase the share of renewable energy sources in the overall energy balance from 6% in 2010 up to 20%, and increase the share of biofuels to at least 10% of all fuels used (Stratan, 2012). A revised version of the Law on Renewable Energy was adopted in 2016, still under a pro-EU government, including the clear establishment of mandatory national targets for renewable energy consumption (Tirsu and Uzun, 2018).

Some of the biggest changes in Moldova's energy sector since my first 2009 visit there have been in terms of EU support for large-scale bioenergy initiatives. This has been reflected in the sharp increase in EU funding to Moldova since 2010: despite the financial crisis, official development assistance contributions per capita nearly doubled between 2009 and 2010 (see Annex to the introductory chapter). Much of this financial support has been directed toward the development of bioenergy, including a €23 million Energy and Biomass Project (2011–2017), the €42 million Moldovan Sustainable Energy Efficiency Financing Facility (2012–2017), €35 million Moldova Residential Energy Efficiency Finance Facility, and Moldova's participation in the €120 million Eastern Europe Partnership for Energy Efficiency and Environment (IRENA, 2019: 28; Tirsu and Uzun, 2018: 28–29). Finally, in one of the few initiatives related to climate finance, the Moldovan government is party to the EBRD Sustainable Energy Financing Facilities—a Green Climate Fund project with $1.4 million in financing for 10 developing countries (IRENA, 2019: 28). But curiously, EU funding for renewables has otherwise side-stepped the climate change regime, including NAMAs.

To summarize, Moldova has consistently and clearly pursued renewable energy. This is, in part, related to its dependency on Russian natural gas and a resulting state development interest in energy security. Despite this clear state development interest, its pursuit of the CDM in the energy sector would be hampered, while NAMAs it has proposed in the energy sector have failed to attract international financial support.

6.5. Conclusion

Looking back on my review of state development interests in the forest sectors of Tanzania, Uganda, and Moldova, variation can be observed that is helpful in explaining the effectiveness of climate finance instruments in later chapters. In Tanzania, the central government did not itself show significant interest in expanding timber plantations during the mid-2000s. This might be explained by the fact that the supply of industrial forest plantations under the FBD outstripped available timber-processing capacity until the reopening of major timber-processing facilities around 2005. However, we have also seen that since at least 2016, there has been renewed attention accorded to the forest sector. At first glance this might be attributed to improved understanding of the extent of forest resources scarcity, a more likely explanation is that with timber-processing facilities again viable, a business rationale now exists to expand Tanzania's industrial timber plantations. As for Tanzania's energy sector, the Tanzanian central government has largely pursued large-scale hydroelectric and fossil fuel power generation that draw on its domestic resources endowments, though with some limited interest in large-scale wind and solar. Decentralized renewable energy projects have largely been a focus of development agencies and international NGOs.

Forest resources in Uganda, particularly timber to support a domestic forest industry, have been scarce since Museveni first came to power in 1986 and have attracted considerable government attention since. Efforts to improve fuelwood supply and demand at the local level have been more limited, however. Instead, the Ugandan government has prioritized large-scale hydroelectric power and is looking to tap recent oil discoveries for domestic power generation. While there has been some interest in decentralized renewables, most notably through a series of REFITs, state resources available for them have been limited. With abundant natural resources for centralized, large-scale power generation facilities, the central government has not been significantly interested in pursuing alternatives, though it has proven open to working with the donor community on renewables if funding is made available.

The forest sector in Moldova has been consistently accorded priority development status by successive communist and pro-EU governments, albeit as an effort to tackle land degradation. While the country has been making progress with a number of afforestation projects, it is still nearly 800 km2 below its 2020 forest-cover target of 15% of the national territory. In the energy sector, successive central governments have identified national energy security as a priority issue over the past 20 years. Even the Party of Communists broke with Russia and embraced the need for diversifying Moldova's supply of natural gas while also pursuing renewables, particularly biomass, as an integral part of this strategy. While recent EU support for renewables has galvanized such interests, including in June 2022 when the EU officially confirmed Moldova's EU candidate status, such interests can be traced back to Moldova's strategic interest in energy security—something that transcends its fragmented political settlement.

7

Development Policy Paradigms in Tanzania, Uganda, and Moldova

7.1. Introduction

In Chapter 4, I mapped the evolution of development policy paradigms as they emerged in the developing world since World War II. In this chapter I focus on their evolution in my three case-study countries in order to chart divergences between countries in terms of ideas about the process of economic development. I pay particular attention to state responses to liberal economic reforms during the neoliberal period, given that it has been promoted by the international community relatively consistently until at least the 2008 global financial crisis. However, due to the more stable political situation in Tanzania, my analysis extends back to the policies of the first president after independence, Julius Nyerere. In Uganda, my analysis focuses largely on the period since Yoweri Museveni came to power, while in Moldova I focus on policy since its independence from the Soviet Union in 1991. The available evidence suggests a hybrid paradigm combining elements of classic developmentalism and neodevelopmentalism have emerged in Tanzania, while liberal neodevelopmentalism best characterizes the prevailing development policy paradigm in Uganda and Moldova. This divergence helps explain, in conjunction with state development interests discussed in Chapter 6, climate finance effectiveness in later chapters.

Of importance for my argument about liberal neodevelopmentalism are differences in economic reforms in the forest and energy sectors of Uganda and Moldova. As we shall see, in both countries the state has retained a role for itself in the forest sector, largely in the form of state agencies, while embarking on extensive privatization of the energy sector. The divergence in state intervention in these two sectors suggests that the central governments determined that the state could be an effective economic actor in the forest sector but not the energy sector. Liberal neodevelopmentalism in the energy sector is indistinguishable from neoliberalism; it is only when comparing the reforms in the forest and energy sectors that liberal neodevelopmentalism becomes apparent.

As ideas, development policy paradigms are difficult to observe directly. I inferred them from analysis of policies, institutions, and organizations established in the forest and energy sectors as well as over 60 elite interviews in

The Political Economy of Climate Finance Effectiveness in Developing Countries. Mark Purdon, Oxford University Press. © Oxford University Press 2024. DOI: 10.1093/oso/9780197756836.003.0007

Tanzania, Uganda, and Moldova from 2008 to 2018. I argue that development policy paradigms are reflected by different rates of liberal economic reform, the degree to which liberal economic policies and institutions have been adopted in various sectors (forest and energy), and the establishment of different types of domestic organizations as a result of these reforms. As Karl Polanyi famously asserted: "The rate of change is often of no less importance than the direction of the change itself" (Polanyi, 2001 [1944]: 39). My analysis is organized around the four key strategic economic development policies from Chapter 4: national assets management (nationalization/privatization), agricultural price controls, state coordination, and international trade. While my approach is vulnerable to Daigneault's (2014) "revealed ideas" critique of much research into policy paradigms, my analysis of each country's development policy paradigm starts by charting the history of economic ideas, generally from the time of their independence (Mahoney and Rueschemeyer, 2003), and then focuses on institutions of the forest and energy sectors since the neoliberal period.

7.2. Tanzania

Evolution of Tanzania's Development Policy Paradigm

Among the three case-study countries, Tanzania has proven most resistant to neoliberal economic ideas. The development policy paradigm that currently pervades Tanzania can be best described as a hybrid of aspiring neodevelopmentalism and classic developmentalism. This can be attributed to the influence of Julius Nyerere, Tanzania's first president, whose legacy is an enduring affinity for classic developmental thinking across the state apparatus. However, Nyerere's version of classic developmentalism, *ujamaa*, was rather unorthodox given his (at least) initial preference for agricultural over industrial modernization.

The concept of *ujamaa* is often translated as "familyhood" or explicitly as "African socialism" (Hunter, 2015). It would form the basis of the 1967 Arusha Declaration, which announced the direction that Nyerere's political party and government would pursue throughout his tenure. While the Marxist influences are obvious, *ujamaa* also incorporated strands of classical liberalism and Fabianism along with an emphasis on pre-colonial African communalism: "Ujamaa in contrast to [capitalism and doctrinaire socialism] was to represent a third way—a synthesis of what is best in traditional African peasant society and the best the country had acquired from its colonial experience" (Nyerere cited in Ibhawoh and Dibua, 2003: 63). In pointed contrast to Marxist materialism, Nyerere would also argue in a 1962 speech that "socialism—like democracy—is essentially an attitude of mind" (Metz, 1982: 388). Donors were highly supportive of Nyerere's efforts, especially those from Scandinavian countries, given the apparent affinities between his African socialism and Scandinavian social democracy. Partially as a result, donor contributions rose to among the highest in sub-Saharan Africa from the 1960s through 1970s (Edwards, 2014).

One important feature of *ujamaa* was its emphasis on modernization of the peasant agricultural sector rather than (urban) industrialization (Metz, 1982: 390). This tended to distinguish *ujamaa* from classic developmentalism and orthodox Marxism, as both underscored industrialization as the preeminent economic development goal. A preference for agriculture characterized at least the first decade of the Nyerere administration. For example, one section of the 1967 the Arusha Declaration reads, "The mistake we are making is to think that development begins with industries" (TANU, 1967: 11). Rather, "the only road through which [Tanzanians] can develop their country is by increasing agricultural production" (p. 14). This emphasis on agriculture would have important implications for Tanzania's forest policy, which I discuss in a separate section below.

Despite this distinction, the four main policy strategies I associate with classic developmentalism are readily observable among policies introduced by Nyerere. The first was nationalization and collectivization of the means of production. While nationalization was not immediately launched upon Tanganyika's independence in 1961, it would become the keystone of *ujamaa*. As stated in the 1967 Arusha Declaration: "The way to build and maintain socialism is to ensure that the major means of production are under the control and ownership of the Peasants and the Workers themselves through their Government and their Co-operatives" (TANU, 1967: 3). Important for the argument of this book, the Arusha Declaration reaffirmed state ownership of land, forests, mineral resources, and electricity—among others—as "major means of production" (p. 3). It should also be noted that just prior to the Arusha Declaration, in 1965, the Tanzanian central government established the National Development Corporation as a parastatal investment organization (Mramba and Mwansasu, 1972). After the Declaration, the National Development Corporation acquired majority shares of various domestic and foreign firms operating in Tanzania.

State ownership of land would allow Nyerere to undertake his Villagization Policy, a form of collectivization implemented from 1968 to 1975. With its aim of modernizing peasant society by grouping often geographically dispersed peasants into organized villages, villagization was a signature policy of Nyerere's *ujamaa* vision (Hydén, 1980; McHenry, 1979). Villagization sought to collectivize agricultural production and concentrate rural populations for service delivery. However, when voluntary approaches failed to motivate peasants to relocate (only 15% of the rural population had been resettled as of 1973), more coercive tactics were used. While Schneider (2007a) convincingly argues that Nyerere's *ujamaa* was not guilty of high modernist hubris, villagization is generally now seen as a heavy-handed attempt by the Nyerere administration to reorganize peasant society.

Second, to control agricultural commodity prices, the Tanzanian central government initially introduced a system of cooperative and marketing boards (Ellis, 1982). These, however, became caught up in the villagization effort. In 1973, they were reorganized as more powerful and centralized parastatal crop authorities. It is not clear how effective these institutions were. In one analysis, prices that smallholders received for their crops were "low and arbitrary" (Nindi, 1989: 98). While into the 1990s, such agricultural controls were unwound as part of broader structural adjustment policies, efforts to liberalize export crop markets were significantly hindered by the state administration (Cooksey, 2011).

Third was Nyerere's affinity for central planning. Nyerere unveiled a first Five-Year Plan for Economic and Social Development for 1964–1968 that was still largely private-sector driven (Edwards, 2014: 67). However, in the second Five-Year Plan for Economic and Social Development (1969–74), the Tanzanian government focused on developing a long-term industrial policy as the initial focus on agriculture modernization gave way. This culminated in the 1975 Basic Industry Strategy (Whitfield et al., 2015). By the early 1980s, Tanzania had the second-highest number of state-owned enterprises in Africa.

Finally, integral to Nyerere's concept of *ujamaa* was self-reliance, which lent itself to protectionist measures such as import substitution industrialization (ISI). This did not happen immediately. From independence through 1967, the industrial strategy of Tanzania continued to rely on foreign capital flows (Skarstein and Wangwe, 1986). However, the Arusha Declaration deemed foreign capital "inconsistent with the principles of socialism and self-reliance" (pp. 6–7). Nyerere also famously ejected an IMF mission in 1979, after the organization made the devaluation of the Tanzanian schilling a condition for lending (Edwards, 2014: 63–64).

However, by the early 1980s, Tanzania's economy was struggling, while relations with donors were strained given Nyerere's standoff with the IMF and exposure of the harshness of Tanzania's villagization policy. Donor funding fell considerably, and pressure to adopt neoliberal structural reform policies mounted. Key policies of classic developmentalism were unwound, including Tanzania's experiment with villagization as well as ISI. Indeed, the World Bank would attribute much of Tanzania's economic difficulty to its industrial policy (Gray, 2013). Soviet-style five-year plans were replaced by a number of modest economic reform programs drawn up by the Tanzanian government in an attempt at economic revival (Wuyts and Kilama, 2016: 320).

Liberal economic reform was not really initiated until Nyerere stepped down from power in 1985 (Amani et al., 2007: 211). Yet donors perceived his successor, President Mwinyi, to be implementing structural adjustment policies grudgingly. Strained relations between the Tanzanian central government and donors reached crisis levels during a major tax scandal in 1994; the fallout of which saw donor levels sink to their lowest levels (Edwards, 2014: 174). In response, the donor community and Tanzania government agreed to convene a special commission that ultimately saw the Tanzanian government embrace neoliberal structural adjustment policy. The first Poverty Reduction Strategy Paper for the World Bank was launched in 2000 while the second was launched in 2005, known through its Kiswahili acronym of MKUKUTA, while MKUKUTA 2 was adopted in 2010.

Despite such institutional reforms, skepticism about globalization and neoliberalism endures. In a 2012 assessment, observers concluded that a sentiment of "economic nationalism" permeates Tanzania's political culture:

> Despite an official government commitment to liberal market policies and foreign investment, within the state administration and the ruling party on different levels, as well as in wide sections of the society, there is obviously a growing hostility toward foreign business due to the perceived "sellout" of Tanzanian enterprises, in the form of privatization and foreign investment. (BTI, 2012: 14)

It is fair to say that neoliberalism never prevailed as a development policy paradigm in Tanzania.

The shift toward a hybrid classic developmental/neodevelopmental policy paradigm was first most clearly on display when, in 2011, the central government published its first Five-Year Development Plan since the Nyerere era. Significantly, it was developed independent of donors, in contrast to the MKUKUTA process (Furukawa, 2018). In the Introduction to the first Five-Year Development Plan, President Kikwete declared that "Tanzania is reverting back to the practice of defining a roadmap towards its development aspirations" and that the Plan "implies transiting from a needs-based planning framework to opportunity-based planning. In the former, the nation's ambition to develop is solely limited to available resources, while in the case of the latter, resources are merely a means to realize the country's aspiration" (POPC, 2011: i). The second Five-Year Development Plan was released under President Magufuli in 2016, which is distinguished by even more explicit commitments to industrial transformation, the "developmental state" model, and a pivot toward Asian economic integration (MPF, 2016: 26). The recently deceased President Magufuli was much more assertive about the economic management of Tanzania. For example, new mining laws adopted in 2017 raised mining royalties, gave the government the right to renegotiate mining contracts, and required that they undertake greater mineral processing in Tanzania (Economist, 2017).

Overall, it is difficult to accept that Tanzania ever really embraced neoliberalism, and we now see some of the ideas associated with classic developmentalism re-emerge, including a revival of central planning and a more assertive role for the state in the economy. But there are also important distinctions from the Nyerere era. The most important being the near absence of ISI, and, rather, a reorientation toward an export economy targeting growing Asian markets. The Magufuli administration has even gone so far to invoke the developmental state model. In this sense, I argue it is best to describe Tanzania's development policy paradigm as one aspiring toward neodevelopmentalism, though the tense relationship between the state and private sector under Magufuli is also suggestive of classic developmentalism. Given this ambiguity, I refer to Tanzania's development policy paradigm as a hybrid of classic developmentalism and neodevelopmentalism.

Tanzania Forest Sector Policy

The evolution of forest policy, institutions, and organizations in Tanzania has been different than that in Uganda and Moldova. Under the classic developmentalism of the Nyerere regime, the forest sector would only be embraced reluctantly given Nyerere's initial unorthodox focus on agricultural modernization. It was only by the 1970s that the central government would organize in support of the forest sector via the establishment of the Forest and Beekeeping Division (FBD) at the Ministry of Natural Resources and Tourism (MNRT), as well as take up active efforts to cultivate a forest industry. Until quite recently, FBD has been the custodian of the government's forest reserves and industrial forest plantations (Kangalawe, 2018; Purdon et al., 2014: 95; World Bank, 2003: 73). While the operationalization in 2014 of the Tanzanian Forest Service (TFS), a state forest agency, would suggest that the central government sought a new role in the forest sector, the available evidence suggests that the TFS has not performed differently from FBD. Despite neoliberal economic reforms of the sector, the Tanzanian central government has been reluctant to view the forest sector as a significant business opportunity.

Tanzania's forest industry can trace its origins to the colonial regime. In 1953, the British introduced the National Forest Policy and in 1957 the first Forest Ordinance, which were responsible for expanding forest reserves, as mentioned in Chapter 6 (Hurst, 2003: 361; Kangalawe, 2018). The newly independent Tanganyika government under Nyerere initially retained most of the colonial era National Forest Policy. However, there were important departures from it that can be grasped via the classic developmentalism of Nyerere's *ujamaa* philosophy.

First, given Nyerere's preference for agricultural over industrial modernization during the country's first decade of independence (1961–1971), the forest sector tended to be marginalized in economic policy discussions (Hurst, 2003). It was difficult for foresters to position themselves within the *ujamaa* discourse. For example, the Nyerere regime opened up forest reserves established during the colonial period for agricultural development. Relatedly, the central government also nationalized all colonial era forest plantations after the 1967 Arusha Declaration, including the 6,700 ha Sao Hill timber plantations. Similarly, government foresters drew up a Forestry Development Plan 1964–1969 that identified strategies for establishing a pulp and paper industry; however, Tanzania's first Five-Year National Plan only committed to taking "exploratory steps" to establish it. Finally, forestry was also marginalized within the bureaucracy as the Forest Division was under the ministry responsible for agriculture.

However, by the early 1970s, industrial forestry in Tanzania began to attract the attention of the central government, which increasingly recognized it as an export crop capable of generating foreign exchange (Kashwan, 2017: 71; Pedersen, 2017). In 1971, the Forestry Division was established at the new MNRT and combined with the Beekeeping Department in 1985 to establish the Forestry and Beekeeping Division (FBD). That same year, the Nyerere government established the Tanzania Wood Industry Corporation (TWICO). TWICO became the main parastatal in the forest sector, coming to own a number of sawmills. In the mid-1970s, the National Development Corporation embarked on the development of a major paper-mill adjacent to Sao Hill plantations in the Mufindi district, initially known as Souther Paper Mills. First operational by 1985, what would later be known as Mufindi Paper Mill was connected via the Tanzania-Zambia Railway (itself completed only in 1975) to the port of Dar es Salaam and, from there, reach markets in Asia (Christiansson and Åshuvud, 1985: 123; Håkanson, 1982: 109; Kangalawe, 2018). The hybridity of Tanzania's development policy paradigm was evident here, with the export orientation of the forest industry aligning more with neodevelopmentalism than classic developmentalism.

Tanzanian forest policy during the neoliberal period of the late 1980s and 1990s is noteworthy for undertaking limited economic reforms and a pivot toward participatory forest management. Reforms, however, were not motivated by a strong interest of the central government in the forest industry, which, as we saw in the previous chapter, declined into the 1980s. In an insightful investigation of the political economy of Tanzania's private forest sector, Pedersen concluded: "The programs that have indeed targeted the [private forest] sector over the last few years seem to be driven more by donors than by the government" (Pedersen, 2017: 3). Indeed, the Tanzanian central government would continue to manage sizeable state-owned forest plantations through FBD. But plantation management deteriorated. For example, the World Bank concluded: "Plantation projects are under-funded and cannot fully take care of their management responsibilities" (Pedersen, 2017: 73). Similarly, the state-run Mufindi Paper Mill would close its doors in 1997 and subsequently be privatized.

Participatory forest management would also rise to prominence during the 1990s, while state-supported tree-planting initiatives at the village level were de-emphasized. Participatory forest management has also been heavily promoted by the conservation and development community as a means of promoting sustainable use and conserving forest resources (Blomley and Iddi, 2009; Ponte et al., 2020). It was one of the key institutional innovations introduced through the 1998 National Forest Policy and 2002 National Forest Act. Participatory forest management was also facilitated by the establishment of the Village Land category under the Land Act and Village Land Act (Purdon, 2013). Strikingly, perhaps because of their focus on managing standing forests, no organizations undertaking participatory forest management in Tanzania have been involved with the CDM, though a few were involved with piloting REDD+ in Tanzania in the 2010s, as discussed in Chapter 9.

An organization worth mentioning in discussion of participatory forest management is the Ministry of Regional Administration and Local Government, currently housed with the President's Office and referred to as PO-RALG (Participedia, No Date). Formerly within the Prime Minister's Office, PO-RALG is responsible for coordinating regional and district policy—including forest policy (PMO-RALG, 2008). It is does so through a regional planning and budgeting process, representing an important conduit for local governments, including village councils in rural areas, to receive conditional transfers from the national government (Lifuliro et al., 2018). In many ways, PO-RALG is a more important central government partner at the local level for participatory forest management than either FBD or TFS.

In 2010, the central government established the TFS as a semi-autonomous forest agency under MNRT according to Tanzania's Executive Agencies Act (MNRT, 2010: 3; TFCMP, 2005: 2). Operational since 2014, TFS has divested FBD of its mandate for the management of forest reserves and government-owned plantations, while FBD is to retain a role in policy, legislative development, and monitoring (TFS, 2015a). While ostensibly similar to state forest agencies in Uganda and Moldova, discussed later, I note that TFS was established about the same time that the central government unveiled, in 2011, its first Five-Year Development Plan (FYDP) and began to overtly pivot away from neoliberalism.

There continues to be questions about the business acumen of TFS. One recent study found that "TFS officials' understanding of market demands and market standards is still limited" (Pedersen, 2017: 21). Notably TFS would identify nearly 22,000 ha of new plantation areas in its 2014–2019 Strategic Plan, but it provided few details about how they will be planted and few references to climate finance (TFS, 2014). This suggests that the TFS is not significantly different from FBD, and that its establishment has been less about a commitment to liberal economic reforms by the Tanzanian central government than pleasing donors. Thus, while I view state agencies in Uganda and Moldova as indicative of liberal neodevelopmentalism, the establishment of TFS does not warrant the same interpretation.

Reflecting renewed interest in the Tanzania forest sector since 2016, forest policy in Tanzania is currently under review. In 2018, MNRT produced a new draft National Forest Policy, National Forest Policy Implementation Strategy, 2018–2028 and, in 2020, a new draft National Forest Management Act for government consideration (FAO, 2021; MNRT, 2018a,b). To the best of my knowledge, these policy documents are, however, still being reviewed by the central government and not yet finalized (see FAO, 2021). Tellingly, however, the government anticipates playing a leading role in the policy's current form. For example, half of the new industrial forest plantations are to be planted by government and the remainder by the private sector (MNRT, 2018b: 23). Furthermore, these draft policy documents continue to demonstrate limited engagement with climate finance instruments. For example, the draft National Forest Policy only refers to REDD+ briefly under a section entitled "Ecosystem Conservation and Service" (MNRT, 2018a: 14), while the section "Forest Investment and Financing" refers to payment for ecosystem services but omits reference to REDD+ and other climate finance instruments (p. 16).

Overall, since independence, Tanzanian policy in the forest sector has reflected a hybrid development policy paradigm that includes elements of classic developmentalism and neodevelopmentalism. A distinguishing feature of this hybrid paradigm has been the priority status it accorded agricultural modernization over forestry, at least in the first decade after independence. While there was a pivot toward liberal economic reform from the 1980s to 2000s, including establishment of a state forest agency in 2010, in practice skepticism of neoliberalism remained strong. While since about 2016 there has been renewed interest in the forest sector, the central government also appears inclined to play a leading role in plantation establishment. Important for our argument about development policy paradigms, neither recent forest strategy documents nor the TFS have clearly pursued climate finance instruments including neither the CDM nor REDD+.

Tanzania Energy Sector Policy

Turning to Tanzania' energy sector, the central government would also resist institutional reforms that would undercut its capacity to intervene, in a manner similar to what has been observed in the forest sector. This contrasts with the situation in Uganda and Moldova, where, as we shall see, the governments extensively liberalized their energy sectors. The legacy of classic developmentalism and recent efforts to pivot toward neodevelopmentalism also intermingle with strong state development interests in exploiting recent fossil fuel deposits—what Pedersen et al. (2020) have referred to as "resource nationalism." Such a confluence of state ideas and interests help explain Tanzania's retention of significant state organizational capacity in the sector, despite tremendous pressure from Western development partners to liberalize it.

Classic Developmental Energy Policy in Tanzania

Conforming with classic developmentalism, after independence, the two power companies established during the colonial period (TANESCO and DARESCO) were nationalized in 1964 and merged in 1968 as TANESCO (Gore et al., 2018; Mwandosya and Luhanga, 1993: 445). As discussed earlier, the Arusha Declaration had listed the power sector for state ownership as a "major means of production" justifying nationalization. As I discuss later in this section, TANESCO remains a state-owned enterprise. The most significant achievement in the energy sector during the period of classic developmentalism, however, was the 200 MW Great Ruaha Power project commissioned in the 1970s. Indicative of *ujamaa*'s unorthodox version of classic developmentalism, Nyerere also committed TANESCO to subsidize access to electricity—a practice that continues: Tanzania's consumer tariffs are considerably lower than Uganda's (TANESCO, 2013; Twesigye, 2022). However, into the 1980s, the challenges facing the Tanzania economy limited the development of significant new power-generating capacity.

Neoliberal Energy Policy in Tanzania

As has already been suggested, Tanzania reluctantly embarked on neoliberal economic reforms in the 1990s. In 1992, the central government published a new National Energy Policy that contained many provisions associated with the World Bank's standard model of power sector reform. This included a commitment to allowing independent power producers to enter the market and the unbundling of TANESCO (Gore et al., 2018). In 1994, two private firms were invited to build fossil fuel power plants, though, as discussed earlier, both were delayed considerably and only commenced operations in 2002 and 2004, respectively (Gratwick et al., 2006). Such delays would contribute to sapping enthusiasm for neoliberalism.

Also discouraging, TANESCO's operations "barely improved" over the 10-year period from 1990 to 2000: the parastatal was barely profitable, and national access to electricity had risen to only 10% while access in rural areas remained below 3% (Gore et al. 2018: 8; also see Marandu and Luteganya, 2004: 143). Under pressure from donors, President Mkapa began the process of privatizing TANESCO in 1999, resulting in its management being transferred to Eskom, a South African firm in 2002 (Johnson, 2010; Kapika and Eberhard, 2012: 56–57).

Reassertion of Classic Developmental Energy Policy in Tanzania

In a startling reassertion of classic developmentalism in Tanzania, efforts to privatize TANESCO were reversed. One of President Kikwete's first acts upon entering office in 2005 was to remove TANESCO from the list of companies to be privatized. In 2006 the Tanzanian government argued it would not renew Eskom's contract because of dissatisfaction with the "quality of management provided" while noting that "the government was obliged to listen to the views of the public following complaints about the quality of service being offered" (TANESCO, 2013). Notably, the reversal took place despite a commitment to liberalizing the power sector and providing incentives for foreign investment in MKUKUTA (VPO, 2005: annex, p. 13). While the shift to a hybrid classic development/neodevelopment policy paradigm would not be officially unveiled until the publication of the first FYDP in 2011, it arguably manifested in the governance of the energy sector at least six years earlier. Importantly, TANESCO remains responsible for about 60% of the country's electricity-generating capacity and ownership of all Tanzania's transmission and distribution services.

In addition to the refusal to privatize TANESCO, classic developmentalism in the energy sector is also evidenced by how energy prices were to be regulated. As Gore et al. (2018) note, the 1992 National Energy Policy had omitted to establish a truly independent state agency "to limit or end political influence over tariffs and licensing" (p. 8). The Energy and Water Utilities Regulatory Authority (EWURA) that was eventually established in 2001 has proven prone to political interference. Located with the Ministry of Water, a relatively isolated part of the state apparatus, EWURA performed effectively until 2012 (Pedersen et al., 2020). However, Pedersen et al. argue that EWURA became increasingly compromised as accelerated state development interests in fossil fuel exploitation consolidated. For example, by 2016, EWURA would be obliged to respect Tanzania's tradition of keeping consumer electricity tariffs low, in contrast to the situation in Uganda where tariff subsidies have focused on large industrial players (Kamagi, 2020; Twesigye, 2022). Other semi-autonomous state organizations in the energy sector have also struggled. For example, in 2007, the central government established the Rural Energy Agency to incentivize private investment for rural energy production (REA, 2010). However, the Rural Energy Agency appears to have been more successful in attracting donor funding rather than private financing (see NAO, 2015: 20, 86; Sergi et al., 2018: 66).

Indicative of its neodevelopmental aspirations, however, the Magufuli regime more forcefully asserted a state-led development strategy for the energy sector in the 2015 National Energy Policy (Government of Tanzania, 2015). While acknowledging that the 1992 and 2003 policies the main objective of the 2015 policy was to "provide guidance for sustainable development and utilization of energy resources to ensure optimal benefits to Tanzanians and contribute towards transformation of national economy" (p. 10). Importantly, the policy identifies 11 specific roles for government, while the private sector's role is reduced to "providing substantial capital investment and technologies needed" (pp. 53–54, 60). Magufuli was also not shy about dictating the terms of TANESCO's business. For example, in 2016, he rejected an attempt by TANESCO to increase electricity tariffs by 8.5% and subsequently dismissed the organization's head (Ng'wanakilala, 2017). As a 2014 interviewee explained, "If there is a big investment, then the government will have to come in and provide financing. . . . It's completely through the Ministry of Energy [and Minerals]. Everything with these large investments, it's the government. It's the one that provides the funds. It's the one that looks for funds."[1]

As for natural gas, the 2015 National Energy Policy aims "to develop a competitive and efficient domestic and export market for oil and natural gas" (Government of Tanzania, 2015: 29). While the majority of Tanzania's natural gas is destined for export, the quote from the National Energy Policy reflects the attentiveness of the state to developmental issues. And for good reason, as the use of Tanzania's natural gas has proven politically sensitive: major riots erupted in 2011–2012 in the southeastern cities of Lindi and Mtwara, where the gas originates, over the prospect that it would be shipped to Dar es Salaam or overseas instead of supporting local development (Must, 2018). Furthermore, reflecting the central government's development initiatives, the National Energy Policy also emphasizes cultivation of Tanzanian human and technological capacities (Government of Tanzania, 2015: 31–39).

It is interesting to note that beginning in 2009, Tanzania took modest steps to promote renewable energy. It introduced the Small Power Producer program for renewable energy and cogeneration, which includes a renewable feed-in tariff (REFIT) for microhydro, biomass, and solar that is regulated by EWURA (Moner-Girona et al., 2016; Tenenbaum et al., 2014). The impact of the REFIT appears modest, responsible for attracting 40 MW of decentralized renewable power as of 2016 (Moner-Girona et al., 2016: 309). It is interesting to note that Tanzania is not yet participating in the Global Energy Transfer Feed-in Tariff (GET FiT) program, which was pioneered in Uganda.

Overall, investigation of Tanzania energy policy reveals a skepticism of liberal economic reforms that suggests a preference for a more developmental policy paradigm. This is most evident in the dramatic reversal of TANESCO's privatization, which indicated a return to classic developmentalism. However, the export orientation of state efforts in the natural gas sector in addition to an abiding commitment to Tanzanian capacity building in the sector are suggestive of neodevelopmentalism. While Tanzania has pursued some renewable energy policies, these have been modest and have come to be reliant on donors. Furthermore, when stepping back and considering efforts to establish state agencies in Tanzania, including the EWURA and the Rural Energy Agency, it appears that their autonomy and, thus, ability to pursue liberal neodevelopmental policy are more limited than in Uganda and Moldova.

7.3. Uganda

Evolution Toward Liberal Neodevelopmentalism in Uganda

Uganda's development policy paradigm is best characterized as liberal neodevelopmentalism. While I first review the history of economic ideas about development in terms of the four policy strategies outlined in Chapter 4, liberal neodevelopmentalism is most evident when comparing economic reforms in the forest and energy sectors. The decision to retain state organizational capacity in the forest sector and near complete privatization of the energy sector is difficult to explain in light of other development policy paradigms identified. While I am unable to identify the specific decision-making process resulting in this divergence, the difference in how state organizational capacity is distributed suggests some internal evaluation of the state's capacity in each sector.

When considering the evolution of Uganda's development policy paradigm, it is important to point out that the preceding regimes of Obote and even Amin were characterized by classic developmentalism. For example, Obote set up marketing boards and government cooperatives for cash crops, and both leaders nationalized existing industries. Amin infamously expulsed Uganda's Asian community and transferred their assets to the state while declaring all land to be under state ownership (Whitfield et al., 2015). Early in his career, President Museveni was also a proponent of Afro-Marxism, as mentioned earlier.

However, later Museveni's mode of thinking about economic development would change, and Uganda would distinguish itself as one of the first countries in sub-Saharan Africa to embrace neoliberal structural adjustment reforms (Kiiza et al., 2007; Melo et al., 2012). Whitworth and Williams (2009) describe four distinct phases in the development of Uganda's economic policy since Museveni took power: pre-reform (1986–1990); the technocratic era (1990–1995); the poverty-reduction period (1995–2002); and a shift to economic growth from 2002 onward (pp. 3–4). While appearing to strongly embrace neoliberalism, I submit that a closer examination reveals a more nuanced role for the state in the economy that is suggestive of liberal neodevelopmentalism.

Despite initially being disposed to Afro-Marxism, Museveni proved an adroit political leader upon assuming power and embraced neoliberal economic reforms pragmatically. Key to the transformation in Museveni's thinking was a debate on currency exchange rules in 1990 that Museveni organized through the powerful Presidential Economic Council. While Ugandan experts had initially promoted a controlled exchange rate, the debate was prompted by the continued deterioration of the economy in the late 1980s. To the surprise of many, Museveni decided to liberalize exchange rates. As one observer noted, the decision to do so was "unexpected and bold. It was not a result of donor conditionality, but was born of vigorous debate within Uganda" (Byaruhanga et al., 2009: 55). Also significant was the 1990 Action Plan for Public Enterprise Reform and Divestiture developed under the auspices of the World Bank (Nyirinkindi and Opagi, 2009). By 1991 the Action Plan was adopted by the Cabinet, and, by 1993, a number of key state-owned companies had been privatized. Similarly, Museveni initiated significant land reforms that saw freehold and "mailo" land tenure restored (a controversial form of quasi-freehold land inherited from the British colonial period) under the 1995 Constitution as well as the 1998 Land Act (Coldham, 2000; Lastarria-Cornhiel, 2003). Donors would become enraptured with Uganda's apparent embrace of neoliberalism, and the country became a "darling" of the donor community (Kuteesa et al., 2009; Whitworth, 2009a).

But I argue that Museveni and the rest of the Ugandan government apparatus never completely swallowed neoliberal precepts and might be better considered as liberal neodevelopmentalism. Others have described Museveni's thinking during the height of the Ugandan neoliberal period as more pragmatic than ideological (Melo et al., 2012). For example, while embracing many neoliberal economic reforms, Museveni also remained true to a promise of establishing universal private education despite pressure from the World Bank to do otherwise (Melo et al., 2012: 59–62). While restoring freehold and "mailo" land, the 1995 Constitution also recognized customary land tenure. Important for this book's argument is the period from 2002 onward when, as Whitworth and Williamson (2009) observe, the state took "a somewhat more interventionist stance" in the economy in an effort to promote competitiveness in the export sector and promote private sector growth (p. 29). However, when also considering Uganda's innovations in the area of development planning, elements of liberal neodevelopmentalism might be seen to have emerged earlier.

As mentioned in Chapter 4, the paradoxical amalgamation of neoliberal economic policy and state development planning was pioneered in Uganda, which became the model for the Poverty Reduction Strategy Papers (PRSPs) of the World Bank (Mackinnon and Reinikka, 1999; Whitworth, 2009a,b). The need for development planning grew out of necessity. The period after Museveni came to power in 1986 saw a rapid influx of donor funds but also a lack of coordination (Mugambe, 2009). In 1991, a number of reforms were adopted to allow the central government to assert more control over the planning process. Most importantly, the Ministry of Finance, Planning and Economic Development (MFPED) was created by integrating two previously separate government bodies (Whitfield et al., 2015). The central government also began to require that any donor project receive counterparty-funding approval from MFPED, not simply line ministries. By 1995, Uganda had adopted reforms that effectively required all donor financing to pass through an integrated planning and budgeting process.

Still there were increasing concerns that Uganda's initial foray into neoliberal development planning had not done enough to tackle poverty. In response, reflecting liberal neodevelopmentalism, the Ugandan central government developed its innovative Poverty Eradication Action Plan (PEAP). The first PEAP, produced in 1997, was a comprehensive development plan that diverged from neoliberalism in terms of government commitment to tackle poverty through five strategies: (1) free universal primary education, (2) primary healthcare, (3) rural feeder roads, (4) provision of safe water and sanitation, and (5) the modernization of agriculture. The PEAP quickly became the pre-eminent planning document in Uganda. As described by Whitworth:

> Donors loved the PEAP. Here was a government—and a society—which was clearly prioritising poverty reduction and addressing it in a transparent, systematic way. Moreover, the substantial increase in funding for education included in the PEAP following the introduction of universal free primary education in 1997 demonstrated that government was putting its money where its mouth was.

By most measures, the first PEAP was a success (Williamson and Canagarajah, 2003). It was revised in 2000 and became the first PRSP approved by the World Bank and IMF. The PEAP for the period 2004–2009 is noteworthy in that it put more emphasis on economic growth, investment in productive sectors, and a greater focus on results (Mugambe, 2009: 167).

In 2010, the PEAP was replaced by a National Development Plan, a five-year planning document coordinated by the National Planning Authority (NPA), a semi-autonomous government agency established in 2002. The Ugandan government claimed that the "National Development Plan maintains the poverty eradication vision [of the PEAP], but with an additional emphasis on economic transformation and wealth creation thereby intertwining sustainable economic growth with poverty eradication" (NPA, 2010: 3). Notably, the 2010 National Development Plan was also largely developed without donor input, likely because of concerns of rising corruption as Museveni sought to hang on to power (Habraken et al., 2017). Nonetheless, Uganda has persevered, adopting a second National Development Plan in 2015 and a third in 2020.

Overall, Uganda has pursued liberal economic reforms that have diverged from simple deference to the market and sought to maintain some developmental ambition. My review of Uganda's forest and energy sector reforms below also demonstrates divergences that might be best understood via the concept of liberal neodevelopmentalism.

Liberal Neodevelopmentalism in Uganda's Forest Sector

In the previous chapter I demonstrated that the Ugandan central government has been quite aware of the scarcity of its forest resources. But such scarcity is unable to explain, on its own, the form of the state's involvement in the sector. In this section, I review the history of Uganda's forest sector policy to demonstrate how the central government reserved for itself an active role in the forest sector, despite ostensibly appearing to embrace many elements of liberal economic reforms—evidence, I submit, of liberal neodevelopmentalism.

Initially, Museveni's government retained the British colonial administration's approach to forest management. But the Uganda Forestry Department would be linked to declining forest cover and plantation capacity. As early as 1987, Museveni's regime embarked on a process of devolving natural resource management to district governments, though it recentralized much of forest management by 1995 given insufficient district capacity (Turyahabwe and Banana, 2008). This exercise may have underscored the need for more fundamental reform. In 1999, the Ugandan central government embarked on a Forest Sector Umbrella Program—a structural adjustment program of the World Bank—that resulted in the dissolution of the Uganda Forestry Department (LTS, 2010; Petursson and Vedeld, 2018; Turyahabwe and Banana, 2008: 651–653). It produced the Uganda Forest Policy (2001), National Forest Plan (2002), and National Forestry and Tree-Planting Act (2003). These saw the creation of three new institutions in the early 2000s: the National Forestry Authority (NFA), the decentralized District Forestry Services, and the Forest Sector Support Department (FSSD).

While acquiescing to calls for neoliberal economic reform, the striking feature of Uganda's forest sector reforms relative to those of the energy sector, discussed later, is the capacity the state retained for policy implementation via the NFA. The

NFA was established with the primary responsibility of managing Uganda's Central Forest Reserves (CFRs). There are 506 CFRs distributed across the countries that represent a total of 1.2 million ha (MWLE, 2001: 2). Of CFR lands, between 0.3 and 0.5 million ha have been identified for plantation development (Jacovelli, 2009: 120; MWE, 2016; NFA, 2005a; SPGS, 2011: 4). Overall, NFA possesses considerable latent organizational capacity for development, mostly in terms of lands available for afforestation and rudimentary staff across CFRs. Significantly, the National Forest Plan expected that the NFA would be self-sufficient, and it received little donor support since first established (Bjella, 2007; MWLE, 2002: 141)—an issue to which I return in my analysis of the CDM in Uganda.

The District Forestry Services are responsible for local forest reserves as well as regulation of forest resources (including charcoal) on private and customary land (MWLE, 2002). They are comprised of district government agents who report to the Ministry of Local Government. While the extent of local forest reserves is small—estimated at only a total of 5,000 ha—the District Forestry Services are a first point of contact with individual Ugandan citizens who can own land under Uganda's land-tenure system (Coldham, 2000; Lastarria-Cornhiel, 2003). The FSSD was accorded a supervisory role of the forest sector, including oversight of the NFA and the District Forestry Services. A recent analysis observes, however, that both "the [District Forestry Services and FSSD] never became operational to the extent intended by the policy ambition" (Petursson and Vedeld, 2018: loc. 4968). Both have come to play a more important role in REDD+, as I shall demonstrate in Chapter 9.

Significant to this book's argument, the Ugandan central government has repeatedly recognized carbon markets as a means of achieving its development goals in the forest sector. Explicit references to the CDM and carbon markets can be found in both the 2004 PEAP and first National Development Plan produced in 2010 (MFPED, 2005: 77–78; NPA, 2010: 95–96). In its 2015 National Development Plan, the government proposed a "countrywide community based and institutional tree planting initiatives," commercial forest plantations and industry, and a number of elements related to REDD+ (NPA, 2015: 170). The 2015 National Development Plan devotes a section to climate change and explicitly references the implementation of Uganda's National Climate Change Policy, released the same year (NPA, 2015: 60–62). Recall that the National Development Plan has developed largely without input from donors, suggesting that the Ugandan central government treats climate finance as a means of supporting its development efforts.

Overall, while the Ugandan government undertook neoliberal economic reforms, it managed to retain considerable organizational capacity in the forest sector. All major elements of the state forest apparatus appear to have been openly pursuing climate finance.

Liberal Neodevelopmentalism in Uganda's Energy Sector

In the previous chapter, I demonstrated how, in successive development plans, the Ugandan central government prioritized large-scale hydroelectricity and oil production over renewables. Until quite recently, the responsibility for realizing these state development interests was placed on the private sector, in contrast to the situation in Uganda's forestry sector where a state forest agency was retained. Without knowledge of the nature of Uganda's forest sector reforms, the way reforms have unfolded in the energy sector might suggest they were motivated by neoliberalism. But a closer examination suggests more nuance that might be interpreted as liberal neodevelopmentalism.

Some history of Uganda's power sector helps us understand its development policy paradigm (Karekezi and Mutiso, 2000; Kinyanjui et al., 2011). The colonial regime established a strong role for the government in the power sector by creating the Uganda Electricity Board (UEB) in 1948 as a state monopoly; that same year the UEB began construction of the Nalubaale dam, which was completed in 1954. Uganda's hydroelectric resources were first developed not for the benefit of Ugandans but for British colonial settlers in Kenya (Kasaija, 2004: 25). In 1957, a power interconnection was built between the two countries (Kinyanjui et al., 2011: 44).

After independence in 1962, vestiges of classic developmentalism began to emerge. While I mentioned earlier how Obote sought (unsuccessfully) to increase power generation capacity, his regime was more successful in cultivating domestic demand than simply exporting power to Kenya. For example, his government accepted a $14 million loan from the World Bank for a national grid expansion program. However, during Uganda's protracted period of civil conflict, the power sector fell into disrepair and no new significant power generation capacity would be built from 1954 until 2000.

Neoliberal reforms to Uganda's energy sector only began in 1999; indeed, in 1993, the Ugandan central government officially classified the UEB as an organization *not* to be privatized. However, as I have discussed earlier, Museveni made the key decision to adopt neoliberal macroeconomic reforms as early as 1990. According to Gore (2017), one reason for the delay was that the electricity sector had been identified as a strategic one where Museveni initially wanted to retain control, reflecting his initial classic developmentalist orientation. The pivot toward privatization was taken after considerable opportunity for reflection. In support of my argument about liberal neodevelopmentalism, the available evidence suggests that the eventual decision in favor of privatization was based on the recognition by both the Ugandan central government and World Bank that the UEB lacked the requisite capacity for constructing new dams and managing the electricity sector. I elaborate on this below.

As early as 1995, both the Ugandan central government and World Bank had become disenchanted with the UEB given delays in completing the 200 MW Kiira extension to the Nalubaale dam in addition to the general poor operation of the UEB. As Gore (2017) summarizes, "There is little question that in the mid-1990s the [UEB] was performing poorly" (p. 116). The Kiira extension project in particular had been initiated in 1991, but only two of the five planned turbines were functioning by 2000. On the government side, as Gore explains, "The delay in initiating the [Kiira] extension project spurred the Government of Uganda to look for other generation options at the same time that Kiira was under way" (p. 125). As for the World Bank, their country manager "emphasized that the government was unable to mobilize new funds for network expansion or improvement and the UEB could not do anything about unpaid bills from ministries . . . ultimately donors were unwilling to provide more funding for the sector unless dramatic change came about" (Gore, 2017: 117). By the late 1990s, the decision had been made to privatize the UEB.

Once the decision was finally made, energy sector reforms were "deep and fast" (Gore et al., 2018: 5). In addition to the privatization of the UEB, a new Electricity Act was adopted in 1999 which was soon followed by a new Energy Policy in 2002 (Engurait, 2005). A South African utility company, Eskom, acquired rights to the Nalubaale dam and its Kiira extension as well as to Uganda's electricity distribution system under the business name of Umeme. Similarly, a private firm would be contracted to construct the Bujagali dam in 2001. As in Tanzania, the state retained a regulatory role in the power sector by establishing the Electricity Regulatory Agency (ERA) to control electricity tariffs (UETCL, 2008: 39). In contrast to Tanzania, however, the ERA would soon begin to raise electricity consumer prices, often reaching more than 50% higher than those in Tanzania (GPP, 2018).

However, there has been growing dissatisfaction with liberal neo-developmentalism in the energy sector, where it has not been synonymous with neoliberalism. Perhaps most important was Uganda's experience with the Bujagali dam project. It took 10 years between its 2002 ground-breaking and its entry into service in 2012, eventually sapping enthusiasm for liberal economic reforms (Gore, 2017). One reason was the changing succession of investment partners. The central government also chaffed at successful legal challenges to the project's implementation by environmental NGOs and other civil society actors under the neoliberal institutional framework established by the World Bank.

Other institutional reforms inspired by neoliberalism also failed to produce the desired results. The Rural Electrification Agency was established in 2001 in order to lead efforts to reach Uganda's rural electrification targets. Initially, the agency sought to attract investors to rural electrification projects it had identified with subsidies (REA, 2006: 31–38). But similar to the situation in Tanzania, the

Rural Electrification Agency was only marginally effective due to a lack of private sector interest in rural electrification projects because of perceived risks and low returns. The agency reoriented its program toward government and donor financing (OAG, 2011: 17–18). But the funding it received initially—more than 60% from donors over 2006–2009—was only 52% of the amount necessary for expanding rural electrification (OAG, 2011: 19).

Reflecting on Uganda's experience in light of the delays with the Bujagali dam, a former minister of Energy and Mineral Development explained at a World Bank event in 2006: "As we went about implementing reforms, it was assumed that we could break away from the traditional public sector delivery and go straight into private delivery models. . . . Our experience to date has proved this assumption wrong" (cited in Gore, 2017). Similarly, in a 2008 investment conference, Museveni confided: "I no longer spend sleepless nights [worrying] about people coming to build dams in Uganda. If they come, they are welcome. But if they don't, we shall do it ourselves" (Gore, 2017: 149). Such language resonates with more developmental aspirations.

Despite declining enthusiasm for what has amounted to a neoliberal energy policy, there has been little apparent discussion of nationalization of power generation but rather a pivot to new investment partners. For example, the Ugandan central government has partnered with Chinese state-owned enterprises to build upcoming dams on the Nile, including the Karuma, Isimba, and Ayago dams. Similarly, in order to develop Uganda's oil sector, the government has approved licenses to Western and Chinese firms, while the contract for developing the country's first oil refinery was awarded to a Russian firm (Hickey and Izama, 2016). It is difficult to discern if such developments are associated with Museveni's strong dominant party political settlement (suggested by Hickey and Izama, 2016) or a more development policy paradigm in the energy sector. Given the dilution of Museveni's power in recent years, I submit that an explanation at the level of ideas warrants greater consideration.

However, liberal neodevelopmentalism helps explain the shape of Uganda's efforts to pursue decentralized renewable energy. While the interest of the central government in decentralized renewables has been low, as demonstrated earlier, it is noteworthy in that it chose to implement them through a rather effective renewable feed-in tariff (REFIT) managed by the semi-autonomous ERA. A first-phase REFIT was introduced for the period 2007–2009, targeting microhydro and bagasse cogeneration (MEMD, 2007: 113). A more comprehensive second-phase REFIT was released for the period 2011–2016 that, in addition to the two previously mentioned sectors, also targeted solar, wind, and geothermal among other renewable technologies (ERA, 2011: 15). This attracted donor interest, who established the GET FiT Uganda program, discussed earlier, which has led to installed capacity of 125 MW (IEA, 2016). This is triple the amount of decentralized renewables incentivized through Tanzania's REFIT. But Uganda appears to have shied away from pursuing renewable energy directly through the state apparatus. As will become apparent in later chapters, this has reduced the effective implementation of the CDM in the energy sector.

Overall, Uganda has undertaken extensive reforms of its energy sector, resulting in a reduction of state organizational capacity to intervene in the sector, though retaining a regulatory role. However, increasing dissatisfaction with the lack of state organizational capacity appears to be galvanizing interest in more direct intervention and deal-making with less demanding partners, such as those from China.

7.4. Moldova

With the collapse of the Soviet Union, successive Moldovan governments have sought to implement what are largely perceived to be neoliberal economic reforms—including the Party of Communists that dominated Moldovan politics from 2000 to 2009 and pro-EU coalitions that have largely held power since. However, the legacy of Soviet-style classic developmentalism has meant that neoliberal economic reforms met considerable initial resistance. The concept of liberal neodevelopmentalism helps us reconcile the paradox of neoliberal economic reforms being implemented by a nominally communist government. Liberal neodevelopmentalism also helps us understand the different ways that liberal economic reforms have been implemented in Moldova's forest and energy sectors. Similar to what was observed in Uganda, successive central governments in Moldova would retain a state agency in its forest sector, while its energy sector has been largely privatized—though there are some recent signs of agencification as well as the establishment of state-owned enterprises. Different from East Africa, however, liberal economic reforms in Moldova's energy sector also appear to play a more political role in the effort to reassert state control and disrupt Russia's monopoly as well as to meet conditions for EU membership.

Evolution Toward Liberal Neodevelopmentalism in Moldova

Rapid economic reforms were first initiated during the twilight years of the Soviet Union (King, 2000: 177). As elsewhere in the former Soviet bloc, these focused on land reform and de-collectivization but also privatization of state assets. In terms of land, it is important to bear in mind that as part of the former Soviet Union, land had been organized around collective farms (*kolhozes*) and state ownership of other land resources, such as forests. Privatization of land commenced with adoption of the 1991 Land Code, the same year that Moldova declared its independence from the Soviet Union. The Land Code established that agricultural lands of state and collective farms were to be allocated to individual villagers, though the village governments retained ownership of village public lands, including degraded land (Chiriac et al., 2000).[2] While land reforms initially met resistance, they culminated in the National Land Program of 1998 (USAID, 1999). It effectively created nearly 8 million land titles for 2.8 million new landowners (Gorton, 2001: 276; Lerman and Cimpoies, 2006: 441).

The Law on Privatization of 1991 targeted many sectors of the national economy, including the energy sector. It set the stage for the First Privatization Program 1993–1994 and Second Privatization Program 1996–1997 (Ciobanu, 1997). By 1996, over 2,000 enterprises had been privatized, including almost all of the agricultural-processing industry, light industry, and public utilities (Ciobanu, 1997: 72).

These initial liberalization efforts, which were led by the Romanian nationalist Popular Front political party, met resistance from the Agrarian Democratic Party, a party comprised largely of members of the then-defunct Communist Party and emergent Moldovan nationalists (Crowther, 2011; Quinlan, 2004; Way, 2005a). Reforms also took place against the backdrop of a collapsing national economy that saw GDP per capita plummet by almost 60% in the early 1990s. The Agrarian Democratic Party gained a majority in Moldova's first parliamentary elections in 1994 and governed until 1998, after which its members would migrate to a resurgent Party of Communists (King, 2000: 154–159).

Initially, the communists staunchly opposed economic reforms. In their 2001 Economic Revival Program, the party leveled a blistering critique: "Social and economic policies have largely been reduced to the concept of monetary governance of the state. Large-scale destatization, undertaken during the period, failed to increase production efficiency or boost economic and investment activity of new owners" (GoRM, 2001: 2). Rather, their Economic Revival Program asserted a need to strengthen the role of the state in economic development and the importance of rolling-back neoliberal economic reforms (pp. 6–9).

Nonetheless, as discussed in Chapter 5, in 2005 the communists surprised many with a turn toward the EU and an embrace of liberal economic reforms, as major disagreements with Russia over Transnistria emerged. Consequently, Moldova found itself in an odd position whereby the Party of Communists was in the driver's seat for economic reforms necessary for EU integration from 2000 to 2009.

Already in 2004, the communists turned to the IMF and World Bank and produced an Economic Growth and Poverty Reduction Strategy Paper (2004, EGPRSP), embracing the World Bank's PRSP process. Its long-term development policy goals were (1) sustainable socially oriented development, (2) reintegration of the country, and (3) European integration (GoM, 2004: 33–36). In 2007, the Party of Communists also presented the National Development Strategy 2008–2011 where they claimed "to aspire toward Moldova's alignment with European standards" (GoM, 2007: 5).

In some ways, the pivot by the communists toward the EU, as well as the liberal economic reforms that EU membership requires, problematizes my effort to separate development policy paradigms from international influences. The initial pivot was perhaps as much about loosening Russia's control over the Moldovan energy sector as a belief in the market. Notably there were doubts about the commitment of the nominally communist government to neoliberalism and EU integration. The IMF and World Bank, for example, observed "contradictions between [the 2004 EGPRSP] policies and current government actions . . . especially since it represents a radical departure from the government's 2001 Economic Revival program" (IMF, 2004: 7). By 2009, the EU had become dissatisfied with superficial implementation of reforms by the Party of Communists, particularly with regard to the EU-Moldova Action Plan (Nizhnikau, 2018: 136). Nonetheless, while the Party of Communists would ultimately lose both the presidency and Parliament in 2009, it had already set, perhaps grudgingly, Moldova on a path toward liberal neodevelopmentalism.

With pro-EU coalitions largely in control of Parliament from 2009 through 2018, this period was characterized by the acceleration of economic reforms and a surge in EU development funding (Devyatkov, 2012; Shapovalova and Boonstra, 2012). Significantly, 2009 marked the beginning of the Eastern Partnership, an ambitious program of the EU to "deepen and strengthen relations" with Moldova and five other post-Soviet states. Initially conceived as a pathway to EU membership, the ambition was scaled back. Furthermore, and important for efforts to decarbonize Moldova's energy sector, the country would, in 2010, officially join the Energy Community. Established in 2005, the Energy Community has promoted integrated and liberalized energy markets in southeastern Europe as well as the adoption of the EU *acquis communautaire* in the region (Goldthau and Sitter, 2014; Renner, 2009). Furthermore, by 2010, Moldova became the largest per capita recipient of EU funding. These efforts culminated in the signing of the EU-Moldova Association Agreement in 2014, including the Deep and Comprehensive Free Trade Arrangement (Kostanyan, 2016; Matei, 2013).

Overall, Moldova has pursued economic reforms that are difficult to accept as driven only by neoliberal economic ideas. Liberal economic reforms also allowed the Moldovan central government to demonstrate a commitment to EU values and conditions for eventual EU membership, which has been surprisingly popular over nearly the past 20 years given Moldova's competitive political settlement—even amongst the Party of Communists. Despite the benefits of reform, especially in the energy sector, the Moldovan central government has held on to a significant role for itself in the forest sector, which suggests the state adheres to a development policy paradigm of liberal neodevelopmentalism rather than simply neoliberalism. Indeed, liberal economic reforms in the energy sector are, paradoxically, a way of reasserting greater state control over Russia's monopoly in the sector. The political control that such liberal neodevelopmental reforms conferred on the state also helps explain the Party of Communists endorsement of them. It is to a detailed review of how economic reforms have played out in the forest and energy sectors to which I now turn.

Liberal Neodevelopmentalism in Moldova's Forest Sector

Like in Uganda, the Moldovan central government reserved a significant role in the forest sector though liberal economic reforms by retaining a state forest agency, Moldsilva. In contrast to almost complete privatization in the energy sector, Moldsilva would embody a unique combination of developmental and business interests for realizing the state's interest in increasing national forest cover and arresting land degradation.

Moldsilva was established in 1996 as an independent and financially autonomous government agency: partial funding was to be derived from the state, but it was also empowered to generate its own income through forest enterprises under its authority that generate revenue from timber and fuelwood sales (World Bank, 2007: 7). Notably, the precursor to Moldsilva, when Moldova was a republic of the Soviet Union, was 90% financed by the state budget though the state forest agency and received less than 10% of its funding from the state in reality (UNECE, 2005: 112). It should also be noted that the World Bank reported that Moldsilva has been operating at a loss and is "essentially self-financing" with government revenues being "relatively small" (World Bank, 2014: 5).

Liberal developmentalism is also reflected in the paradoxical way that Moldsilva gained lands during the land-reform process. Though the bulk of Moldova's forests were retained under state ownership during the transition period (Gulca, 2010b: 84), forested areas previously under the control of collective farms were transferred to village ownership (EMC, 1998). However, in an effort to control illegal logging, a government decision adopted in 1996 had the effect of placing nearly all village forests under the ownership of Moldsilva, resulting in the transfer of 20,320 ha from village governments to the state forest agency.

Furthermore, in contrast to the situation in Uganda, which saw the unbundling of the Uganda Forestry Department into three different organizations, Moldsilva has retained both administrative and operational roles, including the governance of state-owned forest enterprises and forest reserves across the country as well as the Institute of Forestry Research and Management (Moldsilva, 2019).

This concentration of authority has been the focus of donor calls for further reform. The best example is the EU-supported Strategy for Institutional Reform of the Forestry Sector in Moldova (FIRSM) (Popa et al., 2016). Running from 2009 to 2012, the main thrust of reforms it proposed was to unbundle Moldsilva by separating its administrative and operational duties.

Because of pressure from the EU, Moldsilva made a number of internal reforms under FIRSM, including extending harvesting rights to private forest enterprises and auctioning timber and fuelwood (World Bank, 2014: 14). However, more extensive liberal reforms were resisted, such as unbundling Moldsilva, providing strong evidence of a liberal neodevelopmental policy paradigm. Indeed, the Moldovan government signaled its commitment to Moldsilva and pushed back against FIRSM, arguing that "the state must have [a] strong position and adequate capacity for formulating a clear policy for [the] forestry sector" (Popa et al., 2016: 14).

Overall, the Moldovan central government has retained a significant role in the forest sector through an organization that was, paradoxically, adopted as part of neoliberal economic reforms. While there has been pressure to divest Moldsilva of some of its powers, it has been resisted by the central government in a way that reflects a policy paradigm that the state should remain directly involved in the forest sector.

Liberal Neodevelopmentalism in Moldova's Energy Sector

Similar to Uganda, structural adjustment in Moldova during the 1990s and early 2000s saw the state cede power over the energy sector to private actors and retain for itself a largely regulatory role. However, as interests in renewable energy have continued to grow, state organizational capacity for renewables has increased, although characterized by market-based features not dissimilar to the agencification observed in its forest sector. Such a finding demonstrates that as state development interests evolves, state organizational capacity changes through predictable pathways associated with a state's development policy paradigm.

Neoliberal Reforms of Moldova's Energy Sector
As in Uganda, initial reforms of Moldova's energy sector were "deep and fast." During the early stages of liberal economic reforms from 1997 to 2001, most of Moldova's main energy assets were privatized. In the electricity sector, the state-owned enterprise Moldenergo was unbundled, with generation and distribution assets privatized, though the state would retain control of electricity transmission though a new state-owned enterprise known as Moldtranselectro

(Zadnipru, 2011). Natural gas distribution and supply companies were also privatized (ANRE, 2009: 4).

The main power that the Moldovan state would retain after these reforms would be regulation of the energy sector through the National Energy Regulatory Agency (ANRE), established in 1997. Since 2001, ANRE has taken responsibility for regulating prices for natural gas, petrol, and electricity (ANRE, 2008: 78–79). But given Moldova's dependency on Russian natural gas, ANRE's ability to regulate prices is limited. Strikingly, the Moldovan central government under the Party of Communists did not seek to reverse neoliberal reforms in the energy sector.

Liberal Economic Reform to Assert State Control

Since 2010 there have been numerous changes to Moldova's energy policy, institutions, and organizations as it has more actively pursued EU integration (IRENA, 2019: 6–13; Tirsu and Uzun, 2018: 27). However, the affinity for liberal economic reforms overlaps with a key state interest in curtailing Russian monopolies in the energy sector. As discussed in Chapter 6, privatization led to the monopolization of Moldsilva's energy assets by Russian interests. Liberal economic reforms have been pursued in a manner consistent with liberal neodevelopmentalism in an effort to claw back state control over in the energy sector by leveling the playing field and establishing state energy agencies and state-owned energy enterprises.

For example, an organization similar to a state agency, Energy Efficiency Agency, was created to support renewables, notably while the central government was led by the Party of Communists. The 2007 Energy Strategy and Law on Renewable Energy established it with the authority and responsibility to manage all activities related to energy efficiency and renewable energy. Despite its name, the Energy Efficiency Agency is not an independent body but a state organization subordinate to the Ministry of Economy (Ciofu et al., 2014; Stratan, 2012). While not a fully autonomous state agency like Moldsilva in the forest sector, the similarities are quite apparent.

Similarly, in 2016, the Moldovan central government adopted the Law on Electricity to ensure the liberalization of the electricity market and transpose all principles of the EU's Third Energy Package. That same year saw the adoption of the Law on Natural Gas that aimed to liberalize the Moldovan gas market and diversify gas sources, in particular by unbundling Moldovagaz, where Russia's Gazprom is a majority owner.

But the Moldovan central government has also pursued a strategy that is more clearly developmental in its efforts to diversify natural gas sources through state-owned enterprises. The Iasi-Ungheni-Chisinau natural gas pipeline to Romania has been developed by a fully state-owned enterprise known as

VestMoldTransgaz, established in 2014 as a joint venture between the Romanian Transgaz and Eurotransgaz (Nuțu and Cenușă, 2016: 8). Similarly, under legislation adopted in 2016, a new central electricity supplier, Energocom, was created to purchase and provide grid access to renewable electricity, as well as provisions for the import of biofuels.

Overall, I observe a political dynamic in Moldova's energy sector similar to that in Uganda. While the state would initially embrace "deep and fast" neoliberal reforms, these would ironically undermine Moldova's energy security as it allowed major energy assets to be acquired by Russian actors. The Moldovan central government has since embraced further reform in part to level the playing field and assert itself into the domestic energy market while establishing a number of state-owned enterprises and state agencies in sensitive areas in the energy sector. The paradoxical use of liberal economic reforms to improve state control of the energy sector can be understood via a liberal neodevelopmental policy paradigm.

7.5. Conclusion

In this chapter I have reviewed in considerable detail the recent evolution of development policy paradigms in Tanzania, Uganda, and Moldova. I have presented evidence that the Tanzanian state has aspired to a hybrid neodevelopmental paradigm that remains strongly influenced by the classic developmentalism of its first president Julius Nyerere. In contrast, Uganda and Moldova gradually shifted from an embrace of neoliberalism to a more nuanced paradigm of liberal neodevelopmentalism. This saw both countries retain a degree of direct state control over their respective forest sectors, where capacity requirements for effective state intervention are lower, albeit in the form of state agencies, hence demonstrating a certain degree of conformity with neoliberal precepts. In the energy sectors, both Uganda and Moldova extensively privatized state assets; although, especially in the case of Moldova, the state is seeking to reassert a more direct role for itself, paradoxically, through tools often associated with neoliberal economic reforms including state energy agencies and state-owned energy enterprises. Liberal neodevelopmentalism helps us understand initially divergent strategies in the two sectors of Uganda and Moldova as well as the paradoxical role liberal economic reforms continue to play.

By shaping the allocation of state organizational capacity, such divergent development policy paradigms are of key importance to explaining differences in the effectiveness of forest and energy climate finance instruments across the three case-study countries, which I report on in the next three chapters.

PART III
EVALUATING CLIMATE FINANCE EFFECTIVENESS

8

Pockets of CDM Effectiveness

8.1. Introduction

This chapter is the first of Part III where I report on my evaluation of the effectiveness of climate finance instruments, beginning with the CDM and similar carbon offset projects in the three case-study countries. In Part I, I discussed the evolution of global environmental norms about climate and development cooperation that circulated within the UN climate change regime, arguing for an important shift from liberal environmentalism to developmental environmentalism. In Part II, I discussed different domestic political economy factors that shaped the process of development—including political settlements, state development interests, and development policy paradigms—in the Tanzania Uganda and Moldova. Each might be considered a potential independent variable for explaining climate finance effectiveness, which is the dependent variable explored in the chapters of Part III.

In this chapter I summarize findings from my comparative investigation of the actual effectiveness of carbon offset projects in the forest and bioenergy sectors in the three countries, initiated in 2009. Recalling the different stages of policy effectiveness, presented in the Introduction, I consider effectiveness here in terms of policy outcomes in the form of GHG emission reductions or sequestration. This was based on a counterfactual "additionality" evaluation of each carbon offset project: Would the carbon offset projects have been implemented if not for climate finance?

The most important finding is that while some projects were rather ineffective, others appear highly effective—"pockets of CDM effectiveness." I submit that such variation can be attributed to a unique combination of interests and capacities of project developers involved, which play a larger role in carbon offset project effectiveness than often assumed given low carbon prices obtained during the first commitment period of the Kyoto Protocol. It is important to bear in mind that carbon prices associated with carbon offset projects considered in this chapter range from \$2.5 to \$12.5 per tonne CO2 equivalent (tCO2e). However, the presence of such highly effective CDM project developers—particularly state agencies—is not by chance. In this chapter I also argue that attributes project-level effectiveness to state-level variables of development policy paradigms and state development interests.

Fieldwork was key in evaluating project effectiveness by providing information about development contexts that is not included in available project documents. Findings presented in this chapter are based on field investigation of seven carbon offset projects in operation in 2009 in Tanzania, Uganda, and Moldova, with analysis carried through 2014. Each project was evaluated using what I describe as an *ex-post comparative baseline method*, which I briefly elaborate in the first section following this introduction. Projects investigated include large-scale and small-scale tree-planting efforts, improved cookstoves, and biomass heating as well as biomass cogeneration (the usage of biomass to generate electricity). Importantly, my sample included a range of different types of project developers—state organizations, including state agencies and other government bodies, NGOs as well as private firms. See Table 8.1 for an overview of projects, while a map showing locations of projects in Tanzania, Uganda, and Moldova is found in Figure 8.1. While seven projects may not appear to be a large number, they represent a near complete sample of carbon offset projects operating in the forest and bioenergy sectors in the three countries at the time I initiated fieldwork in 2009. Consequently, the presence or absence of effective carbon offset project developers is, I submit, meaningful.

Briefly, I found only three of seven carbon offset projects to be highly additional, where all of the carbon credits appeared to be genuine: a small-scale NGO-led reforestation project in Uganda operating under the Plan Vivo standard of the voluntary carbon market and two CDM afforestation projects led by state agencies in Uganda and Moldova. The other CDM projects investigated were far less effective. Another NGO-led CDM project, this one for improved cookstoves in Tanzania, appeared highly additional but collapsed as its financial agreement fell through in 2010. The ineffectiveness of a CDM rural energy modernization project in Moldova, a project led by a unit of the Ministry of Environment, demonstrates that not all state organizations are capable of implementing carbon offset projects effectively. Finally, of the two projects led by the private sector, one in Tanzania and the other Uganda, I found only a one-quarter to one-third of carbon credits to be genuine.

Variation in the effectiveness of observed carbon offset projects point to the importance of the interests and capacities of project developers themselves. Aside from a rather small-scale NGO agroforestry project, the most effective carbon offset projects have been those aligned with a state's development interests and which the state has already been striving to tackle through state agencies. I submit that state agencies have been instilled by the state leadership with a unique combination of business and development interests as well as organizational capacities that predisposed them to effectively seize low-carbon development opportunities made available through the CDM in order to advance state development interests.

Table 8.1 Summary of Carbon Offset Projects

Country	Project	Project Developer	Technical Support/ Financial Brokerage	Climate Finance		Carbon Credit Evaluation				Crediting Period		
				Estimated Carbon Value	Carbon Price*	Expected Credits	Genuine Credits	Financial Additionality Bogus Credits	Development Additionality Bogus Credits	Implementation Period	Crediting Period	Crediting Window
				(M$)	($/tCO2e)	(tCO$_2$e)	(% Expected)	(% Expected)	(% Expected)			
NGO-led Project												
Uganda	Plan Vivo Reforestation	NGO	NGO	2.3	4.6**	178,221****	Very high	Negligible	Unknown	2003–modular 2008–2010	2003–modular 2009–2020	20 years 10 years
Tanzania	CDM Cookstove	NGO	UNDP	7.4	12.5	587,200	Not implemented	Negligible	Unknown			
State-led Projects												
Moldova	CDM Afforestation	State agency	World Bank	11.0	2.5–3.3***	7,575,000	Very high	Negligible	Negligible	2002–2008 2006–2010	2002–2035 2006–2029	20 years and 30
Uganda	CDM Afforestation	State agency	World Bank	1.1	4.15	647,745	Very high	Negligible	Negligible			years 20 years each
Moldova	CDM Rural Energy Modernization	Moldovan Carbon Finance Unit	World Bank	1.4	5.7	357,768	0%	95%	Negligible	2005–2007	2006–2017	10 years

(continued)

Table 8.1 Continued

Country	Project	Project Developer	Technical Support/ Financial Brokerage	Climate Finance		Carbon Credit Evaluation				Crediting Period		
				Estimated Carbon Value	Carbon Price*	Expected Credits	Genuine Credits	Financial Additionality Bogus Credits	Development Additionality Bogus Credits	Implementation Period	Crediting Period	Crediting Window
				(M$)	($/tCO2e)	(tCO$_2$e)	(% Expected)	(% Expected)	(% Expected)			
Private Sector-led												
Tanzania	CDM Afforestation	Private Sector	Private Sector	8.4	6.0	8,508,155	26%	Negligible	74%	1997–2004 2006–2013	2000–2025	20 years each
Uganda	CDM Biomass Cogeneration	Private Sector	World Bank	1.5	4.0	378,793	34%	35%	31%	2004–2008	2008–2014	7 years

* Price estimated from volume of credits purchased by World Bank and total price paid, except where indicated. See Appendix 2 for further information.

** Based on household surveys of individual smallholders, see Purdon (2018a: 4).

*** Sources: CDM-PDD (2008a, 2010); Moldsilva (2009); World Bank (2010a, No Date).

**** The Uganda Plan Vivo project is a modular project whose basic unit is the individual smallholder. Thus in contrast to the CDM projects, it has grown in size over time as new smallholders became involved in the project. It was launched in 2003 in Bitereko subcounty of southwestern Uganda in which year it claimed 11,819 tCO2e in carbon credits while in 2016 it has expanded across Uganda and now claims 991,589 tCO2e. In 2009, cumulative carbon credits stood at 178,221. See Purdon (2018a: 2) for details.

(a) Tanzania

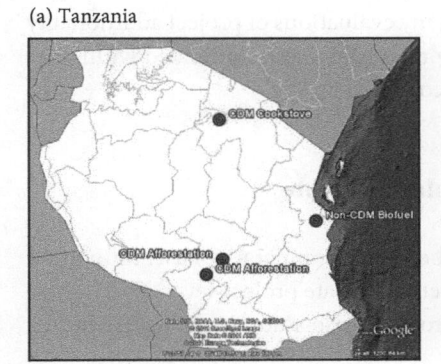

(b) Uganda

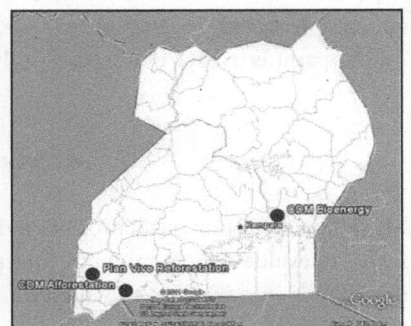

(c) Moldova

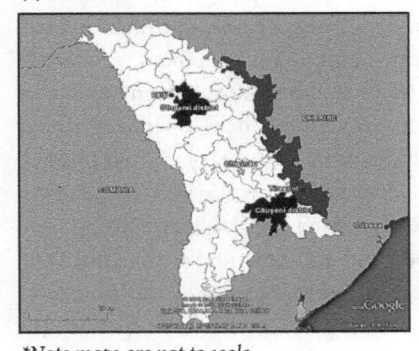

*Note maps are not to scale

Figure 8.1 Maps of Carbon Offset Projects Across Tanzania, Uganda, and Moldova

This chapter is structured as follows. In the next section I elaborate on my methodological approach and field efforts in order to justify the significance I attribute to empirical findings. I then summarize in Section 8.3 my empirical findings about the effectiveness of the carbon projects to have resulted in emissions reductions or sequestration. Supplementary technical information offering support of my evaluations can be found in Appendix 1. In Section 8.4, I describe organizations in each country that were implementing projects with climate mitigation potential but which were not involved with the CDM. It is important for this book's overall argument to be able to explain why certain organizations in a country that were ostensibly capable of reducing emissions did not engage with the CDM. In Section 8.5, I take stock of findings and present a typology of carbon offset project developers based on their organizational interests and capacities. Identification of the types of effective carbon offset project developers allows us to link with broader political economy factors in Tanzania, Uganda, and Moldova, which I elaborate upon in Section 8.6 where I offer an explanation of pockets of CDM effectiveness. Finally, my evaluations of project additionality are complemented by evaluation of how the CDM was coordinated within the state apparatus in each of the case-study countries.

8.2. Methodological Note

My sample of carbon offset projects and the *ex-post* comparative baseline method I used to evaluate them might be interpreted to relate project-level effectiveness to variation in state ideas and interests across the case-study countries in a meaningful way for two reasons.

First, results presented here are based on a near complete sample of carbon offset projects in operation in the forest and bioenergy sectors in the three case-study countries in 2009. They were identified through a systematic process in which I sought to investigate *all* forest (afforestation/reforestation) and bioenergy carbon offset projects in operation—including those operating under the CDM and similar carbon offset standards of the voluntary carbon market. Climate finance experts will note that I technically investigated 15 projects, though I treated as single projects those that used similar technology, were administered by the same project developer, and implemented at the same time (see Table A.1 in Appendix 1). To the best of my knowledge, I was unable to visit only three forest and bioenergy carbon offset projects that were operating in 2009: one other CDM biomass cogeneration project in Uganda, The International Small Group and Tree-Planting Program (TIST) voluntary carbon offset forest project in Tanzania and Uganda, and the UgaStove voluntary carbon offset project in Uganda.[1] I also mention that the heavily criticized but well-known Face Foundation project in Uganda was closed in 2004 (Fisher et al., 2018).

Second, the *ex-post comparative baseline method* I used allowed me to better evaluate the additionality of a project's baseline emission relative to its context. Critics of the CDM often claim that counterfactuals are impossible to measure and, hence, the entire CDM evaluation framework is suspect. However, the general solution for verifying counterfactuals is to use comparative methods, which allow one to reasonably infer what the counterfactual actually would have been (Langbein and Felbinger, 2006: 59). Comparative approaches are used routinely in policy analysis and other scientific domains. While important challenges remain to the construction of reasonable counterfactual baselines, including data availability and changing contextual conditions over time, my ex-post comparative baseline method attenuates such concerns.

The first step of the method was to compare baseline conditions used in project documents with those informed by investigation of changes over the course of a carbon offset project's implementation and crediting period. I focused on two types of baseline conditions: (1) a project's economic development context, and (2) a project's financial environment. I refer to these as development additionality and financial additionality. To the best of my knowledge, the only parallel to what I call development additionality is the "comparison group method" for ex-post baseline emissions evaluations, developed by WRI for their *GHG Protocol: Policy and Action Standard* (WRI, 2014a: 91–92). Distinguishing between development and financial baseline conditions allowed me to create a timeline for each project indicating significant departures from them.

Development additionality considers conditions that are driven by social, economic, and political events outside the control of a project developer. This was undertaken to determine if activities similar to those being implemented via carbon offset projects but not claiming carbon credits were observable within a project's development context. For example, the Tanzanian government's forest plantations that were adjacent to the CDM afforestation project I investigated, mentioned in Chapter 2, suggested that tree planting was not uncommon in area. Financial additionality is concerned with the financial barriers that would have prevented a project from proceeding if not for the support provided by the CDM. I established a financial baseline by reconstructing the financial history of each project in order to determine if funding sources not reported in the CDM project documents were used. Recall that all CDM projects required that the project developer affirm that "any public funding does not result in a diversion of ODA and is separate from and is not counted towards [ODA commitments of developed countries]" (UNFCCC, 2005b: appendix B, para(f)). As I demonstrate, project developers often interpret the rules to mean that ODA *cannot* be used in CDM projects—thus underreporting the use of ODA. My focus was on the identification of what Asuka (2000) refers to "ODA-baselines," using methods akin to forensic accounting to scour donor involvement in climate finance projects.

The second step of the ex-post comparative baseline method was to quantitatively evaluate the extent any such departures from claimed baseline conditions affected the amount of genuine carbon credits generated. To do so, I overlaid the timeline of baseline variations onto each project's emissions removals reported in CDM project documents. If I found ex-post baseline conditions for a specific year to be violated, I deemed the ex-ante emissions reductions or removals from that year onward to be bogus and subtracted them from the project's total claimed carbon credits. Overall, by considering each CDM project in its development context, the ex-post comparative baseline method allowed me to observe changes in socioeconomic conditions over a project's crediting period, determine when breaches of additionality occurred, and gauge their significance. It is possible that a project would have been implemented later, "anyway," but such violations become less important the further along into the crediting period because less bogus credits are at play. The key time for evaluating additionality is a project's implementation period, typically the first few years of its crediting period.

There is a certain limitation to my use of the ex-post comparative baseline method as it was based on fieldwork undertaken in 2009 and subsequent analysis through 2014, which is before the close of the crediting period of all projects investigated. Nonetheless, I have confidence in the evaluations because they were concluded after the implementation phase of all projects except for one. For example, the Tanzania CDM afforestation project was slated to continue tree planting through 2014; however, as discussed below, the most important changes in its baseline conditions occurred before this.

Information to inform my evaluation of CDM additionality was gathered at local, district, and national levels. In each country, I was able to purchase or rent a vehicle that allowed me to visit projects. Local-level fieldwork included household surveys as part of a broader investigation into the sustainability of carbon offset projects. This included investigation of the impact of carbon offset projects on livelihoods in a total 21 villages, including 14 project villages and seven control villages. Villages were almost always coupled with control villages located nearby (under 30 km), in the same jurisdiction and, to the extent possible, of comparable size. In each village I collected quantitative and qualitative information through household surveys ($n = 25$–30), focus groups, and interviews. Altogether, at the local level, I undertook 454 household surveys in addition to key informant interviews and focus groups with local actors ($n = 46$). See Table A.2 in Appendix 1. Fieldwork was always undertaken with a research assistant who also served as a translator when necessary.

Finally, I also sought to interview various relevant actors at the district, regional, and national levels. A total of 95 such interviews were also undertaken in 2009: 39 in Tanzania, 34 in Uganda, and 22 in Moldova. A secondary stage of fieldwork was undertaken in August 2013 (Moldova) and May–June 2014 (Tanzania and Uganda), which allowed follow-up interviews with key national stakeholders ($n = 31$). See Table A.3 in Appendix 1.

8.3. Carbon Offset Project Additionality Under Low Carbon Prices

In this section I present empirical findings from my investigation into the effectiveness of the seven carbon projects that were the focus of my fieldwork as summarized in Table 8.1. Additional technical detail in support of my evaluations can be found in Appendix 1. I organize this section around different types of project developers—including state agencies and other special government bodies, non-governmental organizations (NGOs), and private firms.

State Agencies

In my investigation, I found two CDM afforestation projects in Uganda and Moldova to be highly effective and all CDM credits generated to be genuine. Implemented by state forest agencies, climate finance allowed these organizations to extend their efforts to realize state development interests.

Uganda CDM Afforestation Project

The first CDM project that I found to be highly effective was as the Uganda Nile Basin Reforestation Project undertaken at the Rwoho Central Forest Reserve (CFR) by the National Forestry Authority (NFA) in southwestern Uganda. The project is comprised of five "small-scale" CDM afforestation projects that together were expected to sequester 647,745 tCO2e over 20 years from 2006 to 2029 (CDM-PDD, 2006a,b,c,d, 2009). It was being implemented with technical support from the World Bank and financed through its Biocarbon Fund. The World Bank agreed to buy the first 261,220 tonnes of carbon credits at a unit price of \$4.15 per tCO2e—a payment totaling \$1.1 million (NFA and Biocarbon Fund, 2006). Overall, I found the project to be highly effective: tree-planting rates significantly increased during the CDM implementation period, and climate finance appeared to be the only source of funding outside the limited in-house organizational resources to which the NFA had access.

Important for understanding my additionality evaluation, Rwoho CFR comprises 9,073 ha of which two-thirds (6,000 ha) were available for afforestation (NFA, 2007: 14–15). Of the lands available for afforestation, only about one-third (2,015 ha) were being used in the CDM project with NFA seeking to plant the remainder (3,985 ha).[2] In order to engage local communities an agreement was reached between the NFA and a local NGO. The vast majority of the CDM project area (90%) was being managed by NFA, while the NGO managed a 200 m buffer strip (RECPA & NFA, 2006: 16). I note that NFA also manages the much smaller Bugamba CFR, located just 5 km to the north. This more accessible forest reserve was initially planted by Uganda's then Forestry Department in the 1950s; it reached Rwoho only in the 1960s (NFA, 2007; Uganda Forest Department, 1984).

NFA claimed that without climate finance the project in Rwoho CFR would not have been able to proceed for two primary reasons: a lack of financing, and the inability to attract it (CDM-PDD, 2006d: 15–16). Consequently, it claimed that the baseline afforestation rate in the 2,015 ha CDM project area was effectively zero: no afforestation would have happened in this area if not for the CDM during the project's 20-year crediting period. How well does this claim stand up to scrutiny?

First, in support of NFA's financial additionality claim, the CDM was the only source of funding I could identify. The Bank of Uganda did not consider forestry an attractive investment option (JACO CDM, 2009: 10). Alternative investments that yield higher expected returns include treasury bills (15%) and even agricultural activities like maize (24%). The internal rate of return (IRR) of the CDM project is 13.6% without carbon finance and only 14.7% with carbon finance (JACO CDM, 2009: 14).

Second, in terms of development additionality, tree planting led by NFA significantly increased relative to a comparative baseline I established. The CDM planting rate could be verified by comparing NFA's non-CDM planting effort in Rwoho CFR and planting rates in nearby Bugamba CFR. These results from 1956 to 2012 are presented in Figure 8.2, which generally support the additionality claims of the CDM: planting has historically been restricted to approximately 100

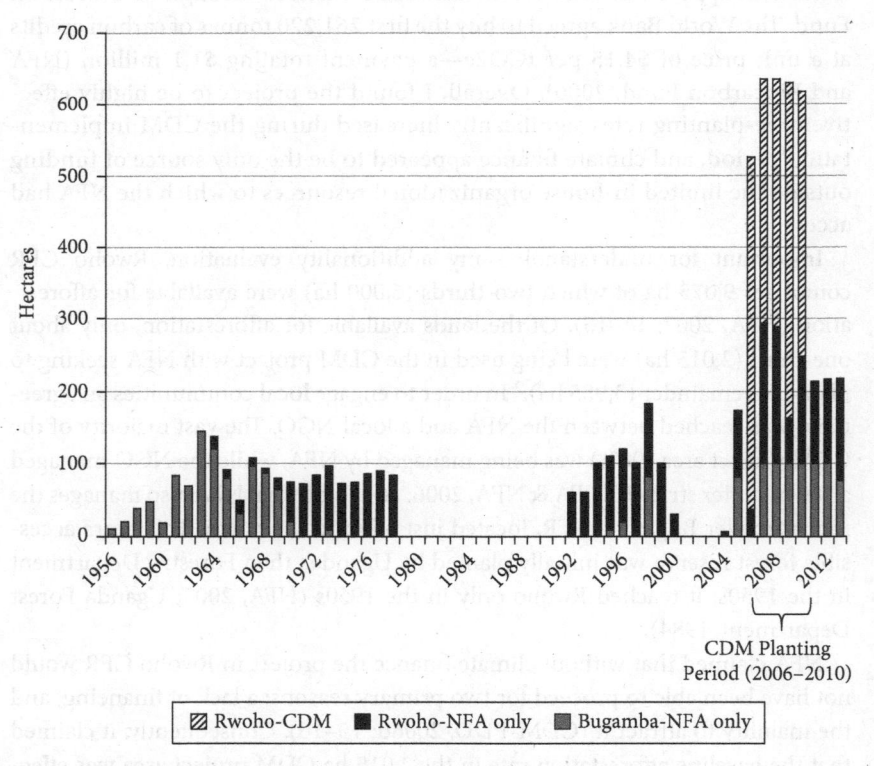

CDM Planting
Period (2006–2010)

☒ Rwoho-CDM   ■ Rwoho-NFA only   ■ Bugamba-NFA only

Figure 8.2 Planting Effort in Rwoho and Bugamba Central Forest Reserves, 1956–2012

Sources: 1956–1980: Uganda Forest Department (1984: Appendix 1, Bugamba and Rwoho Area Statements); NFA (NFA, 2007: Tables 3, 4, 17 & 18); CDM-PDD (2006a; b; c; d; 2009).

ha/yr in each reserve, though there were important gaps during the 1980s and early 2000s. These trends continued in the non-CDM planting zones in Rwoho CFR. However, planting in the CDM zone of Rwoho was associated with an average planting rate of 403 ha/yr. Furthermore, planting in the adjacent Bugamba CFR averaged 100 ha/yr over the CDM implementation period.

The available evidence also suggests that NFA was highly motivated to experiment with the CDM. As Uganda's state forest agency, NFA had been instilled with a unique combination of developmental and business interests that led it to treat the CDM as an attractive policy option. This might be attributed to the state's development interest in the forest sector as well as a development policy paradigm of liberal neodevelopmentalism, discussed in Chapters 6 and 7. While the Ugandan central government was quite aware of the scarcity of forest resources and attached a high development priority to them, it established NFA as one of the primary state organizations to address this state development priority via liberal economic forms initiated in the late 1990s.

Significantly, NFA was expected to sustain itself largely from revenues derived from its forest activities. In particular, CFRs were to be opened to planting by private actors that would generate revenue through timber licensing fees and timber sales (Bjella, 2007). NFA has received little donor support since first established in 2003—of the $15.1 million that NFA initially received, nearly 70% was allocated in the first two years (MWLE, 2002: 141). When donor support dried up in the mid-2000s, NFA struggled to remain solvent. A 2010 review concluded that NFA's afforestation targets and planned programs had not been implemented due to lack of finance (LTS, 2010: 15). A more recent ministerial review of Uganda's forest sector concluded that the NFA "has failed to become self-financing and continues to derive funding from both government and donors" (MWE, 2016: 17). Despite recent improvements in NFA's management, donors were put off by a major corruption scandal in 2009 as well as Museveni's questionable involvement in NFA's affairs, including awarding at least two CFRs for palm oil production and undermining NFA's efforts to address encroachment (Petursson and Vedeld, 2018). Donors would instead support an alternative, public-private partnership known as the Sawlog Production Grant Scheme (SPGS).

With a goal of spurring tree planting and plantation establishment among private landholders in Uganda, SPGS tends to compete with NFA. Established as a joint project of the EU and central government in 2004, SPGS has provided grants to individuals and companies (local and foreign) to establish timber plantations. While SPGS has collaborated with NFA to afforest CFRs, it has also targeted private and customary lands. Significantly, SGPS has consistently outperformed NFA. Of plantations established between 2014 and 2020, NFA has only directly planted an estimated 11,000 ha while SPGS planted approximately

Table 8.2 Tree-Planting Efforts of NFA and SPGS in Uganda, 2004–2020

Phase	NFA Planting (ha)	SPGS Planting (ha)
2004–2008	5,800	10,000
2009–2014	3,800	32,000
2015–2016	1,400	10,700
2017–2020 (expected)	4,000	21,300
Total	11,000	74,000

Sources: Based on numbers presented in Kawooya (2011), Tugumisirize (2011), SPGS (2018), NFA (2016a: 28–29), Dickens (2014: 2), and NFA (2016b: 48).

74,000 ha (Table 8.2). Given its superior performance, SPGS received an additional $20.8 million from donors in 2009 to plant 30,000 ha of plantations by 2013 (SPGS, 2009) and additional funding in 2016 to plant 32,000 ha more (SPGS, 2018). A midterm review found SPGS "over and above the set [planting] target" (MWE, 2016: 87). However, as I discuss later in this chapter, despite undertaking activities that contributed to climate change mitigation, SPGS has not been involved in CDM afforestation efforts.

As a state agency with a mandate to manage Uganda's CFRs and address Uganda's scarcity of forest resources, but with limited support from donors, the CDM was one of the few means available to the NFA for attracting financing for afforestation efforts. I conclude that these contextual factors instilled the organization with a unique combination of developmental and business interests that resulted in it treating the CDM as a real development opportunity. In combination with its latent organizational capacity, including land available for afforestation/reforestation, NFA was predisposed to engage effectively with the CDM to further state development interests to address forest resource scarcity.

Moldova CDM Afforestation Project

A second CDM project that I found highly effective was also an afforestation project implemented by a state forest agency, though this time in Moldova. Climate finance appeared to have been the only source of financing outside the limited in-house resources to which Moldsilva had access, while tree planting significantly increased during the CDM implementation period in a manner that contrasted with prevailing forest-related economic trends.

What I refer to as the Moldova CDM afforestation project was comprised of three carbon offset projects implemented over 2002–2009, including two CDM projects as well as a third project of the voluntary carbon market. Because of similarities in project design and timing, I consider them together as a single project for evaluation. The first CDM project is a 20,290 ha tree-planting effort (CDM-PDD, 2008a) entitled the Moldova Soil Conservation Project, which became the second afforestation project in the world to be approved (World Bank, 2009c). The second CDM project, entitled Moldova Community Forestry Development Project, aimed to afforest 10,589 ha (CDM-PDD, 2010). The third afforestation effort to plant 8,170 ha was financed through a forward contract from the World Bank for the purchase of voluntary carbon credits (Moldsilva, 2009: 18). Altogether, a total of 39,049 ha was planted between 2002 and 2009 under the three projects with a combined crediting period extending until 2035 that would claim to generate approximately 7.6 MtCO2e of carbon credits. In an important contrast to projects in Tanzania and Uganda, the Moldova afforestation projects are national in scope. The two CDM projects alone comprised 3,431 parcels with an average parcel size of 15 ha involving three-quarters of all villages in Moldova (CDM-PDD, 2008a; 2010).

The World Bank played a key brokerage role in the project through two of its climate finance programs: the Prototype Carbon Fund and BioCarbon Fund. The main difference between the two programs is that the former allocated financing upfront, while the BioCarbon Fund provided payment only upon delivery of carbon credits (Lecocq, 2003; Ranade, 2009).[3] For the first two CDM projects, the Prototype Carbon Fund and BioCarbon Fund agreed to purchase 1.3 and 1.9 $MtCO_2e$ of carbon credits, respectively—representing approximately $10.6 million at an estimated $3.3 per tCO_2e (WB Carbon Finance Unit, 2014a,b). As for the voluntary carbon project, the World Bank has purchased 175,000 tCO2e at $2.5 per tCO2e (Moldsilva, 2009: 18). Altogether, the World Bank purchased nearly half of the CDM credits claimed to be generated from the project.

The additionality claim of the Moldova CDM afforestation project was that in the absence of climate finance, the land targeted for afforestation would see "further degradation under growing population demands and will result in adverse impacts on adjoining lands" (CDM-PDD, 2008a: 40–42, 2010: 46–52). Apart from climate finance, it was argued, there were limited financial resources for tree planting apart from what Moldsilva's forest enterprises could generate themselves. How does this additionality claim stand up to scrutiny?

A first piece of evidence in support of the financial additionality claim is that the Moldovan central government was reliant on the CDM to achieve is afforestation policy objectives. As we have seen in Chapter 6, the Moldovan government identified land degradation as a development priority since the early 2000s and set itself a goal of increasing forest cover to 15% of the national territory by 2020—which would require the additional establishment of approximately

130,000 ha of forest cover (Gulca, 2006: 126, 2010a: 87; ICAS, 2007). Nearly three-quarters of this (95,118 ha) was to be undertaken with funds provided under the State Program for Afforestation and Reforestation of the Lands from the Forest Estate for the Period 2003–2020 (CDM-PDD, 2008a: 54–57, 2010: 57–60; FAO, 2007a: 4). But this program was largely supported by climate finance. The remainder of the forest-cover target was to be met through forest restoration techniques, such as assisted natural regeneration, that do not require tree planting *per se* (UNECE, 2005: 111)—though it is also the subject of a recent NAMA proposal that I discuss later. Relatedly, government support of Moldsilva peaked in 2008 at about 20% of Moldsilva's total revenues, while Moldsilva's non-governmental revenue rose from $5 million to over $17 million from 2002 through 2008 (Figure 8.3).

A second piece of evidence in favor of the financial additionality claim of the project was obtained during 2009 interviews. As an official of Moldsilva explained, in the absence of the carbon offset project, afforestation would have proceeded, but at a much smaller scale:

> The CDM was a financial supplement for the project, without these carbon credits, they would have still implemented this kind of a project but on a smaller

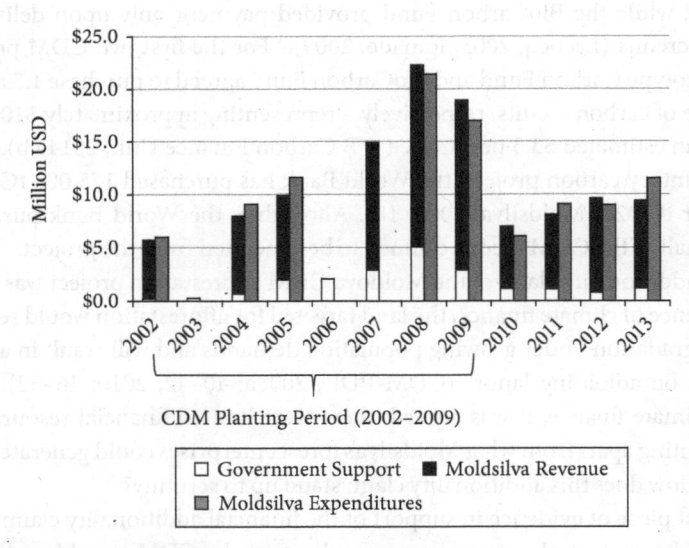

Figure 8.3 Moldsilva's Internal Financing, 2002–2013

Sources: Government Support obtained from Ministry of Finance. Moldsilva Revenue and Expenditures: 2002 (Moldsilva, 2013c); 2004–2005 (Curtea de Conturi, 2006); 2007–2009 (Curtea de Conturi, 2010; Moldsilva, 2011); 2010–2013 (Moldsilva, 2013a). Note that for 2003, 2006, and 2007 available data are incomplete.

area. The profit margin [for afforestation] is very small. The internal rate or return, even with financial support from carbon credits is [still] very small. But there were exact and direct orders from the President of Moldsilva, who said that this project should be implemented. . . . The financial means which are obtained through selling carbon credits isn't the goal of the project, it's just a way of reducing expenditures. The implementation would have still taken place in Moldova, but the carbon credit transactions are a method of reducing costs, not the purpose itself.[4]

Even with climate finance included, the project was not particularly attractive as an investment opportunity. The carbon offset project had a negative IRR over a 20-year horizon and only a 5.6% IRR over the long term; yet to qualify for commercial loans in Moldova requires an IRR of 15–20% (CDM-PDD, 2008a: 50–54).

What kind of project would have been implemented in the absence of the CDM? Individuals interviewed from a district forest enterprise, as well as the World Bank, estimated that CDM financing allowed Moldsilva to double its tree-planting efforts between 2002 and 2009, the project's implementation period, from 30,000 ha without the CDM to 60,000 ha with it.[5] These estimates, which were provided during interviews with different actors, correspond with official numbers. Over the projects' implementation period of 2002–2009, Moldsilva planted a total of 65,545 ha: 26,495 ha independently under the State Program for Afforestation and Reforestation while the carbon offset projects led to the planting of 39,049 ha.

As for development additionality, tree planting undertaken during the CDM implementation period contrasts with rates before and after it (Figure 8.4). Moldsilva's average total planting effort stood at 1,000 ha/yr ahead of 2002, the start of the climate finance project, but climbed to over 8,000 ha/yr during the implementation period from 2002 to 2009. Moldsilva's *non-climate-finance* tree-planting effort also increased to 3,312 ha/yr during the climate finance implementation period. But a key indicator of development additionality was that Moldsilva's non-climate-finance planting effort dropped again to 1,221 ha/year in 2010—approximately pre-CDM levels. Other available evidence supports this conclusion. For example, total tree-planting efforts jumped between 2001 and 2002, before a rise in the price of forest products (Figure 8.4). Between 2002 and 2009, the price of timber rose by 50% to 90% while the price of firewood increased from $8.2 to $34.3 per m3 (Moldsilva, 2011: 31, 2013). In other words, tree-planting efforts rose prior to local market signals for forest products.

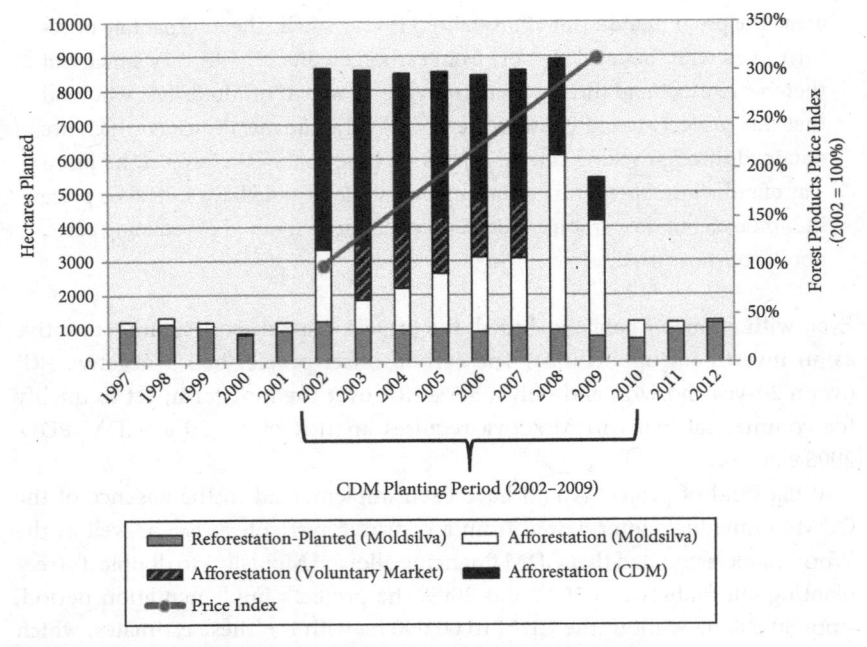

Figure 8.4 Total Tree-Planting Efforts in Moldova, 1997–2012

Sources: Tree-planting: CDM-PDD (2008a: Tables 13 & 22); CDM-PDD (2010: Table 13); Moldsilva (2010a; b; 2013b): Forest Products Price Index derived from Moldsilva (2011: 31; 2013c).

Special Government Units

While the two CDM afforestation projects led by state forest agencies in Uganda and Moldova proved highly effective, a CDM project to modernize rural energy installations in Moldova demonstrated that not all state-led organizations were suited to the task. This CDM project was implemented by a special unit of Moldova's Ministry of Environment and Natural Resources known as the Moldovan Carbon Finance Unit (MCFU). The MCFU was established with donor support to facilitate CDM implementation and related climate finance projects (Gobjila, 2007). The project in question sought to reduce emissions by promoting fuel switching—including from coal to renewable biomass and coal to natural gas—and energy efficiency installations in public buildings (such as schools and hospitals) among rural villages across the country (CDM-PDD, 2005a: 10, 2005b: 10). Comprised of two small-scale CDM projects entitled Moldova Biomass Heating in Rural Communities-No. 1 and 2, the Moldova CDM rural energy modernization project aimed to generate 357,768 tCO_2e of carbon credits over a 10-year period from 2006 to 2015. The project was developed as part of the World Bank's Community Development Carbon Facility

(CDCF, 2007). Total funding for the CDM project was likely in the range of $1.4–2.5 million, which suggests that the World Bank paid between $4–7 per tCO2e.

The MCFU and World Bank sought to graft the CDM project onto another existing donor project: the Social Investment Fund (SIF). SIF was a major donor partnership, which aimed to support social and economic development projects identified by Moldovan villages and vulnerable groups (World Bank, 2004: 2). It was under the authority of the Moldova Social Investment Fund, an autonomous non-profit organization administered by a committee headed by the prime minister (MSIF, No Date). An initial SIF1 ran over 1999–2004 and was extended into SIF2 with a combined budget of nearly $30 million (World Bank, 2004, 2008: 15, 2010a). Significant for my evaluation of additionality, SIF2 was expected to finance 400 projects in rural Moldova, with an estimated 250–300 related to energy infrastructure for village public buildings (CDM-PDD, 2005a: 5). Also important, SIF2 required local villages to contribute 15% to total project costs (World Bank, 2004: 6).

The additionality claim of the Moldova CDM rural energy modernization project was largely a financial one: in the absence of climate finance, donor financing through SIF2 would not have gone toward energy modernization but other village development priorities. It was argued that the 15% co-financing requirement from villages was a significant barrier, which was something that CDM financing would overcome (CDM-PDD, 2005b: 16). However, my analysis suggests this additionality claim was not justified.

In terms of development additionality, an initial piece of evidence was that none of the villages involved with the CDM project had adopted biomass boilers; rather, most had adopted natural gas boilers and energy efficiency installations.[6] While a total of 240 project installations were anticipated—including 106 bioenergy installations—a 2007 monitoring report revealed that only 66 energy efficiency and 49 coal-to-gas installations were completed (MCFU, 2007). The adoption of natural gas and hybrid coal-gas boilers is itself not an indication that the CDM project was not additional. Cleaner natural gas boilers can lead to reductions in emissions relative to coal, and this pathway is anticipated in the CDM methodology used for this project. But the available evidence suggests that switching from coal to natural gas was financially attractive without CDM financing.

In financial analysis prepared for the CDM project, the most financially attractive type of project in the absence of climate finance was switching from coal to natural gas (CDM-PDD, 2005a: annex 4, 2005b: annex 4). Fieldwork supported this conclusion. For example, one village council had signed a climate finance contract with the MCFU for $2,059, less than 5% of the $75,721 used toward the new boilers.[7] Another reason that natural gas boilers were attractive was that they allowed villages to demonstrate local demand for natural

Table 8.3 Frequency of Fuel Use Across Four Villages in Moldova

Region	Village	Control Village	Fuelwood	Charcoal	Dung	Crop Residues	Gas Tanks
Southern	Săiţi	No	77%	10%	50%	30%	80%
	Tocuz	Control	69%	3%	41%	55%	76%
Northern	Bursuceni	No	70%	13%	57%	37%	70%
	Chiscareni	No	93%	40%	3%	10%	60%

Table 8.4 Projects Implemented Under the SIF2 Project

Project Type	Total Proposals	Approved for Implementation	Identification Stage	Evaluation Stage	Rejected
Water	52	37	0	2	13
School	195	177	2	5	11
Roads	71	48	0	1	22
Gas	89	82	0	1	6
Other	15	10	0	0	5
Total	422	354	2	9	57

Source: FISM (2009: 11).

gas and, therefore, influence the central government during negotiations to extend the national gas network.[8] Many of Moldova's rural regions lacked direct pipeline access to natural gas, which might be a legitimate obstacle to some components of the CDM project. The majority of households in villages I visited in 2009 had purchased propane tanks instead but also used fuelwood extensively (Table 8.3).

A more important piece of information challenging development additionality was the fact that a significant number of villages involved with SIF2 appeared to have undertaken natural gas and energy efficiency projects under the donor program (Table 8.4). Of the 354 projects approved under SIF2, 50% involved school renovations and 23% involved natural gas. Though it is not possible to tell if school renovations under SIF2 involved measures to improve energy efficiency, it seems likely that a large part of SIF2 projects had already been directed toward energy modernization prior to the CDM. Interviews also suggested that it was difficult to coordinate the CDM project with the much larger SIF2 program: "There was a little bit of a lack of synchronization in timing between the [the CDM project] and [SIF2]. It was a really good idea on paper, but when we tried to implement it on the ground, SIF2 just zipped through very quickly, over-subscribed."[9] In other words, by the time the MCFU had sought to implement the CDM project, SIF2 funds had already been committed to natural gas boilers among village governments.

Overall, I found that there were valid reasons for villagers to adopt natural gas boilers independent of climate finance, while the CDM project was outcompeted by a much larger donor program seeking similar objectives. None of the CDM credits claimed under the project appear genuine. The low organizational capacity of a small unit at the Ministry of Environment and Natural Resources saw its project overshadowed by a much larger government-donor project.

NGO Project Developers

Among carbon offset projects investigated, only NGOs were found capable of implementing effective projects almost exclusively on climate finance. But given their reliance on climate finance, they were also more vulnerable to the vagaries of the global carbon market than projects led by state organizations and the private sector. Projects observed here included a reforestation program in Uganda operating under the Plan Vivo standard of the so-called voluntary market and, the second, a promising improved CDM cookstove project in Tanzania that collapsed when climate finance was no longer secure.

Uganda Plan Vivo Reforestation Project

The Plan Vivo reforestation project that I investigated in Uganda was highly additional but precariously reliant on climate finance. Known as the Trees for Global Benefit (TFGB) Programme, it has been implemented by a Ugandan NGO Environmental Conservation Trust of Uganda (EcoTrust). While EcoTrust initiated the project in Bitereko subcounty of Mitooma district (formerly Bushenyi district) in 2003, which was the subject of my fieldwork in 2009, it has since expanded to other districts of Uganda. The project is not a CDM project administered by the UNFCCC, but it generates carbon credits for sale on the voluntary carbon market under the Plan Vivo standard. In contrast to the large-scale CDM afforestation projects that I investigated, Plan Vivo has sought to use climate finance to encourage planting indigenous tree species by working directly with smallholder farmers on lands they hold (Plan Vivo, 2008).

Given its focus on smallholders, I interviewed local informants and undertook household surveys with those participating in the Plan Vivo project and

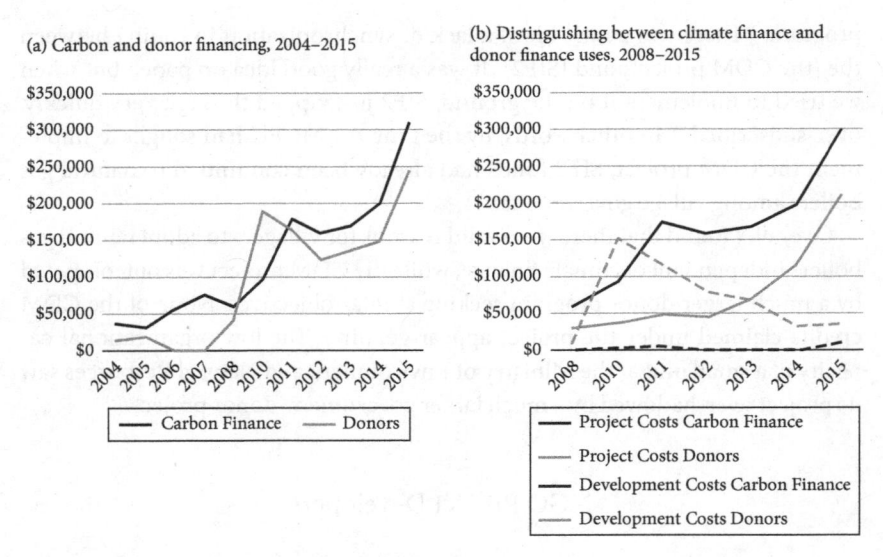

Figure 8.5a and 8.5b Change in Plan Vivo Reforestation Project Financing Over Time

Sources: Annual reports for the TFGB programme from 2004–2015, available online at the website of EcoTrust. Unfortunately, no such data were reported in the project's 2009 annual report.

those not, including approximately 30 households of each group. This was important because, as I demonstrate below, household surveys indicated that those participating in the Plan Vivo project were relatively wealthier and controlled more land than non-participants.

Importantly, Plan Vivo provides upfront carbon financing but also allows smallholders to retain timber and non-timber benefits from trees over the long term. My household surveys confirmed that participants were paid about $4, based largely on carbon contracts entered into prior to 2008. Significantly, smallholders remain contractually bound to maintain Plan Vivo trees until 20 years of age, after which they might be selectively harvested. Most residents of Bitereko subcounty were able to demonstrate customary land rights through informal local documentation (Plan Vivo-PDD, 2009), which was confirmed through my household surveys.[10]

Were the carbon credits generated under this Plan Vivo project genuine? In an important point of contrast to the CDM, there is little formal analysis of additionality in official Plan Vivo documentation. Nonetheless, my evaluation of financial additionality suggests that donor financing was used to launch the project, though it subsequently came to be largely supported by climate finance. As can be seen in Figure 8.5a, already by 2004, climate finance surpassed donor financing as the project's most important source of revenue—except for 2010 which may be attributed to the financial crisis (no data on 2009 were available). Figure 8.5b demonstrates that the majority of climate finance was going toward direct project costs, while donor costs were split between project costs and development costs. It is important to bear in mind that as a project of the voluntary carbon market, the Plan Vivo project was not required to exclude ODA support from its efforts to implement the project as has been the case for the CDM.

A second administrative feature that might assuage additionality concerns is that Plan Vivo issues credits for less than half of the estimated carbon sequestered. In the technical methodologies prepared for this project, Plan Vivo estimated that indigenous tree species would sequester a total of 458 tCO2 per ha over a 20-year period while only 224 tCO2 per ha is accredited (Plan Vivo, No Date: Figure 2). Finally, 10% of the credits were set aside as a buffer pool, further reducing the number of carbon credits issued.

As for development additionality, I considered whether participation in the project changed smallholder land-use practices. Regression analysis of 2009 household survey data suggests that participation in the Plan Vivo program was associated with a significantly more indigenous Plan Vivo tree planting but also tended to reduce the amount of land set aside for agriculture (Table 8.5). However, household surveys suggested that food security was not a risk for households involved with the project, who tended to be the relatively more well-off smallholders in the community: over 90% of participants in the Plan

Table 8.5 Regression of Household Land-Use Practices, Controlling for Participation in TFGB Project, Household Total Land, and Household Income ($n = 57$)

Variable	Eucalyptus Planting	TFGB Planting	Total Tree Planting	Agricult.	Fallow	Uncultiv.	Grazing
Project dummy	0.061	0.643***	0.662***	-0.737**	0.081	0.058*	−0.097
Household total land	0.037	0.066**	0.094***	0.733***	0.155**	0.002	0.006
Household income	0.000*	−0.000**	0.000**	0.000	0.000	0.000	-0.000
Constant	0.075	−0.117**	−0.071*	0.280*	−0.292**	−0.010	0.0603
R2	41.2%	76.5%	83.9%	94.4%	57.0%	4.8%	3.2%

Notes: Project dummies, Plan Vivo = 1 and Non-Plan Vivo = 0. Total tree planting includes Eucalyptus and Plan Vivo indigenous species.

Standard errors in parentheses. All models estimated with robust standard errors: * $p < 0.1$, ** $p < 0.05$, *** $p < 0.001$.

Vivo project reported that their households were food secure, while only 66% of non-participant households reported the same. The implication here is that smallholders saw the Plan Vivo project as an opportunity to use surplus land for tree planting rather than cultivate cash crops.

Overall, my analysis suggested that TFGB project activities in the region investigated were highly additional. While EcoTrust benefited from donor financing during the start-up phase of the project, it became more reliant on climate finance, which alleviates concerns about financial additionality. In terms of development additionality, though the project delivered only modest carbon payments to smallholders, this appeared sufficient to change their land-use practices to plant indigenous Plan Vivo trees rather than Eucalyptus or cash crops. Finally, accounting safeguards built into the project—where under half the carbon sequestered is issued as carbon credits—act as a significant buffer to the risk of generating bogus carbon credits. Notably, other studies of this project have also found it to be highly additional, including a 2019 revisit by the author (Purdon and Byakagaba, 2022).

However, while the project appeared highly additional, there are concerns that the potential long-term benefits of tree planting might not be viable for smallholder farmers, given that poor individuals are more likely to discount future costs for more immediate benefits (such as upfront carbon payments) (Fisher, 2012; Purdon and Byakagaba, 2022). When I reinvestigated Bitereko subcounty in 2019, participant satisfaction with the project had declined significantly from 2009, though not entirely, which might be attributed to participants having discounted the actual long-term costs of the project (Purdon and Byakagaba, 2022). While some strategies might be introduced to alleviate this situation, such as upfront payments for future timber harvested, better communication of the long-term nature of the project is also necessary.

Finally, while EcoTrust has been proactive in promoting its project and securing carbon offset buyers, questions might be asked about the financial viability of the project. As the Plan Vivo project focused on indigenous species among smallholder farmers, this may have limited industrial potential. In Chapter 6 we have seen that the Ugandan central government was highly interested in cultivating a forest industry, which helps explain the government's establishment of NFA and SPGS, discussed earlier.

Tanzania CDM Cookstove Project
The second NGO-led project investigated, the Tanzania CDM cookstove project, also relied largely on climate finance. Known as the Karatu Energy Efficient Stove Project, it was implemented by a local NGO known as the Karatu Development Association (KDA). The project aimed to disseminate improved cookstoves in

Karatu and Mbulu districts of northern Tanzania (KDA, 2008).[11] KDA piloted the project in 2004 with a grant from donors, which led to the construction of 1,800 cookstoves in 11 villages.[12] By 2008, the project had attracted the attention of the UNDP's Millennium Development Goals Carbon Facility to expand it under the CDM.[13] Over 10 years, the CDM project expected to distribute 22,000 cookstoves among 50 villages and generate nearly 600,000 tonnes of emission reductions by reducing non-renewable fuelwood consumption (UNDP, 2008a).

When I first visited the project in April 2009, it was scheduled to scale up efforts significantly, building 5,970 cookstoves that year in a bid to reach 22,000 by 2012 (KDA, 2008). With UNDP able to broker a deal with a major European bank, KDA expected to receive a premium price for its carbon credits, at $12.5 per tCO2e. This puts the value of the entire climate finance project at $7.4 million. Significantly, climate finance was found to have a major impact on its viability: it had a with-carbon-finance IRR of over 150% (UNDP, 2008b: Financial Analysis).

But the project was delayed and not yet operational when I first visited; it would shortly thereafter be suspended. One reason for the initial delay was that KDA was still in the process of negotiating a permit (Letter of Approval) for the project from the Tanzanian CDM authorities. Another related reason was that an official CDM methodology for improved cookstove projects was only adopted in late 2007 (Purdon, 2010: 1036–1037). Regardless, during a return visit to Karatu in 2011, I learned that the local technical advisor to KDA had withdrawn and, along with him, financial support for the project. The project was suspended. Through follow-up interviews, I learned that KDA was seeking assistance from the Tanzania Rural Energy Agency to implement the project, despite the Rural Energy Agency's focus on rural electrification.[14] To the best of my knowledge, the cookstove project has not been implemented since. Compelling evidence of the financial additionality of the CDM cookstove project is, then, the fact that it came to a halt when climate finance fell through by 2011.

What about development additionality? As I discuss in more detail in Appendix 1, there is considerable evidence that if the project had been able to be implemented, it would have changed household behavior. An initial field survey undertaken by KDA found that average daily household firewood consumption was reduced by almost 70% as a result of the project (KDA, 2009). Such results regarding fuelwood consumption were reflected in my household surveys. The project even appeared to dissuade villagers from adopting charcoal stoves, which is usually the next stage in the "energy ladder" (Kammen and Lew, 2005: 3). Women interviewed explained that the cookstove reduced their exposure to smoke and extended the amount of time they were able to cook with a single headload of firewood.[15] For example, the frequency of firewood collection was reduced from once every two days to once every eight days; some respondents traveled as far as 16 km to fetch fuelwood.

However, a concern with this project was whether reducing fuelwood consumption actually reduced emissions and pressure on forests. CDM methodologies for improved cookstove projects only permitted the generation of carbon credits from woody biomass derived from non-renewable sources (Purdon, 2010: 1036–1037). The Tanzania CDM cookstove project claimed that all biomass was derived from non-renewable sources (UNDP, 2008a). Was this really the case? Various studies dating from the 1970s, 1980s, and 1990s report a worsening fuelwood situation in Karatu district (see Axelsson and Hagborg, 1994). District government officials interviewed in 2009 indicated that fuelwood continued to be a major problem.[16] A tree-planting program was being discussed at the time by the district government, which would require each village to establish a forest reserve to secure fuelwood supply.[17] But only two villages had been successful in establishing such reserves, with district support for forest lagging behind other development priorities for health, schools, roads, and water.[18] Furthermore, there were no participatory forest management schemes in the district, including with nearby Marang Forest Reserve. Finally, though there may be some valid concerns about leakage and activity shift, there were viable strategies that KDA might have adopted to address them. These included efforts to improve the governance of forests from where fuelwood was sourced, such as through participatory forest management, and make efforts to promote fuelwood consumption technologies outside the household sector.

Overall, it appeared that the CDM cookstove project would have been highly effective if it had been implemented. But without other sources of support than the CDM, the project collapsed when climate finance fell through. Limited alignment between the cookstove project and state development interests in large-scale hydro and fossil fuel development, discussed in Chapter 6, also explains why the cookstove project received little government support.

Private Project Developers

Tanzania CDM Afforestation Project

What I refer to as the Tanzania CDM afforestation project was composed of two CDM afforestation projects located along the Udzungwa escarpment of Mufindi district in central Tanzania: (1) Afforestation in grassland areas of Uchindile & Mapanda and (2) Reforestation at the Idete Forest Project (CDM-PDD, 2007a, 2008b). Both afforestation projects were being implemented by Green Resources Limited (GRL), a Tanzanian subsidiary of a Norwegian forest company (GRAS,

2010; Nambombe and Mussami, 2007). In 2009, GRL had still found no buyer for its carbon credits and was implementing the projects using in-house resources—thus absorbing the risk that climate finance might not materialize. Together, the two projects represent a total area of about 30,000 ha of which 20,000 ha was to be made available for afforestation. Over a 20-year crediting period, the two projects were expected to generate 8.4 million tCO2e in carbon credits. The actual implementation period of the projects, which is important for our additionality evaluation, extended from 1997 through 2014.[19]

With its relatively humid conditions, Mufindi district has been an attractive location for forestry and tea. As suggested in Chapter 6, where I reviewed Tanzania's state development interests, there are at least three major government forest reserves in the district, including the central government's Sao Hill Plantations, which are the largest in Tanzania at 41,600 ha (World Bank, 2003: 3). In addition, a number of mills are located in Mufindi district including Mufindi Paper Mill and the former Sao Hill timber mill, now owned by GRL, which are currently East Africa's largest paper mill and sawmill, respectively (Christiansson and Åshuvud, 1985; Kangalawe, 2018; MNRT, 2001; World Bank, 2003). Both mills were constructed as government parastatals in the 1980s but were shut down in the 1990s during structural adjustments (Murison, 2002; World Bank, 2003). Mufindi Paper Mill was shut down in 1997, though later purchased by a Kenyan firm and resumed operations in 2005 (Kangalawe, 2018; Kulekana, 2008). GRL acquired and reopened the much smaller Sao Hill sawmill in 2003 (GRL, 2011: 5). All these elements are important for my additionality analysis below.

GRL argued that a lack of domestic financing prevented afforestation in the CDM project areas: "local farmers are usually not able to fully finance forest establishment because it is hard for them to get loans from banks for the purpose of reforestation activities (CDM-PDD, 2007a: 33–34). GRL also maintained that no public funding was used and that a large private investment was needed, which "is only possible with the incentive from the CDM" (CDM-PDD, 2007a: 36, 2008b: 24). In the absence of the CDM project, GRL claimed that the CDM project area would remain grassland (CDM-PDD, 2007a: 37). How does this additionality claim stand up to scrutiny?

In contrast to its financial additionality claim, GRL actually received considerable amounts of donor financing in 2003 and 2010. The first was a $2 million loan from Norfund in 2003 (2011a), a development finance institution that is a key part of Norwegian development policy (Norfund, 2011b). To be conservative, I assume that the 2003 loan was *not* used toward GRL's afforestation efforts. However, in 2010, GRL received loans worth $25 million from the World Bank ($18 million) and Norfund ($7 million), including funds for planting 12,000 ha of forest in the Mufindi district (GRL, 2009: 5; Norfund, 2011a). The funding package also included a $6.5 million "carbon loan" from the World Bank for delivery of an undisclosed amount of carbon credits (IFC, 2010).

While my analysis of financial additionality raises questions, this was overshadowed by significant changes in the project's development context. As indicated above, Mufindi district is home to Tanzania's forest industry, including Mufindi Paper Mill and Sao Hill sawmill. While this timber process capacity had been in various stages of disrepair since the 1990s, available evidence points to important changes in incentives for tree planting around 2005 as mills reopened. For example, a World Bank analysis published in 2003— before the mill's sale—found that the government's plantations in the district were losing money (World Bank, 2003: 76). But if the mill were to come online, the economic value of its plantations would rise from effectively zero to an estimated value of $10.8–14.7 million (World Bank, 2003: 76). GRL's 2003 reopening of the sawmill might be expected to have had a similar, though smaller effect.

Furthermore, around this time, the central government had also taken steps to increase royalty rates for forest products through its control of sizeable government forest plantations. Royalty fees and other permits are set out in "Schedule 14" of the 2004 Forest Regulations, which can only be changed through an act of Parliament (Milledge et al., 2007). The vast extent of government plantations affords the Tanzanian central government the power to set prices across the forestry sector. While the royalty rates are supposed to conform to market forces, the actual method of their determination was, in the words of one government official interviewed, "totally political."[20] In 2006, an attempt was made by the then minister of Ministry of Natural Resources and Tourism (MNRT) to raise royalty rates nearly fourfold, arguably to reflect the environmental value of forest products and approach global market prices.[21] However, the proposed rate hike sparked a political backlash that ultimately saw the minister removed from his post (Mbunda, 2007). Parliament eventually assented in 2007 to a rate hike that only doubled royalty rates.[22]

The effect of changing local tree-planting incentives might be gleaned from data on tree-planting efforts by individual villagers across the district provided to me by the Mufindi District Natural Resource Office during 2009 fieldwork. These data show that villager tree-planting rates jumped from under 4,000 ha in 2005 to approximately 10,000 ha in 2006 (Figure 8.6). This corroborates with the reopening of Mufindi Paper Mill and efforts to raise royalty fees, discussed above. Another indicator was the fact that in 2006 a second afforestation company (a Kenyan firm) had arrived to one of the villages where one of the CDM afforestation projects was located and acquired an additional 1,700 ha of land.[23] Finally, during my field visits, I observed smallholder farmers recently planting a significant amount of trees on their household lands.

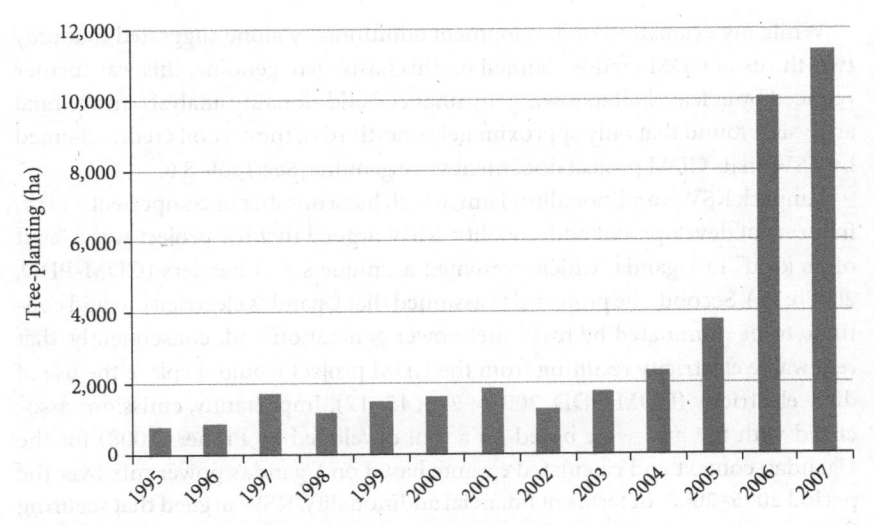

Figure 8.6 Villager's Afforestation Effort in Mufindi District, 1995–2007
Source: Mufindi District Natural Resource Office (personal communication, 2009).

I conclude that only one-quarter of the CDM credits claimed through this project are genuine. The CDM afforestation project, which began in 1997, was additional until 2005 when the Mufindi Paper Mill reopened, after which time it became profitable to practice forestry in the area. To be conservative, I ignore the sawmill that GRL opened in 2003. However, I deem that all trees planted from 2006 onward are not additional—undermining much of the additionality claim of this CDM project.

Uganda CDM Biomass Cogeneration Project

The final CDM project that I evaluated proved to be one of the most complex, and I provide much more detail on my analysis of the project's additionality in Appendix 1. Through the Kakira Sugar Works Ltd. (KSW) Cogeneration Project, a private Ugandan sugar mill, KSW sought to expand its bagasse cogeneration capacity to sell additional surplus electricity to Uganda's national grid in a way that would reduce emissions. Bagasse is the biomass residue left after processing raw sugarcane. Using bagasse to generate electricity through the CDM project would permit KSW to produce an additional 12–14 MW of clean electricity for Uganda's national grid and displace 378,793 tCO2e of emissions over a seven-year crediting period from 2008 to 2014. In 2007, an emission reductions purchase agreement was signed with the World Bank's Community Development Carbon Fund for $3.6 million for these credits at an estimated carbon price of $4 per tCO2e (CFU, 2008: 30; Katoomba Group, 2007).

While my evaluation of development additionality alone suggested that only two-thirds of CDM credits claimed on this basis were genuine, this was further reduced by at least half following my financial additionality analysis. In the final analysis, I found that only approximately one-third of the carbon credits claimed by KSW in its CDM project document were genuine. See Table 8.6.

I unpack KSW's additionality claim, which has a number of components. First, in terms of development additionality, KSW argued that the project was a "first of its kind" in Uganda, which presented a unique set of barriers (CDM-PDD, 2007b: 15). Second, the project also assumed that Uganda's electricity would continue to be dominated by fossil fuel power generation and, consequently, that renewable electricity resulting from the CDM project would displace the use of dirty electricity (CDM-PDD, 2007b: 2–3, 15–17). Importantly, emissions associated with the grid were based on a tool developed by Praher (2008) for the Ugandan context and calculated ex-ante based on Uganda's power mix over the period 2005–2007. In terms of financial additionality, KSW argued that securing financing through traditional private sector channels was not possible because Uganda "has limited access to global capital markets while local banks charge high interest rates" (CDM-PDD, 2007b: 14). Finally, KSW also argued that "there is no [developed country] public funding in the Uganda KSW Cogeneration project activity. . . . The project shall not make use of Official Development Assistance (ODA), nor result in the diversion of such ODA" (CDM-PDD, 2007b: 8).

Based on detailed analysis presented in Appendix 1, I found that both the development additionality and financial additionality claims to be problematic. First, consider the claim for development additionality. A survey of sugar mills in Uganda that I undertook found a number of them harnessing cogeneration, while changes in Uganda's power mix affected the representativity of the grid emissions factor in an important way. Recall that the grid emissions factor was based on Uganda's power mix over 2005–2007. It is true that fossil fuel generators dominated at the time the CDM project was initiated because of a severe drought in the region from 2004 to 2006, but there were important changes to Uganda's electricity mix after the CDM project was initiated—the most important being the Bujagali dam, which finally came online in 2012 (Kasita, 2012). Revising the grid expansion factor to accommodate transformations in Uganda's power mix alone results in a reduction of carbon credits expected over the crediting period 2008–2014 from 378,793 to 261,692 tCO2e—only two-thirds of carbon credits claimed are genuine based on development additionality analysis.

In terms of financial additionality, I estimate that only half of the emission reductions originally claimed in each of the first six years of the CDM crediting period from 2008 to 2014 might reasonably be attributed to the CDM project. While I provide much more detail in Appendix 1, essentially I conclude that

Table 8.6 Calculation of Genuine Carbon Credits After Combined Development and Financial Additionality Evaluation

Year	Ex-Ante Additionality			Ex-Post Development Additionality			Ex-Post Financial Additionality	
	Ex-ante Generating Capacity	Ex-Ante Emissions Factor	Original CERs	Ex-Post Generating Capacity	Ex-Post Emissions Factor	Ex-Post Developmental Additionality CERs	Financial Additionality Emissions Factor	Ex-Post Developmental and Financial CERs
	MWh		tCO2e	MWh		tCO2e		tCO2e
2008	103,606	0.5223	46,025	55,100	0.5209	28,703	0.5	14,351
2009	103,606	0.5223	46,025	87,900	0.9332	82,025	0.5	41,012
2010	103,606	0.5223	57,349	80,300	0.9499	76,276	0.5	38,138
2011	103,606	0.5223	57,349	57,900	0.7601	44,009	0.5	22,005
2012	103,606	0.5223	57,349	85,300	0.2037	17,376	0.5	8,688
2013	103,606	0.5223	57,349	84,646	0.1041	8,812	0.5	4,406
2014	103,606	0.5223	57,349	82,420	0.0545	4,491	1.0	0
Genuine carbon credits			378,793			261,692		128,600
Genuine						69%		34%

donor financing was responsible for 5–7 MW of the 12–14 MW that KSW exported onto Uganda's national grid (5–7 MW ≈ one-half of 12–14 MW). But expansion of export capacity to 32–34 MW in 2014 surpasses the increase in generating capacity that might have reasonably been attributed to the CDM. KSW actually received considerable donor financing both before and during the CDM crediting period. In retrospect, a renewable energy feed-in-tariff (REFIT) has, since 2011, risen to a level sufficient to have incentivized KSW to expand co-generation capacity in the absence of the CDM.

Interviews that I undertook in 2009 support the argument that CDM financing was not essential as KSW was able to fund the project through other channels. For example, one key informant intimate with the project explained in an interview in 2009:

> As a matter of fact this whole project was conceived without any carbon credit funding. I don't know if I'm shooting myself in the mouth, because it has certain commercial implications, but it is the truth. Reality is reality. . . . We are already making money out of the power we are generating. Obviously we are trying to fight with the state utility for a higher tariff, but that is a different issue. But [the CDM's] role is more like a catalyzer, more like an encourager. It's not as if without [the CDM], the world will not go on.[24]

This argument is corroborated through an interview with a representative at the Ministry of Energy and Mineral Development: "The issue is that [CDM renewable energy projects] would [have gone] ahead but at a very high price. A very high tariff. So when they get their carbon financing, they have a fair tariff to charge to the consumer."[25]

Overall, my findings suggest that the CDM may have accelerated KSW's capacity to export electricity and reduce emissions on Uganda's national grid, though not at the rate claimed in the CDM project documents. Only approximately one-third of carbon credits initially claimed were additional under low CDM credit prices fetched during my initial field effort. Perhaps sensing potential challenges to its additionality claims, the firm withdrew from the CDM process in 2011. Ostensibly this was because of changes in the CDM methodology that had reduced the amount of carbon credits the project could generate (Naus, 2010: 91), but my analysis suggests that the project was quite viable without it.

8.4. Unengaged Potential Project Developers

In the preceding section, I evaluated the additionality claims of carbon offset projects that were being implemented in Tanzania, Uganda, and Moldova in

2009. In this section I describe organizations identified during the course of my fieldwork that were implementing projects whose basic activities were very similar to the carbon offset projects investigated (i.e., tree planting, renewable energy provision) but were *not* seeking to claim carbon credits. The types of organizations that did not engage with the CDM are also insightful.

In Uganda and Moldova, a number of government-donor projects had climate mitigation potential but were not involved with climate finance. Since 2004, international donors in Uganda had been supporting tree-planting efforts in partnership with the Ugandan government through an initiative known as the Sawlog Production Grant Scheme (SPGS), which was mentioned in the context of my evaluation of the Uganda CDM afforestation project. During a 2014 interview, a representative of SPGS explained that the organization had not pursued the CDM because of concerns that it would make them ineligible for donor funding.[26] Thus SPGS appeared to consider itself ineligible for the CDM despite having considerable organizational capacity for large-scale tree-planting programs. But it might also be surmised that given the extensive amounts of donor financing SPGS was already receiving, it may simply not have been interested in the relatively low amounts of CDM financing available.

Similarly, in Moldova, as discussed in the context of the CDM rural energy modernization project, a government-donor program known as the aforementioned Social Investment Fund (SIF) was involved in energy modernization efforts across the country but was not involved in the CDM. As was suggested, SIF actually appeared to outdo the CDM in terms of its ability to incentivize energy efficiency and fuel-switching projects among public buildings in Moldova. Overall, in both Uganda and Moldova, special organizations had been established as partnerships between government and donors for activities that were aligned with state development interests. SPGS and SIF were, I submit, not interested in exploring climate finance because either they already had enough resources at their disposal through traditional donor channels or were concerned that engaging the CDM would compromise their access to donor support. Furthermore, during 2009 interviews I also found National Energy Regulatory Agency (ANRE) not to be interested in the CDM because of the financial risks involved.[27] While as a regulatory agency lacking organization capacity for policy implementation, ANRE was itself not able to implement CDM projects, a representative explained that the government would not take responsibility for setting a price on renewable energy when it was more expensive than traditional energy.[28]

In contrast, in Tanzania, the interests and capacities of organizations with capacity for climate mitigation projects were different, as elaborated in Chapter 7. I found that the state maintained organizational capacity in both the forest and energy sectors, though few of the organizations were interested in the CDM in either sector. Capacity for afforestation was found in the Forest and Beekeeping Division (FBD) at the Ministry of Natural Resources and Tourism (MRNT), which still had responsibility for plantation management at the time of my investigation of the CDM in 2009. It was striking that FBD was not engaged with the CDM, given that it was undoubtedly aware of the opportunity that the CDM represented. The CDM afforestation project investigated in Tanzanian was being implemented on lands directly adjacent to state-owned Sao Hill plantations. Similarly, the Tanzania Electric Supply Company Limited (TANESCO)— a state-owned enterprise responsible for electricity generation, transmission, and generation—also had the capacity to implement certain low-carbon energy projects but was not involved with the CDM. Finally, as I discuss in more detail later in this chapter, during interviews undertaken in 2009 I found Tanzania's Rural Energy Agency to be interested in the CDM but was puzzled by the initial lack of support by Tanzania's CDM authority at the Division of Environment at the Vice-President's Office (DoE-VPO). It would subsequently devise a renewable energy program under the CDM; though, with the collapse of the CDM market most of its funding has come from World Bank loans (World Bank, 2018b). Overall, both FBD and TANESCO appeared uninterested in climate finance through the CDM, while there appeared to be a lack of support from Tanzania's CDM authority that delayed if not dissuaded other actors interested in the mechanism.

8.5. Typology of Carbon Offset Project Developers

Findings from my empirical investigation into the effectiveness of carbon offset projects in the forest and bioenergy sectors of Tanzania, Uganda, and Moldova that were in operation in 2009 have revealed an important level of variation. Some projects were highly effectively implemented, where nearly all carbon credits claimed were found to be genuine and representing emission reductions and sequestration above what would have happened in the absence of climate finance. Others were much less effective, with only a third or quarter of credits genuine. See Table 8.1 at the beginning of this chapter.

Earlier, I also suggested that an explanation for such variation can be found in the different characteristics of project developers themselves: the interests and capacities of organizations undertaking projects with climate mitigation potential. Table 8.7 summarizes the seven carbon offset projects identified as well as unengaged potential project developers in terms of their organizational interests and capacities. In terms of interests, I differentiate between developmental interests, motivated to supply public goods and address market failures, and business interests associated with profit-making. A second factor was

Table 8.7 Organizational Interests and Capacities of Carbon Offset Project Developers and Other Organizations with Climate Mitigation Potential

Organizational Capacity	Organizational Interests		
	Business	Business and Developmental	Developmental
Active organizational capacity	CDM afforestation (Tz) CDM biomass cogen (Ug)		
Latent organizational capacity		CDM afforestation (Ug) CDM afforestation (Md)	SPGS (Ug) SIF (Md) TANESCO (Tz) FDB-MNRT (Tz)
Low organizational capacity		Plan Vivo reforestation (Ug) CDM cookstove (Tz) Rural energy modernization (Md)	

organizational capacity, where I distinguish active, latent, and low organizational capacity.

I submit that while state forest agencies, such as NFA and Moldsilva in Uganda and Moldova, were not created with the CDM in mind, they embodied a unique combination of developmental and business interests in addition to a latent organizational capacity that resulted in their using climate finance effectively. First, in terms of interests, state forest agencies in Uganda and Moldova were created by the state to address priority development issues. As we saw in Chapter 6, the central governments of Uganda and Moldova were quite aware of the extent and severity of forest resource scarcity and associated environmental issues such as land degradation. This led them to prioritize afforestation and tree-planting policies, despite that they were not very profitable. But in addition to such developmental interests, state agencies were instilled with a business interest to explore the carbon market. Both state agencies lacked sufficient government resources to realize state development mandates, but their relative independence and self-sufficient institutional character predisposed them to experimenting with the opportunity that the CDM presented.

A second factor distinguishing state agencies was their organizational capacity. Because profit-making was not the primary goal of state agencies, the organizational capacities they possessed might be maintained despite not generating profit. Such latent organizational capacity constitutes a basic level of personnel, equipment, information, and other resources—such as land—for pursuing development objectives, though it may not be sufficient for seeing these objectives fully realized. Many of the activities of the state are directed precisely to areas where market incentives are weak and, consequently, private firms less active. As discussed in Chapter 7, NFA in Uganda possess considerable operational resources, including extensive land resources in the form of central forest reserves, but insufficient government and donor financing to fully afforest them. Similarly, Moldsilva has retained administrative and operational roles and resisted further liberal economic reforms. It has personnel, equipment, and offices distributed across the country while remaining responsible for the governance of state-owned forest enterprises and forest reserves across the country as well as the Institute of Forestry Research and Management (Moldsilva, 2019).

The finding that state forest agencies in Uganda and Moldova implemented highly effective CDM projects was all the more surprising given prevailing concerns about corruption and mismanagement in the forest sectors of the two countries. However, my argument that "pockets of CDM effectiveness" emerge as a result of the convergence of particular state ideas and interests appears credible when we consider the modest incentives offered through the CDM. The afforestation projects in Moldova were offered CDM financing at prices of between \$2.5 and \$3.3 per tCO2e, while I estimate that prices received by NFA for the CDM afforestation project there at \$4.15. Under these conditions, CDM finance could not fully support state agencies in their efforts to realize state development goals in the forest sector. Indeed, CDM financing was effectively used because it did not launch entirely new projects but fed into existing afforestation efforts that governments were pursuing.

The upshot is that when state forest agencies received climate finance, they were able to leverage their latent organizational capacity to extend development efforts, for which the agency was already responsible, in a way that was highly effective and led to genuinely additional emission reductions—even if state agencies themselves failed to generate a profit. This was perhaps clearest in the CDM afforestation project in Moldova where an official of the state forest agency explained how CDM financing, while not generating a significant profit, reduced expenditures that allowed Moldsilva to double the afforestation effort it would have otherwise achieved. This dynamic is significantly different from how highly non-additional projects were implemented, which in my sample were associated with the private sector.

Other carbon offset project developers investigated did not possess such interests and capacities, which resulted in less effective carbon offset project implementation. Some organizations had interests similar to state agencies but had lower capacity. This included the specialized climate finance unit at the

Moldovan Ministry of Environment and Natural Resources, which had limited experience with project implantation in the forest and energy sectors and was outperformed by other policy actors. The NGOs observed also possessed a combination of business and developmental interests that saw them engage with carbon offset opportunities, but their reliance on climate finance (and absence of other revenue streams and assets) left them vulnerable. As in the example of the CDM cookstove project, if climate finance fell through, projects risked coming to a halt because alternative revenue streams were unavailable.

Because NGO-led projects generated little profit apart from carbon offset finance, businesses tended to not be involved in these types of projects. Central governments also did not seem particularly interested. This may be because the activities promoted in my two NGO-led projects, indigenous tree planting among smallholders and improved cookstoves, were largely removed from efforts toward industrialization and state development interests in Uganda and Tanzania, as discussed in Chapter 6. This might be because these projects catered more to individual investors in developed countries through transnational environmental organizations and international development agencies. The upshot is that while domestic NGOs investigated had a set of developmental and business interests similar to state agencies, they had lower organizational capacity.

Private firms were found to be the least effective CDM project developers observed, which might be attributed to their business interests and, relatedly, how their organizational capacities were deployed. Projects that private firms were seeking to undertake appeared largely feasible without climate finance offered through the CDM. This can be attributed to low carbon prices that prevailed at the time, which made it difficult to build a business case for CDM projects on the basis of carbon offset alone. While managers of firms investigated would likely support the provision of public goods and combatting poverty in Tanzania and Uganda, I think it fair to assume that they were focused on the bottom line. Private firms were therefore cautious about becoming dependent on the CDM, particularly given low carbon prices. Consequently, while private firms retained capacity for projects that might lead to emission reductions and sequestration, such capacity could not be left latent as this would sap resources necessary for profit-making activities. In contrast to government organizations, businesses faced pressure to actively deploy their organizational capacities where they were most effective in generating profit. At low carbon prices incentives associated with the first commitment period of the Kyoto Protocol, the CDM did not appear to influence decision-making about whether to undertake a project. Consequently, firms developed CDM projects that were largely profitable on their own. While the CDM financing may have accelerated the implementation of emission reduction actions by private firms earlier than would have otherwise been the case, it was not the primary motivation for project implementation.

It is fair to raise questions about the attempts by both private firms investigated in this chapter to obtain CDM financing while also seeking donor financing and thereby flouting the CDM financial additionality rules. But this points to a fundamental problem with the CDM's architecture. Without an accounting option to accommodate donor contributions, the CDM has promoted obfuscation of financial accounts as project developers have concluded that either that they need to claim that no donor financing was used or else render themselves ineligible for the CDM.

Finally, I return to organizations undertaking activities in the forest and energy sectors that could, ostensibly, be tied to emission reductions and, thus, eligible for the CDM, but which were not engaged with the climate finance instrument. While such organizations possessed a latent organization capacity similar to state agencies, absence of business interests predisposed them to disregard the CDM. In Uganda and Moldova, organizations identified were created by central governments in partnership with international development partners. The implication is that, with sufficient donor funds, such organizations were simply not interested in securing more financing through the CDM. In contrast, in Tanzania, organizations that were responsible for forest and energy were largely unmotivated to engage with the CDM, though they likely did have organizational capacity to do so. This suggests that the reasons for their lack of interest had less to do with financial interests and was, rather, due to skepticism about the CDM process in the first place. In both cases, these organizations were involved in activities that might lend themselves to climate change mitigation—including tree planting and increasing the production of renewable energy—but lacked the business motivation to seek out the CDM.

The discussion above about organizational interests and capacities allows us to create a typology of carbon offset project developers, which I map out in Figure 8.7. Here I show a climate finance layer that might be added to the in-house resources of each country, which is a proxy for their capacities. We can see that for NGOs the contribution of climate finance to project implementation is high relative to available in-house resources, whereas this is less for other policy actors given their larger in-house resources. The main difference between state agencies and private firms is that the former aims to implement projects despite their lack of profitability. In this situation, climate finance offered through the CDM has been able to extend ongoing project activities. As for private firms, they pursue projects that are profitable even in the absence of climate finance, with such business financing largely sufficient for project implementation in the absence of climate finance. This is because the climate finance layer is too thin to deliver sufficient profits on its own. While climate finance does not lead firms to extend climate mitigation activities, it increases the financial attractiveness of

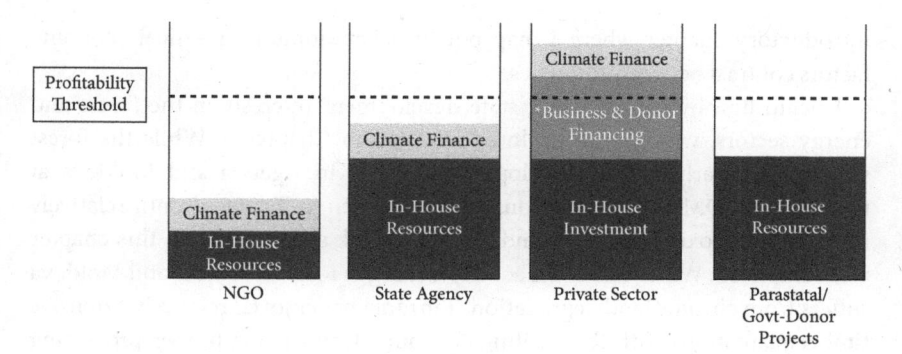

Figure 8.7 Typology of CDM Project Developers

existing activities that may lead firms to implement them earlier than might otherwise be the case.

Figure 8.7 was also created on the basis of carbon market prices available to project developers that were obtained on the CDM carbon market during the first commitment period of the Kyoto Protocol. In my sample, these ranged from $2.5 to $12.5 per tCO2e, though most hovered between $4 to $7 per tCO2e. The implication is that, at a certain level, climate finance might on its own be sufficient motivation to be the basis of effective emission reduction projects regardless of other financial resources and related capacities available to project developers. I return to this issue in the Conclusion of this book as prices on major carbon markets have grown considerably in recent years. In late 2023, while completing this manuscript, prices of $35 per tCO2e were observed on the Western Climate Initiative (California-Quebec) carbon market and $90 per tCO2e on the European Union Emissions Trading System.

8.6. Explaining CDM Pockets of Effectiveness

While I was able to identify characteristics of effective carbon offset project developers in the previous section, a larger question remains about the presence of highly effective ones, especially state forest agencies observed in Uganda and Moldova. What explains such CDM "pockets of effectiveness"? I attribute the characteristics of effective carbon offset project developers to state-level variables, namely the convergence of development policy paradigms and state development interests—at least at the low carbon prices that characterized the first commitment period of the Kyoto Protocol. While I elaborate on this causal mechanism in this section, the reader might want to return to Table 1.2 in the introductory chapter where I map out how key domestic political economy factors contrast between countries.

I begin first by summarizing state development interests in the forest and energy sectors, which were explored in detail in Chapter 6. While the forest sector was clearly a state development interest in Uganda and Moldova at the time of CDM implementation, it has not been in Tanzania until relatively recently—approximately 2016 and after fieldwork summarized in this chapter was completed. While Uganda is acutely lacking in forest resources and Moldova suffers from chronic land degradation, Tanzania has enjoyed relatively extensive timber plantations with the limiting economic factor being timber-processing capacity. In terms of energy, only the Moldovan central government has accorded priority status to renewable energy development, whereas the Tanzanian and, to a lesser extent, Ugandan central governments have been generally less interested in decentralized renewables and focused on developing large-scale hydroelectric and fossil fuel resources.

Recall that in Chapter 7's analysis of development policy paradigms across the case-study countries, I was able to demonstrate that in Uganda and Moldova the state retained state agencies in the forest sector while reserving itself a largely regulatory role in the energy sector. Indeed, both Uganda and Moldova had privatized most major assets for energy generation and distribution during the 1990s and into the mid-2000s. I attributed different responses to liberal economic reforms in the forest and energy sectors to a liberal neodevelopmental policy paradigm. The state has pursued a comparative advantage following development strategy, perceiving the state apparatus to have capacity to be competitive in the forestry sector but not in the more capital-intensive and complex energy sector. This explains the modicum of organizational capacity that state forest agencies retained in Uganda and Moldova, while the state largely privatized the energy sectors of each country at the time the CDM projects considered were being implemented.

As elaborated upon in more detail in Chapter 7, liberal economic reforms in Uganda have allowed the state to retain an active, though limited, role for afforestation in the form of a state agency, the NFA. The existence of such a "pocket of effectiveness" contrasts with the situation in Uganda's energy sector, where the state privatized almost all major energy assets. Indeed, in Uganda's energy sector, especially during the period corresponding to my investigation into the CDM from 2009 to 2014, the state had largely divested itself of any real capacity to directly implement projects in the energy sector. This selective deployment of state organizational capacity is one of the key characteristics of a liberal neodevelopmental policy paradigm. Under neoliberalism one would not expect the state to retain organizational capacity for policy implementation in any sector and instead defer to markets, while both classic developmentalism and neodevelopmentalism anticipate the state endeavoring to be active in all. In contrast, liberal neodevelopmentalism suggests that states will undertake an assessment of where they possess comparative advantage and might deploy limited state organizational capacities accordingly.

Turning to Moldova, I found that the central government retained an important role for itself in the forest sector at the time of my CDM investigation through Moldsilva despite embracing many elements of liberal economic reforms. Similar to Uganda, the state forest agency was found to be an effective CDM project developer. The main difference between Moldsilva and Uganda's NFA appears to be in terms of state organizational capacity. While Moldsilva would use climate finance to plant 39,000 ha of forest across the country, the CDM afforestation project in Uganda would total only approximately 2,000 ha. Despite the difference in the scale of operations, the underlying causal mechanism for climate finance effectiveness in the two countries is similar.

If state development interests alone were sufficient for effective CDM implementation, I should have observed the CDM rural energy modernization project in Moldova to also have been highly additional. Instead, this project highlights the importance of the convergence of state interests and ideas. While renewable energy was clearly also a state development interest in Moldova, as it reduced dependency on Russian natural gas, the CDM project that I investigated in this sector was highly ineffective. While the Moldova Carbon Finance Unit was responsible for project implementation, due to its low capacity it was unable to do so effectively. Indeed, the project was the most ineffective CDM project that I investigated, where I evaluated nearly no carbon credits generated to be genuine. However, no other state organization in the energy sector in Moldova retained sufficient capacity for CDM project implementation at the time as liberal economic reforms had seen the near complete privatization of the sector, in contrast to the forest sector where the state retained the state forest agency Moldsilva. And while at least one government-donor program was involved in renewable energy provision at the time, SIF2, it was uninterested in CDM financing given sufficient donor financing.

While decentralized renewable energy in Uganda was not a state development priority, it shared with Moldova the vast privatization of the energy sector in the late 1990s and early 2000s. Instead, I observed a CDM biomass cogeneration project to be implemented rather ineffectively by the private sector. In Uganda and Moldova there were simply few state organizations that had capacity for implementation of CDM projects in the energy sector during the first commitment period of the Kyoto Protocol.

In contrast, in my review of Tanzania's development policy paradigm in Chapter 7, I demonstrated how the Tanzanian state has striven to remain more directly involved in both the forest and energy sectors and has resisted neoliberal economic reforms; the Tanzanian central government was not directly involved with implementation of any CDM project. While this might be attributed to my assessment that neither the forest sector nor decentralized renewable energy were priority state development interests, the way that liberal economic reforms had been adopted in Tanzania differed from Uganda and Moldova. No state agency was found in either sector during 2009 fieldwork, though Tanzania would grudgingly establish a state forest agency, the Tanzanian Forest Service (TFS), in 2010.

Rather, the most important player in the forest sector at the time of my CDM fieldwork was the FBD, which was responsible for government forest reserves and state-owned industrial forest plantations—including Sao Hill plantations adjacent to the private-sector-led CDM project that I investigated. But at least at low carbon prices, the private sector was not found to be a highly effective climate finance partner. As for the TFS, the available evidence suggests that it has not demonstrated management improvements over its predecessor. Notably, in contrast to state forest agencies in Uganda and Moldova, the TFS has demonstrated little interest in climate finance.

Similarly, in the energy sector, Tanzania has retained a key strategic position through a parastatal (TANESCO) that also appeared uninterested in exploring opportunities with the CDM nor, as we shall later see, NAMAs. The energy policies pursued by President Kikwete and, more stridently, President Magufuli attest to a genuine interest in realizing the potential of domestic hydroelectric, gas, and coal resources; however, the particular form they have embodied—centered on state-owned enterprises with capacity for power generation, transmission, and distribution—is reflective of a particular set of ideas that have emphasized developmental approaches to economic development and been skeptical of neoliberalism. Permeated by a hybrid policy paradigm aspiring toward neodevelopmentalism though still influenced by classic developmentalism, the Tanzanian state was directly involved in both the forest and energy sectors, but organizations of the state apparatus were not instilled with a combination of development and business interests for treating the CDM as a genuine opportunity for developing either.

Overall, my findings lead to the conclusion that the CDM has been most effective in those states adhering to a liberal neodevelopmental policy paradigm where the state has created organizations with capacity for CDM projects but also a combination of business and development interests to harness the climate finance instrument toward the pursuit of state development interests. In other words, the convergence of state ideas and interests can produce different types of state organizational capacity, certain forms of which are predisposed to more effectively engage with the CDM. Indeed, my results suggest that development policy paradigms are important in shaping not just the sectors where limited state organizational capacity is allocated but also the form that state organizational capacity takes.

Among the case-study countries, conditions for effective engagement with the CDM were found in Uganda and Moldova, resulting in highly effective CDM projects being implemented in countries with considerably different levels of state organizational capacity. In areas where the state perceives itself to be competitive in the market, liberal neodevelopmental states tend to establish and confer, albeit limited, capabilities to state organizations that embody a combination of developmental and business interests. But under such a development policy paradigm, the state might be expected to be more prudent about where it allocates limited state capacities, which helps explain that effective CDM projects were found in the forest sectors of both countries and not in the energy sector—especially striking in Moldova as renewable energy was clearly one of its state development interests. In states adhering to more developmental policy paradigm, such as Tanzania, a comparably capable state apparatus is not imbued with the same combination of interests, resulting in the state not engaging with this climate finance instrument.

My emphasis on the state is not to ignore the important efforts that NGOs and the private sector have made in implementing the CDM. However, at low carbon prices, where the carbon finance layer is unlikely to be convincing in shaping business decision-making, such nonstate actors have struggled to implement highly additional and financially sustainable CDM projects.

In bringing this section to a close, I note that the conclusions drawn here are based on a small sample of seven carbon offset projects, they are supported by evaluation of how the CDM was coordinated within the state apparatus in each of the case-study countries, which is the focus of the next section.

8.7. State Coordination of the CDM

The above interpretation distinguishing Uganda and Moldova from Tanzania in terms of development policy paradigms is further supported by investigation of the relationship between the CDM's Designated National Authority (DNA) and the rest of the state apparatus. Recall that, influenced by global norms of liberal environmentalism, the UNFCCC originally accorded the governments of countries hosting CDM projects very limited authority in the form of a DNA. While the role of the DNA has since expanded, its primary function in 2009 was limited to providing Letters of Approval for individual CDM projects on the grounds of their contribution to sustainable development (see Olhoff et al., 2004). Many countries also produced a list of criteria for assessing sustainable development in the initial CDM approval process (Tewari, 2012), including Tanzania and

Uganda (see Appendix 2, Boxes A.1 and A.2). In contrast to the two East African countries, the Moldovan DNA had not established any such criteria. However, it was explained during 2009 interviews that the CDM project should conform to development priorities indicated in Moldova's National Development Strategy 2008–2011.[29]

In the rest of this section, I demonstrate that the CDM was most tightly interwoven with other parts of the state apparatus, particularly state investment agencies, in Uganda and, to a lesser degree, in Moldova. This supports arguments about liberal neodevelopmentalism. In contrast, close inspection of the DNA in Tanzania finds a lack of coordination if not evidence of political infighting.

Uganda's CDM Administration

I begin with Uganda where the DNA was initially housed at the Ministry of Water and Environment (MWE) with a Secretariat known as the Climate Change Unit (CCU). While physically located within the Department of Meteorology, it was explained to me that the Climate Change Unit was akin to a division directly under the permanent secretary of the Ministry of Water and Environment and therefore granted a certain degree of autonomy.[30]

Interviews with project developers and members of the Uganda bureaucracy suggested strong coordination between the DNA and the rest of the government. To begin with, the Ugandan DNA was favorable to carbon markets. As the head of the Climate Change Unit explained to me during a 2009 interview, "we feel that the country could tap some opportunities in either the voluntary carbon markets or regulated carbon markets, including the complicated CDM."[31] This was matched by the Uganda Investment Agency that actively cooperated with the DNA to promote CDM projects. For example, the Uganda Investment Agency even maintained a list of CDM projects available for investment on its website (UIA, 2011b). The Uganda Investment Agency was established under the 2000 Investment Code Act to be a "one-stop shop" allowing investors to register, obtain investment license, and secure necessary secondary clearances (UIA, 2009: 8). The sustainable development criteria of the DNA also complimented the Uganda Investment Agency's investment criteria—including more detailed social criteria for evaluation and additional economic ones (see Appendix 2, Box A.1).

Moldova's CDM Administration

Moldova's DNA was an interdepartmental authority headed by the Ministry of Environment and Natural Resources known as the National Commission for the

Implementation of the UN Climate Change Convention and the Kyoto Protocol (hereafter "National Commission"). Comprised of 18 members from various ministries, NGOs, and the private sector,[32] the National Commission appointed two experts to undertake a technical evaluation of any CDM project submitted.[33]

The DNA's relationship with Moldova's equivalent to an investment promotion agency was more tepid than what was observed in Uganda. A nonprofit agency under the Ministry of Economy established in 1999, the Moldovan Investment and Export Promotion Organization (MIEPO) appeared to aspire to a full investment facilitation organization like in Uganda but lacked fundamental powers to issue business licenses and incentives (Republic of Moldova, 1999: s. 6–7). In 2009, I observed little direct relationship between the Moldovan DNA and MIEPO, which suggested that CDM financing was not perceived as a serious investment opportunity in 2009. However, neither was the Moldovan DNA blocking CDM projects, which appeared to be the case in Tanzania.

Tanzania's CDM Administration

The situation in Tanzania contrasted with what was observed in Uganda and Moldova, conforming with expectations of a development policy paradigm more skeptical of neoliberalism but also Tanzania's weak dominant party political settlement. In 2009, the Tanzanian DNA was housed at the Division of Environment at the Vice President's Office (DoE-VPO). The Vice President's Office's (VPO) mission included "coordinating environmental management for the improvement of the welfare of Tanzanians" (VPO, 2010b). However, the Division of Environment (DoE) was itself first established in 1991 under MNRT and only transferred to the VPO in 1995 in order "to give high priority to the environmental agenda" (VPO, 2010a).

Some observers have argued that the Division of Environment's move to the VPO offered it "strategic functions" for effective interministerial cooperation and coordination (Pallangyo, 2007). However, closer inspection revealed unclear lines of authority surrounding the DNA. Indeed, there remains ambiguity over the legal status of the Division of Environment. The 2004 Environmental Management Act (s. 16), the most important legislation in Tanzania's environmental sector, does not make any reference to a *Division* of Environment but only a *Director* of Environment (s. 14). The *Director* of Environment is to "coordinate various environment management activities . . . and promote the integration of environment considerations into development policies . . . and undertake strategic environmental assessment" and "advise the Government on . . . the implementation of relevant international agreements in the field of environment" (2004 EMA: s. 15(a)&(b)).

More disconcerting, and in stark contrast to the situation in Uganda, the Tanzanian DNA appeared at odds with the country's investment promotion agency, the Tanzania Investment Center. Established under the 1997 Investment Act, the objective of the Tanzania Investment Center has been "to co-ordinate, encourage, promote and facilitate investment in Tanzania and to advise the Government on investment policy and related matters" (Investment Act: s. 5). The Tanzania Investment Center has been vested with important powers for coordination and authority to grant positive incentives to foreign investors.[34] Similar to its Ugandan counterpart, one of the Tanzania Investment Center's primary activities has been to screen investment projects to ensure they meet Tanzania's development objectives (TIC, 2008: 45–50). But the policies of the Tanzania Investment Center did not appear well coordinated with the DNA.

For example, consider the screening criteria of the DNA and Tanzania Investment Center (see Appendix 2, Box A.2). The DNA's criteria require that a project conform to Tanzania's National Strategy for Reduction of Poverty and Vision 2025 but give few concrete criteria for its measurement. Other DNA criteria overlap with that of the Tanzania Investment Center. For example, the DNA criteria for technology transfer overlaps with the Tanzania Investment Center's, though with the additional request that the technology be "environmentally benign"—a term that remains undefined. Two of the DNA's criteria stand out: energy projects in rural areas are accorded the highest priority, while the DNA requested that afforestation/reforestation projects be undertaken in semi-arid and arid areas—quite the contrast to the relatively humid Mufindi district where the CDM project that I investigated was located. Overall, the CDM screening criteria accord the DNA considerable discretion and were not well coordinated with those for foreign investment.

There is also evidence that the Tanzania CDM regulatory authority sought to delay if not obstruct the few CDM projects being implemented. Perhaps the most vehement critique came from an individual in the donor community. As he explained, "[The DNA] is not only the bottleneck, but I mean, [the DNA's] the cork in the bottleneck. Seriously. And we seriously don't understand why that is. We cannot find out."[35] This was corroborated by other interviews at the time. One CDM project developer frankly stated: "[The DNA is] not cooperative."[36] Interviews with the Rural Energy Agency in 2009 revealed an interest in tapping the CDM as a new source of financing. However, the Tanzanian DNA proved unreceptive:

We went to the DNA's office, and we asked for us to work together. Because we are all government agencies, we can just work with them and see how we can push up these projects together. But I don't know if this works out . . . everyone has been disappointed by the [DNA at the] Vice President's Office.[37]

The Rural Energy Agency subsequently initiated a CDM program of activities titled Tanzania Renewable Energy Programme (CDM-SSC-PoA-DD, 2011), which was approved by the DoE-VPO in 2012. However, as has already been established, the CDM carbon market has largely collapsed since 2012, and most funding for this program has been sourced from the World Bank's Energy Small and Medium Enterprises Trust Fund (World Bank, 2018b).

Respondents in Tanzania offered many explanations for the CDM authority's lack of cooperation. First was overlap between its responsibilities for the CDM and international climate change negotiations. [38] Another reason might have been that the country's climate change priority has been adaptation and not mitigation.[39] A third possible explanation was skepticism about foreign investment at the DNA. As one informant explained: "The priority [for the DNA was] environment and that was it. Forget investment. [They] never saw that. And if you talk to them now, CDM is more or less about climate. Policymakers don't see it from an investment angle."[40]

What remains unexplained is why the Tanzanian DNA was able to impede foreign investment projects into climate change mitigation though the government had also established a strong investment promotion agency. Part of the reason might be attributed to Tanzania's political settlement, which is characterized by weak dominant party control of the state apparatus. Under such conditions, it is difficult to assure the sharing of information between different parts of the state apparatus. This resonates with a statement made by a Tanzania expert interviewed: "[the DNA] tend to keep [the CDM] their private show . . . that's where the real constraint comes and that's why [agencies such as Tanzania Investment Center are] not in the process."[41] But another question is, why would such infighting be tolerated by those in higher positions of authority? A hybrid development policy paradigm of classic developmentalism and neodevelopmentalism helps explain why poor governance of the CDM by the DoE-VPO was tolerated.

8.8. Conclusion

In this chapter I have demonstrated that there has been variation in the effectiveness of carbon offset projects implemented in Tanzania, Uganda, and Moldova. (See summary of carbon offset projects in Table 8.1 and summary findings in Table 8.8.) This is important given the tendency of many observers to make sweeping claims about the effectiveness (and ineffectiveness) of the CDM and similar carbon offset projects. Based on my empirical analysis, I have also offered a typology of project developers that attributes variation in project effectiveness to the interests and capacities of project developers involved.

Table 8.8 Summary Findings of CDM Additionality and State Strategic Coordination in Tanzania, Uganda, and Moldova

Sector	Tanzania		Uganda		Moldova	
	Forest	Energy	Forest	Energy	Forest	Energy
1. Project additionality	Project implemented by private sector less effective	Project implemented by NGO appeared additional but overly dependent on climate finance (project collapsed)	Project implemented by state forest agency highly effective; project implemented by NGO appeared additional but overly dependent on climate finance	Project implemented by private sector less effective	Project implemented by state forest agency highly effective	Project implemented by specialized government unit less effective
2. State coordination	Reports of uncooperative DNA, including accusations of blocking projects; CDM not well coordinated with investment promotion		DNA appeared cooperative; CDM tightly coordinated with investment promotion agency		DNA appeared cooperative; CDM not explicitly coordinated with investment promotion agency	

Overall, findings suggest the following causal mechanism at least at carbon prices obtained during the first commitment period of the Kyoto Protocol: carbon offset projects have been most effective when clearly aligned with state development interests and which the state treats as a genuine development opportunity as the result of having created organizations—state agencies—that retain at least minimal capacity for project implementation and harbor a unique combination of business and development interests. The establishment of such state agencies, however, was only observed in states demonstrating a liberal neodevelopmental policy paradigm and in sectors where the evidence suggests the state still perceives itself to have a comparative economic advantage vis-à-vis other policy actors. The convergence of state ideas and interests in states adhering to liberal neodevelopmentalism leads to a form of state organizational capacity that is predisposed to engaging effectively with the CDM. Furthermore, in support of arguments about variation in development policy paradigms across the case-study countries, this chapter has also included analysis of the relationship between the CDM and the rest of the state apparatus that supports my identification of liberal neodevelopmentalism in Uganda and Moldova and a hybrid development policy paradigm of classic developmentalism and neodevelopmentalism in Tanzania.

Given how low carbon prices that project developers had access to were during the first commitment period of the Kyoto Protocol, the conditions I observed for highly effective CDM projects might be expected to change under higher carbon prices currently observed on major carbon markets in North America and Europe. I return to these issues in this book's Conclusion. For the moment, I close this chapter by foreshadowing that the causal mechanism relating state ideas and interests to the form of state organizational capacity generated across the case-study countries also helps explain the implementation of REDD+ and programming of NAMAs, which are addressed in the next two chapters.

9

Explaining REDD+ Effectiveness

9.1. Introduction

Does the causal mechanism underpinning CDM effectiveness observed in the previous chapter carry over into the first of the new climate finance mechanisms under developmental environmentalism, REDD+? Recalling the different stages of policy effectiveness, presented in the Introduction, I consider effectiveness here in terms of REDD+ implementation including type of donor engaged and level of donor support received, the rigor of climate finance evaluation frameworks adopted as well as the character of the state's coordination of the climate finance instrument. I note that with limited forest cover, the government of Moldova has focused on afforestation/reforestation and has not been involved in REDD+. Instead, as I show in the next chapter, Moldova has sought to implement additional afforestation projects akin to its successful CDM projects as a NAMA.

Based on Tanzania's skepticism of neoliberalism, as demonstrated in our review of its development policy paradigm in Chapter 4, it might have been assumed that REDD+—with its more developmental underpinnings—would have been more effectively implemented in the country than the CDM. However, my results suggest that the Tanzanian central government never treated REDD+ as a genuine development opportunity—despite a major effort by the international community to promote it in the country. While Tanzania would receive a staggering $86 million over 2008–2018, Uganda saw only approximately $10 million (Table 9.1).

Given the poor performance with the CDM in Tanzania, I was initially surprised by the amount of donor attention the country was attracting. Furthermore, as demonstrated in Chapter 6, the Tanzanian central government has had very limited interest in the forest sector—at least until 2016. Yet by 2014 Tanzania had completed significant REDD+ milestones, including adopting a National Strategy for REDD+, and appeared poised for implementation and result-based payments.[1] However, problems would subsequently emerge, and donor support began to dry up. By 2018, Norway had effectively withdrawn from its REDD+ engagement in Tanzania.[2] In the words of one close observer of Norway's experience with REDD+ in Tanzania, whom I interviewed in 2018, it had all become a "sad story."[3]

The Political Economy of Climate Finance Effectiveness in Developing Countries. Mark Purdon, Oxford University Press.
© Oxford University Press 2024. DOI: 10.1093/oso/9780197756836.003.0009

Table 9.1 Estimated REDD+ Finance in Tanzania and Uganda, 2008–2018

	Bilateral	Multilateral	Total
TANZANIA			
World Bank Forest Carbon Partnership Facility (WB-FCPF)		$3.8*	$3.8
Germany's International Climate Initiative	$3.2		$3.2
Norway's International Climate and Forest Initiative (NICFI)	$68.6		$68.6
FAO and Finland		$6.0	$2.0
UN-REDD Program		$4.3	$4.3
Total	**$71.8**	**$14.1**	**$81.9**
UGANDA			
World Bank Forest Carbon Partnership Facility (WB-FCPF)		$7.6	$7.6
UN-REDD Program		$1.8	$1.8
Norway's International Climate and Forest Initiative (NICFI)	$0.2		$0.2
Austria Development Agency	$0.7		$0.7
Total	**$0.9**	**$9.4**	**$10.3**

Sources: ClimateFundsUpdate.Org (2015); MWE (2017a); NORAD (2014b: 309) as well as other sources discussed in the text.

* Reported by ClimateFundsUpdate.Org (2015) but no grant funding requested by Tanzanian government (NORAD, 2014b: 308; WB-FCFP, 2014).

The withdrawal of Norway and other donors from REDD+ in Tanzania was based on the perception that Tanzania was not implementing REDD+ effectively. My analysis suggests that this was because the forest sector—especially forest conservation and fuelwood—has not been a prominent state development interest, while Tanzania's development policy paradigm would lead the central government to pursue REDD+ in a way that would not convince donors that REDD+ efforts would lead to emission reductions.

The Tanzanian central government opted for the development of the relatively less rigorous capacity-building program offered through UN-REDD while also increasingly voicing a preference for fund-based approaches associated with softer evaluation frameworks. Tanzania's REDD+ efforts have also been marked by feuding between the Division of Environment at the Vice President's Office (DoE-VPO) and other, more capable government bodies such as the Forest and Beekeeping Division (FBD) of the Ministry of National Resources and Tourism (MNRT). The inability of state apparatus to strategically coordinate REDD+, I submit, reflects Tanzania's development policy paradigm as well as its political settlement. While classic developmentalism and, to a lesser degree, neodevelopmentalism would legitimize a strong centralized role for the state in policy implementation, REDD+ implementation has been frustrated by the weak dominant party political settlement in Tanzania. This all transpired as the Norwegian government pumped in millions of dollars to build REDD+ capacity, albeit mostly into nonstate actors in an effort to avoid government mismanagement.

In contrast, in Uganda, with forests a scarce resource and a development policy paradigm of liberal neodevelopmentalism, I found the central government to be taking constructive steps toward implementing a strategic and comprehensive REDD+ program. Despite receiving considerably less funding for REDD+ implementation, Uganda would surpass Tanzania in terms of the rollout of REDD+ institutions. During my fieldwork in 2018, it was evident that donor interest in Uganda had been picking-up and there was a palpable feeling that the effective implementation of REDD+ in Uganda was a real possibility—despite the fact that Uganda's REDD+ potential in terms of emission reductions is considerably less than in Tanzania. Relative to Tanzania, Uganda has steadfastly partnered with the World Bank Forest Carbon Partnership Facility (WB-FCPF), demonstrating a willingness to pursue a more rigorous evaluation framework that might lend itself to a future carbon market for REDD+ while still professing agnosticism on the market-fund debate. Finally, Uganda has developed a more bottom-up approach to coordinating REDD+ that allows different stakeholders to play to their respective strengths and is being implemented in manner that is integrated in the country's national development planning process. Overall, the Ugandan central government has appeared willing to submit to an administrative process that is capable of demonstrating to Western donors that their funds have been used effectively.

In the rest of this chapter, I first review patterns of donor support for REDD+ in Tanzania and Uganda before moving to an analysis of the evaluation framework for REDD+ being pursued in each country, and, finally, concluding with an analysis of the coordination of REDD+ across the state apparatus. I explain each of these implementation outcomes in terms of political economy factors of political settlements, state development interests, and development policy paradigms.

9.2. Donor Support for REDD+ in Tanzania

With relatively large tracks of forested areas, Tanzania has been one of the largest beneficiaries of REDD+ finance in the world, along with Brazil, Indonesia, and Peru (Sunderlin et al., 2015: 3). By far the most important supporter of REDD+ in Tanzania has been Norway. Through Norway's International Climate and Forest Initiative (NICFI), Norway invested at least $68.6 million over 2008–2018 (NCMC, 2015, 2016; NORAD, 2014b: 309).[4] Since NICIF has been designed to support various multilateral initiatives, Tanzania has been able to use Norwegian funding to pursue engagement with UN-REDD, which is more in alignment with its development policy paradigm given the weak affinity between UN-REDD and the expectations of a potential carbon market.

One reason for Norway's support was hope that Tanzania might demonstrate the feasibility of REDD+ in miombo, dryland forests that predominate in sub-Saharan Africa (Jodoin, 2017). Norway's support also stemmed from a long-established affinity for Tanzania given the social democratic values reflected in Nyerere's policies (Edwards, 2014: 32–53; 81–88).[5] However, perhaps cognizant of Tanzania's weak dominant party political settlement, NICFI funding was largely directed toward nonstate actors. NICFI's strategy in this regard has been consistent with transnational climate governance.

Among the first activities Norway supported was the establishment in 2008 of the National REDD+ Taskforce. It was headed by the Division of Environment at the Vice President's Office (DoE-VPO), though its Secretariat was initially located at the University of Dar es Salaam's Institute for Resource Assessment.[6] By August 2009, the DoE-VPO had prepared the National Framework for REDD+ (VPO, 2009). With an additional $4.3 million received from UN-REDD, the Taskforce was able to produce a National Program Document in November 2009. The National Program Document is a key initial element of UN-REDD. It is intended to provide an overview of the deforestation challenges in a country and propose a program for tackling it. Significantly, this first policy output of the UN-REDD process was signed by the permanent secretary of the MNRT and not DoE-VPO (UN-REDD, 2009b). Later I discuss tensions between DoE-VPO and MNRT over REDD+.

Tanzania was also involved in the WB-FCPF process at the same time. Interestingly, the Tanzanian central government reportedly declined $3.8 million in financial support from the World Bank to prepare a Readiness Preparation Proposal, using Norwegian funding instead to produce it (NORAD, 2014b: 308; WB-FCFP, 2014). Submitted in 2010, the Readiness Preparation Proposal represented the high-water mark of Tanzania's engagement with the WB-FCPF process. At the time of completing this manuscript, in late 2023,

Tanzania appeared to still not have submitted its Readiness Package for World Bank endorsement, the last step before being eligible for the Carbon Fund (WB-FCPF, 2022: 20–21). I detail the contents of the UN-REDD National Program Document and WB-FCPF Readiness Preparation Proposal in greater detail below.

By 2013 the National REDD+ Taskforce had produced a National Strategy for REDD+ along with an Action Plan (VPO, 2013a)—absorbing $7.3 million of REDD+ financing (NORAD, 2014b: 309).[7] This was a considerable achievement as few countries had yet produced a national REDD+ strategy. Indeed, Uganda would take four more years to produce one. With these strategic documents completed, the REDD+ Secretariat was physically relocated to the DoE-VPO, which had, by that time, consolidated its authority over REDD+.[8]

A significant amount of Norwegian REDD+ financing was accorded not to the central government but to universities and NGOs. This included three research programs. The first initiative was known as the Climate Change Impact, Adaptation, Mitigation (CCIAM) research program, a second supported the development of a remote-sensing system (often referred as the LIDAR project), and the third funded a new forest inventory in Zanzibar (NORAD, 2014b: 309). In addition, Norway contributed approximately $5.5 million to the establishment of the National Carbon Monitoring Center (NCMC) to coordinate its REDD+ evaluation framework (NCMC, 2015; 2016).[9] The NCMC was initially conceived as an independent state agency to be housed at Sokoine University (NORAD, 2014b: 310; SUA, 2013).[10] However, critics pointed out that the National Strategy for RDD+ did not mention such an agency, and there were concerns it would become a burden if international REDD+ finance failed to materialize.[11] In any case, the process was abruptly brought to a halt by high-level intervention.[12] In early 2014, the NCMC was established as a center, not as a state agency, under the authority of the DoE-VPO.[13]

From 2009 to 2015, Norway also funded nine REDD+ pilot projects, at a total cost of nearly $30 million (NORAD, 2014b: 309; TNRF, 2011).[14] The projects were chosen from a pool of 46 proposals through a competitive process led jointly by the Norwegian Embassy and the National REDD+ Taskforce (Jodoin, 2017: 159–160). They were selected with the goal of focusing on different technical elements including benefit sharing, REDD+ baselines, different approaches to evaluation frameworks, and REDD+ drivers (VPO, 2013b: 6). Almost all the projects sought to tap climate finance through the voluntary carbon markets, notably through the Verified Carbon Standard (VCS).

Though I was unable to visit the REDD+ pilot projects in the field, existing research indicates that most collapsed when Norwegian funding for them expired (Sunderlin et al., 2015: 6). A 2015 review prepared for the Norwegian Embassy found that project developers had vastly underestimated the costs and complexity of entering the voluntary carbon market (Mäkelä et al., 2015). To the best of my knowledge, only two of these REDD+ projects have been successful in submitting the required documentation to VCS, and only one has been implemented and generating a modest amount of carbon credits.[15] Interestingly, these REDD+ projects on the voluntary carbon market have also been subject of recent research that raises questions about the validity of the emission reductions claimed (West et al., 2023). Overall, there are few who have been satisfied with Tanzania's experience with REDD+ pilot projects. In an important critique, Sunderlin et al. (2015) present them as evidence of the failures of transnational climate governance (pp. 9–10).

Overall, there is a striking pattern to Norway's support for REDD+ in Tanzania. Characterized by a skepticism of the Tanzanian government, Norwegian funding was largely directed toward nonstate actors including NGOs and universities. In some ways this approach was justified—as I discuss below, the DoE-VPO struggled with implementing REDD+. But over the long term, Norway's unwillingness to directly support the Tanzanian government undermined REDD+ implementation. As NORAD reported in a midterm review of Norway's REDD+ efforts:

> The decision to channel most funds via non-governmental channels was understandable but has made securing national ownership of REDD+ more challenging. . . . Government respondents also agreed that the process had initially been driven by NICFI funds and the UN agencies. Government stakeholders highlighted the fact that funds had by-passed Tanzania institutions and this was a reason for lower government ownership. (NORAD, 2014b: 312, 316)

However, the reference to "government ownership" of the REDD+ process in the quote above arguably papers over internal divisions within the Tanzanian government regarding REDD+, which I discuss later in this chapter.

Finally, significant donor resources were also directed to building Tanzania's forest-monitoring capacities. With in-kind contributions from the Food and Agriculture Organization (FAO) and Tanzania Forest Service (TFS), Finland agreed to sponsor the National Forest Resources Monitoring and Assessment (NAFORMA) project, discussed in Chapter 6 on Tanzania's state development interests. Originally conceived in 2007 as a national forest inventory exercise in partnership with FBD, the project was reoriented in 2009 toward REDD+ and its emerging evaluation framework (Alegria et al., 2011: 4). As discussed in Chapter 6, NAFORMA's results for mainland Tanzania were released in 2015, providing estimates of forest carbon stocks and hence facilitating the calculation of emissions associated with deforestation. Significantly, however, data collected under the NAFORMA project is retained by TFS and not NCMC mentioned above.[16]

9.3. Evolution of Tanzania's Evaluation Framework for REDD+

Though the Tanzania government initially appeared open to a carbon market and the more rigorous evaluation framework that this would require, the country has come to adopt a softer approach that has de-emphasized REDD+ drivers. Though Tanzania submitted a first REDD+ baseline to the UNFCCC in late 2016 and a revised one in 2017, in practice there have been few signs that the country is developing much more than a national forest inventory to monitor forest carbon with little concrete strategy for measuring the effect of policy interventions. In particular, the lack of attention to REDD+ drivers frustrates the formulation of policy interventions that can convincingly claim to halt deforestation and forest degradation.

When Tanzania initially embarked on REDD+, it did so in anticipation of a global carbon market. This is apparent in the 2009 National Framework for REDD+, which had an entire section entitled "Forest Carbon Trading Mechanisms" (VPO, 2009: 3). The National Framework for REDD+ also provided considerable discussion of REDD+ baselines and related elements of a robust evaluation system—including an initial list of 13 drivers of deforestation (pp. 7–9). Similarly, the initial National Program Document prepared for UN-REDD in 2009 clearly anticipated the generation of REDD+ carbon credits through a carbon market. Released just prior to the UN climate change talks in Copenhagen, vestiges of liberal environmentalism are clearly discernible in it. For example, in detailed discussion of what is referred to as a "National REDD Production Chain," the National Program Document asserted that it would be necessary to have in place "a transparent, robust, equitable and reliable delivery of carbon credits from REDD" (UN-REDD, 2009a: 29). The National Program Document is replete with language expressing deference to markets that is uncharacteristic of thinking about development in Tanzania, which I discussed in Chapter 7.

Deference to carbon markets was matched by acknowledgement of the need for a robust REDD+ baseline demonstration and attention to information on drivers. In terms of the former, the National Program Document states:

> A key part of the monitoring will be to develop an assessment of [the REDD+ emission baseline] for Tanzania. Work to develop the [REDD+ baseline] will involve a combination of remote sensing, ground truthing and local level

resource assessments. Capacity will also be required at the national level to assess specific forest areas under REDD that need to be monitored and the result reported upon. (UN-REDD, 2009a: 24)

As for drivers, the National Program Document asserted that "it is likely that past, present and future trends in forest loss can be modelled as a function of population expansion, soils, rainfall, existing agriculture, and accessibility" (UN-REDD, 2009a: 26). It identified four root causes of deforestation and degradation in Tanzania that lead to the development of measurable REDD+ drivers: smallholder agricultural expansion, energy needs, plantation development, and building materials. There is even brief mention of REDD+ cost curves that would plot abatement costs against abatement potential for different land uses "including deforestation drivers" (UN-REDD, 2009a: 46). However, there is little discussion about how to actually collect data on drivers in the National Program Document.

Relative to the UNFCCC and UN-REDD processes, Tanzania's 2010 Readiness Preparation Proposal prepared for the WB-FCPF process reveals considerably more technical sophistication. First, the Readiness Preparation Proposal identified a larger number of drivers than in the UN-REDD's National Program Document (United Republic of Tanzania, 2010b: 23). Second, and more significantly, the Readiness Preparation Proposal also identified a number of "REDD+ Strategic Options" that might plausibly be deployed in order to address each of the REDD+ drivers. Drivers and strategic options are themselves discussed in considerably greater detail in an annex to the Readiness Preparation Proposal, including a proposal for a detailed study of drivers (United Republic of Tanzania, 2010b: annex 2a.2). To the best of my knowledge, this study has not yet been produced. Third, the development of Tanzania's REDD+ baseline is discussed in a more rigorous, data-driven manner:

> In developing a reference scenario, we have planned to attempt to model how the drivers of deforestation and forest degradation (markets, policies, infrastructure) could change over time to produce a set or array of different emission scenarios. (United Republic of Tanzania, 2010a)

The contrast between Tanzania's involvement in the UN-REDD and WB-FCPF processes is also apparent when comparing their budget outlays (UN-REDD, 2009a: 38–42; United Republic of Tanzania, 2010b: 67–69). The budget for the UN-REDD's National Program Document was considerably smaller than the Readiness Preparation Proposal, $4 million versus $9 million, and its activities focused predominantly on elements of a REDD+ institutional framework. In the Readiness Preparation Proposal, the proposed budget for technical matters such as development of a REDD+ baseline, design of a monitoring system, as well as specific efforts to collect information on drivers alone stood at approximately $3.5 million. Furthermore, the Readiness Preparation Proposal was anchored by a Program Monitoring & Evaluation Framework—a component lacking in the UN-REDD process.

However, as mentioned earlier, the Readiness Preparation Proposal produced for the WB-FCPF in 2010 would be the high-water mark of Tanzania's active participation in this initiative of the World Bank. With publication of its National REDD+ Strategy in 2013, much of the rigor and emphasis on data in the World Bank's Readiness Preparation Proposal gave way to the less-demanding UN-REDD process that Tanzania was also pursuing, which I discuss in more detail below.

The key inflection point in the gradual watering down of Tanzania's evaluation framework for REDD+ was the 2009 UN climate change conference in Copenhagen, where the global climate governance complex would shift from liberal environmentalism to developmental environmentalism. The Tanzanian central government appeared to welcome the new emphasis on fund-based approaches. For example, while the 2009 National Framework spoke favorably of carbon markets, the 2013 National REDD+ Strategy would seek to position Tanzania strategically vis-à-vis the new climate funds that had emerged after Copenhagen, including recognizing a potential "new financial stream" for REDD+ (VPO, 2013b: 17). Most explicitly, the Tanzania government clearly voiced a preference for funds-based approaches:

> The government of Tanzania considers the REDD+ policy a viable option for providing opportunities for the country to meet its obligations of managing her forests and woodlands on a sustainable basis and at the same time responding to poverty reduction initiatives accordingly. *In this regard, the government is envisaging Tanzania's participation in the REDD+ policy and in its development under fund-based financing arrangements.* However, the on-going global processes through UNFCCC will inform the appropriate financing mechanism. (VPO, 2013b: 17, emphasis added)

In terms of drivers, the 2013 National REDD+ Strategy would largely reflect those identified in the WB-FCPF's Readiness Preparation Proposal. However, neither the National REDD+ Strategy nor its Action Plan discusses the status of available data on drivers nor a plan to acquire them.

The last major REDD+ policy document prepared by the Tanzanian government was the country's official REDD+ baseline submitted to the UNFCCC. As per guidance set out in the Warsaw Framework for REDD+ negotiated at the 2013 UN climate change conference, discussed in Chapter 3. This was initially submitted to the UNFCCC for review in late 2016 and then resubmitted in 2017 (United Republic of Tanzania, 2016, 2017). One immediate concern with the REDD+ baseline is that the estimate of Tanzania's forest cover significantly exceeds previous studies. The size of Tanzania's forests were estimated to be 48.2 million ha in the REDD+ baseline submission made to the UNFCCC (United Republic of Tanzania, 2016: 6, 2017), though Tanzania's forests have generally reported at around 33–35 million ha, as indicated in Chapter 6 (FAO, 2007b; MNRT, 1998: 8). Similar concerns arise from estimations of deforestation rates. Deforestation rates for mainland Tanzania were estimated at 589,000 ha/year in the 2016 submission and only 469,420 ha/year in the 2017 submission (United Republic of Tanzania, 2016: 19, 2017: 23). However, deforestation rates had previously been estimated at 412,000 ha/year for the period 1990–2005 (FAO, 2007b; MNRT, 1998: 8). Taken together, these raise concerns that Tanzania's REDD+ has been inflated.

Another concern with the REDD+ baseline that Tanzania submitted to the UNFCCC is the absence of any discussion of drivers. In developing the REDD+ baseline submission, the DoE-VPO established various technical working groups focusing on (1) a forest definition, (2) REDD+ activity data, (3) emission factors, and (4) comparative review of other country's REDD+ baseline efforts (United Republic of Tanzania, 2016: 27, 2017: 2–3). But there was no working group on drivers. The lack of information on drivers of deforestation remained a matter of concern among experts interviewed in 2018; some NGOs were commissioning their own research into the matter.[17] Finally, while Tanzania has indicated that the REDD+ baseline would contribute to its Third National Communication and first Biennial Update Report (BUR) to the UNFCCC (United Republic of Tanzania, 2017: 5), these reports have yet to be produced—which we see stands in contrast to the REDD+ efforts of Uganda.

At the end of the day, it is difficult to accept that Tanzania has developed a robust REDD+ evaluation framework. Such an approach aligns with the development policy paradigm of Tanzania, which has been characterized by considerable skepticism of neoliberalism. Furthermore, by offering almost unconditional support for Tanzania's participation in UN-REDD, Norway found itself with little leverage over the development of Tanzania's evaluation framework.

9.4. State Coordination of REDD+ in Tanzania

The emphasis that developmental environmentalism has placed on the role of the state in REDD+ implementation is challenging for countries like Tanzania where the political settlement is characterized by a weak dominant party. While indicative of Tanzania's development policy paradigm, Tanzania's efforts to implement

REDD+ have been characterized by the intention of the DoE-VPO to centralize authority over REDD+ despite lacking the capacity for forest policy implementation. Key fault lines would emerge between DoE-VPO and other government bodies over elements of REDD+ governance, while few real efforts have been made to engage with regional and district governments on the issue.[18]

A first fault line would emerge between the DoE-VPO and the FBD at the MNRT. Initially, MNRT was seen as the primary government actor for REDD+ by the international community. Both the UN-REDD and WB-FCPF initially recognized it as the key national partner for REDD+, while the NAFORMA project was first conducted under the auspices of the FBD before gradually being transferred to the TFS—both organizations under MNRT. The language of both the UN-REDD's National Program Document and WB-FCPF's Readiness Preparation Proposal indicates that donor agencies anticipated working largely with MNRT. The director of FBD was even identified as the "REDD national authority" in the National Program Document (UN-REDD, 2009b: 29) and "REDD+ Focal Point" in the Readiness Preparation Proposal (United Republic of Tanzania, 2010b: v). This seems appropriate, given that FBD and, more recently, TFS have been responsible for government forest reserves and state-owned industrial forest plantations. MNRT even convened the initial meeting of the National REDD Taskforce in 2009 at the University of Dar es Salaam (VPO, 2009: 27).

However, by the time the 2013 National Strategy was produced, the DoE-VPO had effectively regained authority over the REDD+ process. One indication is that MNRT is scarcely mentioned in the document. But furthermore, as was explained during interviews already in 2009, the DoE-VPO had taken the MNRT to court over the jurisdiction of REDD+ and won.[19] The DoE-VPO would point to a 2007 official decision of President Kikwete that mandated the DoE-VPO "to coordinate all climate change issues including adaptation and mitigation" (VPO, 2009: 16; also see United Republic of Tanzania, 2010b: 6). Consequently, both the 2009 National Framework for REDD+ and 2013 National Strategy for REDD+ have accorded an important role to the DoE-VPO, who authored both documents. Indeed, as can be seen in an organigramme in the 2013 National Strategy for REDD+ (VPO, 2013b: 22), the DoE-VPO would present itself as the central actor in Tanzania's existing forest governance system. Ultimate authority over REDD+ is now officially claimed by the DoE-VPO where the Director of Environment serves as the "National Climate Change Focal Point."

A second REDD+ fault line would emerge between the DoE-VPO and Tanzania's regional governance framework, particularly the Ministry of Regional Administration and Local Government, currently housed at the President's Office and referred to as PO-RALG. The experience of participatory forest management in Tanzania has suggested that REDD+ will require substantial governance capacity at the subnational level. As explained by one official, a key bottleneck confronting participatory forest management has been a lack of village land-use plans officially approved by district governments.[20] But these subnational governance issues had not received significant attention in REDD+ discussions in Tanzania. The implication was that the DoE-VPO was less interested in cultivating subnational governance capacity for participatory forest management than has been the case for PO-RALG. Indeed, there has been increasing concern that REDD+ has become disconnected from Tanzania's existing forest policy efforts and overly focused on establishing new national REDD+ institutions under the DoE-VPO (Lund et al., 2017).

A third fault line emerging already in 2014 was between the DoE-VPO and the Tanzania Ministry of Finance. Interviews in 2014 indicated that the national government preferred a specific climate change fund going through the Ministry of Finance with funds earmarked for items such as REDD+.[21] However, in Tanzania's National Strategy for REDD+, the DoE-VPO envisioned a special National REDD+ Fund that would "consolidate and distribute funds to different stakeholders based on efforts in implementing REDD+ strategy" (VPO, 2013b: 37–38). In advancing this position, the DoE-VPO argued that the 2004 Environmental Management Act had established an Environmental Trust Fund, which was a more appropriate vehicle for the National REDD+ Fund (para.: 213–218).[22] Significantly, the director of the environment at the VPO would be responsible for the REDD+ Fund's administration (para.: 215(3)).

The DoE-VPO's proposal for a REDD+ Fund did not appear to attract much support from donors. As was explained during 2018 interviews, though the Environmental Trust Fund "was legally recognized . . . there [was] no tangible body which is operational," while the Ministry of Finance had greater experience managing international financing.[23] As of 2018, no REDD+ Fund had been constituted. Rather, donors were instead championing the Ministry of Finance and Planning for accreditation to other multilateral climate funding bodies, such as the Green Climate Fund in an apparent attempt to bypass the REDD+ Fund issue.[24] However, it would be noted that the official National Designated Authority for the Green Climate Fund in Tanzania is currently the DoE-VPO.

Overall, I have observed a certain level of disfunction within the Tanzanian government with regard to the DoE-VPO's efforts to centralize control over REDD+ governance. The question is, how was the DoE-VPO able to retain authority over REDD+ and resist changes to Tanzania's legal and policy framework? Earlier I described Tanzania's political settlement as one of a weak dominant party system. This is consonant with difficulties of the central government to exert effective control across the various elements of REDD+ governance. But a lack of significant government control over 10 years of climate finance efforts suggests factors other than bureaucratic turf wars. Such political maneuvering reflects a hybrid development policy paradigm of classic developmentalism/ neodevelopmentalism, which has remained circumspect of development opportunities presented by the international community.

9.5. Donor Support for REDD+ in Uganda

In comparison to Tanzania, Uganda has attracted considerably less donor interest for its REDD+ efforts. It has also prioritized the World Bank Forest Carbon Partnership Facility (WB-FCPF) process, with the prospect of eventually participating in its results-based Carbon Fund. Notably, the Ugandan central government pursued this strategy even when donor support was limited. I describe the history of donor engagement on REDD+ in Uganda in this section.

The REDD+ process in Uganda was initiated in 2008, when the Ministry of Water and Environment (MWE) agreed to join the WB-FCPF, receiving $0.2 million for the development of a Readiness Plan Idea Note. This was supplemented with $0.18 million from Norway.[25] However, Norway reportedly found the WB-FCPF process slow and did not allocate additional funding.[26] Between 2008 and 2012, donor interest in REDD+ in Uganda stagnated. Nonetheless, demonstrating a commitment to the REDD+ process, MWE kept the initiative afloat by submitting a Readiness Preparation Proposal in 2012 (MWE, 2017c: 1). In it, MWE estimated that funding necessary for REDD+ capacity building stood at $10.7 million (Government of Uganda, 2011: 17).[27]

By 2013, the funding situation began to change. The WB-FCPF agreed to support the implementation of the Readiness Preparation Proposal with a $3.6 million grant while the Austrian government committed $0.7 million (WB-FCPF, 2013a: 1).[28] In 2014, UN-REDD agreed to support Uganda's REDD+ efforts by contributing $1.8 million for the production of certain readiness activities.[29] However, Uganda would continue to hue most closely to the WB-FCPF.[30] In 2016, Uganda was successful in obtaining $3.8 million in additional funding from the WB-FCPF, more than half of which was to be allocated to its evaluation framework (MWE, 2017c: 36). Using these funds, MWE was able to complete its REDD+ National Strategy in late 2017 (MWE, 2017a). Experts interviewed in 2018 expected Uganda would submit its "R[eadiness]-Package" to the WB-FCPF later that year; the Readiness Package was officially endorsed by the World Bank in October 2018 (WB-FCPF, 2018).[31] Uganda's pursuit of WB-FCPF financing instead of UN-REDD, I submit, is consistent with a development policy paradigm of liberal neodevelopmentalism.

Finally, there have been important recent developments outside official REDD+ channels. Perhaps the most important has been endorsement of a $61 million Forest Investment Plan by the Climate Investment Funds in 2017

(MWE, 2017b). While the Forest Investment Plan will be a separate entity, it is closely affiliated with REDD+ efforts. For example, the WB-FCPF has already indicated it will finance emission reductions associated with the Forest Investment Plan as part of Uganda's REDD+ package (MWE, 2017a: 133).

9.6. Uganda's Evaluation Framework for REDD+

The more rigorous evaluation framework being developed in Uganda aligns with the more stringent requirements anticipated by the Carbon Fund of the WB-FCPF.

The central government has treated drivers of deforestation and forest degradation with increasing levels of sophistication over time (Table 9.2). Five drivers were identified in the initial Readiness Preparation Proposal submitted in 2012, seven in a REDD+ Options Assessment Report, 11 in the 2017 REDD+ National Strategy, and eight in the 2017 and 2018 REDD+ baseline submission to the UNFCCC. Furthermore, the collection of data on drivers and forest-related emissions has been institutionalized through the establishment of a National Forest Monitoring System, which I discuss in more detail below (MWE,

Table 9.2 Comparing REDD+ Drivers Identified in Various Ugandan Policy Documents

Readiness Preparation Proposal (2012)	REDD+ Strategy (2017)	REDD+ Baseline (2017 and 2018)
i. Charcoal ii. Firewood iii. Timber iv. Agriculture v. Livestock	i. Infrastructure development ii. Timber logging iii. Construction pole harvesting iv. Fuelwood extraction v. Charcoal production vi. Non-wood forest products vii. Smallholder agriculture expansion viii. Large-scale commercial famers ix. Oil extraction and mining x. Wildfires xi. Livestock free-grazing and fodder	i. Expansion/encroachment of smallholder agriculture into forests and bushlands ii. Unsustainable woodfuel extraction (charcoal and firewood) iii. Unsustainable timber harvesting iv. Large-scale commercial agriculture v. Livestock free-grazing vi. Wood harvesting conducted by refugees vii. Wildfires viii. Artisanal mining operations and oil extraction

Sources: MWE (2011: 98, 2017a: 20, 2017c: 7, 34).

2020: 6). In 2018, Uganda was still in the process of establishing the National Forest Monitoring System, while by 2020 it was described as "functional even if not yet completely sustainable" (MWE, 2020: 14).[32]

There are two innovative elements to how drivers are employed. First, the emissions associated with each driver have been quantified (MWE, 2017a: 22–23). For example, energy efficient cooking stoves were expected to tackle fuelwood and charcoal production as drivers of deforestation and forest degradation. While the modeling behind this quantification effort is not discussed, it does allow for a certain ranking of each driver of deforestation. Second, monitoring indicators for drivers were also identified (MWE, 2017a: 98–99). For example, indicators of drivers for fuelwood and charcoal production included the number of households and buildings with energy efficient stoves, improved charcoal stoves, and the amount of charcoal derived from introduced tree species. Indicators on efforts to address drivers of deforestation are first to be reported at the local county level but scaled up through sectoral ministries to produce a district-level and then national-level progress report submitted to the REDD+ Technical Coordination Unit at MWE (MWE, 2017a: 106). By tracking drivers, the central government is able to better design policy interventions that will have a real effect.

Uganda submitted an initial version of its REDD+ baseline to the UNFCCC in early 2017 and a revised version in 2018 (MWE, 2017c, 2018). Compared to what was observed in Tanzania, Uganda's REDD+ baseline estimation shows considerably more sophistication. First, is its technical precision. While Tanzania saw a 25% reduction between its two REDD+ baseline exercises, Uganda's saw only a 3% increase. The small increase in emissions indicates a conservative revaluation of REDD+ baseline emissions. Furthermore, while the 2017 exercise included estimates of emissions from deforestation and forest degradation, the revised 2018 REDD+ baseline restricted its analysis to deforestation citing high levels of uncertainty with data on forest degradation (MWE, 2017c: 16–25, 2018: 42–44). Second, Uganda has the advantage of already possessing data conducive to estimating forest emissions factors. Recall that Uganda undertook a first National Biomass Survey in 1990 with a third recently completed. The data allow for the estimation of emissions factors for deforestation for various forest types: (1) tropical high forest (543 tCO2e per ha), (2) woodlands (90 tCO2e per ha), and (3) plantation forest (260 tCO2e per ha) (MWE 2018: 30). As discussed earlier, Tanzania estimated only one class of forest carbon stock, which was estimated to hold 122 tCO2e.

With due attention to drivers of deforestation and forest degradation, Uganda's evaluation framework for REDD+ is conducive to attracting funding from carbon markets—though the Ugandan central government does not appear to be opposed to the continuation of fund-based approaches. During interviews in 2014 and 2018 on REDD+, representatives of MWE made it clear that with regards to REDD+ there was no preference for one form of climate finance—carbon markets or climate funds.[33] In 2018, experts explained that Uganda was preparing to enter the Carbon Fund, with the hope that the WB-FCPF would receive additional funding.[34] In parallel, Uganda would complete its REDD+ baseline, discussed above, and submit a special Technical Annex on REDD+ to the UNFCCC in early 2020 (MWE, 2020). Upon approval by the UNFCCC, this would also make it eligible to receive results-based payments through the Green Climate Fund's Results-Based Payments Pilot Programme for REDD+.

9.7. State Coordination of REDD+

The Ugandan central government has developed a flexible and comprehensive evaluation framework for REDD+ that introduces a number of elements associated with its experience with bottom-up, liberal neodevelopmental planning. Such a bottom-up approach to strategic coordination of REDD+ reflects a development policy paradigm of liberal neodevelopmentalism. Additionally, with a political settlement characterized by a relatively more effective central authority, I submit that the Ugandan state has been able to avoid the capture of the REDD+ governance apparatus by any one government body and more effectively delegate responsibilities to state and nonstate organizations.

REDD+ is officially governed by the REDD+ Steering Committee at the National Climate Change Advisory Committee (NCCAC), established in 2015 as part of Uganda's National Climate Change Policy (MWE, 2017c: 1). Upon closer inspection however, the Ugandan central government plans on implementing REDD+ through discrete activities delegated to a range of state and nonstate organizations. These are to be coordinated by the Forest Sector Support Department (FSSD), while REDD+ fund management is to be administered by the Ministry of Finance, Planning and Economic Development (MFPED).

While MWE initially accorded the REDD+ file to the National Forestry Authority (NFA), by 2014 a decision had been made to transfer authority to the FSSD. It currently serves as National Focal Point, REDD+ Secretariat, and chairs the REDD+ Technical Coordination Unit (MWE, 2017a: 94). FSSD undertakes day-to-day management and technical coordination, while NFA retains responsibility for data for REDD+ monitoring.[35] The FSDD also leads and coordinates the work of the National Forest Monitoring System, though, as I discuss below, technical responsibilities have also been allocated to NFA and District Forest Services.

As explained during interviews, MWE believed it appropriate to grant oversight to FSSD because of the policing role it plays in national forest policy, including oversight of NFA and District Forest Services.[36] Another reason was that

NFA was focused on public lands, particularly central forest reserves, and had no jurisdiction over local forest reserves and private land, where deforestation has been more pronounced.[37] But there was also concern that REDD+ was a national issue that should be more firmly under the control of the central government, which suggested FSSD rather than the state agency NFA.[38]

There have, nonetheless, been concerns about the appropriateness of the FSSD. One concern raised in 2014 was about capacity: FSSD was staffed by 7–10 people in comparison to NFA that was comprised of approximately 300 employees.[39] In 2018, the National REDD+ Technical Coordination Unit still retained offices at NFA. Perhaps for these reasons, NFA currently retains responsibility for technical elements of the National Forest Monitoring System, including those related to the national forest inventory, technical determination of Uganda's REDD+ baseline, and data related to drivers of deforestation and forest degradation.[40]

District governments are also expected to be important partners in REDD+ activities and are organized into working groups (MWE, 2017a: 115–116). In particular, the District Forest Service is expected to provide forest extension services to incentivize tree planting and other elements of REDD+, while certain REDD+ funds will be distributed to the local level through conditional grants (MWE, 2017a: 119–121). However, ownership of forest carbon assets by individuals, private entities, or government remained an outstanding issue in 2018.[41] The District Forest Service will also contribute to the National Forest Monitoring System by regularly ground-truthing remote-sensing analysis undertaken by NFA (MWE, 2020: 14–15).

The actual implementation of REDD+ is being built on the existing liberal neodevelopmental national planning system. Recall that as early as 1995, Uganda had adopted a development planning system led by the powerful MFPED that required all donor financing to pass through an integrated national planning and budgeting process. As set out in its 2017 REDD+ National Strategy, Uganda does not expect REDD+ to be implemented as a stand-alone program "but as part of a broader national planning framework and linked to the respective financing frameworks" (MWE, 2017a: 114). In contrast to the situation in Tanzania, where REDD+ was centralized under the DoE-VPO, REDD+ in Uganda is envisioned as a number of discrete activities delegated to sectoral ministries with technical coordination provided by the FSSD at MWE while REDD+ funds are to be allocated through Uganda's planning and budget process administered by the MPFED. I enumerate important planning elements for the evaluation framework for REDD+ evident in the REDD+ National Strategy.

The first planning element are policy interventions referred to as "REDD+ Strategic Options" in the REDD+ National Strategy (Table 9.3). A total of eight policy interventions that might plausibly be considered to be causally related to deforestation and forest degradation were identified as REDD+ Strategic

Table 9.3 Strategic Options of Uganda's National REDD+ Strategy

REDD+ Strategic Options	Coordination of Strategic Option	Lead Institutions	Collaborating Institutions	5-Year Costed Action Plan ($US million)
1. Climate Smart Agriculture	MAAIF			20.6
• SLM and agroforestry practices		MAAIF, districts, NAFFORI	CSO/NGO	
• Rainwater harvesting with collection tank and drip irrigation		MAAIF, districts	DWD, CSO/NGO	
• Greenhouse cultivation of vegetables		MAAIF, districts, NARO	CSO/NGO	
2. Sustainable Fuelwood and Charcoal Production	MAAIF			19.4
• Commercial smallholder and community bioenergy woodlots		MEMD, districts, private landowners	CSO/NGO	
• Commercial smallholder and community poles and timber plantations		districts, private landowners	CSO/NGO	
• Improved charcoal kilns linked to bioenergy wood lots		MEMD, districts, private sector	CSO/NGO	
3. Large-Scale Timber Plantations	NFA			1.5
• Commercial transmission poles and timber plantations		Districts, private landowners		
• Commercial pole and sawlog plantations		NFA, private landowners, districts		
• Improved charcoal kilns linked to plantations sites		private sector		
4. Restoration of Natural Forests in the Landscape	NFA			25.9
• Designated areas for natural forest regeneration		NFA, UWA, districts	CSO/NGO	
• Restoration of degraded protected natural forest		NFA, UWA, districts	CSO/NGO	
• Devolution of forest management through participatory forest management (PMF) and similar set ups		NFA, UWA, districts	CSO/NGO	
• Traditional/customary forest management practices		District cultural institutions, community	CSO/NGO	
5. Energy Efficient Cookstoves	MEMD			19.4
• For fuelwood		MEMD, FSSD, districts	CSO/NGO	
• For charcoal		MEMD, FSSD, districts	CSO/NGO	

(continued)

Table 9.3 Continued

REDD+ Strategic Options	Coordination of Strategic Option	Lead Institutions	Collaborating Institutions	5-Year Costed Action Plan ($US million)
6. Integrated Wildfire Management	NFA			6.0
• On timber plantations		Private landowners, plantation owners, NFA	CSO/NGO	
• On woodlands, bush lands and grasslands		Districts, UWA, NFA		
7. Livestock Rearing in the Cattle Corridor	MAAIF			29.0
• Livestock breeding program		DAR, NGBC, districts	CSO/NGO	
• Establishment of drinking water dams for livestock		DWD	CWUAs	
• Establishment of fodder agroforestry plantations		Districts, NFA, Uganda Seeds Ltd.	CSO/NGO	
8. Strengthening of Policy Implementation for REDD+				2.0
REDD+ Technical Coordination Unit/Crosscutting	FSSD			18.1
Total				149.5

NAFFORI: National Forestry Resources Research Institute

DWD: Directorate of Water Development

NARO: National Agricultural Research Organisation

UWA: Uganda Wildlife Authority

CSO: Civil Society Organization

NGBC: National Genomics and Bioinformatics Centre

Source: MWE (2017a: 12–13, 15, 95, 116–119).

Options. For example, large-scale timber plantations (Strategic Option 3), restoration of natural forests (Strategic Option 4), energy efficient cooking stoves (Strategic Option 5), as well as strengthening policy implementation for REDD+ (Strategic Option 8). A separate government body has been delegated coordinating authority for each, including the Ministry of Agriculture, Animal Industry and Fisheries (MAAIF), the Ministry of Energy and Mineral Development (MEMD) as well as NFA and FSSD at MWE. In addition, state and nonstate organizations that are expected to collaborate on the implementation of each strategic option are also identified. As explained by MWE in the REDD+ National Strategy, the REDD+ strategic options were intended to interact synergistically (MWE, 2017a: 12).

Second, as also indicated in Table 9.3, MWE has sought to estimate the cost implementing each REDD+ Strategic Option. The first six of Uganda's strategic options are expected to be cost efficient, meaning that they are expected to generate surplus income even in the absence of climate finance (MWE, 2017a: 78). Examples here include a sustainable land management (SLM) and agroforestry sub-option as well as improved fuelwood cookstoves sub-option. Only a limited number of the proposed REDD+ activities are anticipated to be conducive to carbon markets. Overall, the Uganda central government expects that the national REDD+ program might be implemented at a total cost of $423 million over a 20-year full implementation period (MWE, 2017a: 119–121).

Finally, it is important to observe the extent to which REDD+ efforts have integrated within the budget planning process. A scheme proposed by MWE recommends an autonomous, national REDD+ fund managed under the conditional grants fiscal transfer system already established by MFPED (Indufor, 2017: 9–10).[42] In this way, MFPED would receive REDD+ funds and allocate them to various state and nonstate organizations responsible for REDD+ activities.[43] Similarly, under the National REDD+ Strategy each ministry and government body is expected to include REDD+ in their annual plans and develop a project document to show how they intend to use budget funds for REDD+ operations (MWE, 2017a: 115–118).

Overall, the relationship between REDD+ and the state in Uganda suggests an effort to allocate state organizational capacity for various elements of REDD+ implementation through a bottom-up process of strategic coordination. The ability of the Ugandan central government to maintain what appears to be effective coordination of REDD+ can be explained in part by the stronger central authority offered by its political settlement. However, the bottom-up strategic planning process also reflects a development policy paradigm of liberal neodevelopmentalism.

9.8. Conclusion

I summarize findings from investigation of the effectiveness of REDD+ implementation in Tanzania and Uganda reported in this chapter in Table 9.4. At first blush, the attention and support accorded REDD+ by the Ugandan government and their lack in Tanzania appear to be explained by state development interests. As I discussed earlier in our explanation of CDM effectiveness, the Ugandan government has long been aware of the nationwide scarcity of forest resources, while the forest sector has not been accorded the same level of priority by successive Tanzanian governments. However, with considerably greater forest resources, the Tanzania central government actually stands to gain more in terms of REDD+ financial inflows and has had considerable support from the international community. The institutional characteristics of REDD+ associated with developmentalism environmentalism would also have been thought to align with the hybrid classic developmentalism/neodevelopmentalism in Tanzania. Yet REDD+ implementation would fail in Tanzania as major donors withdrew by 2018. Tanzania's status in various multilateral REDD+ process appears to be in question.

Table 9.4 Summary Findings Regarding the Effectiveness of REDD+ Implementation in Tanzania and Uganda

	Tanzania	Uganda
1. Donor preferred	UN-REDD preferred	WB-FCPF preferred
2. Level of donor support	Extensive donor funding, especially from Norway	Relatively limited donor funding until recently
3. Evaluation frameworks	Measurement of REDD+ emissions and baseline reasonably adequate but lacking attention to drivers	Measurement of REDD+ emissions, national baseline relatively more precise, and considerable attention accorded to REDD+ drivers
4. State strategic coordination	Ineffective effort toward centralized authority by DoE-VPO and evidence of infighting with other state organizations	REDD+ integrated into bottom-up liberal neodevelopmental planning process that accords appropriate governance roles to MWE and MFPED as well as implementation by appropriate state and nonstate organizations

Drawing inspiration from the causal mechanism of CDM effectiveness sketched in the previous chapter, I submit that Tanzania's development policy paradigm predisposed the central government to not treat REDD+ as a genuine development opportunity. While Tanzania received greater REDD+ support than most countries, this was unable to stimulate greater state interest in the forest sector. Rather, REDD+ would raise concerns amongst state elites that resonated with ideas of classic developmentalism that hold sway across the Tanzanian state apparatus, especially aspirations toward economic self-reliance and worries about becoming financially dependent on the international community. With REDD+'s orientation toward forest conservation, it was difficult for REDD+ enthusiasts at FBD-MNRT to win greater support for REDD+, particular from those interested in industrialization. Under these circumstances it has been difficult to convince the state leadership that the climate finance instrument represents a genuine economic opportunity and that it is not a passing fad of the international community. Instead the status quo would prevail, which saw a state organization with limited capacity and interest for implementing forest policy in Tanzania, the DoE-VPO, retain control over the REDD+ file.

A weak dominant party political settlement in Tanzania partially explains the state's inability to rein in the ineffective efforts of the DoE-VPO to centralize authority over the REDD+ file. What is surprising is that Norway continued to commit large amounts of funding to REDD+ in Tanzania despite almost certain awareness of its governance challenges. The strategy Norway adopted now appears to have been ineffective: bypassing the Tanzanian central government by funding nonstate actors almost exclusively while also remaining silent as Tanzania pursued the UN-REDD process over the more rigorous WB-FPCF.

Close observers of the Tanzania REDD+ process have pointed to a need instead of supporting effective state leadership. For example, authors of the final review of the UN-REDD program in Tanzania argued: "During the phases of the REDD+ readiness process, various activities may be hosted in say the Vice President's Office (VPO), academic and research institution[s], but in the long-term under business-as-usual, the appropriate host is a government agency that can sustain the ongoing requirements [such as FBD-MNRT]" (Gapare and William, 2013: 8). The consistent lack of enthusiasm by the Tanzania government for REDD+ as well as other climate finance instruments, including NAMAs which we turn to in the next chapter, is consistent with a hybrid development policy paradigm of classic developmentalism/neodevelopmentalism.

While the Ugandan state is certainly interested in forests for national development, its embrace of the REDD+ process suggests a development policy paradigm that is outwardly oriented to tap global economic opportunities but also cognizant of the role that different state and nonstate actors might make toward reducing deforestation. Indeed, the Ugandan central government has slowly built an innovative REDD+ program that has seen the central government delegate different elements of the REDD+ program to a suite of state and nonstate policy actors, all of which is integrated in its national development planning process. Finally, the central government has developed a relatively robust evaluation framework that meets the more rigorous methods of the WB-FCPF, including those of its Carbon Fund. The country is well-positioned should a carbon market for REDD+ emerge in the near future. By 2018, there were signs that the donor community was awakening to the idea that Uganda is effectively implementing REDD+.

The comprehensive approach to addressing REDD+ in Uganda depends in large measure on the power of the central government to ensure that that the various capacities and authorities of different policy actors necessary for REDD+ are coordinated effectively. This tends to resonate with its political settlement of a strong dominant party that lends itself to pushing through an aggressive developmental agenda. But I maintain that the decision on this comprehensive approach to REDD+ is itself not determined by Uganda's political settlement but rather the manner with which the Ugandan state perceives the REDD+ opportunity as a means of addressing its development interests—that is a causal mechanism that sees state ideas and interests converging to form state organizational and institutional capacity for effectively implementing this climate finance mechanism.

10

Explaining NAMA Effectiveness

10.1. Introduction

In this chapter I consider how Nationally Appropriate Mitigation Actions (NAMAs) have been undertaken in Tanzania, Uganda, and Moldova. Relative to other climate finance instruments considered in this book, NAMA implementation has been the most problematic as they have not attracted funding necessary to get mitigation actions off the ground. Hence my focus on programming elements, including NAMA proposals submitted to the UNFCCC by Tanzania, Uganda, and Moldova; the amount of domestic co-financing committed to them; anticipated evaluation frameworks for NAMAs as well as state coordination approaches.

As their name suggests, NAMAs have been intended to fund climate mitigation efforts that developing countries deem most appropriate for their development. Using language of the theoretical framework guiding this book, states might be excepted to seek to implement NAMAs aligned with their state development interests into the NAMA process. Reflecting a global environmental norm of developmental environmentalism, the state is recognized as an integral partner in NAMA implementation. Donors have also sought to introduce innovations in the evaluation of NAMA effectiveness, including recognition of efforts to reduce emissions that might only take effect indirectly through a long-term process of transformational change. The main challenge with NAMA though has been a lack of international financial support.

My evaluation is based largely on analyzing NAMAs proposals officially submitted to the UNFCCC's NAMA Registry in addition elite interviews in 2014 and 2018. The number of NAMA proposals submitted is itself an indicator of NAMA effectiveness, as such submissions suggest a certain level of buy-in from developing countries. I am, however, being generous by referring to these documents as proposals. Relative to CDM project design documents, NAMA proposals are concise documents with little technical detail. While not perfect, submitted NAMA proposals disclose important programming elements including the amount of domestic co-financing committed to each NAMA, sectors targeted (NAMAs might include all major climate mitigation sectors), evaluation frameworks anticipated, and how the state intended to coordinate them

The Political Economy of Climate Finance Effectiveness in Developing Countries. Mark Purdon, Oxford University Press.

with other development activities. I submit that such programming elements reflect how effectively NAMAs may have been implemented had international financial support been supplied.

Similar to what was expected for REDD+ implementation, it might be assumed that more effective NAMA programming would also be observed in Tanzania given skepticism of neoliberalism there and NAMA's association with developmental environmentalism. What I found, however, is a striking replication of the pattern of country engagement that we have seen for the CDM and REDD+.

Uganda and Moldova have demonstrated relative enthusiasm for NAMAs and submitted a number of NAMA proposals to the UNFCCC's NAMA Registry: eight in Uganda and 12 in Moldova (Table 10.1). Of the two, Moldova is clearly more invested in the NAMA process, with all its entries in the NAMA Registry listed as NAMAs "seeking support for implementation," while Uganda has been seeking support for NAMA preparation. In contrast, Tanzania has expressed little interest in NAMAs: no NAMA proposals have officially been submitted to the NAMA Registry, and it had unsuccessfully submitted only in 2017 a first NAMA proposal to the NAMA Facility, a multilateral donor initiative discussed in Chapter 3. Such varied engagement with NAMAs, I submit, is consistent with the development policy paradigms of the three case-study countries—namely, liberal neodevelopmentalism in Uganda and Moldova and hybrid classic developmentalism/neodevelopmentalism in Tanzania. Review of submitted NAMAs in Moldova and Uganda also reveals,

Table 10.1 NAMA Funding Status in Tanzania, Uganda, and Moldova as of October 2018

Country	Registered NAMAs	Estimated Annual Emission Reductions in 2030 (MtCO2e/yr)	Total Cost (M$US)	Local Support (M$US)	Requested Support (M$US)	Provided Support (M$US)
Tanzania	0	NA	NA	NA	NA	NA
Uganda	8	16.3	2.0	$0	2.0	0
Moldova	12	27.6	2,890	$811	2,079	0

Source: UNEP DTU (2018).

Note: Uganda received notice in early 2018 it was awarded funding from the NAMA Facility, but these figures are not reflected in this table. Tanzania had submitted a first NAMA to the NAMA Facility in late 2017, which has been recorded by UNEP DTU.

surprisingly, a preference for the more rigorous evaluation frameworks associated with carbon offsetting (though not to the exclusion of Intergovernmental Panel on Climate Change (IPCC) emission inventory methods) as well as a more bottom-up approach to state strategic coordination of NAMA programming. Indeed, the CDM lives on in NAMA proposals registered by Moldova and Uganda as well as in the NAMA Support Project submitted by Tanzania to the NAMA Facility.

However, my analysis of submitted NAMA proposals themselves raises questions about the degree to which NAMAs actually reflect state development interests. In Uganda, submitted NAMAs appear at odds with state development interests in pursuing large-scale hydroelectricity and oil, discussed in Chapter 6. This contrasts with Uganda's interest in REDD+, where there is a clearer state development interest in addressing the scarcity of its forest resources. Tellingly, the Ugandan central government has not committed any domestic co-financing toward NAMA programming. In contrast, NAMAs are being used in Moldova to address state development interests of land degradation and energy independence. At least on paper, the central government has committed to sizeable amounts of domestic financing for NAMAs. However, the reliance on the Ministry of Agriculture, Regional Development and Environment (MARDE) for implementation and monitoring (though recognizing that other stakeholders are referred to) suggests limited attention for NAMAs beyond climate policy circles. It is also curious that the Moldovan central government would pursue NAMAs given that EU donor funding, including a sizeable renewable energy component, has largely bypassed the climate finance instrument. This suggests that the Moldovan central government has come to see NAMAs as part of its broader efforts toward EU integration and perhaps, ultimately, integration with the EU emissions trading system.

10.2. NAMA Programming in Moldova

In January 2010, Moldova submitted a first NAMA to the UNFCCC as part of its responsibilities under the Copenhagen Accord. However, like almost all other countries that participated, the Moldovan central government initially submitted an emission reduction target. In Moldova's case, the Ministry of Environment committed to reducing its emissions 75% below 1990 levels by 2020 (ME, 2010). Such an ambitious emissions reduction target was possible because, as discussed earlier, Moldova's emissions plummeted after the collapse of the Soviet Union—like they did in many countries of the former Soviet bloc. In this way, Moldova's 2010 NAMA anticipated the absolute emission reduction target it would later adopt in its Nationally Determined Contribution under the Paris Agreement in contrast to the targets relative to a business-as-usual baseline adopted in the Nationally Determined Contributions of Tanzania and Uganda (see Table 1.3 in the Introduction).

With refinement of the NAMA concept from emission reduction targets to specific mitigation actions, Moldova had the opportunity to revise its initial NAMA proposal. In 2012, the Ministry of Environment "in close cooperation with relevant line ministries" would develop NAMAs under the UNDP's Low-Emissions Capacity Building Programme, identifying 65 actions in its 2020 Low-Emission Development Strategy (LECBP, 2012). These were formally reported to the UNFCCC in Moldova's Third National Communication in 2013 (see Table 10.2).

Separately, in 2014, the Moldovan central government adopted the 2014–2023 Environmental Protection Strategy and Action Plan (EPSAP), where it formally committed Moldova to reducing emissions 20% below a 2020 baseline scenario (GoRM, 2014a: II.4.7). While the EPSAP was a decision of the central government, the Ministry of Environment was responsible for its execution and relevant line ministries were intended to report to it. Note that this is slightly less ambitious than Moldova's previous commitment made toward the Copenhagen Accord. The EPSAP also identified emission reduction targets for a number of economic sectors, with the forest and energy sectors amounting to 50% of planned reductions and removals (GoRM, 2014a: III.6.B.37.1–3; III.6.C.41.1; III.7.45.2.a–d). Notably, NAMAs were identified as the primary vehicle for achieving the sectoral targets in the EPSAP. The EPSAP also assigned the Ministry of Environment the important role of implementing and monitoring the strategy and, by consequence, the NAMAs.

After the publication of the EPSAP, the Ministry of Environment would identify 11 NAMAs for consideration while a final four were flagged for implementation (Table 10.2). These were presented in Moldova's first Biennial Update Report submitted to the UNFCCC in 2016. The 2030 Low-Emission Development Strategy, developed that same year by the Ministry of Environment and with support from the UNDP, identified 51 NAMAs. This is surprising given that the instrument is only formally associated with 2020 emission reduction targets (GoRM, 2016). Indeed, it suggests that NAMA were viewed as integral to the Nationally Determined Contribution process.

However, the actual number of NAMAs submitted to the UNFCCC's NAMA Registry is lower: by 2018, the government of Moldova had submitted only 12 NAMA proposals. Also important, in 2017, responsibility for NAMAs was accorded to the Ministry of Agriculture, Rural Development and Environment (MARDE), which was formed from the consolidation of the Ministry of Environment, Ministry of Agriculture and Food Industry, and

Table 10.2 NAMAs Identified in Various Climate Policy Planning Documents of Moldova, 2013–2018

	2020 LEDS (2012)	Third National Communication (2013)	First Biennial Update Report (2016)		2030 LEDS (2016)	2018 NAMA Registry	
			Considered	Detailed		Prioritized	Also Submitted
Energy sector	14	14	4	2	7	3	3
Transport sector	10	10	1		5		1
Buildings sector	7	7			8		1
Industrial sector	7	7	1		9		1
Agricultural sector	13	13	2		7		2
LULUCF	9	9	2	1	5	1	
Waste	5	5	1	1	10		
Total	65	65	11	4	51	4	8
Sources:	GoRM (2013a: 33–64)	GoRM (2013b: 378–393)	GoRM (2016a: 190–196)	GoRM (2016a: 196)	GoRM (2016b: Annexe 2)		

the Ministry of Construction and Regional Development in 2017 (GoRM, 2014b).

Overview of NAMA Proposal and Sectors Targeted

NAMAs submitted by the Moldova central government to the UNFCCC reflect state development interests, given their focus on expanding afforestation efforts begun under the CDM as well as promoting energy efficiency, bioenergy, and the displacement of natural gas. A total of 12 NAMAs were submitted to the NAMA Registry, though only four have been prioritized by the Moldovan central government. I discuss all 12 below, though the reader should recall that NAMA proposals submitted to the UNFCC are elementary documents with few technical details.

The first prioritized NAMA addresses energy demand by promoting efficient combined heating and power (CHP) generation running on natural gas (UNFCCC, No Date-j). A second NAMA addresses energy demand, though through the promotion of energy efficient lighting (UNFCCC, No Date-g). A third NAMA seeks to reclaim landfill methane gas and use it to generate electricity (UNFCCC, No Date-p). The fourth NAMA prioritized is a new afforestation project (UNFCCC, No Date-n). It proposes to afforest a total of 61,500 ha of degraded land at an annual afforestation rate of 4,393 ha. The NAMA proposal also suggests that Moldsilva will play an important role in implementation, which is striking given recent pressure from the EU to unbundle the state forest agency, as discussed in Chapter 7.

Eight additional NAMAs have been submitted to the NAMA Registry as of 2018, though they have not been accorded priority status by the Moldovan central government. The first two focus on renewable energy, including wind power (UNFCCC, No Date-h) and bioenergy (UNFCCC, No Date-o). A third NAMA seeks to promote soil carbon sequestration through the implementation of improved agricultural tillage techniques (UNFCCC, No Date-m). A fourth NAMA proposes to deploy over 13,000 heat pumps across various buildings in Moldova to replace natural gas and coal-fired boilers. A fifth NAMA proposal that relies on IPCC guidelines would seek to significantly increase the amount of solar hot water heaters across the country (UNFCCC, No Date-i). A sixth NAMA proposal seeks to replace traditional cement production with a new technology that would allow emissions to be reduced by 70% (UNFCCC, No Date-l). A seventh NAMA that relies almost exclusively on IPCC guidelines seeks to introduce hybrid and electric buses in the capital city of Chisinau (UNFCCC, No Date-k). A final NAMA, proposed in 2018, seeks to reduce emissions from Moldovan cattle by introducing grape plant residues into their feeding systems across the country (NAMA, NS-281).

Domestic Co-Financing

NAMA proposals also allow governments hosting them to indicate how much co-financing they anticipate providing. It should be emphasized that there is no further evidence for the financial commitments made by the Moldovan central government other than NAMA proposals available in the NAMA Registry.

Significantly, a high degree of domestic co-financing for NAMAs is reported—averaging 70% of total costs across all 12 NAMAs proposed. State development interests are also reflected in the amount of domestic resources committed to NAMAs. Total estimated costs range from $4 per tCO2e to over $2,000 per tCO2e (Table 10.3). However, costs come down when calibrated according to the amount of international financing requested. These range from $2 per tCO2e for the Waste to Energy NAMA to between $15 to $25 per tCO2e for the other priority NAMAs—all quite competitive with existing prices on major emissions trading systems in the EU and North America. NAMAs not prioritized all have considerably higher costs per tCO2e. The degree of financial support suggests that the Moldovan government has prioritized NAMAs that might be most attractive to international donors. This might also signal to architects of the EU emissions trading system that if Moldova were to be included, there are viable opportunities for mitigation.

NAMA Evaluation Framework in Moldova

The Moldovan central government has pursued an evaluation framework for NAMAs that is surprisingly ambitious, despite the lack of leadership from the UNFCCC. Moldova's efforts suggest a willingness to submit to international scrutiny with regard to the effectiveness of climate finance implementation. Most importantly, an evaluation framework for NAMAs has been proposed as part of UNDP's Low-Emissions Capacity Building Programme process (Pedersen, 2015).

Significantly, the proposed evaluation framework ties into Moldova's governance framework for international climate policy, to which I return in the following section. In the meantime, regarding the NAMA evaluation framework, Moldova anticipated two new organizations to address technical issues associated with the instrument. These include a NAMA Technical Committee and explicit

Table 10.3 Moldova NAMAs Submitted to UNFFC NAMA Registry as of October 2018

NAMA Title	Year Submitted	Estimated Cumulative Reductions (MtCO2e)	Total Cost (M$US)	Requested International Support (M$US)	Local Support (M$US)	Cost of Emission Reductions		Implementation Body	Evaluation Body	Evaluation Framework	Sector
						Total NAMA Costs ($US/tCO2e)	Costs for Portion of International Support ($US/tCO2e)				
NAMAs Selected for Detailed Consideration											
The promotion of small-scale CHP plants in the Republic of Moldova	2018	1.03	23.5	15.0	8.5	22.8	14.6	MARDE (lead) and other state and nonstate stakeholders including EEA, EEF, and Moldsilva	MARDE	CDM EB IPCC(2012a) 2006a)	Energy demand
Promoting energy efficient lighting in the Republic of Moldova	2018	4.6	248.4	117.0	131.3	54.0	25.4		MARDE	(CDM EB, 2013)	Energy demand
Waste to energy (WTE) NAMA in the Republic of Moldova	2018	3.4	15.0	8.3	6.7	.4.4	2.4		MARDE	(CDM EB, 2015)/(CDM EB, 2012b)	Renewable Energy
Afforestation of degraded land, riverside areas, and protection belts in the Republic of Moldova	2018	5.2	150.9	110.6	40.4	29.0	21.3		MARDE	(CDM EB, 2009)	Afforestation and reforestation

Other NAMAs Considered

Promotion of heat pumps in the Republic of Moldova	2018	1.7	180.1	143.9	36.3	105.9	84.6	MARDE (lead) and other state and nonstate stakeholders including EEA, EEF, Chisinau City Hall, MEI, and AIPA	MARDE	IPCC (2006a)	Energy demand
Promotion of wind power plants (WPP) in the Republic of Moldova	2018	0.61	827.9	662.5	165.5	1,357.2	1,086.1		MARDE	(CCO, 2017)/ (CDM EB, 2011a)	Energy industries (renewables)
Use of solar energy for domestic hot water production in the Republic of Moldova	2018	0.80	637.5	578.0	59.5	796.9	722.5		MARDE	IPCC (2006a)	Energy demand
Hybrid and electric buses and minibuses in the city of Chisinau	2018	0.17	344.3	80.7	263.6	2,025.3	474.7		MARDE	IPCC (2006a)	Transport
Clinker substitution at cement production	2018	1.1	105.3	94.2	11.1	95.7	85.6		MARDE	IPCC (2006a)	Manufacturing industries
Reducing GHG emissions from enteric fermentation by including dried grape marc in cattle ratios	2018	0.07	5.6	4.0	1.6	80.0	57.1		MARDE	(Moate et al., 2014)	Agriculture

(continued)

Table 10.3 Continued

NAMA Title	Year Submitted	Estimated Cumulative Reductions (MtCO2e)	Total Cost (M$US)	Requested International Support (M$US)	Local Support (M$US)	Cost of Emission Reductions		Implementation Body	Evaluation Body	Evaluation Framework	Sector
						Total NAMA Costs ($US/tCO2e)	Costs for Portion of International Support ($US/tCO2e)				
Implementation of soil conservation tillage system in the Republic of Moldova	2018	1.2	257.5	180.3	77.3	214.6	150.3		MARDE	"CDM methodologies"	Agriculture
Use of energy willow for heat generation in the Republic of Moldova	2018	4.4–7.1	93.8	84.4	9.4	2,025.3	474.7		MARDE	(Stolarski et al., 2015)/(CDM EB, 2009)	Energy industries (renewables)

Source: UNEP DTU (2018b) and NAMA proposals uploaded to the UNFCCC NAMA Registry and discussed in the text.

Measurement, Reporting and Verification (MRV)-NAMA Group to interface more directly with NAMA developers and verifiers. Reflecting the more flexible nature of NAMAs, the evaluation framework being prepared in Moldova was ready to accept NAMAs on the basis of Moldovan methodologies or other international best practice, including the CDM, EU Emissions Trading System, and the GHG Protocol. The proposed evaluation framework does raise some concerns about the lack of standardization, however: "As NAMA and MRV [i.e., evaluation frameworks] are not well-defined terms internationally, the administrative system in Moldova should be based on the Moldovan interpretation and this is best done through the preparation of standard templates and guidelines" (Pedersen, 2015: 34).

Despite openness to a variety of evaluation methodologies and standards, in practice NAMA programming has relied heavily on the CDM: all four prioritized NAMAs make use of CDM methodologies. Emission reductions of the first prioritized NAMA for combined heating and power have been estimated with IPCC (2006a) emission inventory guidelines as well as a CDM methodology (CDM EB, 2012a). Emission reductions for the second prioritized NAMA are to be based on information provided by the Moldovan Energy Efficiency Fund and on existing CDM methodology (CDM EB, 2013). Emission reductions for the landfill methane gas NAMA will be derived from information provided by the Moldovan Energy Efficiency Agency yet based on existing CDM methodology (CDM EB, 2012b, 2015). The fourth prioritized NAMA makes clear reference to existing CDM afforestation projects in Moldova and emission credits were estimated with a CDM methodology (CDM EB, 2009).

While reference to the CDM is found in three of remaining eight NAMAs, others refer to IPCC guidelines and other more experimental approaches. For the wind power NAMA, emission reductions are based on calculations of Moldova's Grid Emission Factor (CCO, 2017), where wind energy, it is argued, will displace fossil fuel–based electricity that currently dominates the grid. As explained in the official report setting out the Grid Emissions Factor (CCO, 2017: 11), its calculation is based on a CDM methodology (CDM EB, 2011a). The methodology for calculating emission reductions for the bioenergy NAMA is based on an academic study (Stolarski et al., 2015) as well as an existing CDM methodology (CDM EB, 2009). As for the soil carbon sequestration NAMA, emission mitigation will be determined through "CDM methodologies" though none are specified. Four of the remaining NAMAs recently proposed by the Moldovan government are based on IPCC guidelines (IPCC, 2006). Significantly, all make reference to baselines associated with the CDM approach, though they do not describe the precise method of their determination. The evaluation framework of the final NAMA submitted, in the agriculture sector, is based on an academic study demonstrating that grape plant residue can reduce methane production in cattle by approximately 20% by altering their digestive processes and microbiomes (Moate et al., 2014).

State Coordination for NAMAs in Moldova

Like the CDM, NAMAs were to be governed by the National Commission, which is the chief authority over international climate policy in Moldova (Pedersen, 2015). The National Commission was headed by the Ministry of Environment and, later, by MARDE. Little other information on how NAMAs were expected to be coordinated by the Moldovan central government is available, except what might be found in the EPSAP and individual NAMA proposals. Both suggest a reliance on MARDE for NAMA implementation and monitoring, though other state and nonstate actors are referred to in a manner that suggests greater inclusivity. The lack of detail on the role of other stakeholders in NAMA implementation is disconcerting, though, as it suggests that outside climate policy circles, NAMAs have attracted little attention.

For example, MARDE is listed as the implementing body for the afforestation NAMA, while such capacity is clearly borne by Moldsilva, the state forest agency. While Moldsilva is referred to in the NAMA proposal, it is unclear if the agency has been involved in its development and what role it should play in executing the NAMA. Similarly, MARDE is listed as the implementing body for NAMAs promoting energy efficient lighting and waste-to-energy processes. However, a number of other stakeholders are also targeted in the CHP plant NAMA, including residential heat plants, hospitals, campuses, and industry, while trainings will be provided to staff of the Moldovan Energy Efficiency Agency and Moldovan Energy Efficiency Fund.

Overall, while NAMA programming is far from perfect in Moldova, the climate policy instrument is being undertaken with considerable enthusiasm by MARDE despite the lack of real support for NAMAs by the international community. It is worth repeating that no donors have yet come forward to support NAMAs in Moldova. I return to this issue in the conclusion of this section as it suggests that while Moldova's participation in NAMAs is related to development policy paradigms and state development interests, its development policy paradigm of liberal neodevelopmentalism is not only about managing the country's comparative advantage but also entwined with the Moldovan central government's aspirations for EU membership and reducing Russia's monopoly in the energy sector.

10.3. NAMA Programming in Uganda

NAMAs appear to have elicited a modest degree of interest in Uganda, but enthusiasm there is markedly lower than in Moldova. Uganda did not immediately produce a NAMA proposal in response to the Copenhagen Accord, though the Ministry of Water and Environment (MWE) later embarked on a NAMA identification process through the UNDP's Low-Emissions Capacity Building Programme. The number of NAMAs has been reduced over time. Initially, in 2014, the UNDP exercise led to the identification of 40 potential NAMAs (MWE-CCU, 2014; UNFCCC, 2015). In its 2015 National Climate Change Policy, MWE identified 10 mitigation policy responses, though not specifically referring to them as NAMAs (MWE, 2015). Ultimately, Uganda would submit eight NAMA proposals to the UNFCCC's NAMA Registry, with most submitted prior to the 2015 UN climate change conference in Paris (Table 10.4). Only one of these has attracted financial support via the NAMA Facility—and only partial funding in the form of support for a "NAMA Support Project." As discussed in Chapter 3, the NAMA Facility conceives these as sector-wide programs, national in scope that "contribute to the most transformational elements of the overarching NAMA in which they are embedded" (NAMA Facility, 2015: 4). I briefly describe these and their programmatic elements below.

Overview of NAMA Proposals and Sectors Targeted

The only NAMA proposal to receive financial support in Uganda is one proposing to promote improved cookstoves at educational institutions (UNFCCC, No Dates). In 2018, the NAMA Facility awarded $15 million toward a NAMA Support Project related to it (NAMA Facility, No Date; UNDP, 2017). In the full NAMA proposal, demand for cookstoves was to be addressed by (1) providing qualifying institutions with a 50% subsidy to offset cookstove costs, (2) establishing a revolving fund to ensure funds were sustainable, and (3) initiating an awareness-raising campaign for key stakeholders—including head teachers, school management committees, and communities. The NAMA Support Project is to back the introduction of improved cookstoves in approximately three-quarters of all Ugandan schools (NAMA Facility, No Date). For this purpose, a revolving loan fund will be established with 75% of contributions coming from the NAMA Facility and the remainder from the central government.

Aside from the Uganda cookstove NAMA, Uganda's MWE has submitted five other NAMA proposals to the UNFCCC's NAMA Registry for detailed consideration. Two are in the waste management sector. One is focused on improving waste collection, recycling, and reuse in Kampala, the capital (UNFCCC, No Date-e). It is to be managed by the National Environment Management Authority and Kampala Capital City Authority. The second tackles emissions associated with water treatment facilities and is led by the National Water and Sewerage Corporation (UNFCCC, No Date-d-f). Another NAMA submitted for detailed consideration aims to reduce livestock emissions (UNFCCC, No

Table 10.4 Uganda NAMAs Submitted to UNFFC NAMA Registry as of October 2018

NAMA Title	Year Submitted	Estimated Cumulative Reductions (MtCO2e)	Total Cost (M$US)	Requested International Support (M$US)	Local Support (M$US)	Estimated Cost of Emission Reductions		Implementation Body	Evaluation Body	Evaluation Framework	Sector
						Total NAMA Costs ($US/tCO2e)	Costs for Portion of International Support ($US/tCO2e)				
NAMAs Selected for Detailed Consideration											
The Promotion of the Use of Efficient Institutional Stoves in Institutions	2014	0.1	0.2	0.2	0.0	2.0	150.0	MEMD	MWE	Gold Standard Methodology & CDM	Energy industries (renewables)
Reduction, Recycling and Reuse of Solid Waste in Kampala City	2014	NA	0.2	0.2	0.0			NEMA	MWE	None	Waste
Integrated Wastewater Treatment for Agro-process Water in Uganda	2015	0.3	5.0	5.0	0.0	16.7	16.7	DWRM at MWE	MWE	CDM	Waste
Developing appropriate strategies and techniques to reduce methane emissions from livestock production	2014	NA	0.1	0.1	0.0			MAAIF	MWE	None	Agriculture

Bus Rapid Transit (BRT) for Kampala	2015	0.4	1,181	0.3	0.0	2,952.5	2,952.5	KCCA & MTW	MWE	WRI Global Protocol for Community-Scale Emissions Inventory	Transport
Periodic Vehicle Inspection for Emissions and Roadworthiness	2014	NA	0.2	0.2	0.0			MTW & MEMD	MWE	None	Transport
Other NAMAs Considered											
Promoting cultivation of high-yielding upland rice in Uganda	2015	NA	0.25	0.25	0.0			MAAIF	MWE	None	Agriculture
Fuel Efficiency in Motor Vehicles	2015	NA	0.5	0.5	0.0			MEMD & MTW	MWE	2006 IPCC Guidelines	Transport

Source: UNEP DTU (2018b) and NAMA proposals uploaded to the UNFCCC NAMA Registry and discussed in the text.

Date-b). A fourth NAMA would assist Uganda in planning, developing, and financing a bus rapid transit system for Kampala. Led by the Kampala Capital City Authority and the Ministry of Works and Transport, the NAMA envisions the construction of nine rapid bus routes (UNFCCC, No Date-a). The final NAMA submitted for detailed consideration aims to increase the capacity of government to enforce vehicle pollution regulations (UNFCCC, No Date-q). In an innovative move, the NAMA aims to not only enforce regulations on Ugandan national territory but also coordinate with countries from which vehicles are imported to undertake pre-shipment vehicle inspections (UNFCCC, No Date-q: 11). Sub-Saharan Africa is infamous as a final market for second-hand, often more polluting vehicles (Roychowdhury, 2018).

Two other NAMAs have been submitted, though not necessarily for detailed consideration. One focuses on promoting a transition from paddy rice to upland rice (UNFCCC, No Date-r). The second targets vehicle fuel efficiency and is led by the Ministry of Energy and Mineral Development in conjunction with Ministry of Works and Transport (UNFCCC, No Date-c). The exact mitigation actions are, however, not clearly identified in the NAMA proposal, which "could" include a variety of policy incentives.

Donor support for the improved cookstoves NAMA instead of other proposed NAMAs is somewhat surprising. As we saw in Chapter 6, the Ugandan central government has shown only modest interest in improved cookstoves, instead throwing significant state support behind the development of large-scale hydroelectric and oil. Improved cookstove technology has been only highlighted in Uganda's relatively recent Green Growth Development Strategy, which was produced with support from the UNDP's Low Emissions Capacity Building Programme (NPA, 2017: 20–23). That is, the Green Growth Development Strategy was the fruit of the same donor-supported capacity-building program in which NAMAs themselves were developed, which raises questions about whether the Ugandan central government is genuinely committed to this technology. Overall, while submitted NAMAs do identify opportunities to reduce emissions, they appear peripheral to the Ugandan central government's interests in the energy sector. Finally, to avoid any confusion on the part of the reader, note that given attention already accorded to REDD+, there is understandably no forest NAMA in Uganda.

Domestic Co-Financing

Weak interests by the Ugandan central government in submitted NAMAs is further supported by the lack of domestic co-financing committed to them, which also contrasts strongly with the situation in Moldova. Detailed economic analysis and emission reduction potential of proposed NAMAs is also lacking, which contrasts with Uganda's approach to REDD+.

Nonetheless, I am able to rank Uganda's NAMA proposals in terms of costs per emission reduction in Table 10.4. Total estimated costs per tCO2e range from $2 (improved cookstoves NAMA), $17 (wastewater treatment NAMA) to nearly $3,000 (bus rapid transit NAMA). Interestingly, when considering international financial support per tCO2, climate finance offered from the NAMA Facility for the cookstove NAMA is equivalent to a carbon price of $150 per tCO2e, which is higher than carbon prices associated with carbon-pricing scheme in North America and Europe in late 2023. While beyond the scope of this book, this suggests that the NAMA Facility is motivated by much more than the efficiency of emission reductions associated with its projects.

Evaluation Frameworks for NAMAs in Uganda

Relative to Moldova, Uganda has been less enthusiastic about developing a rigorous evaluation framework for the climate finance instrument. This also contrasts to Uganda's treatment of REDD+. For REDD+, I found Uganda to be quite proactive in developing an evaluation framework that would meet the more exacting requirements of the World Bank's Forest Carbon Partnership Facility (WB-FCPF). This divergence might be attributed, in part, to an understanding that the evaluation framework for NAMAs would be less demanding than for the CDM. As explained by one respondent during a 2014 interview:

> We are already engaged in matters like the CDM, which are even more rigorous, which require a lot of information and all that. The regulatory process is just too hectic. But as a country we are still participating in it. And there are quite a number of projects which have been proposed for the CDM, but, because of certain technicalities, we don't seem to pass as CDM. But they can maybe be taken as NAMAs.[1]

Other motivations are possible, such as a lack of confidence in the NAMA process, and its inability to attract significant amounts of funding from donors. This lack of motivation is reflected in submitted NAMAs: only half clearly indicated a methodology for estimating emissions. Interestingly, the improved cookstove NAMA that received donor support builds on existing experience in Uganda with the CDM and other carbon offset initiatives on the voluntary market. This includes one project operating under the Gold Standard on the voluntary market (UgaStove) as well as six others in the CDM pipeline (UNFCCC, No Date-s: 10–11). The NAMA Facility has also sought to design the NAMA

Support Project to deliver transformational change, largely in terms of potential co-benefits, including reduction in forest degradation, increased health benefits, and improved economic conditions of schools, as well as the establishment of a revolving loan fund—to be financed partially through CDM credits (NAMA Facility, No Date). But CDM methodologies also play an important role in other NAMA proposals submitted. The water treatment NAMA draws on an existing, though modest, CDM project promoted since 2015 by the National Water and Sewerage Corporation though never implemented (UNEP DTU, 2018; UNFCCC, No Date-d: 3). A NAMA was considered a more appropriate vehicle than sectoral CDM because wastewater treatment was associated with low emissions, lacked of a clear value chain, and took place over a large geographical area (UNFCCC, No Date-d: 4). Two of the other NAMA proposals submitted relied on emission inventory approaches, including the bus rapid transit NAMA (UNFCCC, No Date-a) and the vehicle fuel efficiency NAMA (UNFCCC, No Date-c).

However, for a number of NAMAs submitted, no evaluation framework is provided. The solid-waste management NAMA includes no estimate of emission reductions nor proposes a strategy for doing so. Similarly, no evaluation framework is provided for the livestock feed NAMA. Though there is a prospect of carbon sequestration, the NAMA is admittedly a "research NAMA [that] will not directly result into reduction of methane or nitrous oxide emissions" (UNFCCC, No Date-b: 3). Finally, the NAMA rice proposal acknowledges that significant methodological challenges will need to be overcome to implement this project, including measurement of emissions associated with different paddy rice management schemes and land-use change. No evaluation framework is proposed, indeed, devising one to appears to have been the main objective of the mitigation action.

Evaluation frameworks for the other remaining NAMAs are specious, and their associated policy impacts and outcomes problematic. The public transport NAMA has estimated that the NAMA could reduce per capita emissions by 20–30% from a business-as-usual trajectory (UNFCCC, No Date-a). But there are a number of concerns with this claim. To begin with, it is difficult to find justification for this estimate in the available documentation. The NAMA proposal only refers to the WRI Global Protocol for Community-Scale Greenhouse Gas Emission Inventories (WRI, 2014b) that, as the name implies, is appropriate for emission inventories but offers little guidance on business-as-usual calculations. The vehicle pollution regulations NAMA would generate baseline information on the number and type of vehicles in Uganda as well as tailpipe emissions, building on vehicle emission standards only recently developed by the Uganda National Bureau of Standards (UNFCCC, No Date-q: 7). However, while the mitigation actions of the vehicle fuel efficiency NAMA are not clearly described, the proposal still claims that reductions in fuel consumption per vehicle will lead to emission reductions relative to a business-as-usual baseline. Finally, miscalculations can be found in the vehicle fuel efficiency NAMA. This includes estimated annual reductions of 883 MtCO2e across Uganda—which is larger than annual emissions in Canada—that is clearly incorrect (UNFCCC, No Date-c: 7). Overall, the sophistication and rigor of strategies to measure what NAMAs are actually achieving varies widely.

State Coordination of NAMAs in Uganda

The state's strategy for coordinating NAMAs in Uganda reflects the more bottom-up, liberal neodevelopmental approach to development planning that has been, arguably, pioneered in the country (discussed in Chapter 7). The advantage of NAMAs was that they could be developed as policies aligned with Uganda's national development plans in contrast to the CDM experience, which had been project based. As explained by one Ugandan expert: "[NAMAs] just help to support our final objectives in the National Development Plan because one of them is to provide low-carbon development."[2] Also recall that Uganda developed its NAMAs under UNDP's Low-Emissions Capacity Building Programme which was twinned with the development of a Low-Emission Development Strategy.

Additional elements of NAMA programming also suggest a relatively more open administrative arrangement that taps the capacities of various state and nonstate organizations in the country. While all submitted NAMA proposals indicate that the Climate Change Unit at MWE will play an important role in the final evaluation of NAMAs, other state organizations have been assigned responsibility for implementation and initial estimates of emission reductions. For example, the improved cookstove NAMA will be led by the Ministry of Energy and Mineral Development with links to Ministry of Education and Sports as well as district education officers. Similarly, the wastewater treatment NAMA is to be implemented by the Directorate of Water Resources Management at MWE, but it also involves the National Environment Management Authority and National Sewage and Water Corporation. The National Water and Sewerage Corporation is a state-owned enterprise that has largely been judged as having responded well to liberal economic reforms (Mukokoma, 2009; Mukokoma and Van Dijk, 2013).

10.4. NAMA Programming in Tanzania

Turning to Tanzania, evaluation of NAMA programming is difficult as the state has consistently shown very little interest in the climate finance instrument. In

2014, a key informant explained to me that Tanzania only reluctantly participated in the UNDP's Low-Emissions Capacity Building Programme and that no NAMAs were being considered.[3] By 2018, the end of the empirical research focus of this book, no NAMA proposals had been submitted to the UNFCCC. However, in 2017, Tanzania had submitted a NAMA Support Project to the NAMA Facility with support of the UNDP (UNDP, No Date)—though this endeavor would prove unsuccessful.[4] I focus on this NAMA Support Project below while recognizing that Tanzania's reluctance to submit any proposal to the UNFCCC's NAMA Registry signals a fundamental lack of interest in this climate finance instrument.

The NAMA Support Project was entitled Support Project to the NAMA for Bus Rapid Transit Systems in Tanzania and was developed by the Division of Environment at the Vice-President's Office (DoE-VPO) in conjunction with the Ministry of Works, Transport and Communications (NAMA Facility, 2018). It aspired to replicate a bus rapid transit system being deployed in Dar es Salaam in other major Tanzania cities over a five-year period from 2019 to 2023. As a point of reference, the Dar es Salaam bus rapid transit system had received over $700 million in donor financing since 2012 (Ndalu, 2017; World Bank, 2013, 2018a). The main activities included developing of a number of policy instruments and establishing an institutional framework for public transport (pp. 12–13). At a total estimated cost of $21.7 million, over 90% of the funds for the NAMA Support Project were requested from the NAMA Facility.

There are limitations to my analysis of NAMA implementation here as it is difficult to draw firm conclusions from a negative case. But based on my understanding of Tanzania's domestic political economy, Tanzania's inaction is not necessarily surprising. While support for NAMAs by the international community has been low, even in the case of REDD+ implementation in Tanzania, significant donor financing can fail to spur effective policy implementation. Thus state development interests do not appear to be the deciding factor in explaining Tanzania's lack of engagement, pointing to the salience of development policy paradigms. This conclusion is also supported by my brief analysis below of the NAMA's anticipated evaluation framework and coordination.

First, while there appears to have been no support for an independent NAMA evaluation framework, it is telling that in the NAMA Support Project, emission reductions were calculated against a baseline scenario of private vehicle growth based on a CDM methodology (NAMA Facility, 2018). While leading to a total of 1.7 MtCO2e of emission reductions, the costs per tCO2e are quite competitive with current emissions trading systems, at $13 per tCO2e on a total cost basis and $12 per tCO2e on the basis of requested international support (p. 22).

The proposal submitted to the NAMA Facility also offers a window into how transformational change is to be evaluated. Recall that the NAMA Facility requires proponents of NAMA Support Projects to describe the potential for transformational change in their proposals. In this case, it was argued that the project would be transformational as it supports "radical change in the urban planning process" by including low-carbon and efficient transport as one of the priorities of city development (p. 19) that "will contribute to improved, climate-conscious urban and transport planning" (NAMA Facility, 2018: 20). That is, transformational change is discussed in terms of policy outcomes, but there is little discussion of how such outcomes will be achieved nor measured.

Finally, in terms of state coordination, the NAMA Support Project anticipated the establishment of a National NAMA Facility in Tanzania. Indeed, the establishment of a National NAMA Facility was one of the UNDP's main objectives in supporting the proposal (UNDP, No Date). Recall, however, that in Uganda and Moldova, NAMAs were built on the governance apparatus first established for the CDM, including Uganda's Climate Change Unit and Moldova's National Commission. In the case of Tanzania, it is not clear whether the NAMA Facility would build on the Designated National Authority for administering the CDM or if it would be a new organization.

10.5. Conclusion

I summarize findings from investigation of the effectiveness of NAMA programming across Tanzania, Uganda, and Moldova reported in this chapter in Table 10.5. Looking back at how NAMAs have been programmed across the three case-study countries, one is struck with how these findings are congruent with the effectiveness of the CDM and REDD+. This cross-national pattern of NAMA programming, I submit, can be best explained by development policy paradigms. Moldova and, to a lesser degree, Uganda have been giving sustained attention to NAMAs since the 2009 Copenhagen Accord in a manner that is consistent with a development policy paradigm of liberal neodevelopmentalism. A willingness to engage the international community in the NAMA process (despite very limited donor financing), relatively robust evaluation frameworks, and a bottom-up planning approach are all indicative of a liberal neodevelopmental policy paradigm. It is also striking how many NAMA proposals have relied on CDM methodologies. Indeed, the only proposal selected for funding by the NAMA Facility across the three case-study countries draws on improved cookstove projects developed through the CDM and related voluntary carbon offset standards in Uganda over the past decade.

Nonetheless, there are important distinctions between NAMA programming in Moldova and Uganda, which might be explained by different interests at play in each country. Based on my analysis of state development interests in

Table 10.5 Summary Findings Regarding the Effectiveness of NAMA Programming in Tanzania, Uganda, and Moldova

	Tanzania	Uganda	Moldova
1. Number of NAMA proposals submitted to UNFCCC NAMA Registry	0 Only one proposal submitted to donors for NAMA support	8 In addition one NAMA support project financed by donors	12 No support for NAMA support projects from donors
2. Sectors targeted	NA	Weak relationship with state development interests in energy sector	Strong relationship with state development interests in forests and energy sectors
3. Domestic co-financing	No co-financing	No co-financing	Considerable co-financing, averaging 70% of total NAMA costs
4. Evaluation framework	No centralized evaluation framework developed [Proposed donor funded NAMA Support Project reliant on CDM methodology]	No centralized evaluation framework; reliance on CDM methodologies and GHG inventories for some proposed NAMAs, none for others Donor-funded NAMA support project reliant on methodologies of CDM and voluntary carbon market	Centralized evaluation framework drafted; reliance on CDM methodologies and GHG inventories for all proposed NAMAs
5. State strategic coordination	NA	Efforts to align with liberal neodevelopmental planning approach	Efforts to align with liberal neodevelopmental planning approach involved various state and nonstate actors, though implementation and monitoring concentrated at MARDE

Chapter 6, submitted NAMA proposals in Moldova reflect state development interests more than those in Uganda. Considerable co-financing has also been offered in Moldova, at least on paper. MARDE has also appeared quite proactive in attempting to develop a NAMA evaluation framework. However, while individual NAMA proposals refer to other state and nonstate actors for policy implementation, the concentration of NAMA implementation and evaluation at the MARDE raises concerns about interest in NAMAs by the rest of the state apparatus. Furthermore, the lack of financial support for NAMAs in Moldova also raises questions about the NAMA process. Curiously, the NAMA Facility, based in Berlin, has not supported any NAMAs in Moldova. With so much funding to Moldova flowing through EU channels, Moldova's support for NAMAs might be interpreted as a signal of commitment to Western priorities and values. Rather than being a vehicle for realizing state development interests, the pursuit of NAMAs might be symbolic of Moldova's commitment to the EU's climate change agenda.

While a number of NAMAs have been proposed by the Ugandan central government, the sophistication of the government's preparations was low relative to Uganda's engagement with REDD+. Few domestic resources have been committed, and evaluation frameworks are rather underdeveloped. Restrained enthusiasm for NAMAs in Uganda might be attributed to the central government's interest in pursuing large-scale hydroelectric and oil resources, which are at odds with the implicit goal of promoting renewable energy and energy efficiency through NAMAs. Nonetheless, NAMAs in Uganda appear to be attracting donor support: Uganda was the only country investigated to actually receive any funding for its NAMAs. Despite this, levels of financial support for NAMAs in Uganda and in the other case-study countries has been exceedingly low. In this light, Uganda's involvement in the NAMA process may also be seen as a means of signaling their willingness to engage with the international community on climate change mitigation.

Turning to Tanzania, I find the state's treatment of NAMAs consistent with its behavior vis-à-vis the CDM and REDD+. Despite being offered capacity building comparable to that received by Uganda, Tanzania has simply not been interested in NAMAs. While the DoE-VPO would endeavor to develop a NAMA recently, it almost appears too little, too late. During interviews in 2018, there was a consensus among development practitioners in Tanzania that climate and environmental issues were not state priorities. Tanzania's lack of engagement with the NAMA process is most consistent with the legacy of classic developmentalism, which is characterized by a certain degree of skepticism about global cooperation efforts.

It is also hard to escape the conclusion that NAMAs have been less rigorous than the CDM and REDD+ in terms of measuring the effectiveness of the instrument. Its current design may be sufficient if those investing in NAMAs do not require measurable results and have confidence in the difficult-to-evaluate claims of "transformational change" of those developing NAMAs. But when donors and investors are serious about funding climate initiatives, they may demand greater stringency of climate finance instruments to demonstrate that they are delivering results (i.e., policy outcomes). The behavior toward Moldova points in this direction. Since 2010, the EU has significantly ramped up official development assistance for Moldova, including significant support for renewable energy (see Annex in introductory chapter). This support has, however, remained independent of the NAMA process as the EU would pursue its renewable energy ambitions in Moldova through bilateral channels where it would appear to have more control than via the UNFCCC.

11
Conclusion

This book has sought to respond to questions about the effectiveness of climate finance instruments developed under the UNFCCC to reduce emissions in developing countries. The effectiveness of the Clean Development Mechanism (CDM), Reducing Emissions from Deforestation and Forest Degradation (REDD+), and Nationally Appropriate Mitigation Actions (NAMAs) has attracted a range of, often polarized, views. But little of this polarized debate has been grounded in comparative fieldwork into the basic issues of policy effectiveness and how instruments devised at the international level are being implemented on the ground. The subject of climate finance effectiveness has remained a *terra incognita* in global climate politics. A clearer understanding of the conditions under which such climate finance instruments are effective in reducing emissions might improve strategies for implementing Nationally Determined Contributions (NDCs) in developing countries, which often rely on these instruments and related mechanisms to finance climate action.

The main research question motivating this book has been to understand the conditions under which such climate finance instruments have been effective. A second major research question has been whether REDD+ and NAMAs, which I argue embody a new set of global environmental norms that I have described as developmental environmentalism, have been more effective than the CDM. While the CDM reflected what Bernstein (2001) has described as liberal environmentalism, REDD+ and NAMAs have placed greater reliance on public donor funds yet rely on softer systems for evaluating results and clearly recognize the state as an essential partner in their implementation. The two sets of climate finance instruments have represented quite different ideas for engaging developing countries on climate change mitigation, a shift that I have attributed largely to the 2008 global financial crisis and loss of neoliberalism's credibility across much of the developing world.

I have sought to respond to these questions by undertaking a comparative, field-based investigation into the effectiveness of three different climate finance instruments in three different countries (Tanzania, Uganda, and Moldova) over a 10-year period that corresponds, I have argued, to a shift in global environmental norms from liberal environmentalism to developmental environmentalism. If

The Political Economy of Climate Finance Effectiveness in Developing Countries. Mark Purdon, Oxford University Press.
© Oxford University Press 2024. DOI: 10.1093/oso/9780197756836.003.0011

important gaps exist between a policy designed in Washington and its implementation in California (Pressman and Wildavsky, 1973), how much greater might be the gap between climate policies designed in Bonn, Copenhagen, or Paris and their implementation and effectiveness in Tanzania, Uganda, and Moldova?

Admittedly, my case-study countries do not do justice to the vast range of different cultures, histories, and geographies of the "developing world." Nonetheless, countries investigated differ significantly in terms of state organizational capacity as well as other, less appreciated political economy elements, including political settlements, development policy paradigms, and state development interests. Nor were all the climate finance instruments considered fully implemented and claiming to have reduced emissions. Rather, they represented different stages along the process of policy effectiveness (Knoepfel et al., 2007), including at the stage of policy outcomes (emission reductions and sequestration) for the CDM, policy implementation for REDD+, and policy programming for NAMAs. The result is a rich and detailed account of how different climate finance instruments have been undertaken in three different case-study countries over a 10-year period stretching from the Kyoto Protocol through implementation of the Paris Agreement.

11.1. Conditions of Climate Finance Effectiveness

In response to my first research question, research points to the importance of domestic politics. The most important finding is that climate finance instruments have consistently been more effective in Uganda and Moldova than in Tanzania, despite considerable differences in state organizational capacity between these two East African countries and a former Soviet Republic. These empirical finds are summarized in Table 11.1; the details of which I discuss in

Table 11.1 Summary of Climate Instrument Effectiveness Across Countries and Sectors

Climate Finance Instrument	Sector	Tanzania	Uganda	Moldova
CDM	Forest	Ineffective	*Effective*	*Effective*
	Energy	Ineffective	Ineffective	Ineffective
REDD+	Forest	Ineffective	*Effective*	NA
NAMAs	Various	Ineffective	*Effective*	*Effective*

more detail below. Importantly, such findings allow me to elaborate a causal mechanism describing how development policy paradigms can combine with state development interests to produce state organizational capacity for effective climate finance instrument implementation—at least at low carbon prices that characterized the period from 2008 to 2018 that I have focused on. This causal mechanism is presented in Figure 11.1. Essentially, states that adhere to a liberal neodevelopmental policy paradigm are more effective partners in global climate mitigation efforts. This is because such states treat climate finance instruments as part of their general strategy of integrating their countries incrementally into the global economy and proactively engaging with the international community in a way that helps realize state development interests.

Causal Model

As might be discerned from Figure 11.1, my causal mechanism differentiates between policy processes of states adhering to different development policy paradigms. This is because the characteristics of state organizational capacity that are formed under liberal neodevelopmentalism differ from those under classic developmentalism and, to a lesser degree, neodevelopmentalism. Given the *comparative advantage following* strategy of liberal neodevelopmental states, they tend to generate state organizations and institutions that harbor development ambitions but are also motivated to be self-sufficient by generating business income. Furthermore, the evidence suggests some sort of internal assessment by liberal developmental states of their comparative advantage in different economic sectors, which informs how they deploy scarce state organizational capacity. While classic developmentalism and neodevelopmentalism differ in certain aspects, such as their orientation toward domestic or export markets, they tend to share a *comparative advantage defying* strategy of economic development. This tends to produce state organizations and institutions that harbor developmental ambitions and are more reliant on state support for their economic activities.

The causal mechanism in Figure 11.1 also recognizes that state development interests are foundational in shaping state organizational capacities. Of course states do not always act in ways that might be considered to further their development interests. Nonetheless, development policy paradigms tend to operate as a filter through which states gauge how to best realize their state development interests. As sets of instrumental beliefs linking different policy organizations and institutions with economic development objectives, development policy paradigms shape state organizational capacity, including the capacities and interests of state organizations, state approaches to coordination and planning,

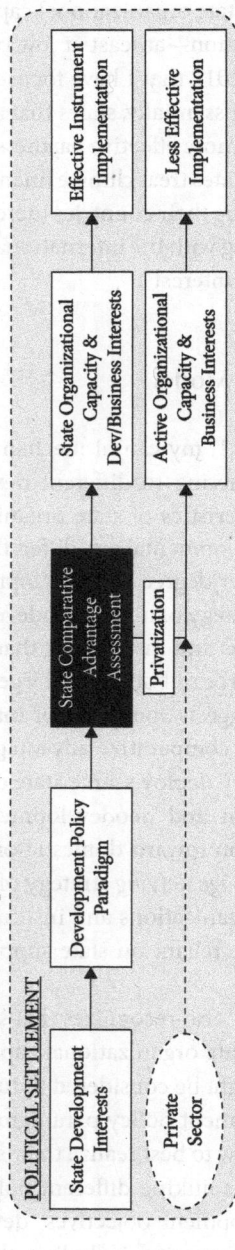

Figure 11.1 Causal Mechanism of Climate Finance Instrument Effectiveness Under Low Carbon Prices

and state institutions for demonstrating to the international community the effects that climate finance instruments have.

My causal mechanism also recognizes that the private sector plays an important role in both types of states. It is characterized by a more active form of organizational capacity, in contrast to the more latent organizational capacity of the state. The private sector also tends to play a relatively more prominent role in the economy of liberal neodevelopmental states. This is because liberal neodevelopmental states tend to defer to the private sector when, based on an assessment of their comparative advantage in specific sectors, they determine that private actors rather than the state are more economically competitive.

Summary of Research Findings

This causal mechanism plays out in each of the climate finance instruments, as indicated in Table 11.1. In the late 2000s, when I first went into the field to investigate the CDM, Uganda and Moldova maintained state organizational capacity in the forest sector but had largely ceded the energy sector to private actors. Such a divergence can be attributed to an assessment by the state that it had sufficient organizational capacity to intervene in the forest sector though not in the more capital-intensive and complex energy sector. But the manner that the state remained engaged in the forest sector in both Uganda and Moldova reflected a similar liberal neodevelopmental policy paradigm. Both states retained state forest agencies that possessed sufficient organizational capacity and unique combination of developmental and business interests that allowed them to engage with the opportunity presented by the CDM. As a result, CDM projects led by state forest agencies in these two countries were highly effective. Projects in their respective energy sectors were led by organizations, such as a special government unit at the Ministry of Environment, and the private sector that did not possess such a combination of organizational capacities and interests, leading CDM projects to be less effectively implemented.

In Tanzania, the CDM was generally less effective. One reason was that the state tended to be uninterested in promoting afforestation/reforestation and decentralized renewable energy projects. While fuelwood is a real problem, Tanzania retains considerable industrial forest plantations and is keen on developing new large-scale hydroelectric and natural gas resources. The central government has also been skeptical of neoliberal development policy, such as that reflected in the CDM. Altogether, the Tanzanian central government did not constructively engage with the CDM. Such behavior vis-à-vis the CDM is difficult to attribute to state organizational capacity, as its level between Tanzania and Uganda is broadly comparable. Rather, given its development policy paradigm, the Tanzanian central government did not perceive climate finance instruments as being a genuine development opportunity.

Similarly, detailed investigation of REDD+ and NAMAs in the three case-study countries suggests that more effective implementation has been taking place in Uganda and Moldova than in Tanzania. Despite considerable enthusiasm by the international community, REDD+ in Tanzania would run into a number of obstacles, leading donors to ultimately withdraw. In contrast, Uganda has slowly but surely implemented an innovative REDD+ program. At one level this might be attributed to different interests in reducing deforestation. While interests of the Tanzanian central government in the forest sector have grown, especially since about 2016, this does not compare with the priority status that has consistently been accorded to the forest sector in Uganda since Museveni first consolidated power in the 1980s. However, a development policy paradigm of liberal neodevelopmentalism in Uganda has also seen the central government adopt a rigorous evaluation framework that might more transparently demonstrate results to the international community. The Ugandan central government has also integrated REDD+ into its comprehensive development planning process, seeking to tap the capabilities of a range of state and nonstate organizations. Thus Uganda has persevered with REDD+ implementation in what appears to be a highly effective manner despite much lower international financial support from the international community than Tanzania.

Similarly, while Uganda and Moldova have submitted numerous potential NAMAs, Tanzania has shown little interest. The former two countries have also actively participated in climate planning processes with the UNDP in order to identify NAMAs that might genuinely reflect politically feasible mitigation opportunities. That Uganda and Moldova pursued NAMA programming in the near complete absence of international financial support suggests that both states value signaling their support for climate change to the international community, perhaps in the hope that this might bring other benefits. As has been indicated, Moldova is actively negotiating with the EU about membership status. However, in support of the causal mechanism I have elaborated, the Moldovan central government has also demonstrated more enthusiasm for NAMAs than Uganda. Moldova has committed considerable levels of co-financing and endeavoring to devise a relatively rigorous evaluation framework for NAMAs (despite the near absence of guidance from the UNFCCC). This might be that the instrument appears to be more conducive to Moldova's development interests in both afforestation and bioenergy.

Overall, given the challenges involved in global climate change politics, it is exciting to report on cases where climate finance appears to be achieving what it was designed to do. But the underlying causal mechanism is also sobering as the conditions under which climate finance instruments were found to be effective are narrower than might have been hoped. However, the exercise of delineating the causal mechanism of climate finance instrument effectiveness provides grounds for optimism. Most importantly, the causal mechanism helps identify international factors that, if they were to change, might improve climate finance effectiveness. Most interesting are levels of climate finance that the international community is willing to allocate toward climate change mitigation in the developing world. It should be stressed that levels of climate finance I observed stood largely between \$4–\$7 per tCO2e, with the lowest price at \$2.5 and highest at \$12.5—all well below the social cost of carbon and prices currently observed on major carbon markets. At such low levels, climate finance instruments have been most effectively implemented when the state treats them as a means of realizing its development interests—what Srivastava and Larizza (2013) call working "with the grain." But not all states were prepared to treat climate finance instruments this way, given their development policy paradigms.

However, if carbon prices were to rise, the causal mechanism identified might be upended such that climate finance itself is sufficient to serve as the basis of effective climate action rather than need to be refracted through development policy paradigms and state development interest. In other words, climate interventions might be effectively implemented across a broader part of the economy rather than only in specific areas where the state is actively intervening to promote developmental goals. I return to this prospect later in my discussion of liberal developmental environmentalism.

11.2. Effectiveness and Instrument Design

A second major research question motivating this book has been whether climate finance instruments whose design has been based on norms of developmental environmentalism have been more effective than the CDM, which reflected ideas of liberal environmentalism. As discussed in the Introduction and Part I, compelling arguments have been made that the climate funds might be expected to perform more effectively than carbon markets. This argument has underwritten many critiques of the CDM; it has, arguably, been one of the major motivations for the shift from liberal environmentalism to developmental environmentalism at the UNFCCC—in addition to the collapse of support for neoliberal ideas after the 2008 global financial crisis.

According to this line of argument, one would have expected the CDM to be less effectively implemented across the case-study countries than REDD+ and NAMAs. However, my findings suggest little meaningful change in policy effectiveness across climate finance instruments in Tanzania, Uganda, and Moldova over the 10-year period considered. In retrospect, despite the uproar over the

CDM's perceived ineffectiveness and bogus credits, such contestation has been healthy: it has led to significant yet underappreciated reforms, such as sectoral CDM, for the (generally forgotten) second commitment period of the Kyoto Protocol. In contrast, detached from carbon markets and thus debates about claiming compensation for emission reductions in developed countries, REDD+ and NAMAs have sailed through the UN process with considerably less controversy despite little evidence to suggest that they are more effective.

Considering differences in the effectiveness of climate finance instruments in this light illuminates other research gaps. While new fund-based climate finance instruments might be disconnected from carbon markets, this avoids the larger question how about to coax rich countries to provide the enormous amounts of climate finance necessary to support the transition to low-carbon development in the developing world in the first place. Lacking such reflection, there is a risk of research critical of carbon markets a priori succumbing to what Harold Demsetz (1969) described as the "nirvana fallacy." Here the researcher "implicitly presents the relevant choice as between an ideal norm and an existing 'imperfect' institutional arrangement" (p. 1).

In this book I have sought to minimize the nirvana fallacy by comparing climate finance effectiveness across different climate finance instruments in a number of different developing countries as the international climate change regime has shifted from liberal environmentalism to developmental environmentalism. Finding little difference in the effectiveness of different climate finance instruments on the ground should prompt calls for greater scrutiny of critiques of actually existing climate finance instruments.

11.3. Alternative Explanations

My research findings and the causal mechanism they point to contrast in certain ways with other prevailing theories about the effectiveness of climate finance instruments in global climate politics. I address four alternative explanations below, including state capacity and political settlements at the domestic level as well as transnational climate politics and other international influences.

State Capacity

As suggested in the Introduction, state capacity has long been identified as a key factor shaping the effectiveness of climate policy, leading Yohe (2001) to coin the term "mitigative capacity" over two decades ago. While state capacity has rightly attracted interest in the climate policy literature, my results suggest that one distinct form of state capacity—state organizational capacity—is shaped by underlying state ideas and interests, which are the key factors shaping climate finance effectiveness.

Based on findings presented in this book, the capacity of states to engage with international climate finance instruments effectively is largely related to underlying ideas about the appropriate strategy of economic development as well as current developmental interests of the state in different economic sectors, which themselves might be largely determined by resource endowments, geography and history. Put differently, state organizational capacity is a resource whose production and deployment by the state is attributable to other underlying political factors.

This is not to say that state organizational capacity is unimportant. Rather, my results suggest that state organizational capacity is related more to the scale and complexity of climate mitigation action and not the actual effectiveness of those actions to achieve what they were set out to do. For example, the effective CDM afforestation project in Moldova was much larger than another effective CDM afforestation project in Uganda. The sophistication of the Moldovan government's engagement with NAMAs relative to Uganda can also be attributed to its higher capacity. The Moldovan state is just more capable than the Ugandan state. However, NAMA engagement in both countries contrasts starkly with that of Tanzania, which essentially did not engage with this climate finance instrument. This points to the saliency of factors other than state organizational capacity.

Also important, my concept of state organizational capacity contrasts with what Meckling and Nahm (2022) have described as state strategic capacity. This draws on Skocpol's (1985) definition of state capacity as a state's ability to achieve its objectives "especially over the actual or potential opposition of powerful social groups" (p. 9). While a useful concept for describing different strategies for using state power, there is considerable overlap with the concept of political settlements I have also used, which I elaborate upon below.

Overall, while political settlements are an important condition shaping state organizational capacity, such capacity is more directly attributable to state ideas and interests that provide direction to how the state should direct its limited capacities.

Political Settlements

To a certain degree, my emphasis on the convergence of development policy paradigms and state development interests contrasts with other research into policy effectiveness among the countries I have investigated. In particular, in their comparative study of a number of sub-Saharan African countries, Whitfield et al. (2015) have attributed "pockets of effectiveness" to countries with a strong dominant party political settlement.

In support of the explanatory power of political settlements, some support comes from the Tanzania case. A weak dominant party political settlement in Tanzania partially explains the state's inability to effectively implement the CDM and REDD+ where there was some evidence that the Division of Environment at the Vice President's Office (DoE-VPO), which was officially in charge of climate policy issues, was not effectively collaborating with other parts of the state apparatus. Some even argued that it was unnecessarily delaying some CDM projects. But key fault lines over REDD+ implementation would also emerge between the DoE-VPO and other government bodies including the Forest and Beekeeping Division at the Ministry of Natural Resources and Tourism, the Ministry of Regional Administration and Local Government at the President's Office, as well as the powerful Ministry of Finance. But a lack of significant government effort to coordinate the CDM and REDD+, as well as a near complete disregard for NAMAs over the 10-year period investigated, suggests factors other than bureaucratic turf wars are at play. I submit that such political maneuvering was possible in a state characterized by hybrid development policy paradigm of classic developmentalism/neodevelopmentalism that has been skeptical about international development opportunities presented by the international community.

Furthermore, the enduring similarities in climate finance effectiveness in Uganda and Moldova relative to Tanzania raise questions about the explanatory power of political settlements. While the relative effectiveness of climate finance instruments is congruent with the strong dominant party political settlement that still lingers in Uganda, instruments have also been implemented relatively effectively in Moldova despite a much more tumultuous recent political history that is more accurately described as competitive clientelism. Such comparative results add support to my argument about the convergence of development policy paradigms and state development interests. While a country's political settlement might help gauge the state's power to push policy implementation through the state apparatus, it does not determine the basic direction of policy itself and whether to engage with climate finance instruments in the first place. The decision on whether to engage is better viewed as a consequence of the convergence of state ideas and interests.

One remaining question—and quite beyond the scope of this book—is about the origins of the political settlements observed in Tanzania, Uganda, and Moldova. Daron Acemoglu and James Robinson have argued that institutions amenable to a market economy arise as the result of inclusive political institutions, but such institutions emerge only at certain critical historical junctures (Acemoglu et al., 2001; Acemoglu and Robinson, 2012b). They have actually been quite pessimistic about the prospects of purposeful, state-led development, such as industrial policy: "The problem is trying to identify the political situations in which industrial policy can actually be used to address these situations, and that is a much taller order" (Acemoglu and Robinson, 2012a). For these authors, even England's success in inciting the Industrial Revolution was a historical anomaly (Acemoglu and Robinson, 2012b).

This critical junctures thesis finds some support in this book. Different political settlements in Tanzania, Uganda, and Moldova may be related to divergent historical processes. Both Uganda and Moldova endured considerable political upheaval in the late 1980s/early 1990s, when the popularity of neoliberal economic ideas were at their zenith. Under these conditions, state elites appear to have been able to implement deep economic reforms without significant resistance. For Museveni in Uganda, this resulted in a cadre of disciplined bureaucrats who were able to organize the state with a surprising degree of purpose (Hickey and Izama, 2016). In Moldova, independence from the Soviet Union in 1991 led to a rapid transition to a market economy that shook the political order significantly, though actors and ideas associated with the Soviet era would find a second life by 2000 through the Party of Communists. In contrast, in Tanzania the transition to independence was more gradual, and vestiges of the past permeates current political life (Gray, 2018). More research into political settlements and their link to state capacity and policy effectiveness would be warranted.

Nonetheless, revisiting the history of economic development offers grounds to be optimistic about state-led low-carbon development and resonates with my main empirical finding about the importance of *state* ideas and interests for climate finance effectiveness. As Karl Polanyi (2001 [1944]) in his classic work *The Great Transformation* argued: "laissez-faire was planned" (p. 147). This insight—that the Industrial Revolution and capitalism were facilitated by the state—allowed for economic transformation to be spread across Europe and later the globe.

Transnational Climate Governance

To the degree that my argument identifies ideas and interests of the state as capable of explaining enduring patterns of climate finance instrument effectiveness in developing countries, it diverges considerably from prevailing theories of transnational climate governance and its emphasis on nonstate actors. Perhaps despite the intentions of its proponents (see Andonova et al., 2017), transnational climate governance has tended to suggest nonstate actors as a substitute for ineffective state-led climate action. While research in developing countries from this theoretical vantage is limited, many have concluded that the state in the developing world is inappropriate actor for catalyzing the broad transformation to low-carbon development.

For example, Newell and Bulkeley (2017) argue with regard to international climate policy and energy transitions in sub-Saharan Africa that "it is clear the state is not in a position to perform key roles in relation to innovation, lacks convening power and resources to deliver targets and goals and often also has only limited autonomy to assert policy preferences that diverge from those of transnational businesses, donors and other powerful states" (p. 655). Similarly, in a recent systematic review of electricity infrastructure development in East Africa, Gregory and Sovacool (2019) claim that a public sector perspective about electricity delivery dominates in East Africa and argue that the "government narrative must be adapted therefore towards a private sector one" (p. 148). Such conclusions are not limited to climate change politics. While a full review is beyond the scope of this book, the limited transnational governance literature addressing developing countries has generally concluded that the state is a rather passive actor in transnational policy processes (Skogstad, 2011: 20–21; Stone, 2017).

In contrast, results presented in this book suggest that nonstate actors have been underperforming, while efforts by the international development community to cater to them, to the exclusion of the state, are counterproductive. To be sure, some nonstate climate activities were beneficial, though efforts tend to be largely incremental as they were not connected to broader efforts of economic development and industrialization. Consider the case of the Plan Vivo reforestation carbon offset project in Uganda that was operating on the voluntary carbon market. Implemented by a Uganda NGO, this project was functioning well, despite relying almost exclusively on climate finance for its operations. The weakness of the project was that while it sought to plant indigenous trees with smallholders and promote biodiversity, it was not well aligned with broader state development interests to cultivate a forest industry and address the penury of timber resources in Uganda. Consequently, though the project was highly additional, it was of a smaller scale than effective afforestation projects led by the state forest agencies in Uganda and Moldova. CDM projects led by private firms were less effective. I estimate that only about one-third of carbon credits that had initially been claimed by the two private-sector-led CDM projects in Uganda and Tanzania were genuine.

Tanzania's experience with REDD+ most clearly exemplifies how a focus on nonstate actors over the central government might prove counterproductive. Norway's reluctance to offer direct financial support to the Tanzanian central government appears to have ultimately contributed to the decline of REDD+ there. While the government infighting over the REDD+ file may have explained Norway's reluctance to engage with the Tanzanian central government, the decision to bypass government appears to have thwarted effective policy implementation. As NORAD (2014b) itself admitted that "the decision to channel most funds via non-governmental channels was understandable but has made securing national ownership of REDD+ more challenging" (p. 312).

Overall, transnational climate governance theory bears an uncanny similarity to neoliberal development policy recommendations of a generation ago. In this regard, it is useful to point to recent debates about the similarities between the thought of French philosopher Michel Foucault, neoliberalism, and transnational climate governance. Foucault's biting critiques of the modern state and the entwinement of knowledge and power are associated with opening up the political process to a plurality of voices that is now seen as a fundamental characteristic of progressive governance. Yet new research puts his political activities in the 1970s/1980s in a new light and has shaken this progressive interpretation by pointing to surprising similarities between his thought and neoliberalism (Dean and Zamora, 2019; Sawyer and Daniel, 2019; Zamora and Behrent, 2016). Indeed, a number of academic works published in recent years have disclosed that Foucault saw in neoliberalism considerable political opportunity and offered it tacit endorsement (Behrent, 2009). In this perspective, transnational climate governance does not differ from liberal developmentalism but rather represents its logical extension if not radicalization.

Other International Influences

While I have argued that development policy paradigms should be viewed primarily through an economic lens, they clearly also have political dimensions that can be subject to international and/or transnational influences. This is most evident in the case of Moldova where a development policy paradigm of liberal neodevelopmentalism is entwined with the Moldovan central government's aspirations of EU membership and reducing Russian monopolies in the energy sector. For example, the initial 2005 pivot from a Russian economic partnership to one oriented toward the EU—and, strikingly, undertaken by the Party of Communists—was perhaps as much about loosening Russia's control over the Moldova economy as a belief in the market.

Despite such international influences, I submit that Moldova and the two East African states still have control over their economic ideas. In other words, they have agency. In the case of Moldova, while economic reforms have been part of efforts toward EU integration, the ultimate decision to do so has resided, in my analysis, with the Moldova people and its leaders. The 2005 decision to pivot away from Russia toward the EU by the Party of Communists came as a surprise to the international community as it demonstrated how a small country might make big decisions in its own interests. But there are other examples. Even under an EU-coalition government, the Moldovan central government has resisted recent EU calls for reform of the forest sector by unbundling Moldsilva, its state forest agency.

A similar pivotal moment took place in Uganda in 1990 when President Museveni, who identified with Afro-Marxism before assuming power, decided to liberalize exchange rates. As one observer noted, the decision to do so was "unexpected and bold. It was not a result of donor conditionality, but was born of vigorous debate within Uganda" (Byaruhanga et al., 2009: 55). Finally, in Tanzania, the country's first president after independence, Julius Nyerere, famously ejected an IMF mission in 1979, after the organization made the devaluation of the Tanzanian schilling a condition for lending (Edwards, 2014: 63–64). Thirty-five years later, President Kikwete would arguably upset neoliberal policy prescriptions by reasserting state control over TANESCO, the main power generation authority in the country.

While international influences on developing countries perhaps weigh relatively more than they do in developed countries, in each of the case-study countries there is evidence that development policy paradigms have been determined largely through an independent process.

11.4. Toward Liberal Developmental Environmentalism?

In the final analysis, findings from my investigation into the effectiveness of climate finance instruments in three developing countries over a 10-year period stretching from the liberal environmentalism of the Kyoto Protocol to developmental environmentalism of the Paris Agreement offers some guidance for moving forward.

As suggested at the outset of this book, the debate about climate finance instruments has become mired in opposing camps about the virtues and vices of more liberal approaches, which are associated with carbon markets, and more developmental approaches, which are associated with climate funds. Findings from this book suggest that an approach to climate cooperation would benefit from combining elements of both, which I describe as *liberal developmental environmentalism*. See Table 11.2.

In practical terms, *liberal developmental environmentalism* would prioritize climate mitigation actions that states are already pursuing, like NAMAs, but also include a more robust evaluation framework to attract resources from an international community that still demands results. Such an approach might go further to attract private finance for climate mitigation efforts in developing countries and avoid current dependency on public financing. Furthermore, instead of

Table 11.2 Characteristics of Liberal Developmental Environmentalism Relative to Previous

	Global Environmental Norm		
	Liberal Environmentalism	Developmental Environmentalism	Liberal Developmental Environmentalism
Principle source of financing	Private sector	Public sector	Public and private sectors at funding levels to (prudently) defy comparative advantage
Role of the state	Limited role	Essential partner	constructive roles between state and nonstate actors
Evaluation frame	Rigorous results-based approach; anticipates need for carbon market fungibility	More traditional approach to development cooperation; independent of carbon markets	Rigorous results-based approach; anticipates need for carbon market fungibility

privileging either state or nonstate actors, this would cultivate synergies between the two in the transition to low-carbon development. Informed by findings presented in this book about the effectiveness of different types of climate finance instruments, I elaborate on liberal developmental environmentalism below.

Balancing the International Needs for Results and Domestic Needs for Development

Most importantly, liberal developmental environmentalism would balance the needs of the international community for results with developing countries needs for development. First would be to establish an evaluation framework that responds to the preferences of transnational private actors, international donors, and central governments hosting climate finance initiatives. To appeal to private sector actors and donors, climate finance instruments would create more rigorous evaluation frameworks that offer greater confidence that interventions supported by climate finance are leading to emissions reductions. However, the developmental dimension of climate finance would be promoted by ensuring that the prices for emission reductions enable a country to defy its comparative advantage, realize its developmental potential and achieve transformational change

In terms of evaluation frameworks of climate finance instruments observed in this book, institutions adhering most closely to liberal developmental environmentalism principles are the World Bank's Forest Carbon Partnership Facility (WB-FCPF), especially its Carbon Fund, and as well as the Brazilian Amazon Fund (BNDES, 2021). While some might view these as similar to the carbon market approach of the CDM, the key difference is that emission reductions are unable to be sold to third parties. However, the rigor of the evaluation frameworks associated with WB-FCPF and the Brazilian Amazon Fund allows policy actors investing in them more credibility regarding their claims about their climate mitigation efforts. At the same time, if a global carbon market does emerge, these types of climate finance instruments are relatively compatible. I note that rules for the Sustainable Development Mechanism, agreed at the UN climate change conference in 2021 in Glasgow and widely seen as the successor to the CDM, also maintains the additionality criterion, suggesting policy effectiveness remains a key preoccupation of segments of the international community (Slaughter and May, 2021).

However, any climate finance instrument based on liberal developmental environmentalism needs to avoid setting the prices of emission reductions only on neoliberal principles, such as the opportunity costs associated with the current comparative advantages of developing countries. Instead, carbon prices should be based on the costs of defying (perhaps prudently) existing comparative advantage. For example, part of the reason that REDD+ has failed in Tanzania, I argue, is because the costs of forest conservation is evaluated by the state relative to the land's potential value in terms of investments in industrial agriculture, forestry, or mining and not in terms of smallholder agriculture, which underlies many REDD+ economic models used by the international community.

The methodological challenges implied in realistically endeavoring to transform a country's comparative advantage is rather uncharted territory and would benefit from more sophisticated economic analysis. This might be informed by the distinction I have sought to introduce between neodevelopmentalism and liberal neodevelopmentalism with regard to a comparative advantage defying and following strategies of economic development (Lin and Chang, 2009). But it is also worth considering how fabulously low carbon prices associated with the CDM and REDD+ initiatives investigated in this book appear now: ranging from $2.5 to $12.5 per tCO2e. Such prices are well below the social cost of carbon as well as prices currently observed on major carbon markets. In late 2023, while completing this manuscript, prices of $35 per tCO2e were observed on the Western Climate Initiative (California-Quebec) carbon market and $90 per tCO2e on the European Union Emissions Trading System. A price floor starting at approximately $12.5 per tCO2e and rising with inflation could be considered as a point of departure for discussion of a liberal developmental environmental global price for carbon. Notably, such carbon price floors serve to stabilize prices in other emissions-trading systems, such as that of the California-Quebec carbon market (Purdon et al. 2021).

Among the various climate policy instruments considered in this book, NAMAs might serve as a model for identifying climate mitigation actions with transformational developmental potential given the instrument's focus on supporting climate mitigation actions prioritized by states themselves. But NAMAs have been handicapped by a lack of leadership from the UNFCCC about what the instrument is intended to achieve and an insufficiently stringent evaluation framework for demonstrating that NAMAs have been doing what they were set out to achieve. The climate finance instrument appears to be failing to attract meaningful climate finance investments from public or private actors. Rather, the CDM continues to be a lodestar for NAMAs in practice, particularly those NAMAs attracting the most actual funding. *The CDM is dead, long live the CDM!* Despite growing interest in transformational change, most policy actors interested in investing in climate finance instruments still want results. Grafting some elements of the CDM evaluation framework onto the NAMA development process might be an appropriate strategy moving forward.

Significantly, the results-based approach and developmental aspects described above are mutually beneficial. Higher carbon prices might be expected to allay the regulatory burden as they would allow effective climate actions to be more easily distinguished from counterfactual business-as-usual scenarios. Under currently low carbon prices, the tools to measure the effectiveness of climate finance instruments—such as the CDM's counterfactual baseline measurement system—are not of sufficient resolution to separate the wheat from the chaff. In this light, climate finance instruments have been caught in a vicious circle whereby concerns about climate finance effectiveness y have dampened interest on the part of international community, bringing down carbon prices that have only further frustrated the efforts to measure additionality. But with prices on many carbon markets in North America and the EU rising, perhaps this vicious circle might soon be broken. Put differently, at higher carbon prices, climate finance might on its own represent sufficient resources to serve as a basis for effective climate action by firms, states, and a variety of other actors rather than being limited to state organizations.

An alternative institutional arrangement might be to build emissions-trading systems in developing countries. As suggested in Chapter 3, the advantage of emissions-trading systems is that the actual causal processes necessary to drive emission reductions at the firm level do not need to be identified by the regulator (Tietenburg, 2006). Rather, it is important that the regulator has comprehensive, firm-level information on emissions in a jurisdiction and, importantly, who is emitting them. Once emissions are measured and responsibility assigned to actors emitting them (via allocation of emission allowances), the regulator might let the market "figure out" the most cost-effective strategy to reduce emissions among actors in that jurisdiction. In the developing world, however, information and data constraints have frustrated the production of such detailed emission inventories, making cap-and-trade impractical. However this is changing. China launched a national emissions-trading system in 2020, where prices currently hover at about $10 (Swartz, 2016; You, 2023), while both India and Brazil are considering the development of such systems (ICAP, 2023a,b). Amongst the case-study countries, Moldova is best positioned to develop an emissions-trading systems given its development policy paradigm, state development interests in mitigation actions, and a commitment in its NDC to reduce emissions in absolute terms, rather than reducing them relative to a business-as-usual baseline, which is currently the case in Tanzania and Uganda (see Table 1.3 in the Introduction). In its updated NDC, Moldova is clearly anticipating linkage with EU emissions-trading system (GoRM, 2022). A price floor similar to that suggested above might also be secured for an eventual Moldovan emissions-trading system to ensure it delivers developmental emission reductions. Lacking such comprehensive and timely data on emissions—as well as a need to allow for some growth in emissions under a business-as-usual scenario—the governments of Tanzania and Uganda might need to rely on an alternative baseline instrument like that which I sketched above.

Bringing the State Back In

The important role that I have found the state to be playing in explaining climate finance effectiveness draws attention to certain attributes that allow the state to be an effective partner in decarbonization. Such findings resonate with the literature in comparative political economy and development studies—"No state, no development" (Bates, 2008: 709). But they also add to a growing literature in environmental politics that is also trying to bring the state back in.

For example, Bäckstrand and Kronsell (2015) have called for a fundamental rethinking of the state's role in dealing with environmental challenges, suggesting it has unique power and authority to address many current crises. Similarly, Death (2015) identifies a number of green economy discourses in the Global South, including green resilience, green growth, green transformation, and green revolution, going so far to conclude that the "major commonality in all . . . national strategies and articulations of the green economy is the central role of the state" (p. 2219).

While nonstate actors can play a constructive role, my findings raise fundamental questions about importance accorded them in transnational climate governance, particularly for investigating low-carbon transitions in the developing world. The virtue of transnational climate governance theory is to have identified an important part of the equation for effective climate action: the private sector, subnational governments, and NGOs. Its weakness, however, has been to create an unhealthy binary opposition between "state" and "non-state" actors that casts doubt on the legitimate hierarchical authority that states can embody. As Samuel Huntington once argued: "Authority has to exist before it can be limited" (Huntington, 1968: 7–8).

The notion of inviting the state to play a larger, more developmental role in climate finance may raise alarm. The history of economic development is littered with "win-win scenarios" between international actors and domestic elites at the apex of the state apparatus won at the exclusion of other interests. Such concerns are amplified in the context of investment projects in developing countries involving land, such as climate finance projects in the forest and bioenergy sectors given the relative lack of power of local communities and land tenure issues (Purdon, 2013; Unruh, 2008). As I discussed in our review of development policy paradigms, neodevelopmentalism has often been associated with authoritarian regimes, whether South Korea in the 1960s or China today. The surprising heritage that classic developmentalism shares with the Soviet development model is also profoundly disconcerting. For these reasons, bringing the state more constructively into climate finance should draw on innovative ideas such as the democratic developmental state (Edigheji, 2010) and just transitions (Swilling et al., 2016).

Role for Clean Technology Subsidies

My discussion of liberal developmental environmentalism might still not convince some readers who might ask: Why not just go through traditional markets, taking advantage of rapidly declining costs for decentralized renewable energy technologies including solar, wind, and batteries? Indeed, the 2022 adoption of the Inflation Reduction Act in the US has, arguably, triggered a subsidy war among the US, EU, and China that promises to bring down the costs of clean technology globally as these countries look for markets for their products (Meckling, 2021).

In many ways, this is a valid argument. As suggested earlier, the Inflation Reduction Act is a good example of neodevelopmentalism if not liberal neodevelopmentalism—although commonly referred to as "industrial policy" in the developed world—in the sense that the US federal government is seeking to steer the US economy and build comparative advantage (if not dominance) in new clean energy technologies. As Meckling has argued, such industrial policies tend to proceed more direct regulatory efforts to reduce emissions and provide a technological off-ramp that allows governments to introduce more stringent climate mitigation measures (Meckling, 2021; Meckling et al., 2017).

But there are a few reasons to remain vigilant about the global impact of clean technology subsidies. First, while concerns about the "rebound effect" might be overblown (Gillingham et al., 2016), clean technology subventions do not guarantee emission reductions. Second, it is not clear how subsidized technologies will penetrate markets in developing countries. Climate finance or related development policy instruments might still be necessary to facilitate the transfer of such technologies. Third, clean technology subsidies do little to target emis- · sions in the land-use sector. It is true that declining costs for renewable energy might disrupt existing, often illicit, markets for fuelwood and charcoal in developing countries, but it is difficult to envision their effect on forest management and deforesetation. More research into the spillover effects of clean technology subsidies in the developing world is necessary.

11.5. Recommendations for Further Research

The findings of this book point toward a number of new avenues for research. A first is to undertake greater empirical evaluations of the effectiveness of climate finance instruments to reduce emissions, including the three that have been the focus of this book, while extending the ex post analysis to other instruments and initiatives, such as the activities being financed under the Green Climate Fund as well as NDCs themselves.

Most research into the Green Climate Fund to date has focused on aggregated financial flows and institutional arrangements (Bowman and Minas, 2019; Cui and Huang, 2018; Klöck et al., 2018). However, its core metric remains comparable to the climate finance instruments investigated: emission reductions measured against a country-level business-as-usual trajectory, though costs of reductions and volume of climate finance catalyzed are also important outcomes (GCF, 2014: 5, 13). Similarly, most research into NDCs to date has also been largely prospective and not based on actual implementation (Fawcett et al., 2015; Höhne et al., 2017; Khan et al., 2020; Röser et al., 2020; Siriwardana and Nong, 2021; Vogt-Schilb and Hallegatte, 2017).

A number of empirical strategies might be pursued to investigate this broader array of climate finance instruments. One route might be to undertake fieldwork and validate how initiatives financed through these climate finance instruments have been implemented on the ground, similar to the approach taken in this book. Evaluations of effectiveness might also make better use of sophisticated new statistical methods of causal inference referred to as "synthetic controls."

Some of the more cutting-edge research in climate policy has used such methodological tools, including emission reductions claimed from REDD+ projects on the voluntary carbon market (West et al., 2023), the European Union Emissions Trading System (Bayer and Aklin, 2020), and the British Columbia carbon tax in Canada (Pretis, 2022). To use the terminology of this book, the method is based on the reconstruction of baseline scenarios against which the implementation of climate finance instruments are compared using meticulous econometric methods (Athey and Imbens, 2017). If data for synthetic control methods remain scarce, though, comparative small-N methods remain an appropriate approach for research into the causal claims of new policy instruments (Steinberg, 2007).

It is important to bear in mind that evaluation should not only be limited to direct emission reductions. The concept of transformational change is increasingly drawing attention to the complex and indirect higher-level effects of policy interventions. Climate and development organizations increasingly seek to evaluate their interventions in light of transformational change, including the UNDP (Lütken et al., 2013), Global Environment Facility (GEF) (Batra et al., 2022), NAMA Facility (2015), OECD (2019), and IPCC (2022b). Despite consensus on promoting transformational change, important debates revolve around what constitutes it as well as the relationship of transformational change to sustainability and global governance (Feola, 2015; Mapfumo et al., 2017; Swilling et al., 2016).

Furthermore, as suggested above, it would also be important to gauge the effectiveness of climate finance instruments in light of recent efforts to ramp up subsidies for the development and deployment of clean energy technologies. Might climate finance instruments in developing countries and clean technology subsidies in developed countries be brought together in a manner that is truly transformational? While not a subsidy, a related example is the EU's recently introduced "Regulation on Deforestation-Free Products," which aims to ensure that imported soy, beef, palm oil, wood, cocoa, coffee, rubber, and some of their derived products do not contribute to deforestation in developing countries (European Commission, 2023). In this way, the EU is using its market power to tackle transnational drivers of deforestation.

Answering these questions might benefit from unpacking transformational change and its relationship with incremental change. As suggested by Termeer et al. (2017), transformational change has often been characterized as change that is entrenched, large-scale, and/or quick (also see Bernstein and Hoffmann, 2018). But there are often important trade-offs between these different characteristics: a change that is quickly achieved might be very shallow. Furthermore, incremental changes might accumulate over time to a level that moves a socioeconomic system beyond a threshold and result in transformational change (Levin et al., 2012; Termeer et al., 2017; Winkelmann et al., 2022). Another debate revolves around the measurement of transformational change. Of the characteristics of transformational change, entrenchment is arguably the most difficult to measure because it is associated with complex path-dependent processes that have only begun to attract empirical research attention (Bernstein and Hoffmann, 2018; Mahoney, 2000; Pierson, 1993; Torfing, 2009). More research is required to refine these analytical categories and perhaps introduce new ones. However, given the international community's continued interest in direct effects, such as measurable emission reductions, I would suggest not abandoning traditional evaluation frameworks to focus on transformational change. Instead, agreeing with the strategic orientation of the GEF, the evaluation of direct effects (additionality) should be seen as foundational for evaluating broader impacts and transformational change (Batra et al., 2022: 93–114).

The causal mechanism that I have argued shapes climate finance effectiveness in my three case-study countries would also benefit from further research. The different types of development policy paradigms I have identified will not, I suspect, receive universal acclaim. Some might be uncomfortable with the historical associations I make between classic developmentalism and the Soviet model of economic development. Similarly, critical development theorists might contest the distinction I make between neoliberalism and liberal neodevelopmentalism. Most important, in my view, would be to validate my differentiation between neodevelopmentalism and liberal developmentalism. Given my method for observing policy paradigms as ideas "revealed" in policies, institutions, and organizations (Daigneault, 2014), I cannot claim to have actually observed the decision-making process argued to take place within liberal neodevelopmental states about where to best allocate limited state organizational capacities. As Andreoni and Chang (2019) argue, "a backward economy doesn't really know what it is capable of until it tries new things" (p. 140). I readily admit that my argument about liberal neodevelopmentalism appears to suffer from an omitted variable about how the state makes strategic decisions about the comparative advantage of different firms and sectors and welcome future research in this area.

Finally, legitimate concerns might be raised about the generalizability of my conclusions as they emanate from only three case-study countries. The drawback of research focusing on policy effectiveness is that it requires a deep dive into technical issues, which is difficult to sustain over a large number of cases. Nonetheless, my countries did capture considerable variation in different elements of political economy, including not only state capacity but also political settlements, development policy paradigms, and state development interests. However, it did not capture enough of the universe of cases to be representative of the "developing world." I agree with Hochstetler (2023) that the "developing world" and "Global South" as analytical categories are losing their analytical purchase as the economic gap between developed and many developing countries closes. My feeling is, however, that such an argument is more appropriate when comparing climate policy in developed economies and emerging economies, such as Brazil and China. As suggested in my discussion of political settlements, structural features of least developed countries, which includes Tanzania and Uganda, are fundamentally different from those in developed countries.

In least developed countries, material scarcity and an underdeveloped private sector have the counterintuitive effect of concentrating political and economic power in the state while simultaneously driving politics into informal channels where various groups compete for the state's scarce resources (Khan, 2005). Such recognition has profound implications for understanding the policy process in least developed countries, especially the prevalence of patron-client relations and "corruption." Enjoining my critique of transnational climate governance earlier, policy recommendations that discount the state and favor nonstate actors as a work-around may prove counterproductive because they are based on assumptions about the policy process in the developed world. Mainstream policy theory remains open to the critique that it has been informed overwhelmingly by the experience of Western liberal democracies (Dodds, 2013: 297–314; Maliniak et al., 2018; Steinberg, 2012; Waever, 1998).

To conclude, the findings of this book might be expected to "resonate" (see Steinberg, 2015) with the experience of other countries still in the early process of industrialization where the economy is highly reliant on agriculture and rural peasants are still important. Comparison with other countries of East Africa and the former Soviet Union might be a logical first step. In East Africa, Rwanda is widely recognized as now possessing a strong dominant party political settlement that has developmental potential (Chemouni, 2023), while Kenya is no longer considered a least developed country and might be expected to possess greater state organizational capacity. In Eastern Europe and the former Soviet Union, the CDM was also permitted in Armenia, Azerbaijan, Georgia, and Albania, which might allow comparison with Moldova's experience. Research into climate policy effectiveness in a broader universe of cases might address these outstanding questions.

Appendix 1: Supplementary Information About Carbon Offset Projects

Introduction

This appendix contains supplementary information from my investigation into the effectiveness of carbon offset projects in Tanzania, Uganda, and Moldova presented in Chapter 8. This investigation was based on visits to seven carbon offset projects in operation in 2009 with analysis carried through 2014 (Table A.1). Information for evaluation was obtained through project site visits, review of official project documents, and local-level and district/national-level interviews. Summaries of these interviews are presented in Table A.2 and Table A.3, respectively.

In this appendix, I also present more detailed information on two CDM projects investigated in Chapter 8: the Tanzania CDM cookstove project as well as the Uganda CDM Cogeneration Project.

Tanzania CDM Cookstove Project

I compared the amount of fuelwood consumed among households of a village involved in the pilot project and control village.[1] Households in the control village consumed an average of 12 kg/day of firewood, while in the CDM project village, household consumption was 7 kg/day (Table A.4).[2] Of the households surveyed in 2009, nearly 60% already had stoves and approximately 20% said they were seeking to obtain one.

The history of natural resource management suggests that most of the fuelwood being collected was from non-renewable sources. Prior to German colonialism, the Karatu area had been the domain of Maasai pastoralists whose cattle maintained a grassland ecosystem. However, a major cattle plague in the 1890s wiped out Maasai herds, initiating a political transformation which saw the agro-pastoral Iraqw (Mbulu) people settle in the region. The displacement of the Maasai and their cattle resulted in the reestablishment of miombo woodlands (Rohde and Hilhorst, 2001: 10; Snyder, 1996). But such miombo woodlands are also prime habitat for the tsetse fly, which causes sleeping sickness (Brightwell et al., 1992; Nash, 1937). Mindful of a major sleeping sickness outbreak in Uganda, the British colonial authorities embarked on a tsetse control program in Tanzania during the 1940s–1950s that included the mass relocations of local populations and the clearing of woodland habitat (Hocking et al., 1963; Hoppe, 2003). As a result, Karatu district again became largely devoid of woody vegetation, with most forest resources concentrated in centrally managed forest reserves.

Various studies dating from the 1970s, 1980s, and 1990s report a worsening fuelwood situation in Karatu district (see Axelsson and Hagborg, 1994). Between 1953 and 1987, woody vegetation in the Lake Manyara basin declined by around 14% due to fuelwood

Table A.1 Seven Carbon Offset Projects Investigated Across Tanzania, Uganda, and Moldova

Country	Project Reference Name	Technical Name	Reference
Tanzania	Tanzania CDM Afforestation	• Afforestation in Grassland Areas of Uchindile & Mapanda • Reforestation at the Idete Forest Project	CDM-PDD, 2007a, 2008b
	Tanzania CDM Cookstove	• Karatu Energy Efficient Stove Project	KDA, 2008
Uganda	Uganda CDM Afforestation	• Uganda Nile Basin Reforestation Project—No. 1 • Uganda Nile Basin Reforestation Project—No. 2 • Uganda Nile Basin Reforestation Project—No. 3 • Uganda Nile Basin Reforestation Project—No. 4 • Uganda Nile Basin Reforestation Project—No. 5	CDM-PDD, 2006a,b,c,d, 2009
	Uganda Plan Vivo Reforestation	• Trees for Global Benefits: A Cooperative Community Land-Use Carbon Offset Project	EcoTrust, 2004, 2007, 2008; 2009
	Uganda CDM Biomass Cogeneration	• Kakira Sugar Works Ltd. (KSW) Cogeneration Project	CDM-PDD, 2007b
Moldova	Moldova CDM Afforestation	• Moldova Soil Conservation Project • Moldova Community Forestry Development Project • Voluntary Carbon Project Between Moldsilva and World Bank	CDM-PDD, 2008a, 2010Moldsilva, 2009: 18
	Moldova CDM Rural Energy Modernization	• Moldova Biomass Heating in Rural Communities—No. 1 • Moldova Biomass Heating in Rural Communities—No. 2	CDM-PDD, 2005a,b
Total	7	15	

consumption and timber harvesting while cropland increased by 118% (Mwalyosi, 1991 and Mwalyosi and Mohamed, 1992 cited in Yanda and Madulu, 2005). The Marang Forest Reserve saw 15–20% of its forest degraded into grassland during this time (Meindertsman and Kessler, 1997 cited in Yanda and Madulu, 2005: 723).

Uganda CDM Biomass Cogeneration Project

The Kakira Sugar Works Ltd. (KSW) Cogeneration Project sought to expand bagasse co-generation capacity to sell surplus electricity to Uganda's national grid in a way that would reduce emissions. It was the most complex CDM project investigated and I report on more detailed additionality evaluation here.

Table A.2 Summary of Local-Level Field Efforts

Village	Village Surveys	Household Surveys	Household Interviews				Focus Groups			Dates Visited in 2009
			House holds	Local Govt	Private	NGO	Local Govt	Private	NGO	
TANZANIA										
Luhunga	1	26	12	2	1		1			Jan 3; Mar 1–4
Mapanda	1	22	9	1	2		1			Feb 1; Mar 5–8
Idete	1	25	10	1			1			Feb 2; Mar 10–12
Ipilimo	1	24	1	1						Mar 13–15
Makunga	1						1			Mar 13
Mtamba	1	17	5				1			Apr 30–May 2
Magaruwe	1	24								May 22–24,
Endabash	1	24	3				1			Apr 6–10,
Bassodawish	1	27		1						Aug 17–18,
UGANDA										
Kirungu	1	27	6	1			1			May 19–22
Rwoho/RECPA	1				1					May 19–22, June 2–4
Rwerazi	1	29	12				1	2		May 23–24, June 2–4

(continued)

Table A.2 Continued

Village	Village Surveys	Household Surveys	Household Interviews				Focus Groups			Dates Visited in 2009
			House holds	Local Govt	Private	NGO	Local Govt	Private	NGO	
Biteroko Subcounty	1			2		1				May 26–27, June 7–12
• Plan Vivo HHs		31	9							May 26–27, June 7–12
• Non-Plan Vivo HHs		30	2							May 26–27, June 7–12
Kagogwa	1	29	1				2			June 10–11, 15–16
MOLDOVA										
Săiți	1	30	12	1	3					July 27–Aug 2
Tocuz	1	29	5	1	1			2		Aug 4–6
Ursoaie	1			3		1				July 23
Bursuceni	1	30	17	2						Aug 13–15
Chiscareni	1	30	17	1		1				Aug 18–22
Cotiujenii-Mici	1			2						Aug 17
Prepelița	1			1			1			Aug 17
	21	454	121	20	8	3	11	4		

Table A.3 Summary of District- and National-Level Key Informant Interviews

	District/Region			National					Total
	NGO	Govt	Private	NGO	Govt	Donor	Private	Research	
Tanzania	4	10	6	6	7	2	3	1	39
Uganda	1	8	3	3	10	3	1	5	34
Moldova		3	3	3	9	3	1		22
Total	5	21	12	12	26	8	5	6	95

Table A.4 Fuel Consumption and Associated Costs in Endabash and Bassodawish, Tanzania CDM Cookstove project

Village	Households	Firewood	Charcoal	Crop Residues	Kerosene
Average daily fuel consumption	(N)	(kg/day)	(kg/day)	(kg/day)	(liter/day)
Endabash	22	6.6	0.1	/	0.1
—Improved stove	13 (9*)	5.1 (4.0*)	/	/	0.2
—3-stone hearth	8 (23*)	7.7 (13.0*)	/	/	0.1
—Charcoal	1	13.7	2.5	/	0.1
Bassodawish	25	11.8	1.1	1.4	0.2
—3-stone hearth	21	13.6	/	1.6	0.1
—Charcoal	4	2.6	6.6	/	0.3
Cost		(Tsh/kg)	(Tsh/kg)	(Tsh/kg)	(Tsh/liter)
Endabash	22	22.8	171	/	1,104
Bassodawish	25	17.7	179	13.9	1,216

* Indicates field results reported by KDA (2009).

Development Additionality

I begin evaluation of background additionality with a brief review of the history of Uganda's sugar mills. Though KSW claimed that the project was a "first of its kind," a survey I undertook of Uganda's sugar mills found two additional mills planning cogeneration for export to the national grid (Table A.5).

Technical factors influencing the development baseline also changed. First, the amount of power KSW would actually produce over the CDM project's crediting period from 2008 to 2014 produced only three-quarters as much power as expected, from an expected 103,606 MWh per year to only 76,224 MWh per year (CDM-PDD, 2007b: 24; ERA, 2010; 2014b). Second, the grid emissions factor used to estimate emissions displaced from Uganda's grid also changed. It is true that fossil fuel generators dominated at the time the

Table A.5 Common Practice Analysis of Sugar Factories Across Uganda (2009), Uganda CDM Biomass Cogeneration Project

	Commission Year	Sugar Cane Production Capacity	2011 Annual Sugar Production**	Total Power Generation	Power Generation for Export	District
		Tonnes Cane per Day	Tonnes	MW	MW	
Existing Sugar Factories*						
Sugar Company of Uganda Ltd. (SCOUL)	1924	NA	38,006	16	7.4	Buikwe
Kakira Sugar Works	1930	6,000	132,679	48–51	32–34	Jinja
Sango Bay Estates	1930	NA	15,000	NA	NA	Rakai
Kinyara Sugar Ltd.	1969	NA	88,725	35	22	Masindi
GM Sugar	NA	200	2,500	NA	NA	Jinja
Mayuge Sugar Ltd.**	2005	2,500	5,000	9	NA	Mayuge
Sugar & Allied Industries	2013	2,000	NA	12	8	Kaliro
Newly Licensed Sugar Factories as of 2011[†]						
Tirupati Development Uganda	In development	2,500	NA	NA	NA	Nakasongola
Mukwano Sugar Industry	In development	2,500	""	""	""	Masindi
Uganda Crop Industries	In development	200	""	""	""	Buikwe
Kafu Sugar	In development	800	""	""	""	Masindi
Kamuli Sugar	In development	200	""	""	""	Kamuli
Kenlon Sugar	In development	500	""	""	""	Namasagali
Bugiri Sugar Company	In development	500	""	""	""	Bugiri

* Wikipedia (2014)

** M&P Group of Industry (2011)

[†] Sanya (2011, 2013); SugarOnline (2012)

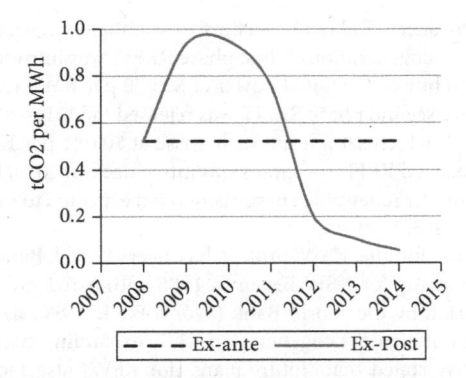

Figure A.1 Uganda's Grid-Based Emissions During the CDM Crediting Period, Uganda CDM Biomass Cogeneration Project

CDM project was initiated in 2007 because a severe drought in the region from 2004 to 2006. But there were important changes to Uganda's electricity mix after the CDM project was initiated—the most important being the Bujagali dam, which finally came online in 2012 (Kasita, 2012). These changes in Uganda's power mix affect the grid emissions factor in an important way.

In recalculating the grid emissions factor, I used a tool developed by Praher (2008) for the Ugandan context as well as appropriate conversion factors found in the CDM project document itself. The tool facilitates the conversion of power generation into emissions based on type of power producer (large hydro, thermal, or renewable energy), fuel consumption, and fuel type (heavy oil, diesel, or natural gas). Figure A.1. presents the ex-ante grid emissions factor from the CDM project in contrast to the ex-post grid expansion factor I modeled. The average grid expansion factor estimated over the CDM crediting period stands at 0.5038 tCO2e per MWh which is slightly below the 0.5223 tCO2e per MWh set in the CDM project document (CDM-PDD, 2007b: 24). The ex-ante CDM baseline grid emissions factor tends to underestimate baseline emissions until 2011 as Uganda became more reliant on thermal power; however, as the Bujagali large-scale hydroelectric plant came fully online in 2012, the emissions factor then overestimates actual grid emissions. This transformation alone results in a reduction of carbon credits expected over the crediting period 2008–2014 from 378,793 to 261,692 tCO2e—only two-thirds of carbon credits claimed are genuine based on development additionality analysis.

Financial Additionality

My evaluation of financial additionality required a method for disentangling emission reductions due to Uganda's renewable energy feed-in tariff (REFIT), donor project financing, and those associated with the CDM. I determined the amount of KSW's generating capacity that might reasonably be attributed to different funding sources through a detailed reconstruction of the different stages of the cogeneration project and corresponding generating capacity associated with each. I then estimated the share of emission reductions claimed by the CDM that are actually due to each of these other interventions (Table A.7).

Uganda would introduce REFITs in an effort to stimulate renewable energy production, including biomass cogeneration. A first phase REFIT was introduced in 2007 by the central government to buy cogenerated power at $0.070 per KWh (MEMD, 2007: 113). A more comprehensive second phase REFIT was released for 2011–2016 (ERA, 2011: 15, 2014a: 27; Gipe, 2011), which set a tariff for bagasse at $0.081 per KWh. In addition, a $130 million donor-backed REFIT program was introduced in 2013, known as GET FIT Uganda, with payments for renewable energy generated expected to extend through 2023 (GET FiT Uganda, 2014: 3, 32–33).

But more important for the KSW project has been World Bank donor financing. Significant donor financing for KSW began in 1988 with a $62 million sugar rehabilitation project supported by the World Bank (World Bank, 1996: ii). The firm has also consistently sought to implement cogeneration while expanding sugarcane production. In the late 1980s, KSW stated that "future plans [for KSW] also include proposals for usefully disposing excess bagasse resulting from continuing expansion of cane production" (World Bank, 1996: iv). In the 1990s, two-thirds of the bagasse produced was used to fuel two turbo generators capable of generating 4 MW of electricity for in-house power consumption while the rest was dumped and burned (Wardrop, 2004: 12; World Bank, 2001: 62). The logical next step would be to harness the excess to produce electricity for the national grid.

KSW's initial efforts to acquire the technology necessary to export additional electricity were unsuccessful. In 1998, KSW submitted a proposal to the Uganda central government to sell 18 MW of electricity at a tariff of $0.080 per KWh (GEF, 2007: 37; Mutambi, 2010: 4). However, the government decided not to pursue this proposal because it was expecting that cheaper hydroelectric capacity would soon come online via the 250 MW Bujagali dam (GEF, 2007: 37; Mutambi, 2010: 4). But with the dam's delay, KSW won a contract in 2003 to export 7 MW but only at a tariff of $0.049 per KWh (Mutambi, 2010: 4). I submit that the firm only agreed to the low tariff rate in 2003 because of support through the World Bank's Energy for Rural Transformation program. In the first phase of the program, awarded in 2003, about $14 million was directed to the cogeneration project (GEF, 2001; Juuko, 2004; Kayizzi, 2004; Mufumba, 2005). This included a $3.3 million tariff subsidy (Kalyango, 2004; Kayizzi, 2004; MEMD, 2004: 10) and a $7.7–$8.6 million loan (Juuko, 2004; KSW, 2010; World Bank, 2009b: 76).[3]

This first phase of the World Bank program abutted the CDM project. While distinguishing emission reductions due to donor and CDM financing is difficult, a careful analysis allows me to attribute generating capacity to different sources of financing. For the first phase of the World program, 14–15 MW of generating capacity was added by refurbishing KSW's existing boilers: installation of two new 20 bar boilers and the addition of a new turbo generator (GEF, 2001; Juuko, 2004; Kayizzi, 2004; Mufumba, 2005). However, of this additional capacity only 5–7 MW were to be exported to the national grid (KSW, 2010; Mufumba, 2005; Wardrop, 2004: 23). *This is of key importance to the evaluation of CDM financial additionality: the 5–7 MW scenario is the appropriate historical, pre-CDM financial baseline scenario for the CDM project—though it is not reported in the CDM documents.*

The CDM subsidized the electricity tariff (CFU, 2008: 30; Katoomba Group, 2007), compensating KSW for the tariff of $0.062 per kWh offered by government, which was considerably less than the $0.110 rate that KSW sought (Mutambi, 2010: 4). Based on the available evidence, the only new power generation components financed through the CDM were two new 45 bar boilers (replacing older 20 bar ones), which have allowed for an increase in sugarcane crushing capacity (CDM-PDD, 2007b: 3). The CDM project also sought to increase sugarcane crushing capacity from 3,500 to 6,000 tonnes cane per day with additional cane being sourced from surrounding smallholder farmers (CDM-PDD, 2007b: 2–3). I conclude from this that the CDM allowed KSW to increase the power generating capacity of the existing turbo generator to 12–14 MW from the initial baseline of 5–7 MW.[4] In other words, the CDM project added 7 MW of export capacity to the initial 5–7 MW made possible through the World Bank program though the CDM project documents claim all 12–14 MW.

In an important sign of the non-additionality of the project, KSW has been able to continue to expand cogeneration capacity after withdrawing from the CDM project. Recall that crediting period of the CDM project ran from 2008 to 2014. In 2010, an increase of in-house generating capacity by 3 MW was achieved through a UNEP-GEF project (AFREPREN/FWD, 2009; GEF, 2007). Furthermore, the World Bank Energy for Rural Transformation program anticipated a second phase of KSW's expansion from 2010 to 2014 to increase KSW exports to 20–25 MW at a cost of $25 million (AFREPREN/FWD, 2009; GEF, 2001: 63). Finally, in early 2014, as the result of a $65 million investment, KSW has been able to increase total generating capacity to 46 MW—with 32–34 MW to be exported to the grid (KSW, 2014). It is not entirely clear what has spurred this second phase expansion in 2014. It seems unlikely that all might be attributed to the World Bank program but rather the second-phase REFIT. This offered a tariff of $0.075 per kWh for bagasse cogeneration (ERA, 2011: 6: 6), which is close to the original tariff rate of $0.080 per kWh originally proposed by KSW in 1998.

Overall, combination of development and financial additionality over the CDM crediting period from 2008 to 2014 finds genuine carbon credits reduced to 128,600 tCO2e—only one-third of that originally claimed (Table A.6). While my evaluation of development additionality suggested that only two-thirds of CDM credits claimed on this basis were genuine, these were further reduced by at least half based on my financial additionality analysis.

Table A.6 Summary of Changes in Project Financial Baseline Conditions, Uganda CDM Biomass Cogeneration Project

Year	Intervention	Total Generation Capacity	In-House Capacity	Export Capacity	Tariff	Donor Support	Financers	Original CERs	Financial Additionality Factor	Ex-Post CER Evaluation
		MW	MW	MW	$/KWh	$M		tCO2e		tCO2e
Late 1990s	In-house	4	4	0	NR	Unknown	Unknown			
1998	(KSW expansion attempt)	(22)	(4)	(18)	(0.080)	(0)	(0)			
1999										
2000										
2001										
2002										
2003	KSW Expansion 1	18–19	11–14	5–7	0.049	23.6	ERT Programme: WB & Netherlands			
2004										
2005										
2006										
2007	CDM	25–26	11–14	12–14	0.062	3.3	CDM/WB			
2008								46,025	0.5	23,013

Year	Project					Source			
2009							46,025	0.5	23,013
2010	Cogen for Africa	28–29	14–17	12–14	Unknown	ERT Programme: UNEP-GEF	57,349	0.5	28,675
2011	RE Feed-in-Tariff				0.07	GofU	57,349	0.5	28,675
2012							57,349	0.5	28,675
2013							57,349	0.5	28,675
2014	KSW Expansion 2	48–51	14–17	32–34		KSW	57,349	0.0	0
Total Emission Reductions 2008–2014							378,795		160,726

Appendix 2: Evaluation Criteria by DNA and by State Investment Agencies

---

Box A.1 Uganda's CDM and Investment Promotion Criteria

A. Uganda's CDM Sustainable Development Criteria

1. Introduction

The Clean Development Mechanism (CDM) defined under Article 12 of the Kyoto Protocol has two main primary objectives:

- Assist non-Annex I parties to achieve sustainable development.
- Assist Annex I Parties to meet part of their commitments under Article 3 of the Kyoto Protocol through implementation of project activities that lead to greenhouse gas emission reduction/uptake.

The CDM Executive Board regulates greenhouse gas emission reduction while a participating party regulates the sustainable development aspects according to its development priority. This criterion is developed to serve this purpose for Uganda.

Uganda adopted the Bruntland definition of sustainable development: "development that meets the needs of the present generation without compromising the ability of future generations to meet their own needs." Uganda's sustainable development criterion is based on environmental, social, economic, and technology transfer. The National Environment Management Authority (NEMA) is responsible for re-enforcing compliance with environmental legislation in close collaboration with other law re-enforcement agencies. It therefore clears projects, including evaluation and approval of environmental impact assessment, where applicable. The guidelines are simple to use and therefore project developers should be able to rate their projects prior to submission to the DNA.

These elements of the criteria are subdivided into sub-elements and each is given a maximum score against which the project is evaluated.

2. The Criterion

The criterion comprises environmental, social, economic, and technology elements and monitoring indicators. The elements are subdivided into sub-elements. Project developers are expected to provide baselines for each sub-element and a monitoring plan.

2.1 Environmental

Clearance from NEMA is a prerequisite for submission of CDM projects to the Designated National Authority (DNA). Some projects mandate environmental impact assessment (EIA) while others do not. The level of EIA varies with size of projects. EIA must be carried out in accordance with the NEMA guidelines. The EIA guidelines emphasize public participation in the entire EIA process, as a way of ensuring public input into the designing of projects. The EIA guidelines do provide for remedial actions for adverse effects of project activities. Project proponents must include a clear description of actions to be taken to address negative effects on the environment and corresponding monitoring plans. The criterion therefore focuses on social, economic, and technology aspects of sustainable development.

2.2 Social Criteria

The criterion emphasizes social benefits in line with Uganda's policy of reducing poverty among its people and therefore this component carries a total score of 40 points. The social criterion is further subdivided into

   i. enhancing community access to essential social services (18 points);
  ii. community participation in project design, implementation, monitoring, and evaluation (15); and
 iii. gender balance and promoting participation of disadvantage groups (7).

2.3 Economic Criterion

Economic contribution is viewed as equally important but rated slightly lower than social and has therefore been allocated a total score of 35 points. The criterion is further subdivided into six sub-elements:

    i. contribution to employment generation (8)
   ii. contribution to saving and generation of foreign exchange (7)
  iii. contribution to increased production of marketable goods and services (6)
  iv. mutual economic benefits accruing from project activities (5)
   v. contribution to increased demand for services (5)
  vi. contribution to redistribution of development to address area imbalances in development (4)

In ii above any project that promotes use of local resources (raw materials and human resources) would get a higher score.

2.4 Technology

Technology transfer has been allocated a total score of 25 points and is further subdivided into four sub-elements:

    i. environmentally friendly technologies (10)
    ii. technology transfer (7)
   iii. efficiency of technology (4)
   iv. acceptability of technology by local community (4)

Technology transfer embraces equipment and imparting of skills required to fully operate the technology. In addition to a technology reducing greenhouse gas emissions it must not cause negative effects on the environment.

3. Application of the Criterion

The general principles for application of the criteria are the following:

    i. The project must have got approval of its EIA from the National Environment Management Authority (NEMA).
    ii. A higher score is given to a project contributes to more than item in a given aspect of the criterion. For example a project that contributes to enhancing community access to energy, safe water and sanitation, and health services would get a higher score than if it contributed to only two items in the list.
   iii. The project developer must establish a baseline for each criteria and clear monitoring plan for evaluation of the performance of the criteria.
   iv. For a project to be selected, it must score an overall minimum score pass of 50% in addition to scoring at least 50% in each aspect of the criterion.
    v. The project developer should be able to score the project based on the SD criteria.
   vi. Where any sub-element of the criteria does not apply to a project by its nature, for example, if the project does not at all have any element of community participation, the project scores zero on this sub-element of the social aspect.
  vii. A positive score implies contribution to any aspect of the criteria, while a negative score implies adverse effects of the project on that aspect.

B. Uganda Investment Authority's Investment Appraisal Criteria

(a) Generation of new earnings or savings of foreign exchange through exports, resource-based import substitution or service activities;
(b) utilization of local materials, supplies and services;
(c) creation of employment opportunities;
(d) introduction of advanced technology or upgrading of indigenous technology;
(e) contribution to locally or regionally balanced socioeconomic development; or
(f) any other objectives that the UIA considers relevant.

Sources: Uganda Climate Change Unit, Ministry of Water, Land and Environment (pers. comm., 2009); Section 12 of the 2000 Investment Code Act.

Box A.2 Tanzania's CDM Sustainable Development Criteria

A. Tanzania's CDM Sustainable Development Criteria

- The CDM project activity should be consistent with National Strategy for Growth and Reduction of Poverty 2005, and it should aim at poverty alleviation by generating additional employment and improving standards of life.
- The CDM project activity should bring in additional financial flows through investment and should be consistent with the Vision 2025 and Vision 2020 for Tanzania mainland and Zanzibar respectively.
- The project activity should be consistent with the Environmental Management Act, 2004 and its Environmental Impact Assessment and Audit Regulations, 2005. The project should reflect resource sustainability and resource degradation if any, impact on biodiversity, human health, and other environmental issues.
- The CDM project activity should lead to transfer of environmentally benign and sound technologies to Tanzania.
- Congruence with the national environmental policy and related action plans and strategies;
- Energy projects particularly in rural areas are accorded the highest priority;
- There should be a partnership between investor country company or institution and the host country local private company, NGO, research/academic institutions or government department (unilateral projects are encouraged) where no additional technology or finance is not requested.
- In Tanzania, priority for undertaking A/R projects is given to semi-arid and arid areas.[a]

B. Tanzania Investment Centre's Social Cost-Benefit Measurement

Social Benefit Measures

1. **Employment Creation.** Will proposed investment create jobs, both directly and indirectly?
2. **Technology, Knowledge, and Skills Transfer.** One important measure for evaluating investment is whether the proposed project has a chance of enhancing technology, knowledge, and skills transfer. Often FDI can bring into the country both hard technology (e.g., equipment, industrial processes) and soft technology (e.g., knowledge, information, expertise, organizational skills, management, marketing and technical know-how). Sometimes some investments are also associated with growth of research and development (R&D) thus increasing the country's technological capacity. All these are important measures in evaluating investment applications.

[a] This final point is not listed under the eligibility criteria but in the section for AR projects. Given its resemblance to a criteria, I have included it here.

3. **Promotion of the country's exports, competitiveness, and markets.** Transnational companies can help boost the country's exports through their foreign affiliates. In general, FDI can be an important intermediary between Tanzanian domestic producers and markets abroad. Foreign investors engaged in export-oriented primary manufacturing and service activities can be particularly useful in enhancing the county's export competitiveness—in part because of their technological superiority and quality consciousness.

4. **Linkages with sectors of the economy.** Is the investment likely to source inputs in the local market? Will the investment improve the supply chain of goods and services? Will the investment add value to domestic resources. These and other considerations that foster linkages within the economy are important for accelerating economic growth.

5. **Improvement in the country's financial inflows and balance of payments.** FDI can inject substantial financial resources into the country beyond those referred to in the statutory requirements. Such resources if channeled to new investments (Greenfield-type investments) or infrastructure (e.g., electricity, telecom, water and sanitation, roads [build-operate principles] can make marked contribution to national development. Under social benefit-cost analysis, investment inflows have to exceed outflows in terms of profit and other remittances).

Social Cost Measures

1. **Crowding out local investors.** Due partly to technological superiority, some FDI investments have squeezed out local producers. For example, a large garment manufacturer that supplies cheap clothes to the domestic market can easily kill local small-scale garment manufacturers. Large foreign banks are known to "crowd out" local banks and due to automation reduce labor considerably.

2. **Holding back local skills development and reducing entrepreneurial growth.** If an investment application demands the use of many expatriate managers and professionals. whose skills are domestically available, this could be regarded as holding back local skills development. Similarly, if FDI investors prefer to use foreign suppliers, this can be taken as reducing entrepreneurial development. In the financial sector, excessive automation by both foreign and local banks has resulted in to reduced employment and lost opportunities for further learning. In situations where investors cut off an existing domestic supply chain due to sourcing abroad (e.g., TBL import of barley from South Africa), this action could be result in killing local entrepreneurial linkages.

3. **Environmental Damage.** Some investments may have negative effects on the environment although the project may be financially profitable. A typical example is the pollution of air or water by industrial plants. The discharge is a by-product of the industrial process that results in net disbenefits to the surrounding population. For such projects an Environmental Impact Assessment (EIA) is mandatory. However, for TIC purposes, it is a good idea to include environmental concerns as one of the measures for investment evaluation.

4. **Social costs related to systemic risk.** Sometimes an economy can be exposed to significant instability due partly to structural and institutional weaknesses of the economy. For example, the entry of foreign financial institutions might undermine the ability of the Bank of Tanzania to exercise control over international capital movements into and out of the country—despite the existence of good regulations.

Sources: DoE (2007: 14–15); TIC (2008: 47–49).

Notes

Chapter 1

1. As of late 2021, the CDM was claimed to represent over 10,500 MtCO2e of emission reductions and removals from over 8,400 projects (UNEP DTU, 2021a; b). For REDD+ under the UNFCCC the impact is difficult to evaluate as the instrument has generally not yet been fully implemented. But REDD+ is believed to have great potential. For example, Norway paid Brazil's REDD+ program about $1.2 billion between 2009 and 2018 for nearly 200 MtCO2e of emission reductions (BNDES, 2021). In addition, as of late 2021, 192 NAMA proposals have been submitted to the UNFCCC (2021) and are associated with an estimated 400 MtCO2e in emission reductions. The GCF only began disbursements in late 2017, and, as of 2021, claims funding total $6.7 billion has been implemented so far will achieve 2,000 MtCO2e of reductions from 190 projects (GCF, 2021; Watson and Schalatek, 2020).
2. NGO Officer, Kampala, Interview U3, 13 June 2014.
3. Formal land titling and surveys have remained around 10% in Tanzania (Bluwstein et al., 2018; Huggins, 2018; Wrottesley, 2017) though reaching approximately 20% in Uganda (Mabikke, 2016). During 2009 interviews, I learned from a central government official in Tanzania that only approximately 10% of village lands had been surveyed and land-use plans produced. Similarly, a district government official in Uganda explained that its district land board had registered fewer than 10% of landowners. In contrast, I received a brief computer demonstration of Moldova's land cadastre at Moldova's Agency for Land Relations and Cadastre (Government Officer, Chisinau, Interview, 25 August 2009).
4. Donor Government Officer, Dar es Salaam, Interview TN2, 30 March 2009.

Chapter 2

1. At a 2010 meeting, the CDM Executive Board updated CDM Validation and Verification Manual to agree that "[auditors] shall apply standard auditing techniques to assess the correctness of the information provided by the project participants, including, where appropriate, but not limited to: (a) Document review . . . (b) Follow-up actions . . . *(c) Reference to available information relating to projects or technologies similar to the proposed CDM project activity under validation*; (d) Review, based on the approved methodology being applied, of the appropriateness of formulae and correctness of calculations (CDM EB, 2010: para.33(a-d, emphasis added).

Chapter 3

1. Paragraph 7 of the Copenhagen Accord reads, "We decide to pursue various approaches, including opportunities to use markets, to enhance the cost-effectiveness of and to promote mitigation actions. Developing countries, especially those with low emitting economies should be provided incentives to continue to develop on a low emission pathway."
2. Even these data are questionable. For example, the NAMA database indicates that all Moldovan NAMAs are in the process of being implemented, though results presented later in this book suggest otherwise.
3. International Consultant, Phone Interview Int1, 5 June 2015.
4. Ibid.
5. Ibid.

Chapter 5

1. Domestic Expert, Dar es Salaam, Interview T7, 30 July 2018.

Chapter 6

1. While Tanzania reports energy statistics to both the International Energy Agency (IEA) and the African Energy Commission (AFREC), Moldova reports only to the IEA and Uganda only to the AFREC. However, only the IEA includes an estimate of the total supply of firewood and modern bioenergy in its measure of bioenergy and waste, while the AFREC only measures charcoal supply.

Chapter 7

1. TANESCO Officer, Dar es Salaam, Interview T8, 2 June 2014.
2. District Government Officer, Căușeni, Interview MD1, 7 August 2009.

Chapter 8

1. For logistical reasons, I was unable to visit a second, more remote CDM biomass co-generation project in Uganda CDM-PDD (2008b). Despite my efforts to reach out to TIST prior to 2009 fieldwork, I was unable to make contact and thus locate projects in the field. Also note that the Tanzania CDM authorities barred TIST from the CDM,

while it was embraced in Uganda as voluntary carbon market project (Reynolds, 2012). I also considered detailed investigation of the cookstove project in Uganda operating on the voluntary markets (Gunther, 2008), though ultimately, I chose not to pursue the project as it was largely urban focused with only a pilot project in a rural area.

2. Source: NFA (2007a: 14–15). Rwoho CFR was decompartmentalized into three management areas totaling 9,060 ha: CDM (2,138 ha), other timber (3,945 ha), and conservation (2,977 ha). Note the small discrepancy between community CDM blocks reported by NFA (346.7 ha) here and those in the CDM documents (194.0 ha).

3. The Prototype Carbon Fund allocated $5.2 million to the first CDM project over 2002–2010, including $1.8 million in terms of carbon credits at $3.3 per tCO_2e (PCF, 2003). The BioCarbon Fund only issued its first payment for this project in 2012, upon completion of the project's first monitoring report when it bought 851,911 tCO_2e of carbon credits for an estimated $2.8 million (World Bank, 2012). The BioCarbon Fund was scheduled to make an additional payment for 550,000 tCO_2e for the second CDM project, which would represent a purchase of $1.8 million (Moldsilva, 2009).

4. Moldova Government Officer, Chisinau, Interview MN9, 10 August 2009.

5. Moldsilva Rayon Agent (MD5), confidential interview; Multilateral Donor Agency Officer, Chisinau, Interview MN4, 26 August 2009: "[In 2008, Moldsilva] claimed they had overall afforested since 2001 about 60,000 ha. . . . Of those 60,000, 30,000 ha have been afforested under [World Bank] projects. So I would again [claim] in the spirit of what we believe is true for additionality. . . that without our carbon finance funds, they wouldn't have afforested the additional 30,000 hectares, and they would have stayed with the 30,000 that they would have afforested on their own. Those 30,000 are beyond our project."

6. Two villages had adopted hybrid coal-natural gas boilers (Cotiujenii-Mici and Prepelița in Sîngerei district), while a third (Ursoaie in Căușeni district) had adopted a natural gas only boiler.

7. Village Government Officer, Cotiujenii-Mici Village, Interview M32, 17 August 2009.

8. Moldova Government Officer, Chisinau, Interview MN5, 26 August 2009; NGO Officer, Chisinau, Interview MN3, 20 August 2009; Business Owner, Chisinau, Interview MN15, 20 July 2009.

9. Multilateral Donor Agency Officer, Chisinau, Interview MN4, 26 August 2009.

10. More than 90% of Plan Vivo participants claimed ownership of their lands, while only approximately 60% of the control group of local residents not participating in the programs. However, I found no formal government-issued land titles of any kind had been issued in the subcounty. As acknowledged by some of those whom I was able to interview, while the additional security offered through formal land titling was attractive, the process was found to be too expensive (Villager, Bitereko Subcounty, Interview U20, 27 May 2009).

11. NGO Officer, Karatu Town, Interview TD6, 3 April 2009.

12. NGO Officer, Karatu Town, Interview TD3, 4 April 2009.

13. Ibid.

14. NGO Officer, Karatu Town, Interview TD22, 21 October 2011.

15. Villager, Endabash Village, Interview T40, 6 April 2009; Villager, Endabash Village, Interview T42, 8 April 2009; NGO Officer, Karatu Town, Interview TD3, 4 April 2009; Village Government Focus Group (T43), Bassodawish Village, 17 August 2009.

16. Karatu District Government Officer, Karatu Town, Interview TD4, 16 April 2009.

17. Ibid.

18. Ibid.

19. The Mapanda-Uchindile project was initiated in 1997 and scheduled to be completed in 2004, yet was found during fieldwork to have been pushed back to 2014. For the second CDM project, its implementation period is officially slated from 2006 to 2013.

20. Tanzania Government Officer, Dar es Salaam, Interview TN6, 30 March 2009.

21. Ibid.

22. See Schedule 14 (Part II, Section B) under regulation 29(i) of the Forest Act.

23. Villager, Mapanda Village, Interview T20, 5 March 2009.

24. Business Manager, Kakira District, Interview UD1, 8 June 2009.

25. Ugandan Government Officer, Kampala, Interview UN20, 12 May 2009.

26. SPGS Officer, Kampala, Interview U4, June 13, 2014

27. Business Owner, Chisinau, Interview MN15, 20 July 2009.

28. Moldova Government Officer, Chisinau, Interview MN5, 26 August 2009.

29. Moldova Government Officer, Chisinau, Interview MN2, 10 July 2009.

30. Ugandan Government Officer, Kampala, Interview UN1, 12 May 2009.

31. Ugandan Government Officer, Kampala, Interview UN14, 8 May 2009.

32. Moldova Government Officer, Chisinau, Interview MN1, 10 July 2009.

33. Ibid.

34. Tanzania Government Officer, Dar es Salaam, Interview TN8, 30 May 2010.

35. Donor Government Officer, Dar es Salaam, Interview TN2, 30 March 2009.

36. NGO Officer, Karatu Town, Interview TD3, 4 April 2009. The interviewee would continue: "We have been sending [a] request for letter of no objection for this CDM project. [In over a year's time], [we] have still not heard anything about it. So we tried to remind [the DNA], and [the DNA] said [the DNA] has never received anything from us. [The DNA claims they don't] know anything about our project, and that's not true."

37. Tanzania Government Officer, Dar es Salaam, Interview TN7, 28 April 2009.

38. NGO Officer, Karatu Town, Interview TD3, 4 April 2009.

39. Tanzania Government Officer, Dar es Salaam, Interview TN5, 2 February 2009.

40. Tanzania Government Officer, Dar es Salaam, Interview TN8, 30 May 2010.

41. Ugandan Government Officer, Kampala, Interview UN14, 8 May 2009.

Chapter 9

1. Donor Government Officer, Dar es Salaam, Interview T6, 20 May 2014.

2. International Expert, Dar es Salaam, Interview T4, 2 August 2018.

3. International Expert, Dar es Salaam, Interview T5, 3 August 2018.

4. International Expert, Dar es Salaam, Interview T4, 2 August 2018.

5. As one interviewee explained, "I don't think NICFI would have chosen Tanzania, but NORAD had this longstanding relationship with Tanzania." International Expert, USA, Telephone Interview Int1, 4 June 2015.

6. Academic Expert, Dar es Salaam, Interview T3, 16 May 2014; Donor Government Officer, Dar es Salaam, Interview T6, 20 May 2014.

7. Academic Expert, Dar es Salaam, Interview T3, 16 May 2014.

8. Ibid.

9. NGO Officer, Dar es Salaam, Interview T4, 16 May 2014.

10. Ibid.; Donor Government Officer, Dar es Salaam, Interview T6, 20 May 2014.

11. Academic Expert, Dar es Salaam, Interview T3, 16 May 2014.

12. Donor Government Officer, Dar es Salaam, Interview T6, 20 May 2014.

13. Ibid.

14. NGO Officer, Dar es Salaam, Interview T4, 16 May 2014.

15. Websites accessed 19 December 2021, for VCS registered projects (http://www.vcs projectdatabase.org/#/projects) and projects submitted to the VCS pipeline (http:// www.vcsprojectdatabase.org/#/pipeline).

16. Donor Government Officer, Dar es Salaam, Interview T6, 20 May 2014.

17. Domestic Expert, Dar es Salaam, Interview T3, 31 July 2018.

18. Ibid.

19. Tanzania Government Officer, Dar es Salaam, Interview TN6, 30 March 2009.

20. International Expert, Dar es Salaam, Interview T4, 2 August 2018.

21. NGO Officer, Dar es Salaam, Interview T4, 16 May 2014; Donor Government Officer, Dar es Salaam, Interview T6, 20 May 2014.

22. NGO Officer, Dar es Salaam, Interview T4, 16 May 2014; Donor Government Officer, Dar es Salaam, Interview T6, 20 May 2014.

23. NGO Officer, Dar es Salaam, Interview T4, 16 May 2014; Donor Government Officer, Dar es Salaam, Interview T6, 20 May 2014; International Donor Officer, Dar es Salaam, Interview T9, 3 June 2014.

24. Domestic Expert, Dar es Salaam, Interview T2, 31 July 2018.

25. Uganda Government Officer, Kampala, Interview U9, 17 June 2014.

26. Ibid.

27. Ibid.

28. Ibid.

29. Domestic Expert, Kampala, Interview T2, 9 August 2018.

30. Uganda Government Officer, Kampala, Interview U9, 17 June 2014.

31. Domestic Expert, Kampala, Interview T2, 9 August 2018.

32. Ibid.

33. Domestic Expert, Kampala, Interview 14, 20 June 2014; Domestic Expert, Kampala, Interview T2, 9 August 2018.

34. Domestic Expert, Kampala, Interview T2, 9 August 2018.

35. Uganda Government Officer, Kampala, Interview U9, 17 June 2014; NGO Officer, Kampala, Interview U5, 13 June 2014.

36. Uganda Government Officer, Kampala, Interview U9, 17 June 2014; NGO Officer, Kampala, Interview U5, 13 June 2014.
37. NGO Officer, Kampala, Interview U5, 13 June 2014; Uganda Government Officer, Kampala, Interview U1, 12 June 2014; Academic, Kampala, Interview U7, 16 June 2014.
38. NGO Officer, Kampala, Interview U5, 13 June 2014; Uganda Government Officer, Kampala, Interview U1, 12 June 2014; Academic, Kampala, Interview U7, 16 June 2014.
39. NGO Officer, Kampala, Interview U5, 13 June 2014.
40. Domestic Expert, Kampala, Interview T2, 9 August 2018.
41. Uganda Government Officer, Kampala, Interview U1, 12 June 2014.
42. Domestic Expert, Kampala, Interview T2, 9 August 2018.
43. Ibid.

Chapter 10

1. Uganda Government Officer, Kampala, Interview U14, 20 June 2014.
2. Ibid.
3. *Tanzania Government Officer, Dar es Salaam, Interview T10, 4 June 2014; Academic Expert, Dar es Salaam, Interview T3, 16 May 2014.*
4. *Domestic Expert, Dar es Salaam, Interview T2, 31 July 2018.*

Appendices

1. Specifically, I compared the village of Endabash, the only village where a cookstove workshop had been set up as of early 2009 (NGO Officer, Karatu Town, Interview TD6, 3 April 2009) with Bassodawish, a village 15 km away, but not involved with the CDM project. Because of logistical constraints, Endabash was surveyed in April 2009 but Bassodawish in August 2009. Bassodawish is larger than Endabash with populations of 9,400 (1,391 households) and 5,036 (920 households), though in terms of landholdings and household expenditures (a proxy for household income) only slightly greater.
2. Note that this is based on survey questions regarding weekly fuel consumption. For conversion, headloads were assumed to be 24 kg and sacks of charcoal 35 kg, as reported in KDA (2009). But Endabash's average of 6.6 kg/day represents households using improved cookstoves, traditional 3-stone hearths and charcoal. However, while the data are less robust due to the smaller sample size, a significant difference is maintained within Endabash data themselves: improved cookstove users consumed less than those using 3-stone hearths, 5.1 and 7.7 kg/day, respectively. Given that the KDA sample size for traditional stove users was more robust (n = 23) and involved direct measurement of fuelwood consumption, a 13 kg/day consumption rate for

traditional 3-stone hearths in Endabash appears appropriate. This is important because it demonstrates that without the cookstove project, fuelwood consumption in Endabash and the control villages of Bassodawish was at comparable levels.

3. The $3.3 million tariff subsidy was allocated in 2003 through the Rural Electrification Agency (REA) using funds from the GEF (Kalyango, 2004; Kayizzi, 2004; MEMD (2004). The second disbursement of $7.7-$8.6 million loan provided by the East African Development Bank and backed by the Bank of Uganda (Juuko, 2004; KSW, 2010; World Bank 2009b).

4. The only new project elements financed through the CDM were two new 45 bar boilers (replacing older 20 bar ones), which have allowed for an increase in sugarcane crushing capacity from 3,500 to 6,000 tonnes cane per day.

References

Aakre S (2016) The political feasibility of potent enforcement in a post-Kyoto climate agreement. *International Environmental Agreements: Politics, Law and Economics* 16:145–159.

Abbott KW and Snidal D (2009) Strengthening international regulation through transmittal new governance: overcoming the orchestration deficit. *Vanderbilt Journal of Transnational Law* 42:501.

Abdallah JM and Monela GG (2007) Overview of Miombo Woodlands in Tanzania. *Working Papers of the Finnish Forest Research Institute* 50:9–23.

Abdulai A-G (2017) The political economy of regional inequality in Ghana: do political settlements matter? *The European Journal of Development Research* 29:213–229.

Acemoglu D, Johnson S and Robinson JA (2001) The colonial origins of comparative development: an empirical investigation. *American Economic Review* 91:1369–1401.

Acemoglu D and Robinson J (2012a) Industrial policy déjà vu. Why Nations Fail: The Blog, Website (accessed 12 August 2014): http://whynationsfail.com/blog/2012/4/12/industrial-policy-deja-vu.html.

Acemoglu D and Robinson J (2012b) *Why nations fail: the origins of power, prosperity and poverty*, Crown Publishing, New York.

AFREC (2019) *Africa energy database*, African Energy Commission, Algiers.

AFREPREN/FWD (2009) *Minutes of 7th Cogen for Africa Project Steering Committee teleconference meeting*, Energy, Environment and Development Network for Africa. Website (accessed 10 June 2011): http://www.afrepren.org/cfadownloads/PSC_Minutes/Minutes%20of%207th%20Cogen%20for%20Africa%20PSC%20Teleconference%20Meeting%2008Jun09.pdf, Nairobi.

Ahlbäck AJ (1988) *Forestry for development in Tanzania*, International Rural Development Centre (IRDC), Swedish University of Agricultural Sciences, Uppsala.

Ahlbäck AJ (1995) Mobilizing rural people in Tanzania to tree planting: why and how. *Ambio* 24:304–310.

Ahram AI, Köllner P and Sil R (2018) *Comparative area studies: methodological rationales and cross-regional applications*, Oxford University Press, New York.

Alegria J, Chamshama SAO and Erkkilä A (2011) *National Forest Monitoring and Assessment of Tanzania (NAFORMA): Mid-Term evaluation report*, FAO, Rome.

Allen RC (2003) *Farm to factory: a reinterpretation of the Soviet industrial revolution*, Princeton University Press, Princeton.

Amani HKR, Wangwe SM, Rweyemamu D, Aiko R and Wanga GG (2007) Understanding economic and political reforms in Tanzania, in *Understanding economic reforms in Africa: a tale of seven nations* Mensah J (ed), 205–236, Palgrave Macmillan, Basingstoke, Hampshire.

Amars L, Fridahl M, Hagemann M, Röser F and Linnér B-O (2017) The transformational potential of Nationally Appropriate Mitigation Actions in Tanzania: assessing the concept's cultural legitimacy among stakeholders in the solar energy sector. *Local Environment* 22:86–105.

Amsden AH (1989) *Asia's next giant: South Korea and late industrialization*, Oxford University Press, Oxford.

Anckar C (2008) On the applicability of the most similar systems design and the most different systems design in comparative research. *International Journal of Social Research Methodology* 11:389–401.

Andersen OW, Hansen H and Rand J (2021) *Evaluating financial and development additionality in blended finance operations*, OECD Development Cooperation Working Paper #91, Paris.

Andonova LB, Hale TN and Roger CB (2017) National policy and transnational governance of climate change: substitutes or complements? *International Studies Quarterly* 61:253–268.

Andreoni A and Chang H-J (2019) The political economy of industrial policy: structural interdependencies, policy alignment and conflict management. *Structural Change and Economic Dynamics* 48:136–150.

Andresen S and Hey E (2005) The effectiveness and legitimacy of international environmental institutions. *International Environmental Agreements: Politics, Law and Economics* 5:211–226.

Angelsen A, Ainembabazi JH, Bauch SC, Herold M, Verchot L, Hänsel G, Schueler V, Toop G, Gilbert A and Eisbrenner K (2013) *Testing methodologies for REDD+: deforestation drivers, costs and reference levels etc.*, Department of Energy and Climate Change & Ecofys, London.

Angelsen A, Brockhaus M, Kanninen M, Sills E, Sunderlin WD and Wertz-Kanounnikof S, eds (2009) *Realising REDD+*, Center for International Forestry Research, Bogor Barat.

ANRE (2008) *Activity report 2008*, National Energy Regulatory Agency, Chisinau.

ANRE (2009) *Activity report 2009*, National Energy Regulatory Agency, Chisinau.

Antonio A (2019) A generalized linkage approach to local production systems development in the era of global value chains, with special reference to Africa, in *The quality of growth in Africa*, Akbar N, Joseph ES and Ravi K (eds), 264–294, Columbia University Press, New York, Chichester, West Sussex.

Aryeetey E and Moyo N (2012) Industrialisation for structural transformation in Africa: appropriate roles for the state. *Journal of African Economies* 21:55–85.

Asselt H and Zelli F (2014) Connect the dots: managing the fragmentation of global climate governance. *Environmental Economics and Policy Studies* 16:137–155.

Asuka J (2000) ODA baseline as a criterion for financial additionality. *Joint Implementation Quarterly* 6:8.

Athey S and Imbens GW (2017) The state of applied econometrics: causality and policy evaluation. *Journal of Economic Perspectives* 31:3–32.

Axelsson AL and Hagborg L (1994) *Karatu yarir a Karatu gantsar. Great Karatu is green Karatu. A follow-up study of a tree-planting project in Karatu, Tanzania*, Swedish University of Agricultural Sciences, Uppsala.

Babeiya E (2012) Multiparty elections and party support in Tanzania. *Journal of Asian and African Studies* 47:83–100.

Bach DC and Gazibo M (2013) *Neopatrimonialism in Africa and beyond*, Routledge, New York.

Bäckstrand K and Kronsell A (2015) *Rethinking the green state: environmental governance towards climate and sustainability transitions*, Routledge, New York.

Ban C (2012) Brazil's liberal neo-developmentalism: new paradigm or edited orthodoxy? *Review of International Political Economy* iFirst:1–34.

Barbier EB (2010) *A global green new deal: rethinking the economic recovery*, Cambridge University Press, Cambridge.

Barkan JD (2011) *Uganda: assessing risks to stability*, Centre for Strategic and International Studies, Washington, DC.

Barletti JPS and Larson AM (2017) Rights abuse allegations in the context of REDD+ readiness and implementation: a preliminary review and proposal for moving forward. *CIFOR InfoBrief* 190:1–8.

Bates RH (2005 [1981]) *Markets and states in tropical Africa: the political basis of agricultural policies*, University of California Press, Berkeley.

Bates RH (2008) The role of the state in development, in *The Oxford handbook of political economy*, Weingast BR and Wittman D (eds), 708–722, Oxford University Press, Oxford.

Batra G, Uitto JI and Feinstein ON (2022) *Environmental evaluation and global development institutions: a case study of the Global Environment Facility*, Taylor & Francis, New York.

Bättig MB and Bernauer T (2009) National institutions and global public goods: are democracies more cooperative in climate change policy? *International Organization* 63:281–308.

Baum WC (1978) The World Bank project cycle. *Finance and Development* 15:10–17.

Bayer P and Aklin M (2020) The European Union emissions trading system reduced CO2 emissions despite low prices. *Proceedings of the National Academy of Sciences* 117:8804–8812.

Beach D and Rohlfing I (2018) Integrating cross-case analyses and process tracing in set-theoretic research: strategies and parameters of debate. *Sociological Methods & Research* 47:3–36.

Behrent MC (2009) Liberalism without humanism: Michel Foucault and the free-market creed, 1976–1979. *Modern Intellectual History* 6:539–568.

Beissinger MR and Young C eds (2002) *Beyond state crisis: postcolonial Africa and post-Soviet Eurasia in comparative perspective*, Woodrow Wilson Press Center, Washington, DC.

Bel G and Joseph S (2015) Emission abatement: untangling the impacts of the EU ETS and the economic crisis. *Energy Economics* 49:531–539.

Béland D and Cox RH (2011) Introduction: ideas and politics, in *Ideas and politics in social science research*, Béland D and Cox RH (eds), 3–20, Oxford University Press, Oxford.

Berazneva J and Lee DR (2013) Explaining the African food riots of 2007–2008: an empirical analysis. *Food Policy* 39:28–39.

Berend TI (2009) *From the Soviet bloc to the European Union: the economic and social transformation of Central and Eastern Europe since 1973*, Cambridge University Press, Cambridge.

Bernoux M, Eschenbrenner V, Cerri CC, Melillo JM and Feller C (2002) LULUCF-based CDM: too much ado for . . . a small carbon market. *Climate Policy* 2:379–385.

Bernstein S (2001) *The compromise of liberal environmentalism*, Columbia University Press, New York.

Bernstein S, Betsill M, Hoffmann M and Paterson M (2010) A tale of two Copenhagens: carbon markets and climate governance. *Millennium: Journal of International Studies* 39:161–173.

Bernstein S and Cashore B (2012) Complex global governance and domestic policies: four pathways of influence. *International Affairs* 88:586–604.

Bernstein S and Hoffmann M (2018) The politics of decarbonization and the catalytic impact of subnational climate experiments. *Policy Sciences* 51:189–211.

Bester A (2012) Results-based management in the United Nations Development System: progress and challenges. A report prepared for the United Nations Department of Economic and Social Affairs, for the Quadrennial Comprehensive Policy Review 2730, New York.

BFC (2018) *Start-up of sawmill in Uganda*, Busoga Forestry Company-Green Resources Limited. Website (accessed 10 May 2018): http://www.busoga-forestry.com/start-up-of-sawmill-in-uganda.html, Jinja.

Bialer S (1988) Gorbachev's program of change: sources, significance, prospects. *Political Science Quarterly* 103:403–460.

Biermann F and Simonis UE (1999) The multilateral ozone fund: a case study on institutional learning. *International Journal of Social Economics* 26:239–273.

Biney A (2011) *The political and social thought of Kwame Nkrumah*, Springer, New York.

Birch K and Mykhnenko V eds (2010) *The rise and fall of neoliberalism: the collapse of an economic order?* Zed Books, London.

Birdsall N and Fukuyama F (2011) The post-Washington Consensus—development after the crisis. *Foreign Affairs* 90:45.

Bjella O (2007) *Erfaringer etter tre år som Statskogsjef i Uganda: institusjonsbygging, plantasjeinvesteringer og politisk maktkamp*, Norwegian University of Life Sciences.

Blomley T and Iddi S (2009) *Participatory forest management in Tanzania: 1993–2009 Lessons learned and experiences to date*, Ministry of Natural Resources and Tourism, Forestry and Beekeeping Division, Dar es Salaam.

BNDES (2021) *Donations*, Amazon Fund. Website (accessed March 14, 2021): http://www.fundoamazonia.gov.br/en/donations/, Brasília.

Bluwstein J, Lund JF, Askew K, Stein H, Noe C, Odgaard R, Maganga F and Engström L (2018) Between dependence and deprivation: the interlocking nature of land alienation in Tanzania. *Journal of Agrarian Change* 18:806–830.

Bodansky D (2010) The Copenhagen climate change conference: a postmortem. *American Journal of International Law* 104:230–240.

Böhm S and Dhabi S (2009) *Upsetting the offset: the political economy of carbon markets*, Mayfly, London.

Boincean B (2009) Farming practices in Moldova for Preventing pollution and degradation of the environment, in *The role of ecological chemistry in pollution research and sustainable development*, Bahadir AM and Duca G (eds), 157–164, Springer, Netherlands.

Boodoo Z and Olsen KH (2018) Assessing transformational change potential: the case of the Tunisian cement Nationally Appropriate Mitigation Action (NAMA). *Climate Policy* 18:794–812.

Bou-Habib P (2019) Climate justice and historical responsibility. *The Journal of Politics* 81:1298–1310.

Bourguignon F and Sundberg M (2007) Aid effectiveness: opening the black box. *The American Economic Review* 97:316–321.

Bowman M and Minas S (2019) Resilience through interlinkage: the green climate fund and climate finance governance. *Climate Policy* 19:342–353.

Bradshaw YW (1987) Urbanization and underdevelopment: a global study of modernization, urban bias, and economic dependency. *American Sociological Review* 52:224–239.

Brandt P, Herold M and Rufino MC (2018) The contribution of sectoral climate change mitigation options to national targets: a quantitative assessment of dairy production in Kenya. *Environmental Research Letters* 13:034016.

Breitmeier H, Underdal A and Young OR (2011) The effectiveness of international environmental regimes: comparing and contrasting findings from quantitative research. *International Studies Review* 13:579–605.

Breslin S (2011) The 'China model' and the global crisis: from Friedrich List to a Chinese mode of governance? *International Affairs* 87:1323–1343.

Brightwell R, Dransfield RD and Williams BG (1992) Factors affecting seasonal dispersal of the tsetse-flies Glossina-Pallidipes and G-Longipennis (Diptera, Glossinidae) at Nguruman, South-West Kenya. *Bulletin of Entomological Research* 82:167–182.

Bruer V, Castro M and McCormick M (2014) *"Numbers, people, papers": components and linkages of monitoring, reporting and verification (MRV) at different levels*, International Partnership on Mitigation and MRV, Bonn.

BTI (2012) *BTI 2012: Tanzania country report*, Bertelsmann Stiftung, Berlin.

Buchner B, Brown J and Corfee-Morloti J (2011) *Monitoring and tracking long-term finance to support climate action*, OECD, Paris.

Buchner B, Clark A, Falconer A, Macquarie R, Meattle C, Tolentino R and Wetherbee C (2019) *The global landscape of carbon finance 2019*, Climate Policy Initiative, Berlin.

Bulkeley H, Andonova L, Betsill MM, Compagnon D, Hale T, Hoffmann MJ, Newell P, Paterson M, Roger C and VanDeveer SD (2014) *Transnational climate change governance*, Cambridge University Press, Cambridge.

Businge J (2020) Why Karuma dam commissioning has been extended again, 29 January 2020, *The Independent*. Website (accessed 10 August 2020): https://www.independent.co.ug/karuma-dam-commissioning-extended-again/.

Byaruhanga C, Henstridge M and Kasekende L (2009) Exchange rate, fiscal, and monetary policy, in *Uganda's economic reforms: insider accounts*, Kuteesa F, Tumusiime-Mutebile E, Whitworth A and Williamson T (eds), 52–88, Oxford University Press, Oxford.

Byres TJ (1979) Of neo-populist pipe-dreams: Daedalus in the Third World and the myth of urban bias. *Journal of Peasant Studies* 6:210–244.

Calel R, Colmer J, Dechezleprêtre A and Glachant M (2021) Do carbon offsets offset carbon?, in CESifo Working Paper No, 9368, Munich Society for the Promotion of Economic Research-CESif, Munich.

Całus K (2016) Moldova: from oligarchic pluralism to Plahotniuc's hegemony. *OSW Commentary* 208:1–9.

Całus K (2018) Moldova's political theatre: the balance of forces in an election year. *OSW Commentary* 258:1–6.

Całus K, Delcour L, Gazizullin I, Iwański T, Jaroszewicz M and Klysiński K (2018) Interdependencies of eastern partnership countries with the EU and Russia: three case studies. EU-STRAT Working Paper Series, Berlin.

Cames M, Harthan RO, Füssler J, Lazarus M, Lee CM, Erickson P and Spalding-Fecher R (2016) *How additional is the Clean Development Mechanism?* Öko-Institut, Berlin.

Cardoso F and Faletto E (1979 [1969]) *Dependency and development in Latin America*, University of California Press, Berkeley.

Cashore B and Howlett M (2007) Punctuating which equilibrium? Understanding thermostatic policy dynamics in Pacific Northwest forestry. *American Journal of Political Science* 51:532–551.

CCO (2017) *Moldova: grid emissions factor assessment*, Ministry of Environment, Republic of Moldova, Chisinau.

CDCF (2007) Moldova: Biomass Heating and Energy Conservation, World Bank Community Development Carbon Fund. Website (accessed 11 January 2011): http://wbcarbonfinance.org/Router.cfm?Page=CDCF&FID=9709&ItemID=9709&ft=Projects&ProjID=24890, Washington DC.

CDM-PDD (2005a) Moldova biomass heating in rural communities no. 1, in *CDM small-scale project design document*, UNFCCC, Bonn.

CDM-PDD (2005b) Moldova biomass heating in rural communities no. 2, in *CDM Small-Scale Project Design Document*, UNFCCC, Bonn.

CDM-PDD (2006a) Uganda Nile basin reforestation project no. 1 (v. 2), *CDM afforestation and reforestation project design document*, UNFCCC, Bonn.

CDM-PDD (2006b) Uganda Nile basin reforestation project no. 2 (v. 2), *CDM afforestation and reforestation project design document*, UNFCCC, Bonn.

CDM-PDD (2006c) Uganda Nile basin reforestation project no. 4 (v. 2), *CDM afforestation and reforestation project design document*, UNFCCC, Bonn.

CDM-PDD (2006d) Uganda Nile basin reforestation project no. 5 (v. 2), *CDM afforestation and reforestation project design document*, UNFCCC, Bonn.

CDM-PDD (2007a) Afforestation in grassland areas of Uchindile, Kilombero, Tanzania & Mapanda, Mufindi, Tanzania (v. 01), in *CDM project design document form for afforestation and reforestation project activities (v. 3)*, UNFCCC, Bonn.

CDM-PDD (2007b) Kakira Sugar Works (1985) Ltd. (KSW) cogeneration project, in *Clean Development Mechanism project design document form (v. 3)*, UNFCCC, Bonn.

CDM-PDD (2008a) Moldova soil conservation project (v. 5), *CDM afforestation and reforestation project design document*, UNFCCC, Bonn.

CDM-PDD (2008b) Reforestation at the Idete forest project in the southern highlands of Tanzania, in *CDM project design document form for afforestation and reforestation project activities (v. 4)*, UNFCCC, Bonn.

CDM-PDD (2009) Uganda Nile basin reforestation project no. 3 (v. 6-1), *CDM afforestation and reforestation project design document*, UNFCCC, Bonn.

CDM-PDD (2010) Moldova community forestry development project (v. 1), *CDM afforestation and reforestation project design document*, UNFCCC, Bonn.

CDM-SSC-PoA-DD (2011) *Tanzania renewable energy programme*, UNFCCC, Bonn.

CDM EB (2005) *Report of CDM Executive Board, 22nd Meeting, Annex 3 "Clarifications on the consideration of national and/or sectoral policies and circumstances in baseline scenarios (v. 2),"* UNFCCC, Bonn.

CDM EB (2009) *Report of CDM Executive Board, 50th Meeting, Annex 16 "AR-AM0002 – restoration of degraded lands through afforestation/reforestation (v. 3),"* UNFCCC, Bonn.

CDM EB (2010) *Report of CDM Executive Board, 55th Meeting, Annex 1 "Clean Development Mechanism validation and verification manual (v. 2),"* UNFCCC, Bonn.

CDM EB (2011a) *Report of CDM Executive Board, 61st Meeting, Annex 12 "Tool to calculate the emission factor for an electricity system" (v.2.2.0)*, UNFCCC, Bonn.

CDM EB (2011b) *Report of CDM Executive Board, 62nd Meeting, Annex 8 "Guidelines for the establishment of sector specific standardized baselines (v. 1.0),"* UNFCCC, Bonn.

CDM EB (2011c) *Report of CDM Executive Board, 65th Meeting, Annex 23: "Guidelines for the establishment of sector specific standardized baselines (v. 2.0),* UNFCCC, Bonn.

CDM EB (2012a) *Installation of co-generation or tri-generation systems supplying energy to commercial buildings (II.K./v. 2.0)*, UNFCCC, Bonn.

CDM EB (2012b) *Report of CDM Executive Board, 66th Meeting, Annex 46 "Methodological tool emissions from solid waste disposal sites (v. 06.0.1)*," UNFCCC, Bonn.

CDM EB (2013) *Report of CDM Executive Board, 75th Meeting, Annex 20 "AMS-II.L: demand-side activities for efficient outdoor and street lighting technologies (v. 2.0)*, UNFCCC, Bonn.

CDM EB (2014) *Standard: CDM validation and verification standard (v. 7.0)*, CDM-EB65-A04-STAN, UNFCCC, Bonn.

CDM EB (2015) *Report of CDM Executive Board, 83rd Meeting, Annex 9 "AMS-III.G.: emission reductions by electric and hybrid vehicles (version 15.0)*," UNFCCC, Bonn.

Centeno MA, Kohli A, Yashar DJ and Mistree D (2017) Unpacking states in the developing world: capacity, performance, and politics, in *States in the developing world*, Centeno MA, Kohli A, Yashar DJ and Mistree D (eds), 1–35, Cambridge University Press, Cambridge.

CFU (2008) *Carbon finance for sustainable development*, World Bank Carbon Finance Unit, Washington, DC.

CFU (2017) The funds, ClimateFundsUpdate.Org: Overseas Development Institute & Heinrich Boll Stiftung. Website (accessed 10 Sept 2017): http://www.climatefundsupd ate.org/data/the-funds-v2, London.

Chang H-J (2003) *Kicking away the ladder: development strategy in historical perspective*, Anthem Press, London.

Chang HJ and Andreoni A (2020) Industrial policy in the 21st century. *Development and Change* 51:324–351.

Chemouni B (2023) The politics of state capacity in post-genocide Rwanda: "pockets of effectiveness" as state-building prioritizations?, in *Pockets of effectiveness and the politics of state-building and development in Africa*, Hickey S (ed), 146–172, Oxford University Press, Oxford.

Chichilnisky G and Bal P (2019) *Reversing climate change: how carbon removals can resolve climate change and fix the economy*, World Scientific Publishing, Hackensack, NJ.

Chiriac L, Munteanu I, Popa V and Mocanu V (2000) Local government in Moldova, in *Stabilization of local governments*, Kandeva E (ed), 289–349, Local Government and Public Sector Service Initiative (LGI), Open Society Institute, Budapest.

Christiansson C and Åshuvud J (1985) Heavy industry in a rural tropical ecosystem. *Ambio* 14:122–133.

Christoff P (2010) Cold climate in Copenhagen: China and the United States at COP15. *Environmental Politics* 19:637–656.

Chu A and Roeder O (2023) "Transformational change": Biden's industrial policy begins to bear fruit, *Financial Times*, 17 April 2023. Website (accessed 4 May 2023): https://www.ft.com/content/b6cd46de-52d6-4641-860b-5f2c1b0c5622.

CIF (2018) *Donors & MDBS*, Climate Investment Funds. Website (accessed October 14, 2018): https://www.climateinvestmentfunds.org/finances, Washington, DC.

Ciobanu C (1997) The supply side of mass privatization: the case of Moldova, in *Between state and market: mass privatization in transition economies*, Lieberman IW, Nestor SS and Desai RM (eds), 61–73, World Bank, Washington, DC.

Ciofu A, Plamadeala I, Popa O, Luchian S and Ursul A (2014) *Energy sector in the Republic of Moldova*, ener2i. Website (accessed 12 December 2017): http://ener2i.archiv.zsi.at/page/34/attach/0_Moldova_Country_Report.pdf, Vienna.

Clapham CS (1985) *Third World politics: an introduction*, University of Wisconsin Press, Madison.

Clapp C, Briner G and Karousakis K (2010) *Low-Emission Development Strategies (LEDS): technical, instititutional and policy lessons*, OECD, Paris.

Clemens MA and Moss TJ (2007) The ghost of 0.7 per cent: origins and relevance of the international aid target. *International Journal of Development Issues* 6:3–25.

Clough L (2012) *Improved cookstove sector in East Africa: Experience from the Developing Energy Enterprise Programme (DEEP)*, GVEP International, London.

Coetzee K and Winkler H (2013) The international policy context for mitigation actions. *Climate and Development* 6:4–11.

Coldham S (2000) Land reform and customary rights: the case of Uganda. *Journal of African Law* 44:65–77.

Conquest R (1986) *The harvest of sorrow: Soviet collectivization and the terror-famine*, Oxford University Press, New York.

Cooksey B (2011) Marketing reform? The rise and fall of agricultural liberalisation in Tanzania. *Development Policy Review* 29:s57–s81.

Cosbey A, Parry J-O, Browne J, Babu YD, Bhandari P, Drexhage J and Murphy D (2005) *Realizing the development dividend: making the CDM work for developing countries*, IISD, Winnipeg.

Cox M (2018) *The Post Cold War World*, Routledge, New York.

Craig D and Porter D (2003) Poverty reduction strategy papers: a new convergence. *World Development* 31:53–69.

Crane Paper Bags L (2018) About us. Website (accessed 10 October 2018): http://cranepaperbags.com/aboutus.php, Kampala.

Crowther W (2007) Moldova, Transnistria and the PCRM's Turn to the West. *East European Quarterly* 41:273.

Crowther W (2011) Semi-presidentialism and Moldova's flawed transition to democracy, in *Semi-presidentialism and democracy*, Elgie R, Moestrup S and Wu Y-S (eds), 210–228, Palgrave MacMillan, New York.

Cuesta Fernández I (2018) Kilowatts, megawatts and power: electric territorialities of the state in the peripheries of Ghana and Tanzania. PhD Thesis, School of Social and Political Science, University of Edinburgh.

Cui L and Huang Y (2018) Exploring the schemes for green climate fund financing: international lessons. *World Development* 101:173–187.

Cullenward D and Victor DG (2020) *Making climate policy work*, John Wiley & Sons, New York.

Curnow P and Hodes G (2009) *Implementing CDM projects a guidebook to host country legal issues*, UNEP Risoe Centre, Roskilde, Denmark.

Curtea de Conturi (2006) Hotărîre Nr. 20 din 12.05.2006 Privind raportul asupra activității economico-financiare și eficienței administrării gospodăriei silvice în anul 2004 și semestrul I al anului 2005, Republica Moldova Curtea de Conturi. Website (accessed 14 January 2014): http://lex.justice.md/index.php?action=view&view=doc&lang=1&id=317316, Chisinau.

Curtea de Conturi (2010) Hotărîre Nr. 25 din 22.04.2010 privind Raportul auditului gestionării patrimoniului public de către Agenția "Moldsilva" și întreprinderile subordonate în perioada anilor 2008–2009 și auditului de atestare a situațiilor financiare privind mijloacele alocate de la bugetul de stat pe anul 2009, Republica Moldova Curtea de Conturi. Website (accessed 14 January 2014): http://lex.justice.md/index.php?action=view&view=doc&lang=1&id=335064, Chisinau.

Daigneault P-M (2014) Reassessing the concept of policy paradigm: aligning ontology and methodology in policy studies. *Journal of European Public Policy* 21:453–469.

Davies RW (1990) *From tsarism to the new economic policy*, Palgrave Macmillan, n.p.

Dean M and Zamora D (2019) *Le dernier homme et la fin de la révolution*, Lux Éditeur, Montréal.

Death C (2015) Four discourses of the green economy in the global South. *Third World Quarterly* 36:2207–2224.

Deininger K and Binswanger H (1999) The evolution of World Bank's land policy: principles, experience, and future challenges. *World Bank Research Observer* 14:247–276.

Demsetz H (1969) Information and efficiency: another viewpoint. *The Journal of Law and Economics* 12:1–22.

Devyatkov A (2012) Russia: relations with Moldova under a paradigm of ambiguity, in *Moldova: Arena of international influences*, Kosienkowski M and Schreiber W (eds), 183–204, Lexington Books, Lanham, MD.

Dewees PA (1989) The woodfuel crisis reconsidered: observations on the dynamics of abundance and scarcity. *World Development* 17:1159–1172.

Dimitrov RS (2010) Inside Copenhagen: the state of climate governance. *Global Environmental Politics* 10:18–24.

Dodds A (2013) *Comparative public policy*, Palgrave MacMillan, London.

DoE (2007) A Handbook for Clean Development Mechanism (CDM) Project Activities in Tanzania, Government of the United Republic of Tanzania, Vice President's Office (Division of Environment), Dar es Salaam.

Doelle M (2002) From Kyoto to Marrakech: a long walk through the desert: mirage or oasis? *Dalhousie Law Journal* 25:113–167.

Dongier P, Van Domelen J, Ostrom E, Ryan A, Wakeman W, Bebbington A, Alkire S, Esmail T and Polski M (2003) Community driven development. *World Bank Poverty Reduction Strategy Paper* 1:303–327.

DonVito PA (1969) *The essentials of a planning-programming-budgeting system*, RAND Corp., Santa Monica, CA.

Dosman E (2008) *The life and times of Raúl Prebisch, 1901–1986*, McGill-Queen's Press, Montreal.

Doucouliagos H and Paldam M (2009) The aid effectiveness literature: the sad results of 40 years of research. *Journal of Economic Surveys* 23:433–461.

Drahokoupil J (2009) After transition: varieties of political-economic development in Eastern Europe and the former Soviet Union. *Comparative European Politics* 7:279–298.

Duménil G and Lévy D (2011) *The crisis of neoliberalism*, Harvard University Press, Cambridge.

Dutschke M and Michaelowa A (2006) Development assistance and the CDM—how to interpret "financial additionality." *Environment and Development Economics* 11:235–246.

Dye BJ (2021) Unpacking authoritarian governance in electricity policy: understanding progress, inconsistency and stagnation in Tanzania. *Energy Research & Social Science* 80:102209.

Dykstra DP (1983) Forestry in Tanzania. *Journal of Forestry* 81:742–746.

Easterly W and Pfutze T (2008) Where does the money go? Best and worst practices in foreign aid. *Journal of Economic Perspectives* 22:29–52.

ECA (2011) *Governing development in Africa: the role of the state in economic transformation*, Economic Commission for Africa, Addis Ababa, Ethiopia.

Ece M (2021) Creating property out of insecurity: territorialization and legitimation of REDD+ in Lindi, Tanzania. *The Journal of Legal Pluralism and Unofficial Law* 53:78–102.

Eckstein H (1975) Case study and theory in political science, in *Handbook of political science*, Greenstein FI and Polsby NW (eds), 79–138, Addison-Wesley, Reading, MA.

Economist (2017) *Tanzania: mining sector in crisis*, Economist Intelligence Unit. Website (accessed 18 October 2017): http://country.eiu.com/article.aspx?articleid=1845689 568&Country=Tanzania&topic=Economy, London.

Economist (2020) Maia Sandu, a reformist ex-prime minister, becomes president, *The Economist*, 19 November 2020.

EcoTrust (2004) A Plan Vivo Carbon offset Project with Small-Scale Farmers in Bushenyi District: Annual Progress Report 2003/2004, The Environmental Conservation Trust of Uganda, Kampala.

EcoTrust (2007) Trees for Global Benefits Program in Uganda: A Plan Vivo Project, 2006 Annual Report, The Environmental Conservation Trust of Uganda, Kampala.

EcoTrust (2008) Trees for Global Benefits Program in Uganda: A Plan Vivo Project, Annual Report, The Environmental Conservation Trust of Uganda, Kampala.

Ecotrust (2009) Trees for Global Benefits, in Plan Vivo Project Design Document, Plan Vivo Foundation, Edinburgh.

Edigheji O ed (2010) *Constructing a democratic developmental state in South Africa: potentials and challenges*, HSRC Press, Cape Town.

Edmonds J, Forrister D, Clarke L, de Clara S and Munnings C (2019) *The economic potential of Article 6 of the Paris Agreement and implementation challenges*, IETA, University of Maryland and CPLC, Washington, DC.

Edwards S (2014) *Toxic aid: economic collapse and recovery in Tanzania*, Oxford University Press, Oxford.

Egypt Today (2021) *Q&A: all you need to know about Julius Nyerere dam Egypt is building in Tanzania*, Egypt Today. Website (accessed 20 December 2021): https://www.egypttoday.com/Article/1/110689/Q-A-All-you-need-to-know-about-Julius-Nyerere, Cairo.

Ellerman AD and Buchner BK (2008) Over-allocation or abatement? A preliminary analysis of the EU ETS based on the 2005–06 emissions data. *Environmental & Resource Economics* 41:267–287.

Ellis F (1982) Agricultural price policy in Tanzania. *World Development* 10:263–283.

Ellis J (2006) *Issues related to implementing "Programmatic CDM"*, OECD/IEA, Paris.

EMC (1998) *Summary environment state in the Republic of Moldova 1998*, Ecological Monitoring Centre of the National Institute of Ecology, Chisinau.

enerCEE (2011) *Moldova: energy sources*, Energy in Central & Eastern Europe. Website (accessed 10 December 2010): http://www.enercee.net/moldova/energy-sources.html, Vienna.

Engeli I and Rothmayr C (2014) *Comparative policy studies: conceptual and methodological challenges*, Palgrave Macmillan, London.

Engurait SP (2005) Power sector reforms in Uganda: status and achievements. *International Journal of Global Energy Issues* 23:110–118.

ERA (2010) *Transmission energy purchases*, Electricity Regulatory Agency. Website (accessed 30 June 2011): http://www.era.or.ug/TransmissionPurchases.php, Kampala.

ERA (2011) *Uganda renewable energy feed-in tariff (REFIT) phase 2: approved guidelines for 2011–2012*, Electricity Regulatory Agency, Kampala.

ERA (2014a) *Developments and investment opportunities in renewable energy resources in Uganda*, Electricity Regulatory Agency, Kampala.

ERA (2014b) *UETCL total volumes purchased across all suppliers of electricity (MWh) 2006–2013*, Electricity Regulatory Agency. Website (accessed 10 January 2014): http://www.era.or.ug/files/UETCLSPurchasesMWh1.xlsx, Kampala.

Erickson A (2012) Peace in Tanzania: an island of stability in sub-Saharan Africa. *Jackson School of International Studies* 3:18–31.

Erickson P, Lazarus M and Spalding-Fecher R (2014) Net climate change mitigation of the Clean Development Mechanism. *Energy Policy* 72:146–154.

Ericson RE (1991) The classical Soviet-type economy: nature of the system and implications for reform. *Journal of Economic Perspectives* 5:11–27.

EU & GoM (2005) *EU-Moldova action plan*, European Union & Government of Moldova. Available at (accessed 12 June 2017): https://library.euneighbours.eu/content/eu-moldova-action-plan, Brussels & Chişinău.

EurActive (2010) Moldova's presidency referendum flops, *EurActivecom*, 6 September 2010, Website (accessed 10 September 2011): http://www.euractiv.com/east-mediterranean/moldovas-presidency-referendum-flops-news-497454, Brussels.

European Commission (2015) *International carbon market*, Commissioner for Climate Action. Website (accessed 10 February 2015): http://ec.europa.eu/clima/policies/ets/linking/index_en.htm, Brussels.

European Commission (2023) *Deforestation-free products*, European Commission. Website (accessed 18 September 2023): https://environment.ec.europa.eu/topics/forests/deforestation/regulation-deforestation-free-products_en, Brussels.

Evans P (1995) *Embedded autonomy: states and industrial transformation*, Princeton University Press, Princeton.

Evans P (2010) Constructing the 21st century developmental state: potentials and pitfalls, in *Constructing a democratic developmental state in South Africa: potentials and challenges*, Edigheji O (ed), 37–58, HSRC Press, Cape Town.

Evans PB, Rueschemeyer D and Skocpol T (1985) *Bringing the state back in*, Cambridge University Press, New York.

Expert-Grup (2017) *Mid-term evaluation of National Development Strategy "Moldova 2020": key findings*, Expert-Grup, Chişinău.

FAO (2007a) *Some aspects of forestry policy and forestry institutional framework from the Republic of Moldova*, FAO, Rome.

FAO (2007b) *State of the world's forests*, FAO, Rome.

FAO (2021) *Support for the development of the national forest policy implementation strategy and forest legislation in Tanzania*, FAO, Rome.

FAOSTAT (2018) *Forest land*, FAO. Website (accessed 10 April 2018): http://www.fao.org/faostat/en/#data/GF, Rome.

Fawcett AA, Iyer GC, Clarke LE, Edmonds JA, Hultman NE, McJeon HC, Rogelj J, Schuler R, Alsalam J, Asrar GR, Creason J, Jeong M, McFarland J, Mundra A and Shi W (2015) Can Paris pledges avert severe climate change? *Science* 350:1168–1169.

FBD (2021) *The contribution of forest sector to the national economy*, Forestry and Beekeeping Division, Ministry of Natural Resources and Tourism, Dar es Salaam.

Fearon J and Wendt A (2002) Rationalism v. constructivism: a skeptical view, in *Handbook of international relations*, Carlsnaes W, Risse-Kappen T, Risse T and Simmons B (eds), 52–72, SAGE, London.

Feola G (2015) Societal transformation in response to global environmental change: a review of emerging concepts. *Ambio* 44:376–390.

Figueres C, Schellnhuber HJ, Whiteman G, Rockström J, Hobley A and Rahmstorf S (2017) Three years to safeguard our climate. *Nature News* 546:593.

Fisher J (2012) No pay, no care? A case study exploring motivations for participation in payments for ecosystem services in Uganda. *Oryx* 46:45–54.

Fisher J, Cavanagh C, Sikor T and Mwayafu D (2018) Linking notions of justice and project outcomes in carbon offset forestry projects: insights from a comparative study in Uganda. *Land Use Policy* 73:259–268.

FISM (2009) Raport Semianual 2009 (ianuarie–iunie 2009), Fondul de Investiţii Sociale din Moldova, Chisinau.

Fole AG (2003) The historical origin of African debt crisis. *Eastern Africa Social Science Research Review* 19:59–89.

Fridahl M, Hagemann M, Röser F and Amars L (2015) A comparison of design and support priorities of nationally appropriate mitigation actions. *The Journal of Environment & Development* 24:237–264.

Friman M and Hjerpe M (2015) Agreement, significance, and understandings of historical responsibility in climate change negotiations. *Climate Policy* 15:302–320.

Fritz V (2007) *State-building: a comparative study of Ukraine, Lithuania, Belarus and Russia*, Central European University Press, Budapest.

Furukawa M (2018) Management of the international development aid system: the case of Tanzania. *Development Policy Review* 36:O270–O284.

Gapare N and William C (2013) *Final evaluation of the UN-REDD Tanzania national programme—final report*, UN-REDD, Geneva.

Gavard C, Winchester N and Paltsev S (2016) Limited trading of emissions permits as a climate cooperation mechanism? US-China and EU-China examples. *Energy Economics* 58:95–104.

Gazibo M and Moumouni C (2017) *Repenser la légitimité de l'État africain à l'ère de la gouvernance partagée*, Presses de l'Université du Québec, Montreal.

GCB (2022) *Global carbon budget: powerpoint and figures on budget 2022*, Earth System Science Partnership. Website (accessed 10 February 2023): https://www.globalcarbon project.org/carbonbudget/22/presentation.htm, Canberra.

GCF (2014) *Initial results management framework of the fund*, Green Climate Fund, Songdo, Republic of Korea.

GCF (2021) Project Portfolio, Green Climate Fund, Seoul-Incheon. Website (accessed 15 December 2021): https://www.greenclimate.fund/what-we-do/portfolio-dashboard.

GEF (2001) *Energy for rural transformation project: project appraisal document*, Global Environment Facility, Washington, DC.

GEF (2006) *Evaluation of incremental cost assessment (GEF/ME/C.30/2)*, Global Environment Facility, Washington, DC.

GEF (2007) *GEF project document: Cogen for Africa (Project ID: 2597)*, Global Environment Facility, Washington, DC.

GEF (2008) *Manual for calculating GHG benefits of GEF projects: energy efficiency and renewable energy projects (GEF/C.33/Inf.18)*, Global Environment Facility, Washington, DC.

GEF (2018a) *Updated co-financing policy (GEF/C.54/10/Rev.01)*, Global Environment Facility, Washington, DC.

GEF (2018b) *Updated results architecture for GEF-7 (GEF/C.54/11/Rev.02)*, Global Environment Facility, Washington, DC.

GEF (2023) *Climate change mitigation*, Global Environment Facility. Website (accessed 10 May 2023): https://www.thegef.org/what-we-do/topics/climate-change-mitigation, Washington, DC.

GEF STAP (2011) *Manual for calculating GHG benefits of GEF transportation projects*, GEF Scientific and Technical Advisory Panel, Washington, DC.

Gerring J (2007) Is there a (viable) crucial-case method? *Comparative Political Studies* 40:231–253.

GET FiT Uganda (2014) *GET FiT Uganda: annual report 2013*, GET FiT Secretariat, Kampala.

Gillingham K, Rapson D and Wagner G (2016) The rebound effect and energy efficiency policy. *Review of Environmental Economics and Policy* 68–88.

Gipe P (2011) Uganda launches sophisticated feed-in tariff program, Renewable Energy World, 20 January 2011. Website (accessed 30 June 2011): http://www.renewableener gyworld.com/rea/news/article/2011/01/uganda-launches-sophisticated-feed-in-tar iff-program, Peterborough, NH.

Gobjila A (2007) *Carbon finance in practice: public heating biomass systems in Moldovan Rural communities project*, World Bank. Website (accessed 10 January 2010): http://siteresources.worldbank.org/INTALBANIA/Resources/Carbon_finance_in_practice_anatol.pdf, Washington, DC.

Goldthau A and Sitter N (2014) A liberal actor in a realist world? the commission and the external dimension of the single market for energy. *Journal of European Public Policy* 21:1452–1472.

Gordon R (2006) Sub-Saharan Africa and the brave new world of the WTO multilateral trade regime. *Berkeley Journal of African-American Law & Policy* 8:79.

Gore CD (2017) *Electricity in Africa: the politics of transformation in Uganda*, Boydell & Brewer, Woodbridge, UK.

Gore CD, Brass JN, Baldwin E and MacLean LM (2018) Political autonomy and resistance in electricity sector liberalization in Africa. *World Development* 120:193–209.

GoRM (2001) *2001–2005 activity program of the government of the Republic of Moldova "economic revival is revival of the country,"* Government of the Republic of Moldova, Chisinau.

GoRM (2004) *Economic growth and poverty reduction strategy paper (2004–2006)*, Government of the Republic of Moldova, Chisinau.

GoRM (2007) *National development strategy for 2008–2011*, Government of the Republic of Moldova, Chisinau.

GoRM (2012) *National development strategy "Moldova 2020,"* Government of the Republic of Moldova, Chisinau.

GoRM (2014a) *Hotărîre Nr. 301 din 24.04.2014 cu privire la aprobarea strategiei de mediu pentru anii 2014–2023 și a Planului de acțiuni pentru implementarea acesteia*, Government of the Republic of Moldova, Chisinau.

GoRM (2014b) *Hotărîre Nr. 594 din 26.07.2017 cu privire la restructurarea administrației publice centrale de specialitate*, Government of the Republic of Moldova, Chisinau.

GoRM (2014c) *Strategia națională de dezvoltare agricolă și rurală pentru anii 2014–2020 actualizată, aprobată prin hotărîrea guvernului nr.409/2014*, Government of Moldova, Chişinău.

GoRM (2016) *First Biennial Update Report of the Republic of Moldova under the United Nations Framework Convention*, Ministry of Environment, Chisinău.

GoRM (2022) *Updated nationally determined contribution of the Republic of Moldova*, UNFCCC, Bonn.

Gorton M (2001) Agricultural land reform in Moldova. *Land Use Policy* 18:269–279.

GoT (1992) *The energy policy of Tanzania*, Government of the United Republic of Tanzania, Ministry of Water, Energy and Minerals, Dar es Salaam.

GoT (2003) *The energy policy of Tanzania*, Government of the United Republic of Tanzania, Ministry of Energy and Minerals, Dar es Salaam.

GoT (2005) *MKUKUTA: Tanzania's national strategy for growth and reduction of poverty (NSGRP)*, Government of the United Republic of Tanzania, Vice-President's Office, Dar es Salaam.

GoT (2008) *Draft national forest policy*, Government of the United Republic of Tanzania, Dar es Salaam.

GoT (2017) *Energy access situation report 2016, mainland Tanzania*, Government of the United Republic of Tanzania, National Bureau of Statistics and Rural Energy Agency, Dar es Salaam.

Government of Moldova (2007) *Energy strategy of the Republic of Moldova to the year 2020* (English version), Ministry of Industry and Infrastructure, Chisinau.

Government of Tanzania (2015) *National energy policy, 2015*, Government of the United Republic of Tanzania, Dar es Salaam.

Government of Uganda (2011) *REDD readiness preparation proposal for Uganda*, World Bank Forest Carbon Partnership Facility, Washington, DC.

GPP (2018) *Tanzania electricity prices*, Global Petroleum Prices.com. Website (accessed 10 May 2018): https://www.globalpetrolprices.com/Tanzania/electricity_prices/.

GRAS (2010) *Development of Clean Development Mechanism projects in Tanzania by Green Resources AS: lessons learnt*, Green Resources AS, Lysaker, Norway.

GRAS (2011) *Director's report 2010*, Green Resources AS, Oslo.

Gratwick K, Ghanadan R and Eberhard A (2006) Generating power and controversy: understanding Tanzania's independent power projects. *Journal of Energy in Southern Africa* 17:39–56.

Gray H (2013) Industrial policy and the political settlement in Tanzania: aspects of continuity and change since independence. *Review of African Political Economy* 40:185–201.

Gray H (2018) *Turbulence and order in economic development: institutions and economic transformation in Tanzania and Vietnam*, Oxford University Press, Oxford.

Green E (2011) The political economy of nation formation in modern Tanzania: explaining stability in the face of diversity. *Commonwealth & Comparative Politics* 49:223–244.

Green JF (2017) Don't link carbon markets. *Nature* 543:484.

Green JF (2021) Does carbon pricing reduce emissions? A review of ex-post analyses. *Environmental Research Letters* 16:1–17.

Gregersen H, El Lakany H, Karsenty A and White A (2010) *Does the opportunity cost approach indicate the real cost of REDD+?* Rights and Resources Initiative, Washington, DC.

Gregory J and Sovacool BK (2019) The financial risks and barriers to electricity infrastructure in Kenya, Tanzania, and Mozambique: a critical and systematic review of the academic literature. *Energy Policy* 125:145–153.

Grindle MS (1980) *Politics and policy implementation in the Third World*. Princeton University Press.

GRL (2009) *Annual report*, Green Resources Limited, Oslo.

GRL (2011) *Director's report 2010*, Green Resources Limited, Oslo.

Guan-Fu G (1983) Soviet aid to the Third World, an analysis of its strategy. *Soviet Studies* 35:71–89.

Gulca V (2006) Opportunity of small-scale forestry in Moldova, in *Small-scale forestry and rural development: The intersection of ecosystems, economics and society*, Galway-Mayo Institute of Technology and IUFRO, 18 to 23 June 2006, Galway, Ireland.

Gulca V (2010a) Distrust in private forests—main gap in sustainable forest management of Moldova. *Journal of Horticulture, Forestry and Biotechnology* 14:80–90.

Gupta A and van Asselt H (2019) Transparency in multilateral climate politics: furthering (or distracting from) accountability? *Regulation & Governance* 13:18–34.

Gupta J and Thompson M (2010) Development and development cooperation theory, in *Mainstreaming climate change in development cooperation*, Gupta J and Van der Grijp N (eds), 3–30, Cambridge University Press, Cambridge.

Gupta J and Van der Grijp N (2010) Climate change, development and development co-operation, in *Mainstreaming climate change in development cooperation*, Gupta J and Van der Grijp N (eds), 3–30, Cambridge University Press, Cambridge.

Habraken R, Schulpen L and Hoebink P (2017) Putting promises into practice: the new aid architecture in Uganda. *Development Policy Review* 35:779–795.

Haggard S (2018) *Developmental states*, Cambridge University Press, Cambridge.

Håkanson L (1982) Identification and design of industrial development projects. *Geografiska Annaler: Series B, Human Geography* 64:105–118.

Hale T and Roger C (2014) Orchestration and transnational climate governance. *The Review of International Organizations* 9:59–82.

Hale TN, Chan S, Hsu A, Clapper A, Elliott C, Faria P, Kuramochi T, McDaniel S, Morgado M, Roelfsema M, Santaella M, Singh N, Tout I, Weber C, Weinfurter A and Widerberg O (2021) Sub- and non-state climate action: a framework to assess progress, implementation and impact. *Climate Policy* 21:406–420.

Hall PA (1993) Policy paradigms, social learning, and the state: the case of economic policymaking in Britain. *Comparative Politics* 25:275–296.

Hall PA (2010) Historical institutionalism in rationalist and sociological perspective, in *Explaining Institutional Change: Ambiguity, Agency, and Power* Mahoney J and Thelen K (eds), 204–224, Cambridge University Press, Cambridge.

Hansen MC, Potapov PV, Moore R, Hancher M, Turubanova S, Tyukavina A, Thau D, Stehman S, Goetz S and Loveland T (2013) High-resolution global maps of 21st-century forest cover change. *Science* 342:850–853.

Hanson P (2014) *The rise and fall of the the Soviet Economy: an economic history of the USSR 1945–1991*, Routledge, New York.

Hendrix CS (2010) Measuring state capacity: Theoretical and empirical implications for the study of civil conflict. *Journal of Peace Research* 47:273–285.

Hermwille L (2014) *Standardised baselines: Options to Strategically advance national climate policies*, Wuppertal Institute, Wuppertal, Germany.

Hesse J-O (2021) Financial crisis and the recurrence of economic nationalism. *Journal of Modern European History* 19:14–18.

Hickey S (2019) *The politics of state capacity and development in Africa: reframing and researching "pockets of effectiveness,"* Effective States and Inclusive Development (ESID) Research Centre, Manchester.

Hickey S and Izama A (2016) The politics of governing oil in Uganda: going against the grain? *African Affairs* 116:163–185.

Hinostroza M, Cheng C-C, Zhu X, Fenhann J, Figueres C and Avendano F (2007) *Potentials and barriers for end-use energy efficiency under programmatic CDM*, CD4CDM, Roskilde, Denmark.

Hinostroza ML, Lütken S, Aalders E, Pretlove B, Peters N and Olsen KH (2012) *Measuring, reporting, verifying. a primer on MRV for nationally appropriate mitigation actions*, UNEP Risø Centre on Energy, Climate and Sustainable Development, Department of Management Engineering, Technical University of Denmark.

Hirschman AO (1997 [1977]) *The passions and the interests: political arguments for capitalism before its triumph*, Princeton University Press, Princeton.

Hochstetler K (2023) Environment and development: crossing the divide between Global South and Global North, in *The Oxford handbook of comparative environmental politics*, Sowers JL, VanDeveer SD and Weinthal E (eds) 81–92, Oxford University Press, New York.

Hocking KS, Lamerton JF and Lewis EA (1963) Tsetse-fly control and eradication. *Bulletin of the World Health Organization* 28:811–823.

Höhne N, Kuramochi T, Warnecke C, Röser F, Fekete H, Hagemann M, Day T, Tewari R, Kurdziel M, Sterl S and Gonzales S (2017) The Paris Agreement: resolving the inconsistency between global goals and national contributions. *Climate Policy* 17:16–32.

Homer-Dixon T (1999) *Environment, scarcity, and violence*, Princeton University Press, Princeton.

Hood C (1991) A public management for all seasons. *Public Administration* 69:3–19.

Hoppe KA (2003) *Lords of the fly: sleeping sickness control in British East Africa, 1900–1960*, Praeger, Westport, CT.

Hosier RH, Boberg J, Luhanga M and Mwandosya M (1990) Energy planning and wood balances: sustainable energy future for Tanzania. *Natural Resources Forum* 14:143–154.

Huggins C (2018) Land-Use Planning, Digital Technologies, and Environmental Conservation in Tanzania. *The Journal of Environment & Development* 27:210–235.

Hughes A (1992a) The appeal of Marxism to Africans. *Journal of Communist Studies* 8:4–20.

Hughes A (1992b) *Marxism's retreat from Africa*, Frank Cass, London.

Hunter E (2015) *Political thought and the public sphere in Tanzania: freedom, democracy and citizenship in the era of decolonization*, Cambridge University Press, Cambridge.

Hunter J (2003) Broken promises: trade, agriculture and development in the WTO. *Melbourne Journal of International Law* 4:299–322.

Huntington SP (1968) *Political order in changing societies*, Yale University Press, New Haven.

Hurst A (2003) State forestry and spatial scale in the development discourses of post-colonial Tanzania: 1961–1971. *Geographical Journal* 169:358–369.

Hydén G (1980) *Beyond ujamaa in Tanzania: underdevelopment and an uncaptured peasantry*, Heinemann, London.

Ibhawoh B and Dibua JI (2003) Deconstructing Ujamaa: the legacy of Julius Nyerere in the quest for social and economic development in Africa. *African Journal of Political Science* 8:59–83.

ICAP (2023a) *Brazil introduces draft law for cap-and-trade system*, International Carbon Action Partnership. Website (accessed 23 October 2023): https://icapcarbonaction. com/en/news/brazil-introduces-draft-law-cap-and-trade-system, Berlin.

ICAP (2023b) *India establishes framework for voluntary carbon market and outlines pathway towards cap-and-trade system*, International Carbon Action Partnership.

Website (accessed 23 October 2023): https://icapcarbonaction.com/en/news/india-establishes-framework-voluntary-carbon-market-and-outlines-pathway-towards-cap-and-trade, Berlin.

ICAS (2007) *Extinderea pădurilor*, Institutului de Cercetări şi Amenajări Silvice. Website (accessed 10 February 2010): http://www.icas.com.md./index.files/Extind_pad.htm, Chisinau.

IEA (2009) *Sectoral approaches in electricity*, International Energy Agency, Paris.

IEA (2016) Global Energy Transfer Feed-in Tariff (GET FIT) Programme Uganda, International Energy Agency, Website (accessed 30 September 2018): https://www.iea.org/policies/5636-global-energy-transfer-feed-in-tariff-get-fit-programme-uganda, Paris.

IEA (2020) *Total Primary Energy Supply (TPES) by source*, International Energy Agency, Website (accessed 30 August 2020): https://www.iea.org/data-and-statistics?country=WORLD&fuel=Energy%20supply&indicator=Total%20energy%20supply%20(TES)%20by%20source, Paris.

IEGCF (2020) *Delivering on the $100 billion climate finance commitment and transforming climate finance*, United Nations, Independent Expert Group on Climate Finance, New York.

IFC (2010) *Green resources: summary of proposed investment (project no. 26506)*, International Finance Corporation, Washington, DC.

IISD (2009) *G8 Finance ministers support climate investment funds*, International Institute for Sustainable Development. Website (accessed 7 April 2020): http://sdg.iisd.org/news/g8-finance-ministers-support-climate-investment-funds/, Winnipeg.

Ikeme J (2003) Equity, environmental justice and sustainability: incomplete approaches in climate change politics. *Global Environmental Change-Human and Policy Dimensions* 13:195–206.

IMF (2004) *Repubilc of Moldova: joint staff advisory note of the poverty reduction strategy paper*, International Monetary Fund, Washington, DC.

Independent (2020) Chinese firm applies for construction of 840MW Ayago dam, *The Independent*. Website (accessed 10 May 2021): https://www.independent.co.ug/chinese-firm-applies-for-construction-of-840mw-ayago-dam/.

Indufor (2017) *Benefit sharing arrangements for Uganda's national REDD+ strategy: executive summary of BSA options assessment*, Indufor, Helsinki.

IPCC (2003) *Good practice guidance for land use, land-use change and forestry*, IPCC-NGGIP, Kanagawa, Japan.

IPCC (2006a) *2006 IPCC guidelines for national greenhouse gas inventories*, IPPC-NGGIP, Kanagawa, Japan.

IPCC (2006b) *Agriculture, forestry and other land use, volume 4: 2006 IPCC guidelines for national greenhouse gas inventories*, IPPC-NGGIP, Kanagawa, Japan.

IPCC (2019) *2019 refinement to the 2006 IPCC guidelines for national greenhouse gas inventories*, IPPC-NGGIP, Kanagawa, Japan.

IPCC (2022a) Mitigation of Climate Change: Summary for Policymakers, in Climate Change 2022: Contribution of Working Group III to the Sixth Assessment Report of the Intergovernmental Panel on Climate Change, Cambridge University Press, Cambridge.

IPCC (2022b) Point of departure and key concepts, in *Climate Change 2022: Impacts, adaptation and vulnerability contribution of Working Group II to the sixth assessment report of the intergovernmental panel on climate change*, H.-O. Pörtner, D.C. Roberts, M. Tignor,

E.S. Poloczanska, K. Mintenbeck, A. Alegría, M. Craig, S. Langsdorf, S. Löschke, V. Möller, A. Okem, B. Rama (eds), 123–196, Cambridge University Press, New York.

IRENA (2017) *Renewable readiness assessment: United Republic of Tanzania*, International Renewable Energy Agency, Abu Dhabi.

IRENA (2019) *Renewable readiness assessment: Republic of Moldova*, International Renewable Energy Agency, Abu Dhabi.

JACO CDM (2009) *Small-scale a/r validation report: Uganda Nile basin reforestation project no. 3 (report no. GR07W0002D Rev.06)*, JACO CDM, Tokyo.

Jacob T (2017) Competing energy narratives in Tanzania: towards the political economy of coal. *African Affairs* 116:341–353.

Jacovelli PA (2009) Uganda's sawlog production grant scheme: a success story from Africa. *International Forestry Review* 11:119–125.

Jacovelli PA (2014) The future of plantations in Africa. *International Forestry Review* 16:144–159.

Jasny N (1961) *Soviet industrialization, 1928–1952*, University of Chicago Press, Chicago.

Jenkins HC, Nohrstedt D, Weible C and Sabatier PA (2014) The advocacy coalition framework: foundations, evolution, and ongoing research, in *Theories of the policy process*, Sabatier PA and Weible C (eds), 183–222, Westview Press, Boulder, CO.

Jenkins M (2021) *Carbon prices soar in bullish year*, Environmental Finance. Website accessed (10 December 2021): https://www.environmental-finance.com/content/awards/annual-market-rankings-2021/categories/carbon-prices-soar-in-bullish-year.html, London.

Jinnah S, Bushey D, Munoz M and Kulovesi K (2009) Tripping points: barriers and bargaining chips on the road to Copenhagen. *Environmental Research Letters* 4:1–6.

Jirušek M and Kuchyňková P (2018) The conduct of Gazprom in Central and Eastern Europe: A tool of the Kremlin, or just an adaptable player? *East European Politics and Societies* 32:818–844.

Jodoin S (2017) *Forest preservation in a changing climate: REDD+ and indigenous and community rights in Indonesia and Tanzania*, Cambridge University Press, Cambridge.

Johnsen FH (1999) Burning with enthusiasm: fuelwood scarcity in Tanzania in terms of severity, impacts and remedies. *Forum for Development Studies* 1:107–131.

Johnson O (2010) *The evolution of donor-recipient relations in electricity reform: rethinking the principal-agent framework*, PhD thesis, Science and Technology Policy Research, University of Sussex, Brighton, UK.

Jones GA and Corbridge S (2010) The continuing debate about urban bias: the thesis, its critics, its influence and its implications for poverty-reduction strategies. *Progress in Development Studies* 10:1–18.

Jordan A, Huitema D, Van Asselt H and Forster J eds (2018) *Governing climate change: polycentricity in action?* Cambridge University Press, Cambridge.

Jung M (2003) *The role of forestry sinks in the CDM—analyzing the effects of policy decisions on the carbon market*. HWWA Discussion Paper 241.

Juuko S (2004) *EADB gives Kakira $8m loans*, All Africa, 9 August 2004. Website (accessed 10 June 2011): http://allafrica.com/stories/200408090885.html, Kampala.

Kalderen L (1991) The UN and the Bretton Woods institutions: A study for the Nordic UN Project, in *The United Nations: issues and options: five studies on the role of the UN in the economic and social fields commissioned by the Nordic UN Project*, Almqvist & Wiksell International, Stockholm.

Kalumanga E, Olwig MF, Brockington D and Mwamfuge A (2018) Partnerships and governance in forest management in Tanzania: historical and current perspectives. *Nepsus Working Paper* 1–31.

Kalyango Y (2004) Kakira gets $3.5m subsidy for rural electrification, 25 August 2004, All Africa. Website (accessed 10 October 2010): http://allafrica.com/stories/200408250 507.html, Kampala.

Kamagi D (2020) Power generation exceeds demand by 280 MW, *Daily News*, 3 February 2020. Website (accessed 10 August 2020): https://dailynews.co.tz/news/2020-02-035e 37c4f6375a8.aspx, Dar es Salaam.

Kambugu RK, Banana AY and Odokonyero G (2010) Chainsaw milling in Uganda. *European Tropical Forest Research Network News* 52:194–202.

Kammen DM and Lew DJ (2005) *Review of technologies for the production and use of charcoal*, Energy and Resources Group & Goldman School of Public Policy, Berkeley, CA.

Kangalawe H (2018) *Plantation forestry in Tanzania: A history of Sao Hill forests, 1939–2015*, PhD thesis, Stellenbosch, South Africa.

Kapika J and Eberhard A (2012) *Power sector reform and regulation in Africa: Lessons from Ghana, Kenya, Namibia, Tanzania, Uganda and Zambia*, HSRC Press, Pretoria.

Kapur D, Lewis JP and Webb RC (2011) *The World Bank: its first half century*, Brookings Institution Press, Washington, D.C.

Karbozova-Saljnikov E, Funakawa S, Akhmetov K and Kosaki T (2004) Soil organic matter status of Chernozem soil in North Kazakhstan: effects of summer fallow. *Soil Biology & Biochemistry* 36:1373–1381.

Karekezi S and Mutiso D (2000) *Power sector reform: A Kenyan case study*, Springer, London.

Kasaija PA (2004) Regional integration: a political federation of the East African countries? *African Journal of International Affairs* 7:21–34.

Kashwan P (2017) *Democracy in the woods: Environmental conservation and social justice in India, Tanzania, and Mexico*, Oxford University Press, Oxford.

Kasita I (2012) Uganda meets power needs as Bujagali delivers 250 Megawatts, in *The New Vision*, 15 June 2012, Website (accessed 10 September 2012): http://allafrica.com/stor ies/201206151283.html, Kampala.

Kasozi E (2007) Uganda: $12m paper factory starts, in *The Monitor*, 9 November 2007. Website (accessed 10 October 2010): http://allafrica.com/stories/200711081045.html, Kampala.

Katoomba Group (2007) World Bank to buy US $3 million worth of carbon credits from Uganda, *East & Southern Africa Katoomba Group Newsletter*, November 2007, Website (accessed 10 June 2011): http://www.katoombagroup.org/documents/newsletters/Vol1_No11.html#anchor2, Kampala.

Kaufman SJ (1996) Spiraling to ethnic war—elites, masses, and Moscow in Moldova's civil war. *International Security* 21:108–138.

Kay C (2009) Development strategies and rural development: exploring synergies, eradicating poverty. *Journal of Peasant Studies* 36:103–137.

Kayizzi R (2004) Locals want Kakira power rates reduced, 23 April 2004, *The New Vision*, p. 38, Kampala.

KDA (2008) *Business plan: Karatu energy efficient stove project/Clean Development Mechanism project*, Registered Trustees of Karatu Development Association, Karatu, Tanzania.

KDA (2009) *Improved stoves: steps of the project, survey of firewood consumption*, Karatu Development Association. Website (accessed 10 January 2011): http://kda-karatu.org/stoves_steps.htm.

Kelsall T (2011) Rethinking the relationship between neo-patrimonialism and economic development in Africa. *IDS Bulletin* 42:76–87.

Kelsall T (2013) *Business, politics, and the state in Africa*, Zed Books, London.

Keohane R and Victor D (2011) The regime complex for climate change. *Perspectives on Politics* 9:7–23.

Khamzina A, Lamers JPA, Worbes M, Botman E and Vlek PLG (2006) Assessing the potential of trees for afforestation of degraded landscapes in the Aral Sea Basin of Uzbekistan. *Agroforestry Systems* 66:129–141.

Khan KA (2015) Uganda—a country yet to achieve its entity: discovery of oil and future prospects. *Ethiopian International Journal of Multidisciplinary Research* 2:16–24.

Khan M, Mfitumukiza D and Huq S (2020) Capacity building for implementation of nationally determined contributions under the Paris Agreement. *Climate Policy* 20:499–510.

Khan MH (2005) Markets, states and democracy: patron–client networks and the case for democracy in developing countries. *Democratization* 12:704–724.

Khan MH (2010) Political settlements and the governance of growth-enhancing institutions, SOAS Draft Paper, Research Paper Series on Growth-Enhancing Governance, London.

Khan MH and Jomo KS (1999) *Rents, rent-seeking and economic development: theory and evidence in Asia*, Cambridge University Press, Cambridge.

Khan SR and Christiansen J (2011) *Towards new developmentalism: market as means rather than master*, Routledge, New York.

Kihwele S, Hur K and Kyaruzi A (2012) Visions, scenarios and action plans towards next generation Tanzania power system. *Energies* 5:3908–3927.

Kiiza J, Mubazi JKE and Kibikyo DL (2007) Understanding economic and institutional reforms in Uganda, in *Understanding economic reforms in Africa: A tale of seven nations*, Mensah J (ed), 57–94, Palgrave Macmillan, Basingstoke, Hampshire.

Kim RE (2020) Is global governance fragmented, polycentric, or complex? The state of the art of the network approach. *International Studies Review* 22:903–931.

King C (2000) *The Moldovans: Romania, Russia, and the politics of culture*, Hoover Institution Press, Stanford, CA.

Kinyanjui B, Gitau A and Mang'oli M (2011) Power development planning models in East Africa. *Strategic Planning for Energy and the Environment* 31:43–55.

Kleinschnitger K and Knodt M (2018) Asymmetric perceptions of EU relations with the Near Eastern neighbours: the Republic of Moldova, Ukraine and Belarus in comparison. *European Foreign Affairs Review* 23:79–99.

Klöck C, Molenaers N and Weiler F (2018) Responsibility, capacity, greenness or vulnerability? What explains the levels of climate aid provided by bilateral donors? *Environmental Politics* 27:892–916.

Knoepfel P, Larrue C, Varone F and Hill M (2007) *Public policy analysis*, Bristol University Press, Bristol.

Koch N, Fuss S, Grosjean G and Edenhofer O (2014) Causes of the EU ETS price drop: recession, CDM, renewable policies or a bit of everything? New evidence. *Energy Policy* 73:676–685.

Koeberle S (2005) *Conditionality revisited: concepts, experiences, and lessons*, World Bank, Washington, DC.

Kohli A (2004) *State-directed development: political power and industrialization in the global periphery*, Cambridge University Press, Cambridge.

Kostanyan H (2016) *Why Moldova's European integration is failing*, Centre for European Policy Studies (CEPS), Brussels.

Kottasova I (2015) *How to steal $1 billion in three days*, CNN Money. Website (accessed 12 August 2016): http://money.cnn.com/2015/05/07/news/economy/moldova-stolen-billion/.

Krugman P (1995) Cycles of conventional wisdom on economic development. *International Affairs* 71:717–732.

Krupenikov IA (2008) *Chernozems. Vozniknovenie, sovershenstvo, tragediya degradatsii, puti okhrany i vozrozhdeniya (Chernozems: their origin and perfection, the tragedy of their degradation, and the ways of their conservation and revival)*, Pontos, Chisinau.

KSW (2010) Expansion, Kakira Sugar Works. Website (accessed 30 June 2011): http://www.kakirasugar.com/content/expansion, Kampala.

KSW (2014) Kakira expansion update—January 2, 2014, Kakira Sugar Limited Facebook Page. Website (accessed Jan 15, 2014): https://www.facebook.com/KakiraSugarWorks.

Kulekana J (2008) Mufindi Paper Mills in full production, *Daily News*, 8 August 2008. Website (accessed 10 February 2010): http://dailynews.habarileo.co.tz/magazine/index.php?id=6423, Dar es Salaam.

Kulindwa K and Schechambo F (1995) The impact of rural energy use on the environment during the economic reforms period (1981–1992): some evidence from Tanzania. *Utafiti (New Series)* 2:110–131.

Kulovesti K (2012) Negotiations on the new market mechanism and the framework for various approaches: What future role for the UNFCCC in regulating the carbon market. *Carbon & Climate Law Review* 4:373–383.

Kuteesa F, Tumusiime-Mutebile E, Whitworth A and Williamson T (2009) *Uganda's economic reforms: insider accounts*, Oxford University Press, Oxford.

Labbate G (2008) The incremental cost principle and the conservation of globally important habitats: a critical examination. *Ecological Economics* 65:216–224.

Langbein L and Felbinger CL (2006) *Public program evaluation: a statistical guide*, M.E. Sharpe, Armonk and London.

Lastarria-Cornhiel S (2003) Uganda country brief: property rights and land markets, Land Tenure Center, University of Wisconsin–Madison.

LECBP (2012) *Moldova*, UNDP Low Emission Capacity Building Program. Website (accessed March 15, 2014): http://www.lowemissiondevelopment.org/countries/moldova, New York.

Lechevalier S, Debanes P and Shin W (2019) Financialization and industrial policies in Japan and Korea: evolving institutional complementarities and loss of state capabilities. *Structural Change and Economic Dynamics* 48:69–85.

Lecocq F (2003) Pioneering transactions, catalyzing markets, and building capacity: the prototype carbon fund contributions to climate politics. *American Journal of Agricultural Economics* 85:703–707.

Ledesma D (2013) *East Africa gas—the potential for export*, Oxford Institute for Energy Studies.

LEDSGP (2014) *Linkages between LEDS-NAMA-MRV*, LEDS Global Partnership Secretariat, US National Renewable Energy Laboratory, Boulder, CO.

Lee M-K ed (2004) *CDM: information and guidebook*, UNEP Risoe Centre, Roskilde, Denmark.

Lerman Z and Cimpoies D (2006) Land consolidation as a factor for rural development in Moldova. *Europe-Asia Studies* 58:439–455.

Leroy P and Crabb A (2012) *The handbook of environmental policy evaluation*, Earthscan, New York.

Levin K, Cashore B, Bernstein S and Auld G (2012) Overcoming the tragedy of super wicked problems: constraining our future selves to ameliorate global climate change. *Policy Sciences* 45:123–152.

Levine HS (1962) Input-output analysis and Soviet planning. *The American Economic Review* 52:127–137.

Levitsky S and Way LA (2002) The rise of competitive authoritarianism. *Journal of Democracy* 13:51–65.

Lewis JI (2010) The evolving role of carbon finance in promoting renewable energy development in China. *Energy Policy* 38:2875–2886.

Lifuliro C, Zilihona I, Mdendemi T, Kamanzi A, Kinyashi G and van Dijk T (2018) *Tanzania planners' handbook: a guide for development planning*, African Studies Centre, The Netherlands.

Lin J and Chang H-J (2009) Should industrial policy in developing countries conform to comparative advantage or defy it? A debate between Justin Lin and Ha-Joon Chang. *Development Policy Review* 27:483–502.

Lin JY (2011) New structural economics: a framework for rethinking development. *The World Bank Research Observer* 26:193–221.

Lin JY (2021) New structural economics: a framework of studying government and economics. *Journal of Government and Economics* 2:1–4.

Lindblom CE (1959) The science of muddling through. *Public Administration Review* 19:79–88.

Lipton M (1977) *Why poor people stay poor: urban bias in world development*, Temple Smith, London.

Liu X, Strömberg P and Wennler L (2013) *Estimating the additionality of the Swedish climate subsidy program: Klimp*, Örebro University School of Business, Örebro University, Sweden.

Livi-Bacci M (1993) On the human costs of collectivization in the Soviet Union. *Population and Development Review* 19:743–766.

Lopez JJ (1992) Theory choice in comparative social inquiry. *Polity* 25:267–282.

LTS (2010) *Review of the forestry sector in Uganda*, LTS International, Penicuik, UK.

Lund JF, Sungusia E, Mabele MB and Scheba A (2017) Promising change, delivering continuity: REDD+ as conservation fad. *World Development* 89:124–139.

Lütken S, Dransfeld B, Wehner S, Agyemang-Bonsu W, Avendaño F, Babu D, Bonduki Y, Carman R, Forner C and Hinostroza ML (2013) *Guidance for NAMA design-building on country experiences*, UNDP Low Emission Capacity Building Program, New York.

Lymio B (2007) *Improving energy resilience in Tanzania*, HELIO International, Paris.

M&P Group of Industry (2011) Mayuge Sugar Industries, Jinja, Website (accessed 4 March 2014): http://www.mpgroupofindustries.com/mayuge-sugar.html.

Mabikke SB (2016) Historical continuum of land rights in Uganda: a review of land tenure systems and approaches for improving tenure security. *Journal of Land and Rural Studies* 4:153–171.

Mackinnon J and Reinikka R (1999) *Lessons from Uganda on strategies to fight poverty*, World Bank Policy Research Working Papers, World Bank, Washington, DC.

MacLean LM, Gore C, Brass JN and Baldwin E (2016) Expectations of power: the politics of state-building and access to electricity provision in Ghana and Uganda. *Journal of African Political Economy and Development* 1:103–134.

MacNeil R (2017) *Neoliberalism and climate policy in the United States: from market fetishism to the developmental State*, Taylor & Francis, New York.

Mahoney J (2000) Path dependence in historical sociology. *Theory and Society* 29:507–548.

Mahoney J (2008) Toward a unified theory of causality. *Comparative Political Studies* 41:412–436.

Mahoney J and Rueschemeyer D eds (2003) *Comparative historical analysis in the social sciences*, Cambridge University Press, Cambridge.

Mäkelä M, Blomley T, Edwards K, Lukumbuzya K, Kingazi S, Vesa L and Martin J (2015) *Lessons learned from the implementation of REDD pilot projects in Tanzania*, NIRAS Finland Oy, Vantaa, Finland.

Maliniak D, Peterson S, Powers R and Tierney MJ (2018) Is international relations a global discipline? Hegemony, insularity, and diversity in the field. *Security Studies* 27:448–484.

Mapfumo P, Onyango M, Honkponou SK, El Mzouri EH, Githeko A, Rabeharisoa L, Obando J, Omolo N, Majule A, Denton F, Ayers J and Agrawal A (2017) Pathways to transformational change in the face of climate impacts: an analytical framework. *Climate and Development* 9:439–451.

Marandu E and Luteganya R (2004) Tanzania, in *The regulation of the power sector in Africa: attracting investment and protecting the poor*, Marandu E and Kayo D (eds), Chapter 4, Zed Books, London.

Marland G, Fruit K and Sedjo R (2001) Accounting for sequestered carbon: the question of permanence. *Environmental Science & Policy* 4:259–268.

Matei L (2013) Republic of Moldova: toward a European administration, in *Public administration in post-communist countries: former Soviet Union, Central and Eastern Europe, and Mongolia*, Liebert S, Condrey SE and Goncharov D (eds), 191–216, Taylor & Francis, Boca Raton, FL.

Mathews JA (2008) How carbon credits could drive the emergence of renewable energies. *Energy Policy* 36:3633–3639.

Mayne J (2007) Challenges and lessons in implementing results-based management. *Evaluation* 13:87–109.

Mazza F, Falzon J and Buchner B (2016) *Global climate finance: an updated view on 2013 & 2014 flows*, Climate Policy Initiative, Venice.

Mazzucato M (2011) *The entrepreneurial state*, Demos, London.

Mbabazi P and Taylor I (2005) *The potentiality of "developmental states" in Africa: Botswana and Uganda compared*, Council for the Development of Social Science Research in Africa (CODESIRA), Dakar.

Mbunda F (2007) Exporters of electric poles planning legal action on Maghembe, *The Guardian*, 29 October 2007. Website (accessed 4 December 2009): http://216.69.164.44/ipp/guardian/2007/10/29/101393.html, Dar es Salaam.

MCFU (2007) *Annual monitoring report of emission reductions of CDM Project "Moldova biomass heating in rural communities (project design document no. 1),"* Carbon Finance Unit of the Republic of Moldova, Chisinau.

McHenry DE (1979) *Tanzania's ujamaa villages: the implementation of a rural development strategy*, Institute of International Studies, University of California, Berkeley.

McKinsey & Company (2018) Investment and industrial policy: a perspective on the future, in *UNCTAD Trade and Development Board, Sixty-Fifth Session*, UCTAD, Geneva.

McKinsey Global Institute (2016) *Digital globalization: the new era of global flows*, McKinsey, London.

ME (2010) *Association of the Republic of Moldova to the Copenhagen Accord*, Ministry of Environment of the Republic of Moldova. Website (accessed 10 January 2017): https://unfccc.int/files/meetings/cop_15/copenhagen_accord/application/pdf/moldovacph accord_app2.pdf, Chisinau.

Meckling J (2017) The developmental state in global regulation: economic change and climate policy. *European Journal of International Relations* 24:58–81.

Meckling J (2021) Making industrial policy work for decarbonization. *Global Environmental Politics* 21:134–147.

Meckling J and Allan BB (2020) The evolution of ideas in global climate policy. *Nature Climate Change* 10:434–438.

Meckling J and Nahm J (2022) Strategic state capacity: how states counter opposition to climate policy. *Comparative Political Studies* 55:493–523.

Meckling J, Sterner T and Wagner G (2017) Policy sequencing toward decarbonization. *Nature Energy* 2:918.

Mehling MA, Metcalf GE and Stavins RN (2018) Linking climate policies to advance global mitigation. *Science* 359:997–998.

Meindertsman JD and Kessler JJ eds (1997) *Towards better use of environmental resources: A planning document of Mbulu and Karatu districts*, Netherlands Economic Institute (NEI), Rotterdam.

Melo MA, Ng'ethe N and Manor J (2012) *Against the odds: politicians, institutions and the struggle against poverty*, Hurst, London.

MEMD (2002) *The energy policy of Uganda*, Ministry of Energy and Mineral Development, Kampala.

MEMD (2004) *MEMD annual report 2003*, Ministry of Energy and Mineral Development, Kampala.

MEMD (2007) *The renewable energy policy for Uganda*, Ministry of Energy and Mineral Development, Kampala.

Mensah J (2007) Introduction: understanding economic reforms in Africa, in *Understanding economic reforms in Africa: a tale of seven nations* Mensah J (ed), 1–15, Palgrave Macmillan, Basingstoke, Hampshire.

Metz S (1982) In lieu of orthodoxy: the socialist theories of Nkrumah and Nyerere. *The Journal of Modern African Studies* 20:377–392.

Meyer R, Eberhard A and Gratwick K (2018) Uganda's power sector reform: there and back again? *Energy for Sustainable Development* 43:75–89.

MFEA (2010) *MKUKUTA 2: Tanzania's national strategy for growth and reduction of poverty 2*, Government of the United Republic of Tanzania, Ministry of Finance and Economic Affairs, Dar es Salaam.

MFPED (2005) *Poverty eradication action plan (2004/5–2007/8)*, Ministry of Finance, Planning and Economic Development, Kampala.

Miarka A (2020) Transnistria as an instrument of influence of the Russian Federation on the security of Moldova in the second decade of the 21st Century—selected aspects. *Communist and Post-Communist Studies* 53:61–75.

Michaelowa A (2012) Preface: climate finance at the crossroads between market mechanisms and public funding vehicles, in *Carbon markets or climate finance?* Michaelowa A (ed), xviii–xxii, Routledge, Abingdon.

Michaelowa A and Michaelowa K (2011) Climate business for poverty reduction? The role of the World Bank. *The Review of International Organizations* 6:259–286.

Michaelowa A and Sacherer A-K (2022) Is climate finance a meteoric fashion or a stable pillar of the global response to anthropogenic climate change?, in *Handbook of international climate finance*, Michaelowa A and Sacherer A-K (eds), 1–14, Edward Elgar, London.

Michaelowa A, Shishlov I and Brescia D (2019) Evolution of international carbon markets: lessons for the Paris Agreement. *Wiley Interdisciplinary Reviews: Climate Change* 10:e613.

Mihalache AE (2014) *The fairytale that wasn't: The Iași-Ungheni gas interconnector*, Energy Policy Group. Website (accessed 10 July 2018): https://www.enpg.ro/wp-cont ent/uploads/2017/10/EPG_The-Iasi-Ungheni-Interconnector.pdf, Bucharest.

Milledge SAH, Gelvas IK and Ahrends A (2007) *Forestry, governance and national development: lessons learned from a logging boom in southern Tanzania*, TRAFFIC, Tanzania Development Partners Group & Ministry of Natural Resources and Tourism, Dar es Salaam.

Mkandawire T (2001) Thinking about developmental states in Africa. *Cambridge Journal of Economics* 25:289–313.

Mkandawire T (2015) Neopatrimonialism and the political economy of economic performance in Africa: critical reflections. *World Politics* 67:563–612.

MNRT (1998) *National forest policy*, Ministry of Natural Resources and Tourism, Dar es Salaam.

MNRT (2000) *Forestry outlook studies in Africa: United Republic of Tanzania*, Ministry of Natural Resources and Tourism, Dar es Salaam.

MNRT (2001) *National forest programme in Tanzania (2001–2010)*, Ministry of Natural Resources and Tourism, Division of Forestry and Beekeeping, Dar es Salaam.

MNRT (2010) *Tanzania forest service framework document*, Ministry of Natural Resources and Tourism, Dar es Salaam.

MNRT (2018a) *National forest policy (draft 08)*, Ministry of Natural Resources and Tourism, Dar es Salaam.

MNRT (2018b) *National forest policy implementation strategy*, Ministry of Natural Resources and Tourism, Dar es Salaam.

Moate P, Williams S, Torok V, Hannah M, Ribaux B, Tavendale M, Eckard R, Jacobs J, Auldist M and Wales W (2014) Grape marc reduces methane emissions when fed to dairy cows. *Journal of Dairy Science* 97:5073–5087.

Moldsilva (2009) *Carbon sequestration through afforestation: experience of the Republic of Moldova*, Î.E.P. Știința., Chisinau.

Moldsilva (2010a) Extinderea suprafețelor forestiere, Moldsilva. Website (accessed 10 January 2010): http://www.moldsilva.gov.md/md/extension/, Chisinau.

Moldsilva (2010b) Regenerarea pădurii, Moldsilva. Website (accessed 10 January 2010): http://www.moldsilva.gov.md/md/regenerare/, Chisinau.

Moldsilva (2011) *State of the forestry of the Republic of Moldova, 2006–2010*, ENPI Fleg & Agency Moldsilva, Chisinau.

Moldsilva (2013a) Analiza activității economico – financiară a ramurii silvice, semestrul I, 2013, Moldsilva. Website (accessed 14 January 2014): http://www.moldsilva.gov.md/public/files/transparenta_decizionala/Raport_analiza_economico-finaciara_2009-2013_trimestru_I.doc, Chisinau.

Moldsilva (2013b) Regenerarea și extinderea pădurii, Moldsilva. Website (accessed 10 January 2014): http://www.moldsilva.gov.md/pageview.php?l=ro&idc=187&t=/Act ivitati/Regenerarea-si-extinderea-padurilor&, Chisinau.

Moldsilva (2013c) Situația actuală în sectorul forestier național și sarcinile curente de ameliorare, Moldsilva. Website (accessed 14 January 2014): http://www.moldsilva. gov.md/public/files/docs/Raport%20Sarcinile%20curente%20de%20ameliorare%20 03.07.2010.pdf, Chisinau.

Moldsilva (2019) Lista întreprinderilor de stat din subordinea Agenției "Moldsilva," Moldsilva. Website (accessed 12 March 2019): http://www.moldsilva.gov.md/pagev iew.php?l=ro&idc=264&t=/Despre-Agentie/Entitati-subordonate/Lista-Entitatilor-subordonate&, Chisinau.

Molnar S (2012) Romanian government approves gas pipeline between Romania and Moldova, Natural Gas Europe, 6 June 2012. Website (accessed 10 July 2012): http:// www.naturalgaseurope.com/gas-pipeline-between-romania-and-moldova, London.

Moner-Girona M, Ghanadan R, Solano-Peralta M, Kougias I, Bódis K, Huld T and Szabó S (2016) Adaptation of feed-in tariff for remote mini-grids: Tanzania as an illustrative case. Renewable and Sustainable Energy Reviews 53:306–318.

Monitor (2019) Relief for industrialists as 183mw Isimba dam opens, 21 March 2019. Website (accessed 10 August 2020): https://www.monitor.co.ug/News/National/Rel ief-industrialists-183mw-Isimba-dam-opens/688334-5035140-11bnp4az/index.html, Kampala.

Morisset J (2000) Foreign direct investment in Africa: policies also matter, World Bank, Washington, DC.

Mou W, Jiahua P and Ying C (2010) Analysis on American Clean Energy and Security Act. Advances in Climate Change Research 6:307–312.

Mountford H, Waskow D, Gonzalez L, Gajjar C, Cogswell N, Holt M, Fransen T, Bergen M and Gerholdt R (2021) COP26: Key outcomes from the UN climate talks in Glasgow, World Resources Institute (WRI), Washington, DC.

MPF (2016) National five year development plan 2016/2017–2020/2021, United Republic of Tanzania, Ministry of Planning and Finance, Dar es Salaam.

Mramba B and Mwansasu B (1972) Management for socialist development in Tanzania: the case of the National Development Corporation in Tanzania. African Review 1:29–47.

MSIF (No Date) Legal Framework, Moldova Social Investment Fund. Website (accessed 1 February 2011): http://www.msif.md/index.php?option=com_content&view=arti cle&id=9&Itemid=26&lang=en, Chisineau.

Mufumba I (2005) Financiers line up $23.6m for Kakira, All Africa, 25 March 2005. Website (accessed 10 June 2011): http://allafrica.com/stories/200503240940.html, Kampala.

Mugambe K (2009) The poverty eradication action plan, in Uganda's economic reforms: insider accounts, Kuteesa F, Tumusiime-Mutebile E, Whitworth A and Williamson T (eds), 157–171, Oxford University Press, Oxford.

Mukisa P, Tumusiime D, Webersik C, Liwenga E and Tabuti J (2020) Dissenting voices in a consenting village: lessons from implementation of free, prior and informed consent at a REDD+ pilot in Tanzania. International Forestry Review 22:120–131.

Mukokoma MM (2009) Application and effectiveness of new public management in National Water and Sewerage Corporation. Journal of Science and Sustainable Development 2:61–67.

Mukokoma MMN and Van Dijk MP (2013) New public management reforms and efficiency in urban water service delivery in developing countries: blessing or fad? *Public Works Management & Policy* 18:23–40.

Multilateral Fund (2022) Welcome to the Multilateral Fund for the Implementation of the Montreal Protocol, Multilateral Fund for the Implementation of the Montreal Protocol. Website (accessed 1 January 2023): http://www.multilateralfund.org, Montreal.

Munnings C, Leard B and Bento AM (2016) *The net emissions impact of HFC-23 offset projects from the Clean Development Mechanism, RFF DP 16-01*, Resources for the Future, Washington, DC.

Murison K ed (2002) *Africa south of the Sahara 2003*, Europa, London.

Must E (2018) Structural inequality, natural resources and mobilization in southern Tanzania. *African Affairs* 117:83–108.

Mutambi BM (2010) *Successfully regulating electricity from the sugar industry: the case of Uganda*, Electricity Regulatory Agency (ERA). Kampala.

Mwalupinde O (2017) Magufuli's dilemma: corruption and the pursuit of democracy. *The St Andrews Africa Summit Review*. Website: (accessed 20 February 2024)https://ojs.st-andrews.ac.uk/index.php/SAASUM/article/view/1402/1071.

Mwalyosi R (1991) Ecological evaluation for wildlife corridors and buffer zones for Lake Manyara National Park, Tanzania, and its immediate environment. *Biological Conservation* 57:171–186.

Mwalyosi RBB and Mohamed SA (1992) Resource management strategy for Lake Manyara catchment basin, in *Proceedings of the workshop, 5–6 March 1992*, Arusha, Tanzania.

Mwandosya M and Luhanga M (1993) Energy and development in Tanzania: issues and perspectives. *Energy Policy* 21:441–453.

Mwasumbi H and Tzoneva R (2007) Power sector in Tanzania: Performance, trends and reforms, *Institute of Electrical and Electronics Engineers (IEEE) AFRICON 2007*, 1–7.

MWE-CCU (2014) *Uganda's eight priority NAMA's*, Uganda Ministry of Water and Environment-Climate Change Unit, Kampala.

MWE (2015) *Uganda national climate change policy*, Uganda Ministry of Water and Environment, Kampala.

MWE (2016) *State of Uganda's forestry 2016*, Uganda Ministry of Water and Environment, Kampala.

MWE (2017a) *Draft final REDD+ national strategy*, Ministry of Water and Environment, Kampala.

MWE (2017b) *Forest investment program for Uganda*, Ministry of Water and Environment, Kampala.

MWE (2017c) *Proposed forest reference level for Uganda: preliminary document*, Uganda Ministry of Water and Environment, Kampala.

MWE (2018) *Proposed forest reference emission level for Uganda*, Uganda Ministry of Water and Environment, Kampala.

MWE (2019) *Uganda's first Biennial Update Report to the United Nations Framework Convention on Climate Change*, Uganda Ministry of Water and Environment, Kampala.

MWE (2020) *Uganda's technical annex with REDD+ results from reducing emissions from deforestation*, Uganda Ministry of Water and Environment, Kampala.

Mwesigye F and Redd R (2021) Green spaces for "green" energy: what are the implications of damming Murchison Falls National Park in Uganda? Peace Research Institute Oslo (PRIO) Blogs. Website (accessed 10 May 2021): https://blogs.prio.org/2021/04/

green-spaces-for-green-energy-what-are-the-implications-of-damming-murchison-falls-national-park-in-uganda/.

MWLE (2001) *The Uganda forest policy*, Ministry of Water, Lands and Environment, Kampala.

MWLE (2002) *The national forest plan*, Ministry of Water, Lands and Environment, Kampala.

Myers R, Larson AM, Ravikumar A, Kowler LF, Yang A and Trench T (2018) Messiness of forest governance: how technical approaches suppress politics in REDD+ and conservation projects. *Global Environmental Change* 50:314–324.

Nafziger S (2016) Communal property rights and land redistributions in late tsarist Russia. *The Economic History Review* 69:773–800.

NAMA Facility (2015) *Monitoring and evaluation framework*, NAMA Facility, Berlin.

NAMA Facility (2017a) *Inspiring ambitious action on climate change*, NAMA Facility, Berlin.

NAMA Facility (2017b) *The NAMA Facility*, NAMA Facility. Website (accessed August 14, 2018): https://www.nama-facility.org/about-us/, Berlin.

NAMA Facility (2018) *Support project to the NAMA for bus rapid transit systems in Tanzania*, NAMA Facility, Berlin.

NAMA Facility (2021) *Projects*, NAMA Facility. Website (accessed 20 December 2021): https://www.nama-facility.org/projects/, Berlin.

NAMA Facility (No Date) *Uganda—revolving loan fund for the uptake of improved institutional cook stoves (IICS) in Schools*, NAMA Facility. Website (accessed 14 August 2018): https://www.nama-facility.org/projects/uganda-revolving-loan-fund-for-the-uptake-of-improved-institutional-cook-stoves-iics-in-schools/, Berlin.

Nambombe VG and Mussami PM (2007) *Summary of the forest management plan (January 2005–December 2009) for Uchindile forest project*, Green Resources, Dar es Salaam.

Nantongo M, Vatn A and Vedeld P (2019) All that glitters is not gold: power and participation in processes and structures of implementing REDD+ in Kondoa, Tanzania. *Forest Policy and Economics* 100:44–54.

NAO (2015) *Report of the controller and auditor general on the consolidated financial statements of Tanzania Electric Supply Company Limited for the 18-month period ended 30th June 2015*, United Republic of Tanzania, National Audit Office, Dar es Salaam.

Nash TAM (1937) Climate, the vital factor in the ecology of Glossina. *Bulletin of Entomological Research* 28:75–127.

Naus J (2010) *The Clean Development Mechanism (CDM): an analysis of the state of play in Uganda*, Wageningen University and Research Centre, Wageningen, The Netherlands.

NCMC (2015) *Tanzania establishes its National Carbon Monitoring Centre (NCMC)*, National Carbon Monitoring Centre. Website (accessed 22 November 2015): http://www.ncmc.suanet.ac.tz/, Arusha, Tanzania.

NCMC (2016) *The National Carbon Monitoring Centre (NCMC) officially launched*, National Carbon Monitoring Centre, 23 May 2016. Website (accessed 10 September 2016): http://www.ncmc.suanet.ac.tz/?p=431, Arusha, Tanzania.

Ndalu D (2017) *Phase II Dar es Salaam bus rapid transit project to get $159m*, The East African. 28 November 2017. Website (accessed 14 August 2018): https://www.theeastafrican.co.ke/business/Phase-II-Dar-bus-rapid-transit-project--get-159-million-dollars/2560-4205984-146yv4w/index.html, Nairobi.

Nel A (2016) A critical reflection on social equity in Uganda carbon forestry, in *The carbon fix: forest carbon, social justice, and environmental governance*, Paladino S and Fiske SJ (eds), 302–319, Taylor & Francis.

Nel A, Lyons K, Fisher J and Mwayafu D (2018) An environmental justice perspective on the state of carbon forestry in Uganda, in *Conservation and development in Uganda*, Sandbrook C, Cavanagh CJ and Tumusiime DM (eds), 125–147, Routledge, London.

Nemtsova A (2016) Igor Dodon is Vladimir Putin's Moldovan mini-me. *The Daily Beast*, 29 October 2016. https://www.thedailybeast.com/igor-dodon-is-vladimir-putins-moldovan-mini-me

New York Times (2009) Moldova, *The New York Times* 30 July 2009. Website (accessed 10 September 2011): http://topics.nytimes.com/top/news/international/countriesandterritories/moldova/index.html.

Newell P and Bulkeley H (2017) Landscape for change? International climate policy and energy transitions: evidence from sub-Saharan Africa. *Climate Policy* 17:650–663.

NFA (2005a) *Management of central forest reserves*, National Forestry Authority. Website (accessed 10 April 2011): http://www.nfa.org.ug/content.php?submenu_id=4#plant, Kampala.

NFA (2005b) *Uganda's forests, functions and classification*, National Forestry Authority, Kampala.

NFA (2007) *Forest management plan for Bugamba and Rwoho central forest reserves for the period 2006–2026*, National Forest Authority, Kampala.

NFA and Biocarbon Fund (2006) *Biocarbon Fund Clean Development Mechanism verified emission reductions purchase agreement (Uganda Nile Basin Reforestation Project) by and between the National Forestry Authority and the International Bank for Reconstruction and Development, as trustee of the Biocarbon Fund*, 30 June.

NFC (2017) About us: history, New Forests Company. Website (accessed 10 October 2018): http://newforests.net/about-us/history/, Johannesburg.

Ng'wanakilala F (2017) *Tanzania's president sacks head of power firm over tariff hike*, Reuters, 1 January 2017. Website (accessed November 23, 2017): https://www.reuters.com/article/tanzania-politics/tanzanias-president-sacks-head-of-power-firm-over-tariff-hike-idUKL5N1ER0JA, London.

Nguyen NT, Ha-Duong M, Greiner S and Mehling M (2010) Improving the Clean Development Mechanism post-2012: a developing country perspective. *Carbon & Climate Law Review* 4:76–85.

Nindi B (1989) Institutional forms of government agricultural marketing in Tanzania. *Journal of Eastern African Research & Development* 19:95–101.

Nizhnikau R (2016) When Goliath meets Goliath: how Russia and the EU created a vicious circle of instability in Moldova. *Global Affairs* 2:203–216.

Nizhnikau R (2018) *EU induced institutional change in post-Soviet Space: promoting reforms in Moldova and Ukraine*, Routledge, New York.

NORAD (2014a) *Real-time evaluation of Norway's international climate and forest initiative: synthesising report 2007–2013*, Norwegian Agency for Development Cooperation, Oslo.

NORAD (2014b) *Real-time evaluation of Norway's international climate and forest initiative: synthesising report 2007–2013: Annexes 3–19*, Norwegian Agency for Development Cooperation, Oslo.

NORAD (2021) *Norway's international climate and forest initiative*, Norwegian Agency for Development Cooperation. Website (accessed 8 March 2021): https://www.norad.

no/en/front/thematic-areas/climate-change-and-environment/norways-internatio nal-climate-and-forest-initiative-nicfi/, Oslo.

Norfund (2011a) About Norfund, Norfund. Website (accessed 4 December 2011): http:// norfund.no/index.php/en/about-norfund, Oslo.

Norfund (2011b) Industrial partnerships, Norfund. Website (accessed 4 February 2012): http://norfund.no/index.php/en/portfolio/industrial-partnerships, Oslo.

Norman M and Nakhooda S (2015) *The state of REDD+ finance*, CGD Climate and Forest Paper Series #5, Center for Global Development, Washington DC.

NPA (2010) *National development plan (2010/11–2014/15)*, National Planning Authority, Kampala.

NPA (2015) *Second national development plan (2015/16–2019/20)*, National Planning Authority, Kampala.

NPA (2017) *The Uganda green growth development strategy*, National Planning Authority, Kampala.

Nunnenkamp P and Thiele R (2013) Financing for development: the gap between words and deeds since Monterrey. *Development Policy Review* 31:75–98.

Nuţu AO and Cenuşă D (2016) *Interconnecting Moldova's gas market: the Iasi-Ungheni case*, Expert-Grup, Chişinău.

Nygren B (2008) *The rebuilding of greater Russia: Putin's foreign policy towards CIS countries*, Routledge, London and New York.

Nyirinkindi E and Opagi M (2009) Privatization and parastatal reform, in *Uganda's economic reforms: insider accounts*, Kuteesa F, Tumusiime-Mutebile E, Whitworth A and Williamson T (eds), 355–383, Oxford University Press, Oxford.

O'Keefe P, Kikula I and Mascarenhas O (eds) (1990) *Evaluation of Norwegian assistance to the energy sector of SADCC countries—project profile 4: Morogoro fuelwood stove project*, Centre for Development and Technology, University of Trondheim, Trondheim.

OAG (2011) *Value for money audit report: on implementation of rural electrification programme by the Rural Electrification Agency in the Ministry of Energy and Mineral Development*, Office of the Auditor General, Kampala.

OECD (2004) *Statement adopted by members of the OECD's Development Assistance Committee (DAC) high level meeting, 15–16 April 2004*, OECD, Paris.

OECD (2009a) The effectiveness and scope of fiscal stimulus, in *OECD economic outlook—interim report (March 2009)*, 105–150, OECD, Paris.

OECD (2009b) *Green growth: overcoming the crisis and beyond*, OECD, Paris.

OECD (2019) *Better criteria for better evaluation: revised evaluation criteria definitions and principles for use*, OECD, Paris.

OECD (2020) *Climate finance provided and mobilised by developed countries in 2013–18*, OECD, Paris.

OECD (2022) *Net ODA*, OECD. Website (accessed 10 July 2022): https://data.oecd.org/ oda/net-oda.htm, Paris.

OECD (2023) Climate Finance Provided and Mobilised by Developed Countries in 2013– 21. OECD, Paris.

Okubo Y, Hayashi D and Michaelowa A (2011) NAMA crediting: how to assess offsets from and additionality of policy-based mitigation actions in developing countries. *Greenhouse Gas Measurement and Management* 1:37–46.

Olhoff A, Markandya A, K. H and Taylor T (2004) *CDM sustainable development impacts*, UNEP Riso Centre, Roskilde, Denmark.

Ondraczek J (2013) The sun rises in the east (of Africa): a comparison of the development and status of solar energy markets in Kenya and Tanzania. *Energy Policy* 56:407–417.

Otiti T (1992) Tanzania stoves. *Boiling Point* 29.

Pallangyo DM (2007) Environmental law in Tanzania: how far have we gone? *Law and Development Journal* 3:28–39.

Pallot J (1999) *Land reform in Russia, 1906–1917: peasant responses to Stolypin's project of rural transformation*, Clarendon Press, Oxford.

Papua New Guinea and Costa Rica (2005) *Reducing emissions from deforestation in developing countries: approaches to stimulate action* (UN Doc. FCCC/CP/2005/MISC.1.), UNFCCC, Bonn.

Parfitt TW and Riley SP (2010) *The African debt crisis*, Routledge, New York.

Paroussos L, Mandel A, Fragkiadakis K, Fragkos P, Hinkel J and Vrontisi Z (2019) Climate clubs and the macro-economic benefits of international cooperation on climate policy. *Nature Climate Change* 9:542–546.

Participedia (No Date) *President's Office, Regional Administration and Local Government Tanzania (PO-RALG)*, Participedia. Website (accessed 10 February 2021): https://participedia.net/organization/1081, Vancouver.

Patlis JM (1992) The Multilateral Fund of the Montreal Protocol: a prototype for financial mechanisms in protecting the global environment. *Cornell International Law Journal* 25:181.

Paulsson E (2009) A review of the CDM literature: from fine-tuning to critical scrutiny. *International Environmental Agreements* 9:63–80.

PCF (2003) *Moldova soil conservation project: project appraisal document*, World Bank Prototype Carbon Fund, Washington, DC.

Pearse R and Böhm S (2014) Ten reasons why carbon markets will not bring about radical emissions reduction. *Carbon Management* 5:325–337.

Pedersen M (2015) *Conceptual framework for MRV of NAMAs, Republic of Moldova: draft version*, Coordinator ApS, Copenhagen.

Pedersen RH (2017) *The political economy of private forestry in Tanzania: a review*, Danish Institute for International Studies, Copenhagen.

Pedersen RH, Jacob T and Bofin P (2020) From moderate to radical resource nationalism in the boom era: pockets of effectiveness under stress in "new oil" Tanzania. *The Extractive Industries and Society* 7:1211–1218.

Pempel TJ (1999) The developmental regime in a changing world economy, in *The developmental state*, Woo-Cumings M (ed), 137–181, Cornell University Press, Ithaca, NY.

Peskett L and Brockhaus M (2009) When REDD+ goes national: a review of realities, opportunities and challenges, in *Realising REDD+* Angelsen A, Brockhaus M, Kanninen M, Sills E, Sunderlin WD and Wertz-Kanounnikof S (eds) 25–44, Center for International Forestry Research, Bogor Barat.

Petursson JG and Vedeld PO (2018) Lost in the woods? A political economy of the 1998 forest sector reform in Uganda, in *Conservation and development in Uganda*, Sandbrook C, Cavanagh CJ and Tumusiime DM (eds), Chapter 11, 206–226, Routledge, New York.

Pierson P (1993) When effect becomes cause: policy feedback and political change. *World Politics* 45:595–628.

Pitcher A, Moran MH and Johnston M (2009) Rethinking patrimonialism and neopatrimonialism in Africa. *African Studies Review* 52:125–156.

Plan Vivo (2008) *The Plan Vivo standards*, Plan Vivo Foundation, Edinburgh.

Plan Vivo (No Date) *Technical specification for smallholder carbon management project, Bushenyi Uganda*, Plan Vivo Foundation, Edinburgh.

Plan Vivo-PDD (2009) *Trees for global benefits: a cooperative community land-use carbon offset project, Uganda*, Plan Vivo Foundation, Edinburgh.

PMO-RALG (2008) *Strategic plan: 2009/10–2011/12*, Prime Minister's Office-Regional Administration and Local Government, Dodoma.

Polanyi K (2001 [1944]) *The great transformation: the political and economic origins of our time*, Beacon Press, Boston.

Polycarp C, Fransen T, Hatch J, Easton C, Stasio K and Ballesteros A (2012) *Summary of developed country "fast-start" climate finance pledges (updated November 26, 2012)*, World Resources Institute. Website (accessed 10 July 2013): http://pdf.wri.org/clima te_finance_pledges_2012-11-26.pdf, Washington, DC.

Ponte S, Noe C and Mwamfupe A (2020) Private and public authority interactions and the functional quality of sustainability governance: Lessons from conservation and development initiatives in Tanzania. *Regulation & Governance* 15:1270–1285.

Popa B, Halalisan F and Abrudan I (2016) Forestry institutional reform strategy and implementation in Republic of Moldova, in *Legal aspects of European Forest Sustainable Development 17th International Symposium, May 18–20, 2016*, Šulek R, Hrib M and Šodková M (eds), 7–17, Faculty of Forestry and Wood Sciences, Czech University of Life Sciences, Prague, Czech Republic.

POPC (2011) *The Tanzania five year development plan 2011/2012–2015/2016*, United Republic of Tanzania, President's Office, Planning Commission, Dar es Salaam.

Popovici I (2007) Energy (in)security of Moldova, Despite Borders.com, 26 September 2007. Website (accessed 10 October 2010): http://www.despiteborders.com/clanok _an.php?subaction=showfull&id=1190808150&archive=&start_from=&ucat= 35,37,42&, Bratislava.

Potopová V, Boroneanţ C, Boincean B and Soukup J (2016) Impact of agricultural drought on main crop yields in the Republic of Moldova. *International Journal of Climatology* 36:2063–2082.

Praher C (2008) *Calculation of the Grid Emission Factor (GEF) of the electricity grid in Uganda accordant to the "tool to calculate the emission factor for an electricity system,"* Energy Changes Projektentwicklung GmbH, Vienna.

Pressman JL and Wildavsky AB (1973) *Implementation: how great expectations in Washington are dashed in Oakland: or, why it's amazing that federal programs work at all*, University of California Press, Los Angeles.

Pretis F (2022) Does a carbon tax reduce CO2 emissions? Evidence from British Columbia. *Environmental and Resource Economics* 83:115–144.

ProBEC (2010) *ProBEC interventions in Tanzania*, Programme for Basic Energy Conservation in Southern Africa. Website (accessed 10 June 2010): http://www.pro bec.org/displaysection.php?czacc=&zSelectedSectionID=sec1194880064, Pretoria.

Probst B, Westermann L, Anadón LD and Kontoleon A (2021) Leveraging private investment to expand renewable power generation: evidence on financial additionality and productivity gains from Uganda. *World Development* 140:105347.

Purdon M (2009a) Bio-carbon Overview, in *Bio-Carbon in Eastern & Southern Africa: harnessing carbon finance to promote sustainable forestry, agro-forestry and bio-energy*, Kelly R and Purdon M (eds), 2–25, UNDP, New York.

Purdon M (2009b) Implementing forest bio-carbon projects: summary and synthesis of existing CDM methodologies for AR and forest bio-energy, in *Bio-Carbon in Eastern &*

Southern Africa: harnessing carbon finance to promote sustainable forestry, agro-forestry and bio-energy, Kelly R and Purdon M (eds), 50–85, UNDP, New York.

Purdon M (2010) The Clean Development Mechanism and community forests in sub-Saharan Africa: reconsidering Kyoto's "moral position" on biocarbon sinks in the carbon market. *Environment, Development and Sustainability* 12:1025–1050.

Purdon M (2013) Land acquisitions in Tanzania: strong sustainability, weak sustainability and the importance of comparative methods. *Journal of Agricultural and Environmental Ethics* 26:1127–1156.

Purdon M (2014a) *Land and sustainable industrial policy in sub-Saharan Africa: the relationship between land tenure and foreign investment strategy in Uganda and Tanzania*, APSA 2014 Annual Meeting Paper, Washington, DC.

Purdon M (2014b) Neoclassical realism and international climate change politics: moral imperative and political constraint in climate finance. *Journal of International Relations and Development* 17:301–338.

Purdon M (2015a) Advancing comparative climate change politics: theory & method. *Global Environmental Politics* 15:1–26.

Purdon M (2015b) Opening the black box of carbon finance "additionality": the political economy of carbon finance effectiveness across Tanzania, Uganda and Moldova. *World Development* 74:462–478.

Purdon M (2018) Finding common ground: a critique of subsumption theory and its application to small-scale forestry-based carbon offsetting in Uganda. *Society & Natural Resources* 31:1082–1093.

Purdon M and Byakagaba P (2022) *Evaluating the transformational impact of a forest carbon offsetting programme in Uganda: Lessons from a ten-year investigation into the Trees for Global Benefits programme*, Working Paper No. 2022-1, Chaire sur la décarbonisation, Université du Québec à Montréal (UQAM), Montréal.

Purdon M, Lokina R and Bukenya M (2014) Comparing the effectiveness of forest sector reforms in Tanzania and Uganda, in *Forest tenure reform in Asia and Africa: local control for improved livelihoods, forest management, and carbon sequestration*, Robinson E and Bluffstone R (eds), 83–106, Resources for the Future Press, Washington, DC.

Purdon M, Witcover J, Murphy C, Ziaja S, Winfield M, Giuliano G, Séguin C, Kaiser C, Papy J and Fulton L (2021) Climate and transportation policy sequencing in California and Quebec. *Review of Policy Research* 38:596–630.

Quinlan PD (2004) Back to the future: an overview of Moldova under Voronin. *Demokratizatsiya* 12:485–504.

Rajamani L (2011) The Cancun climate agreements: reading the text, subtext and tea leaves. *International and Comparative Law Quarterly* 60:499–519.

Raleigh C, Choi HJ and Kniveton D (2015) The devil is in the details: An investigation of the relationships between conflict, food price and climate across Africa. *Global Environmental Change* 32:187–199.

Ranade M (2009) *Presentation: The BioCarbon Fund—case-study and lessons*, World Bank, Washington, DC.

REA (2006) *Investment guide for rural electrification*, Rural Electrification Agency, Kampala.

REA (2010) *Current Projects*, Rural Energy Agency. Website (accessed 10 June 2010): http://www.rea.go.tz/PROJECTS/CurrentProjects/tabid/70/Default.aspx, Dar es Salaam.

RECPA & NFA (2006) *Collaborative forest management plan*, National Forest Authority, Kampala.

Renner S (2009) The energy community of southeast Europe: A neo-functionalist project of regional integration. *European Integration Online Papers (EIoP)* **13**. https://eiop.or.at/eiop/pdf/2009-001.pdf

Republic of Moldova (1999) *Government decision no. 105 on the creation of the Organization for Promotion of Export of Moldova*, Republic of Moldova, Chisinau.

Reuters (2009) Factbox—U.S., European bank write downs, credit losses, Reuters. Website (accessed 5 November 2009): https://www.reuters.com/article/banks-writedowns-losses-idCNL554155620091105?rpc=44.

Roberts JT, Weikmans R, Robinson S-a, Ciplet D, Khan M and Falzon D (2021) Rebooting a failed promise of climate finance. *Nature Climate Change* **11**:180–182.

Robinson AL (2014) National versus ethnic identification in Africa: modernization, colonial legacy, and the origins of territorial nationalism. *World Politics* **66**:709–746.

Rodrik D (2006) Goodbye Washington Consensus? Hello Washington confusion? A review of the World Bank's economic growth in the 1990s: learning from a decade of reform. *Journal of Economic Literature* **44**:973–987.

Rodrik D (2011) *The globalization paradox: why global markets, states, and democracy can't coexist*, Oxford University Press, New York.

Rogelj J, Schaeffer M, Meinshausen M, Knutti R, Alcamo J, Riahi K and Hare W (2015) Zero emission targets as long-term global goals for climate protection. *Environmental Research Letters* **10**:105007.

Rohde R and Hilhorst T (2001) *A profile of environmental change in the Lake Manyara Basin, Tanzania*, IIED, London.

Roll M ed (2014) *The politics of public sector performance: pockets of effectiveness in developing countries*, Routledge, Milton Park.

Rosefielde S (1996) Stalinism in post-communist perspective: new evidence on killings, forced labour and economic growth in the 1930s. *Europe-Asia Studies* **48**:959–987.

Rosenbloom D, Markard J, Geels FW and Fuenfschilling L (2020) Opinion: Why carbon pricing is not sufficient to mitigate climate change—and how "sustainability transition policy" can help. *Proceedings of the National Academy of Sciences* **117**:8664–8668.

Rosenstein-Rodan PN (1943) Problems of industrialisation of eastern and south-eastern Europe. *The Economic Journal* **53**:202–211.

Röser F, Widerberg O, Höhne N and Day T (2020) Ambition in the making: analysing the preparation and implementation process of the Nationally Determined Contributions under the Paris Agreement. *Climate Policy* **20**:415–429.

Roychowdhury A (2018) *Clunkered: combating dumping of used vehicles—a roadmap for Africa and South Asia*, Centre for Science and Environment, New Delhi.

Sachs JD (2006) *The end of poverty: economic possibilities for our time*, Penguin, New York.

Sachs JD (2012) From millennium development goals to sustainable development goals. *The Lancet* **379**:2206–2211.

Sachs W ed (1992) *The development dictionary: a guide to knowledge as power*, Zed, London.

Sah RK and Stiglitz JE (2002) *Peasants versus city-dwellers: taxation and the burden of economic development*, Oxford University Press, Oxford.

Sanchez WA (2009) The "frozen" southeast: how the Moldova-Transnistria question has become a European geo-security issue. *The Journal of Slavic Military Studies* **22**:153–176.

Sanchez-Sibony O (2014) *Red globalization: The political economy of the Soviet Cold War from Stalin to Khrushchev*, Cambridge University Press, Cambridge.

Sanya S (2011) Eight firms join sugar production, in *The New Vision*, 22 November 2011, Website (accessed 10 September 2012): http://www.newvision.co.ug/news/30198-eight-firms-join-sugar-production.html, Kampala.

Sanya S (2013) Kaliro sugar factory to ease sugar deficit, in The New Vision, 26 January 2013, Website (accessed 10 September 2013): http://www.newvision.co.ug/news/639 237-kaliro-sugar-factory-to-ease-sugar-deficit.html, Kampala.

Sasaki N and Putz FE (2009) Critical need for new definitions of "forest" and "forest degradation" in global climate change agreements. Conservation Letters 2:226-232.

Savoia A and Sen K (2015) Measurement, evoluation, determinants, and consequences of state capacity: a review of recent research. *Journal of Economic Surveys* 29:441–458.

Sawe E (2015) Brief on RE Programmes status and REFITS in Tanzania, Global Renewable Energy Support Programme Focusing on Globally Funded Feed-in Tariffs, 30 March to 1 April 2015, CSE India, New Delhi.

Sawe EN (2009) *Wood fuels stoves development and promotion in Tanzania: some selected experiences*, European Biomass/COMPETE Workshop on Bioenergy for Rural Development in Africa and Asia, 30 June 2009. Website (accessed 10 June 2010): http://www.compete-bioafrica.net/events/events2/hamburg/Session%202/S2-5-COMPETE-REImpact-Hamburg-Sawe-090630.pdf, Hamburg.

Sawyer SM and Daniel S-J eds (2019) *Foucault, neoliberalism, and beyond*, Rowman & Littlefield, Washington DC.

Schlamadinger B, Bird N, Johns T, Brown S, Canadell J, Ciccarese L, Dutschke M, Fiedler J, Fischlin A, Fearnside P, Forner C, Freibauer A, Frumhoff P, Hoehne N, Kirschbaum MUF, Labat A, Marland G, Michaelowa A, Montanarella L, Moutinho P, Murdiyarso D, Pena N, Pingoud K, Rakonczay Z, Rametsteiner E, Rock J, Sanz MJ, Schneider UA, Shuidenko A, Skutsch M, Smith P, Somogyi Z, Trines E, Ward M and Yamagata Y (2007) A synopsis of land use, land-use change and forestry (LULUCF) under the Kyoto Protocol and Marrakech Accords. *Environmental Science & Policy* 10:271–282.

Schlamadinger B, Bosquet B, Streck C, Noble I, Dutschke M and Bird N (2005) Can the EU emission trading scheme support CDM forestry? *Climate Policy* 5:199–208.

Schmidt V (2009) Putting the political back into political economy by bringing the state back yet again. *World Politics* 61:516–548.

Schneider L (2007a) High on modernity? Explaining the failings of Tanzanian villagisation. *African Studies* 66:9–38.

Schneider L (2007b) *Is the CDM fulfilling its environmental and sustainable development objectives? An evaluation of the CDM and options for improvement*, Institute for Applied Ecology, Berlin.

Schneider L (2011) Perverse incentives under the CDM: an evaluation of HFC-23 destruction projects. *Climate Policy* 11:851–864.

Schneider L, Broekhoff D, Fuessler J, Lazarus M, Michaelowa A and Spalding-Fecher R (2012) *Standardized baselines for the CDM—are we on the right track?* Stockholm Environmental Institute, Stockholm.

Scruggs L and Benegal S (2012) Declining public concern about climate change: can we blame the great recession? *Global Environmental Change* 22:505–515.

Sergi B, Babcock M, Williams NJ, Thornburg J, Loew A and Ciez RE (2018) Institutional influence on power sector investments: a case study of on- and off-grid energy in Kenya and Tanzania. *Energy Research & Social Science* 41:59–70.

Shapovalova N and Boonstra J (2012) The European Union: from ignorance to privileged partnership with Moldova, in *Moldova: arena of international influences*, Kosienkowski M and Schreiber W (eds), 51–76, Lexington Books, Lanham, MD.

Sharma S and Desgain D (2014) *Nationally appropriate mitigation action: understanding NAMA cycle*, UNEP, Nairobi.

Shaw TM (2005) Uganda as an African "developmental state"?, in *Global Encounters*, Graham Harrison (ed), 63–73, Springer, Hampshire.

Shi B, Wu L and Kang R (2021) Clean development, energy substitution, and carbon emissions: evidence from Clean Development Mechanism (CDM) project implementation in China. *Sustainability* 13:860.

Shirima DD, Munishi PK, Lewis SL, Burgess ND, Marshall AR, Balmford A, Swetnam RD and Zahabu EM (2011) Carbon storage, structure and composition of miombo woodlands in Tanzania's Eastern Arc Mountains. *African Journal of Ecology* 49:332–342.

Shleifer A (2009) The age of Milton Friedman. *Journal of Economic Literature* 47:123–135.

Shukla P, Skea J, Calvo Buendia E, Masson-Delmotte V, Pörtner H, Roberts D, Zhai P, Slade R, Connors S and Van Diemen R (2019) *Climate change and land: an IPCC special report on climate change, desertification, land degradation, sustainable land management, food security, and greenhouse gas fluxes in terrestrial ecosystems*, IPCC.

Singh N, Finnegan J, Levin K, Rich D, Sotos M, Tirpak D and Wood D (2016) MRV 101: Understanding measurement, reporting, and verification of climate change mitigation. *World Resources Institute* 4–5.

Siriwardana M and Nong D (2021) Nationally Determined Contributions (NDCs) to decarbonise the world: a transitional impact evaluation. *Energy Economics* 97:105184.

Skarstein R and Wangwe SM (1986) *Industrial development in Tanzania some critical issues*, Nordiska Afrikainstitutet, Tanzania Publishing House.

Skjærseth JB, Bang G and Schreurs MA (2013) Explaining growing climate policy differences between the European Union and the United States. *Global Environmental Politics* 13:61–80.

Skocpol T (1985) Bringing the state back in: strategies of analysis in current research, in *Bringing the state back in*, Evans PB, Rueschemeyer D and Skocpol T (eds), 3–37, Cambridge University Press, New York.

Skogstad GD ed (2011) *Policy paradigms, transnationalism, and domestic politics*, University of Toronto Press, Toronto.

Skutsch M (1985) Forestry by the people for the people: some major problems in Tanzania's village afforestation programme. *International Tree Crop Journal* 3:147–170.

Slaughter and May (2021) *Global carbon markets after COP26: The past, present, and future*, Slaughter and May. Website (accessed 20 December 2021): https://www.lexology.com/library/detail.aspx?g=a3ef15e7-280f-4e99-81ef-0d5062cdc2f4, London.

Smith MJ (1990) Pluralism, reformed pluralism and neopluralism: the role of pressure groups in policy-making. *Political Studies* 38:302–322.

Snyder KA (1996) Agrarian change and land-use strategies among Iraqw farmers in Northern Tanzania. *Human Ecology* 24:315–340.

Soederberg S (2005) Recasting neoliberal dominance in the Global South? A critique of the Monterrey consensus. *Alternatives* 30:325–364.

Sowers JL, VanDeveer SD and Weinthal E eds (2023) *The Oxford handbook of comparative environmental politics*, Oxford University Press, New York.

SPGS (2007) *Forestry investment in Uganda: opportunities and challenges*, Sawlog Production Grant Scheme, Kampala.

SPGS (2009) Phase II details. Website (accessed 10 October 2010): http://www.sawlog.ug/index.php?option=com_content&view=article&id=91&Itemid=6, Kampala.

SPGS (2011) What area of timber plantation does Uganda need? *Sawlog Production Grant Scheme Newsletter* 31:4.

SPGS (2018) About SPGS III. Website (accessed 10 October 2018): http://spgs.mwe.go.ug/about-spgs-iii, Kampala.

Srivastava V and Larizza M (2013) Working with the grain for reforming the public service: a live example from Sierra Leone. *International Review of Administrative Sciences* 79:458–485.

Steinberg PF (2007) Causal assessment in small-N policy studies. *The Policy Studies Journal* 35:181–204.

Steinberg PF (2012) Welcome to the jungle: policy theory and political instability, in *Comparative environmental politics: theory, practice, and prospects*, Steinberg PF and VanDeveer SD (eds), 255–284, MIT Press, Cambridge, MA.

Steinberg PF (2015) Can we generalize from case studies? *Global Environmental Politics* 15:152–175.

Steinberg PF and VanDeveer SD (2012) *Comparative environmental politics: theory, practice, and prospects*, MIT Press, Cambridge, MA.

Stern J (2006) *The Russian-Ukrainian gas crisis of January 2006*, Oxford Institute for Energy Studies, Oxford.

Stern N (2007) *The economics of climate change: the Stern review*, Cambridge University Press, Cambridge.

Stewart RB, Kingsbury B and Rudyk B (2009) *Climate finance: regulatory and funding strategies for climate change and global development*, New York University Press, New York.

Stewart RB, Oppenheimer M and Rudyk B (2017) Building blocks: a strategy for near-term action within the new global climate framework. *Climatic Change* 144:1–13.

Stiglitz JE and Lin JY eds (2013) *The industrial policy revolution I: the role of government beyond ideology*, Palgrave Macmillan, New York.

Stiglitz JE, Lin JY and Patel E eds (2013) *The industrial policy revolution II: Africa in the 21st century*, Palgrave Macmillan, New York.

Stolarski MJ, Krzyżaniak M, Warmiński K, Tworkowski J and Szczukowski S (2015) Willow biomass energy generation efficiency and greenhouse gas reduction potential. *Polish Journal of Environmental Studies* 24:2627–2640.

Stone D (2017) Understanding the transfer of policy failure: bricolage, experimentalism and translation. *Policy & Politics* 45:55–70.

Stratan M (2012) *The role of Energy Efficiency Agency in the energy sector of the Republic of Moldova*, German Eastern Business Association (OAOEV). Website (accessed 12 December 2018): https://www.oaoev.de/sites/default/files/eventdocs/E%27efficiency%20Agency_0.pdf.

Strøm-Sedgwick C and Tank P (2022) The impact of the Ukraine war on donor priorities. *PRIO Policy Brief* 17:1–4.

SUA (2013) *Briefing note for REDD+ measurement, reporting and verification (MRV) system and National Carbon Monitoring Centre (NCMC) for Tanzania*, Faculty of Forestry and Nature Conservation, Sokoine University of Agriculture, Morogoro, Tanzania.

SugarOnline (2012) UGANDA: Company plans to set up new sugar factory by 2013, in SugarOnlinecom, 30 April 2012, Website (accessed 10 September 2012): http://www.sugaronline.com/home/website_contents/view/1188230, Kampala.

Summer W and Diernhofer W (2003) Soil erosion in the Republic of Moldova: the importance of institutional arrangements, in *Erosion prediction in ungauged basins: integrating methods and techniques*, de Boer D, Froehlich W, Mizuyama T and Pietroniro A (eds), 24–29, International Association of Hydrological Sciences, Wallingford, UK.

Sunderlin W, Sills E, Duchelle A, Ekaputri A, Kweka D, Toniolo M, Ball S, Doggart N, Pratama C and Padilla J (2015) REDD+ at a critical juncture: assessing the limits of polycentric governance for achieving climate change mitigation. *International Forestry Review* 17:400–413.

Sunseri T (2002) *Vilimani: labor migration and rural change in early colonial Tanzania*, Heinemann, Portsmouth, NH.

Sunseri T (2009) *Wielding the ax: state forestry and social conflict in Tanzania, 1820–2000*, Ohio University Press, Athens.

Swartz J (2016) *China's national emissions trading system: implications for carbon markets and trade*, International Centre for Trade and Sustainable Development, Geneva.

Swilling M, Musango J and Wakeford J (2016) Developmental states and sustainability transitions: prospects of a just transition in South Africa. *Journal of Environmental Policy & Planning* 18:650–672.

TANESCO (2013) History, Tanzania Electric Supply Company. Website (accessed 10 March 2013): http://www.tanesco.co.tz/index.php?option=com_content&view=article&id=38&Itemid=126, Dar es Salaam.

TANESCO (No Date) Historical Background, TANESCO. Website (accessed 10 August 2018): http://www.tanesco.co.tz/index.php/about-us/historical-background, Washington, DC.

Tangri R and Mwenda AM (2010) President Museveni and the politics of presidential tenure in Uganda. *Journal of Contemporary African Studies* 28:31–49.

TANU (1967) *The Arusha Declaration*, Publicity Section, Tanganyika African National Union, Dar es Salaam.

Tenenbaum B, Greacen C, Siyambalapitiya T and Knuckles J (2014) *From the bottom up: how small power producers and mini-grids can deliver electrification and renewable energy in Africa*, World Bank, Washington, DC.

Termeer CJAM, Dewulf A and Biesbroek GR (2017) Transformational change: governance interventions for climate change adaptation from a continuous change perspective. *Journal of Environmental Planning and Management* 60:558–576.

Tewari R (2012) Mapping of criteria set by DNAs to assess sustainable development benefits of CDM projects, in *Report prepared on behalf of the CDM high-level policy dialogue*, Energy and Resources Institute (TERI), New Delhi.

TFCMP (2005) *Tanzania Forest Conservation and Management Project (TFCMP), IDA credit No. 3604-TA: status of implementation 2004/05*, World Bank, Washington, DC.

TFS (2014) *Strategic plan: July 2014–June 2019*, Ministry of Natural Resources and Tourism, Dar es Salaam.

TFS (2015a) *Business plan and associated budget for financial year 2015/2016*, Ministry of Natural Resources and Tourism, Dar es Salaam.

TFS (2015b) *National Forest Resources and Assessment of Tanzania Mainland (NAFORMA): main results*, Ministry of Natural Resources and Tourism, Dar es Salaam.

Thelen K (1999) Historical institutionalism in comparative politics. *Annual review of political science* 2:369–404.

Therkildsen O and Bourgouin F (2012) *Continuity and change in Tanzania's ruling coalition: legacies, crises and weak productive capacity*, Danish Institute for International Studies, Copenhagen.

TIC (2008) *Report on the study of growth and impact of investment in Tanzania*, Tanzania Investment Centre, Dar es Salaam.

Tietenburg TH (2006) *Emissions trading: principles and practice*, Resources for the Future, Washington, DC.

Tirpak D and Adams H (2008) Bilateral and multilateral financial assistance for the energy sector of developing countries. *Climate Policy* 8:135–151.

Tirsu MS and Uzun GN (2018) Renewables as important energy source for Moldova. *The EuroBiotech Journal* 2:24–29.

TNRF (2011) *REDD realities: learning from REDD pilot projects to make REDD work...* Tanzania Natural Resources Forum, Arusha, Tanzania.

Torfing J (2009) Rethinking path dependence in public policy research. *Critical Policy Studies* 3:70–83.

TPDC (No Date) *Songo Songo gas-to-electricity project*, Tanzania Petroleum Development Corporation. Website (accessed 14 September 2015): http://www.tpdc-tz.com/songo_songo.htm, Dar es Salaam.

Tubiello FN, Conchedda G, Wanner N, Federici S, Rossi S and Grassi G (2021) Carbon emissions and removals from forests: new estimates, 1990–2020. *Earth System Science Data* 13:1681–1691.

Tubiello FN, Salvatore M, Ferrara AF, House J, Federici S, Rossi S, Biancalani R, Condor Golec RD, Jacobs H and Flammini A (2015) The contribution of agriculture, forestry and other land use activities to global warming, 1990–2012. *Global Change Biology* 21:2655–2660.

Tucker RC (1992) *Stalin in power: the revolution from above, 1928–1941*, W. W. Norton, New York.

Tumusiime-Mutebile E (2009) Institutional and political dimensions of economic reform, in *Uganda's economic reforms: insider accounts*, Kuteesa F, Tumusiime-Mutebile E, Whitworth A and Williamson T (eds), 35–51, Oxford University Press, Oxford.

Turinawe H (2013) Sawmill technology for yesterday, today & tomorrow. *Sawlog Production Grant Scheme Newsletter* 36:4–5.

Turyahabwe N and Banana AY (2008) An overview of history and development of forest policy and legislation in Uganda. *International Forestry Review* 10:641–656.

Twesigye P (2022) Structural, governance, & regulatory incentives for improved utility performance: a comparative analysis of electric utilities in Tanzania, Kenya, and Uganda. *Utilities Policy* 79:101419.

UEGCL (2018) *Karuma hydropower project*, Uganda Electricity Generation Company Ltd. Website (accessed 10 June 2018): https://www.uegcl.com/business-operations/projects/karuma-hydro-power-project.html, Kampala.

UETCL (2008) *UETCL corporate business plan 2008–2013*, Uganda Electricity Transmission Company Ltd., Kampala.

Uganda Forest Department (1984) *Working plan for Bugamba and Rwoho Central Forest Reserves*, Ministry of Agriculture and Forestry, Kampala.

UIA (2009) *Brief investing guide to Uganda*, Uganda Investment Authority, Kampala.

UIA (2011a) *Forestry sector profile*, Uganda Investment Authority, Kampala.

UIA (2011b) *Uganda: list of CDM projects*, Uganda Investment Authority. Website (accessed 10 September 2011): http://www.ugandainvest.go.ug/index.php?option=com_docman&task=doc_download&gid=25&Itemid=161, Kampala.

UN-REDD (2008) *UN-REDD framework document*, UN-REDD, Geneva.

UN-REDD (2009a) *UN-REDD programme—Tanzania quick start initiative*, UN-REDD, Geneva.

UN-REDD (2009b) *UN Collaborative Programme on reducing emissions from deforestation and forest degradation in developing countries: national programme document Tanzania*, UNDP, Geneva.

UN-REDD (2014) *Emerging approaches to forest reference emission levels and/or forest reference levels for REDD+*, UN-REDD Programme, Rome.

UN-REDD (2015) *Technical considerations for forest reference emission level and/ or forest reference level construction for REDD+ under the UNFCCC*, UN-REDD Programme, Rome.

UN-REDD (2021) *One gigaton of emissions reductions per year—how do we move from ambitions to action?* UN-REDD. Website (accessed 29 December 2020): https://www.un-redd.org/post/one-gigaton-of-emissions-reductions-per-year-how-do-we-move-from-ambitions-to-action, Geneva.

Unruh JD (2008) Carbon sequestration in Africa: the land tenure problem. *Global Environmental Change* 18:700–707.

UNCTAD (2017) *World investment report 2017*, United Nations Press, New York and Geneva.

UNDP (2008a) Karatu Energy Efficient Stove Project, in *MDG Carbon Facility Project Idea Note (PIN)*, UNDP, New York.

UNDP (2008b) Karatu: MDG carbon facility screening stage financial analysis tool, UNDP, unpublished Excel sheet.

UNDP (2010) *How-to guide: low-emission development strategies and nationally appropriate mitigation actions: Eastern Europe and CIS*, UNDP, New York.

UNDP (2013) *Conceptual framework for implementing LEDS & NAMAs: a comparative analysis*, UNDP Low Emission Capacity Building Programme, New York.

UNDP (2017) *Uganda selected by NAMA Facility to advance green school design*, NDC Support Programme. Website (accessed 14 August 2018): http://www.ndcs.undp.org/content/ndc-support-programme/en/home/impact-and-learning/ideas-and-insights/2017/uganda-selected-by-nama-facility-to-advance-green-school-design.html, New York.

UNDP (No Date) *Dar es Salaam urban transport improvement project*, UNDP. Website (accessed 14 August 2018): http://www.tz.undp.org/content/tanzania/en/home/ourwork/environmentandenergy/successstories/UNDP-supports-the-development-of-a-Nationally-Appropriate-Mitigation-Action-NAMA-for-the-transport-sector.html, Dar es Salaam.

UNECE (2005) *2nd environmental performance review, Republic of Moldova*, UN Economic Commission for Europe, New York and Geneva.

UNEP (2011) *Towards a green economy: pathways to sustainable development and poverty eradication*, United Nations Environment Programme, Nairobi.

UNEP (2020) *Handbook for the Montreal Protocol on substances that deplete the ozone layer* (14th ed.), United Nations Environment Programme, Ozone Secretariat, Nairobi.

UNEP DTU (2018) December 2018 Update of NAMA Pipeline Overview Spreadsheet, UNEP-DTU. Website (accessed 10 December 2018): http://namapipeline.org/Publications/NAMApipeline.xlsx, Copenhage, Denmark.

UNEP DTU (2020) August 2020 update of PoA pipeline overview spreadsheet, United Nations Environment Programme. Website (accessed 10 September 2020): https://www.cdmpipeline.org/publications/PoAPipeline.xlsm, Copenhagen.

UNEP DTU (2021a) December 2021 Update of CDM/JI Pipeline Overview Spreadsheet, UNEP-DTU. Website (accessed 23 December 2021): http://www.cdmpipeline.org/publications/CDMpipeline.xlsx, Copenhage, Denmark.

UNEP DTU (2021b) December 2021 Update of PoA Pipeline Overview Spreadsheet, UNEP-DTU. Website (accessed 23 December 2021): http://cdmpipeline.org/publications/PoAPipeline.xlsx, Copenhage, Denmark.

UNFCCC (2001) *Decision 17/CP.7 "Modalities and procedures for a Clean Development Mechanism as defined in Article 12 of the Kyoto Protocol,"* UNFCCC, Bonn.

UNFCCC (2003) *Decision 17/CP.8: Guidelines for the preparation of national communications from parties not included in annex 1 to the Convention,* UNFCCC, Bonn.

UNFCCC (2005a) *Decision 3/CMP.1: modalities and procedures for a Clean Development Mechanism as defined in Article 12 of the Kyoto Protocol,* UNFCCC, Bonn.

UNFCCC (2005b) *Decision 5/CMP.1: Modalities and procedures for afforestation and reforestation project activities under the clean development mechanism,* UNFCCC, Bonn.

UNFCCC (2008a) *Decision 1/CP.13: Bali action plan (FCCC/CP/2007/6/Add.1),* UNFCCC, Bonn.

UNFCCC (2008b) *Decision 2/CP.13: Reducing emissions from deforestation in developing countries: approaches to stimulate action,* UNFCCC, Bonn.

UNFCCC (2009) *Decision 2/CP.15: Copenhagen Accord,* UNFCCC, Bonn.

UNFCCC (2010) *Decision 1/CP.16—Cancun Agreements: Outcome of the work of the Ad Hoc Working Group on Long-term Cooperative Action under the Convention,* UNFCCC, Bonn.

UNFCCC (2011a) *Decision 3/CP.17: Launching the Green Climate Fund,* UNFCCC, Bonn.

UNFCCC (2011b) *Decision 12/CP.17: Guidance on systems for providing information on how safeguards are addressed and respected and modalities relating to forest reference emission levels and forest reference levels as referred to in decision 1/CP.16,* UNFCCC, Bonn.

UNFCCC (2013a) Decision 10/CP.19 "Coordination of support for the implementation of activities in relation to mitigation actions in the forest sector by developing countries, including institutional arrangements," UNFCCC, Bonn.

UNFCCC (2013b) Decision 15/CP.19 "Addressing the drivers of deforestation and forest degradation," UNFCCC, Bonn.

UNFCCC (2014a) *Countries afforestation/reforestation informations,* UNFCCC. Website (accessed 10 January 2015) https://cdm.unfccc.int/DNA/bak/allCountriesARInfos.html, Bonn.

UNFCCC (2014b) *Manual of the NAMA Registry,* UNFCCC, Bonn.

UNFCCC (2015) Uganda's plan for low carbon development. *NAMA Profile* 9:1–7.

UNFCCC (2018a) *Appendix II—Nationally appropriate mitigation actions of developing country Parties,* UNFCCC. Website (accessed 23 March 2018): https://unfccc.int/process/conferences/pastconferences/copenhagen-climate-change-conference-december-2009/statements-and-resources/4, Bonn.

UNFCCC (2018b) *Compilation and synthesis of third biennial reports of parties included in annex i to the Convention,* UNFCCC, Bonn.

UNFCCC (2020) *National communication submissions from non-annex i parties,* UNFCCC. Website (accessed 16 September 2020): https://unfccc.int/non-annex-I-NCs, Bonn.

UNFCCC (2021) *Public NAMA*, UNFCCC, Bonn. Website (accessed 21 December 2021): https://www4.unfccc.int/sites/publicnama/SitePages/Home.aspx.

UNFCCC (No Date-a) *Bus rapid transit (BRT) for Kampala*, UNFCCC, Bonn.

UNFCCC (No Date-b) *Developing appropriate strategies and techniques to reduce methane emissions from livestock production in Uganda*, UNFCCC, Bonn.

UNFCCC (No Date-c) *Fuel efficiency in motor vehicles*, UNFCCC, Bonn.

UNFCCC (No Date-d) *Integrated wastewater treatment for agro-process water in Uganda*, UNFCCC, Bonn.

UNFCCC (No Date-e) *NS-150-Reduction, recycling and reuse of solid waste in Kampala City*, UNFCCC, Bonn.

UNFCCC (No Date-f) *NS-156-Integrated wastewater treatment for agroprocess water in Uganda*, UNFCCC, Bonn.

UNFCCC (No Date-g) *NS-274-The promotion of small scale CHPs in the Republic of Moldova*, UNFCCC, Bonn.

UNFCCC (No Date-h) *NS-276-Promotion of wind power plants (WPP) in the Republic of Moldova*, UNFCCC, Bonn.

UNFCCC (No Date-i) *NS-27-Use of solar energy for domestic hot water production in the Republic of Moldova*, UNFCCC, Bonn.

UNFCCC (No Date-j) *NS-278-Promoting energy efficient lighting in the Republic of Moldova*, UNFCCC, Bonn.

UNFCCC (No Date-k) *NS-279-Hybrid and electric buses and minibuses in the city of Chisinau*, UNFCCC, Bonn.

UNFCCC (No Date-l) *NS-280-Clinker substitution at cement production*, UNFCCC, Bonn.

UNFCCC (No Date-m) *NS-282-Implementation of soil conservation tillage system in the Republic of Moldova*, UNFCCC, Bonn.

UNFCCC (No Date-n) *NS-283-Afforestation of degraded land, riverside areas and protection belts in the Republic of Moldova*, UNFCCC, Bonn.

UNFCCC (No Date-o) *NS-284-Use of energy willow for heat generation in the Republic of Moldova*, UNFCCC, Bonn.

UNFCCC (No Date-p) *NS-285-Waste to Energy (WTE) NAMA in the Republic of Moldova*, UNFCCC, Bonn.

UNFCCC (No Date-q) *Periodic vehicle inspection for emissions and roadworthiness*, UNFCCC, Bonn.

UNFCCC (No Date-r) *Promoting cultivation of high-yielding upland rice in Uganda*, UNFCCC, Bonn.

UNFCCC (No Date-s) *The promotion of the use of efficient institutional stoves in educational institutions—NAMAs proposal*, UNFCCC, Bonn.

UNFCCC Secretariat (2008) *Compilation and analysis of available information on ways and means to enhance equitable regional and subregional distribution of projects under the Clean Development Mechanism*, UNFCCC, Bonn.

United Republic of Tanzania (2010a) *Tanzania readiness preparation proposal (R-PP)—final presentation*, World Bank Forest Carbon Partnership Facility, Washington, DC.

United Republic of Tanzania (2010b) *Tanzania readiness preparation proposal (R-PP), 12th October 2010*, World Bank Forest Carbon Partnership Facility, Washington, DC.

United Republic of Tanzania (2016) *Tanzania's forest reference emissions submission to the UNFCCC*, Office of Vice President, Dar es Salaam.

United Republic of Tanzania (2017) *Tanzania's forest reference emission level submission to the UNFCCC*, Office of Vice President, Dar es Salaam.

Upadhyaya P (2016) Aligning climate policy with national interest: disengagements with nationally appropriate mitigation actions in South Africa. *Journal of Environmental Policy & Planning* 18:463–481.

Urse C (2009) The Caucasus Crisis in 2008 and its Impact on Moldova, in *From fragile state to functioning state: pathways to democratic transformation in a comparative perspective*, Collmer S (ed) pp 308–328, Lit Verlag, Berlin.

USAID (1999) *USAID project to develop land and real estate markets in Moldova*, US Agency for International Development, Washington, DC.

Vähämäki J, Schmidt M and Molander J (2011) *Review: results-based management in development cooperation*, Riksbankens Jubileumsfond, Stockholm.

Van den Bergh J, Castro J, Drews S, Exadaktylos F, Foramitti J, Klein F, Konc T and Savin I (2021) Designing an effective climate-policy mix: accounting for instrument synergy. *Climate Policy* 21:745–764.

Van der Linden M (2014) *Understanding the FCPF Carbon Fund's methodological framework*, World Bank, Open Learning Campus. Website (accessed 10 June 2015): https://olc.worldbank.org/content/understanding-fcpf-carbon-fund%E2%80%99s-methodological-framework.

Van der Ven H, Bernstein S and Hoffmann M (2016) Valuing the contributions of nonstate and subnational actors to climate governance. *Global Environmental Politics* 17:1–20.

Van Lynden GWJ (2000) *Soil degradation in Central and Eastern Europe: the assessment of the status of human-induced soil degradation*, FAO International Soil Reference and Information Centre, Rome.

Vatn A and Angelsen A (2009) Options for a national REDD+ architecture, in *Realising REDD+*, Angelsen A, Brockhaus M, Kanninen M, Sills E, Sunderlin WD and Wertz-Kanounnikof S (eds), 57–74, Center for International Forestry Research, Bogor Barat.

VCS (2011) *AFOLU non-permanence risk tool*, Voluntary Carbon Standard, Washington, DC.

VCS (2013) Jurisdictional and nested redd initiative: Summary of technical recommendations. VCS Association, Washington, DC.

Vedavalli R (2007) *Energy for development: twenty-first century challenges of reform and liberalization in developing countries*, Anthem Press, London.

Verhoest K, Roness PG, Verschuere B, Rubecksen K and MacCarthaigh M (2010) *Autonomy and control of state agencies: comparing states and agencies*, Palgrave Macmillan, New York.

Victor D (2011) *Global warming gridlock*, Cambridge University Press, Cambridge.

Vogt-Schilb A and Hallegatte S (2017) Climate policies and nationally determined contributions: reconciling the needed ambition with the political economy. *Wiley Interdisciplinary Reviews: Energy and Environment* 6:e256.

Voigt C and Ferreira F (2015) The Warsaw framework for REDD+: implications for national implementation and access to results-based finance. *Carbon & Climate Law Review* 9:113–129.

Vokes R (2012) The politics of oil in Uganda. *African Affairs* 111:303–314.

VPO (2005) *MKUKUTA: Tanzania's National Strategy for Growth and Reduction of Poverty (NSGRP)*, Government of the United Republic of Tanzania, Vice-President's Office, Dar es Salaam.

VPO (2009) *National framework for REDD+*, Vice President's Office, Division of Environment, Dar es Salaam.

VPO (2010a) *The Environment Division*, United Republic of Tanzania, Vice-President's Office. Website (accessed 10 July 2010): http://www.vpo.go.tz/environment/utawala.php, Dar es Salaam.

VPO (2010b) *Vision & mission*, United Republic of Tanzania, Vice-President's Office. Website (accessed 10 July 2010): http://www.vpo.go.tz/about_us/mission.php, Dar es Salaam.

VPO (2013a) *Action plan for the implementation of the national strategy for REDD+*, Vice President's Office, Division of Environment, Dar es Salaam.

VPO (2013b) *National strategy for REDD+*, Vice President's Office, Division of Environment, Dar es Salaam.

Vulpe H, Minzatean A, Magidson S, Tocino I, Mindruta-Stratan R, Lönnback LJ, Wagner U, Nazaria V, Ciubotaru E and Minzatean N (2023) Cancer in conflict: the impact of the war in Ukraine on Moldova. *European Journal of Cancer*. doi: 10.1016/j.ejca.2023.05.004

Wade RH (1990) *Governing the market: economic theory and the role of government in East Asian industrialization*, Princeton University Press, Princeton.

Wade RH (2018) The developmental state: dead or alive? *Development and Change* 49:518–546.

Waever O (1998) The sociology of a not so international discipline: American and European developments in international relations. *International Organization* 52:687–727.

Wallbott L and Recio E (2018) Practicing human rights across scale: Indigenous peoples' affectedness and recognition in REDD+ governance. *Third World Thematics: A TWQ Journal* 3:785–806.

Wara M (2008) Measuring the Clean Development Mechanism's performance and potential. *UCLA Law Review* 55:1759–1803.

Wara M and Victor D (2008) *A realistic policy on international carbon offsets*, PSED Working Paper #74, Program on Energy and Sustainable Development, Stanford University, CA.

Wardrop (2004) *Kakira Sugar Works cogeneration expansion environmental assessment—report to the Madhvani Group*, Wardrop Engineering, Mississauga, ON.

Waterbury J (1999) The long gestation and brief triumph of import-substituting industrialization. *World Development* 27:323–341.

Watson C and Schalatek L (2019) Climate Finance Thematic Briefing: REDD+ Finance, ClimateFundsUpdate.Org, London.

Watson C and Schalatek L (2020) Climate Finance Thematic Briefing: Mitigation Finance, ClimateFundsUpdate.Org, London.

Way L (2005a) Authoritarian state building and the sources of regime competitiveness in the fourth wave: the cases of Belarus, Moldova, Russia, and Ukraine. *World Politics* 57:231–261.

Way LA (2003) Weak states and pluralism: the case of Moldova. *East European Politics and Societies* 17:454–482.

Way LA (2005b) Rapacious individualism and political competition in Ukraine, 1992–2004. *Communist and Post-Communist Studies* 38:191–205.

WB Carbon Finance Unit (2014a) *BioCarbon Fund project portfolio*, World Bank Carbon Finance Unit. Website (accessed 14 January 2014): https://wbcarbonfinance.org/Router.cfm?Page=BioCF&ft=Projects, Washington, DC.

WB Carbon Finance Unit (2014b) *Prototype Carbon Fund project portfolio*, World Bank Carbon Finance Unit. Website (accessed 14 January 2014): https://wbcarbonfinance.org/Router.cfm?Page=PCF&ft=Projects, Washington, DC.

WB-FCFP (2014) *REDD readiness progress fact sheet, Tanzania*, World Bank Forest Carbon Finance Partnership Facility, Washington, DC.

WB-FCPF (2013a) *Annex D: REDD+ annual country progress reporting—Uganda (June 2012 to October 2013)*, World Bank Forest Carbon Partnership Facility, Washington, DC.

WB-FCPF (2013b) *Carbon Fund brochure*, World Bank, Washington, DC.

WB-FCPF (2013c) *Carbon Fund methodological framework, final—December 20, 2013*, World Bank Forest Carbon Partnership Facility, Washington, DC.

WB-FCPF (2013d) *A guide to the FCPF readiness assessment framework*, World Bank, Washington, DC.

WB-FCPF (2014) *2014 Annual report*, World Bank, Washington, DC.

WB-FCPF (2017) About FCPF, World Bank. Website (accessed 13 January 2017): https://www.forestcarbonpartnership.org/about-fcpf-0, Washington, DC.

WB-FCPF (2018) *FCPF 26th participants committee meeting: Resolution PC/26/2018/3 (endorsement of Uganda's readiness package)*, World Bank Forest Carbon Partnership Facility, Washington, DC.

WB-FCPF (2022) *World Bank Forest Carbon Partnership Facility annual report 2022*, World Bank Forest Carbon Partnership Facility, Washington, DC.

WB-FCPF (2023) *Donor participants*, World Bank. Website (accessed 22 June 2023): https://www.forestcarbonpartnership.org/donor-participants, Washington, DC.

Webster G, Osmaston HA and Osmaston H (2003) *A history of the Uganda Forest Department, 1951–1965*, Commonwealth Secretariat, London.

Wendt A (1999) *Social theory of international politics*, Cambridge University Press, Cambridge.

Werksman J (1998) The Clean Development Mechanism: unwrapping the "Kyoto Surprise." *Review of European Community and International Environmental Law (RECIEL)* 7:147–158.

West TAP, Wunder S, Sills EO, Börner J, Rifai SW, Neidermeier AN, Frey GP and Kontoleon A (2023) Action needed to make carbon offsets from forest conservation work for climate change mitigation. *Science* 381:873–877.

Wettestad J (2006) The effectiveness of environmental policies, in *Palgrave Advances in International Environmental Politics* Michele M. Betsill, Kathryn Hochstetler and Dimitris Stevis (eds), 299–328, Springer, London.

WFC (2009) *Unleashing renewable energy power in developing countries: proposal for a global renewable energy policy fund*, World Future Council, Hamburg.

Whitfield L, Therkildsen O, Buur L and Kjær AM (2015) *The politics of African industrial policy: A comparative perspective*, Cambridge University Press, Cambridge.

Whitworth A (2009a) How development policy was made in Uganda, *The Guardian*, 3 December 2009. Website (accessed 10 October 2010): http://www.guardian.co.uk/katine/2009/dec/03/alan-whitworth-uganda-policy.

Whitworth A (2009b) Planning and development budget reform, 1990–1995, in *Uganda's economic reforms: insider accounts*, Kuteesa F, Tumusiime-Mutebile E, Whitworth A and Williamson T (eds), 129–156, Oxford University Press, Oxford.

Whitworth A and Williamson T (2009) Overview of the Ugandan economic reform since 1986, in *Uganda's economic reforms: insider accounts*, Kuteesa F, Tumusiime-Mutebile E, Whitworth A and Williamson T (eds), 1–34, Oxford University Press, Oxford.

Wiesmeier M, Lungu M, Hübner R and Cerbari V (2015) Remediation of degraded arable steppe soils in Moldova using vetch as green manure. *Solid Earth* 6:609–620.

Wikipedia (2014) List of sugar manufacturers in Uganda, in Wikipedia Website (accessed 4 March 2014): http://en.wikipedia.org/wiki/List_of_sugar_manufacturers_in_Uganda.

Williamson J (2009) A short history of the Washington Consensus. *Law and Business Review of the Americas* 15:7.

Williamson T and Canagarajah S (2003) Is There a place for virtual poverty funds in pro-poor public spending reform? Lessons from Uganda's PAF. *Development Policy Review* 21:449–480.

Winkelmann R, Donges JF, Smith EK, Milkoreit M, Eder C, Heitzig J, Katsanidou A, Wiedermann M, Wunderling N and Lenton TM (2022) Social tipping processes towards climate action: a conceptual framework. *Ecological Economics* 192:107242.

Winkler H, Baumert K, Blanchard O, Burch S and Robinson J (2007) What factors influence mitigative capacity? *Energy Policy* 35:692–703.

Woehrel S (2009) *Russian energy policy toward neighboring countries*, Congressional Research Service, Washington, DC.

Woo-Cummings M (1999) *The developmental state*, Cornell University Press, Ithaca.

Woods N (2006) *The globalizers: the IMF, the World Bank, and their borrowers*, Cornell University Press, Ithaca, NY.

World Bank (1981) *Accelerated development in sub-Saharan Africa: An agenda for action*, World Bank, Washington, DC.

World Bank (1993) *The World Bank's role in the electric power sector: policies for effective institutional, regulatory, and financial reform*, World Bank, Washington, DC.

World Bank (1996) *Implementation completion report: Republic of Uganda—Sugar rehabilitation project*, World Bank, Washington, DC.

World Bank (1999) *Implementation completion report: Tanzania, forest resources management project*, World Bank, Washington, DC.

World Bank (2001) *Project appraisal document on a proposed credit in the amount of SDR x million (US$49.15 million equivalent) to the Republic of Uganda for an energy for rural transformation project*, World Bank, Washington, DC.

World Bank (2002) *Review of the Poverty Reduction Strategy Paper (PRSP) approach: main findings*, World Bank, Washington, DC.

World Bank (2003) *Project appraisal document on a proposed grant from the Global Environmental Facility Trust Fund in the amount of US$7.0 million to the United Republic of Tanzania for the Eastern Arc Forests Conservation and Management, report no: 23901-TA*, World Bank, Washington, DC.

World Bank (2004) *Updated Project Information Document (PID): MOLDOVA—Social Investment Fund II*, World Bank, Chisinau.

World Bank (2007) *Country review: Moldova—integrating environment into agriculture and forestry progress and prospects in Eastern Europe and Central Asia*, Volume 2, World Bank, Washington, DC.

World Bank (2008) *World Bank in Moldova: 15 years of partnership*, World Bank, Chisinau.

World Bank (2009a) *Climate investment funds*, World Bank. Website (accessed 7 April 2020): https://www.mlit.go.jp/kokusai/MEET/documents/MEETFUM/S3-WorldBank-sup1.pdf, Washington, DC.

World Bank (2009b) *Implementation completion and results report on a credit in the amount of us$49.15 million and a GEF grant in the amount of US$12.12 million to the Republic of Uganda for an energy for rural transformation project in support of the first phase of the Energy for Rural Transformation Program*, World Bank, Washington, DC.

World Bank (2009c) *UN approved forestry project shows role reforestation can play on climate change*, World Bank. Press release. Website (accessed 10 June 2010): http://wbca rbonfinance.org/docs/03062009_RM_BioCF_Moldova_Projec_Registered.pdf), Washington, DC.

World Bank (2010a) *Second Social Investment Fund project—additional financing*, World Bank. Website (accessed 1 Feb 2011): http://web.worldbank.org/external/projects/main?Projectid=P114838&theSitePK=40941&piPK=64290415&pagePK=64283 627&menuPK=64282134&Type=Overview.

World Bank (2010b) *World development report*, World Bank, Washington, DC.

World Bank (2012) W*orld Bank helps Moldova restore degraded lands and earn carbon credits*, 25 October 2012. Website (accessed 10 September 2013): http://www.worldb ank.org/en/news/press-release/2012/10/24/world-bank-helps-moldova-restore-degra ded-lands-and-earn-carbon-credits, Washington, DC.

World Bank (2013) *Additional financing for Tanzania's bus rapid transit system to benefit 300,000 commuters and create 80,000 Jobs*, World Bank. 15 January 2013. Website (accessed 14 August 2018): http://www.worldbank.org/en/news/press-release/2013/01/15/additional-financing-tanzania-bus-rapid-transit-system-benefit-300000-commuters-create-80000-jobs, Washington, DC.

World Bank (2014) *Republic of Moldova: forest note*, World Bank, Washington, DC.

World Bank (2018a) *Dar es Salaam urban transport improvement project*, World Bank. Website (accessed 14 August 2018): http://projects.worldbank.org/p150937/?lang=en&tab=overview, Washington, DC.

World Bank (2018b) *Implementation, completion and results report to the United Republic of Tanzania for Tz-Energy Development and Access Expansion Project (p101645)*, World Bank, Washington, DC.

World Bank (2020a) *State and trends of carbon pricing*, World Bank, Washington, DC.

World Bank (2020b) *World development indicators 2020*, World Bank. Website (accessed 10 March 2020): http://data.worldbank.org/data-catalog/world-development-indicat ors, Washington DC.

WRI (2014a) *Greenhouse gas protocol: policy and action standard, world resources institute*, Washington, DC.

WRI (2014b) *Global protocol for community-scale greenhouse gas emission inventories: executive summary*, World Resources Institute, Washington, DC.

Wrottesley R (2017) RICS Africa summit 2017. *Land Journal* 23.

Wuyts M and Kilama B (2016) Planning for agricultural change and economic transformation in Tanzania? *Journal of Agrarian Change* 16:318–341.

Yanda PZ and Madulu NF (2005) Water resource management and biodiversity conservation in the Eastern Rift Valley Lakes, Northern Tanzania. *Physics and Chemistry of the Earth, Parts A/B/C* 30:717–725.

Yohe GW (2001) Mitigative capacity–the mirror image of adaptive capacity on the emissions side. *Climatic Change* 49:247–262.

You X (2023) *As China's carbon market turns two, how has it performed?* China Dialogue. Website (accessed 23 October 2023): https://chinadialogue.net/en/climate/china-car bon-market-turns-two-how-has-it-performed/#:~:text=The%20carbon%20price%20 of%20China's,euros%20(%24110)%20per%20tonne, London.

Young C (2001) Uganda under Museveni. *African Studies Review* 44:207–210.

Zadnipru R (2011) Energy policy of the Republic of Moldova, Institute of Energy Economics, Tokyo, Japan.

Zakaria F (2011) *The post-American world: Release 2.0*, W.W. Norton, New York.

Zamora D and Behrent MC (2016) *Foucault and neoliberalism*, John Wiley & Sons, New York.

Zdruli P, Eswaran H, Almaraz R and Reich P (1997) Developing the prerequisites for sustainable land use in Albania. *Soil Use and Management* 13:48–55.

Zhang JJ and Wang C (2011) Co-benefits and additionality of the Clean Development Mechanism: an empirical analysis. *Journal of Environmental Economics and Management* 62:140–154.

Index